1 QUOTATION

JAMES ELROY FLECKER, 1884-1915

Between the Pedestals of Night and Morning
Between red death and radiant desire
With not one sound of triumph or of warning
Stands the great sentry on the Bridge of Fire.
O transient soul, thy thought with dreams adorning,
Cast down the laurel, and unstring the lyre:
the wheels of Time are turning, turning, turning,
The slow stream channels deep and doth not tire.
Gods on their bridge above
Whispering lies and love
Shall mock your passage down the sunless river
Which, rolling all it streams,
shall take you, king of dreams,
—Unthroned and unapproachable for ever—
To where the kings who dreamed of old
Whiten in habitations monumental cold

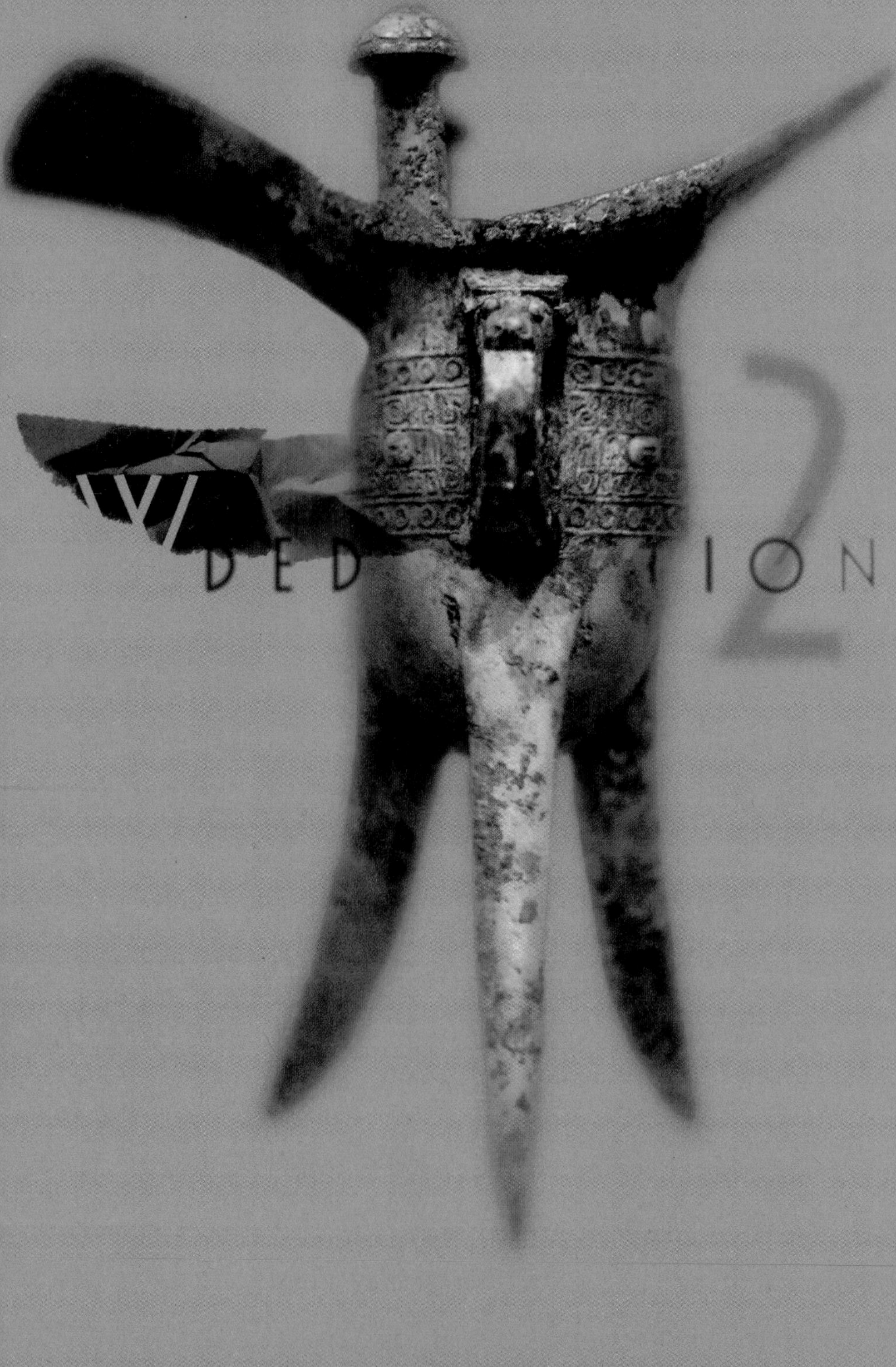

DED
ION
2

This book is for Dave McKean,

as a small token of thanks.

I do not know what Sandman

would have been without Dave,

as our public face - creating the

covers, the typefaces, the design,

all that - and as my hardest critic.

It was a long, strange journey,

and it was the better for having

a friend by my side on the way.

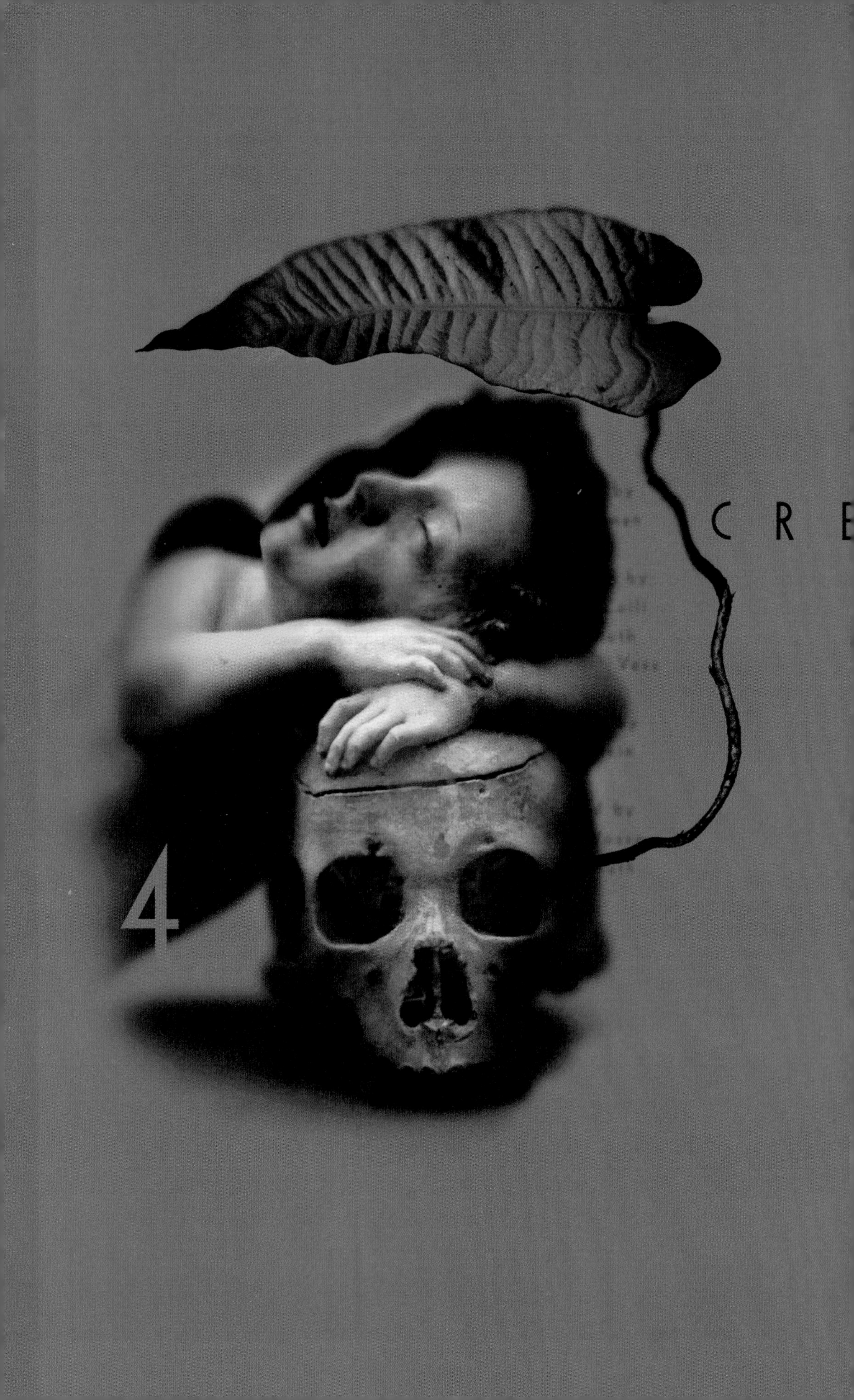
CRE
4

THE SANDMAN: THE WAKE

Written by NEIL GAIMAN
Illustrated by MICHAEL ZULLI.
JON J MUTH & CHARLES VESS
Lettered by TODD KLEIN
Colored by DANIEL VOZZO & JON J MUTH
Separations by DIGITAL CHAMELEON
Covers and design by DAVE MCKEAN
The Wake Title page by MICHAEL ZULLI
Sandman characters created by
GAIMAN, KIETH & DRINGENBERG.

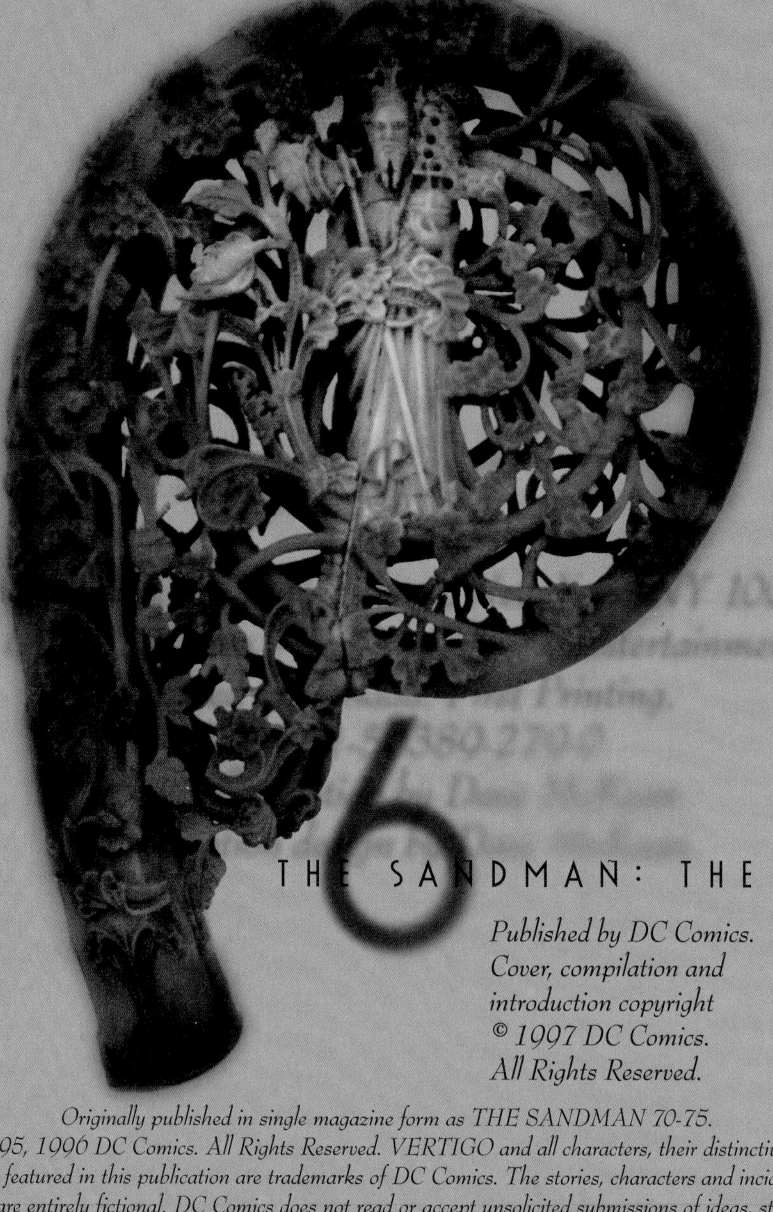

THE SANDMAN: THE WAKE

Published by DC Comics.

Originally published in single magazine form as THE SANDMAN 70-75.

DC Comics, 1700 Broadway, New York, NY 10019
A Warner Bros. Entertainment Company
Printed in Canada. Eighth printing.
ISBN: 978-1-56389-279-0
Cover illustration and publication design by Dave McKean.

CONTENTS

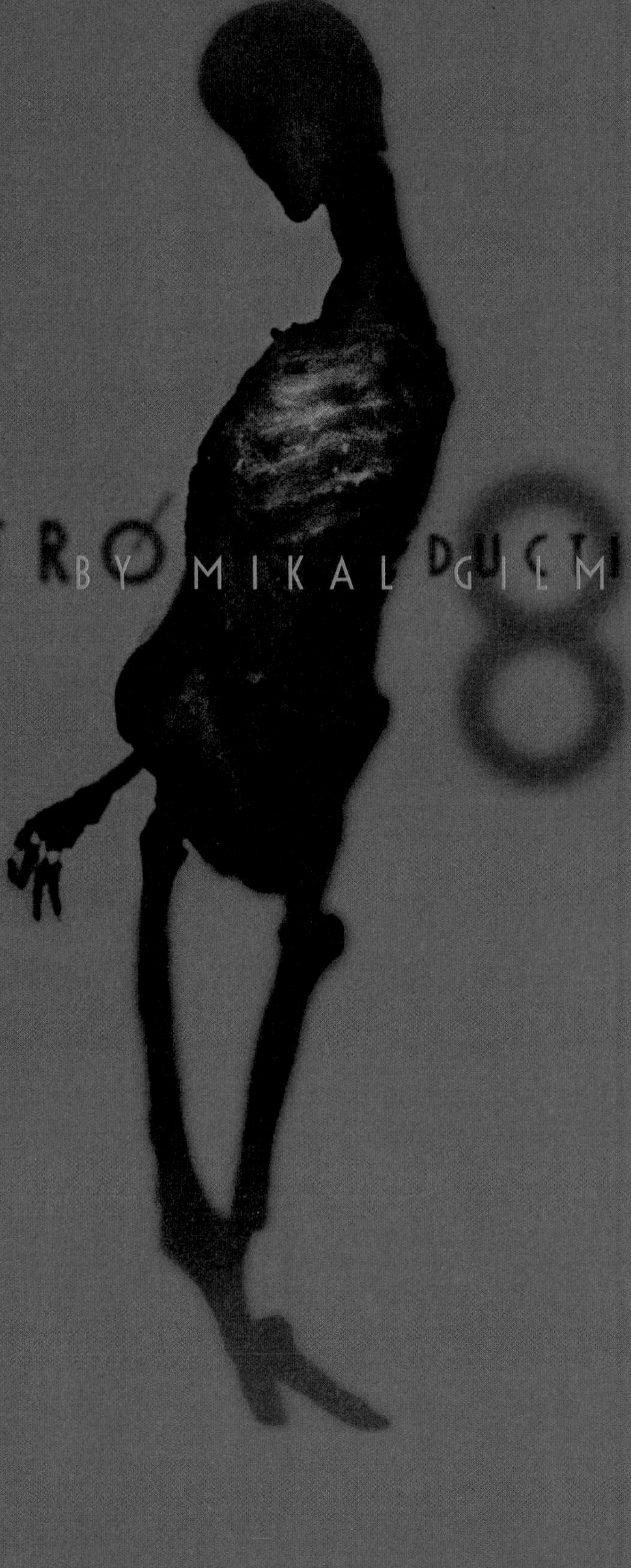

INTRODUCTION

BY MIKAL GILMORE

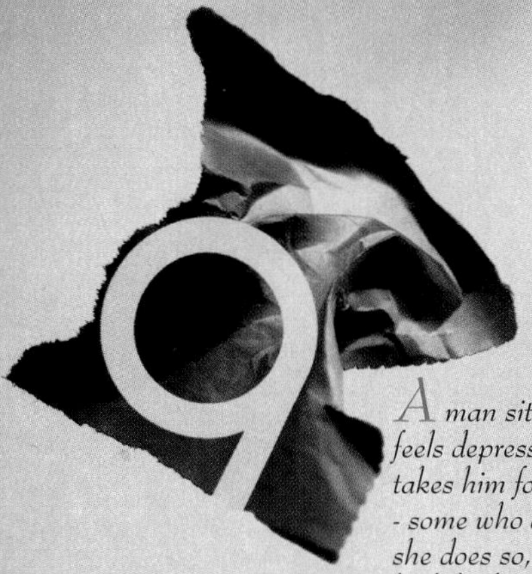
9

A man sits in Washington Square, feeding pigeons. He feels depressed, tired of his existence. His sister shows up, takes him for a walk, and along the way, kills a few people - some who are ready for the killing, some who are not. As she does so, she gives her brother a hard lesson: They are both lords, she reminds him - she, the lord of death; he, of dreams - and what they do isn't always easy. But if they don't do it, the world - or at least life and its meanings - fall into futility. In his own fashion, the Dream Lord cheers up, and decides to go stalk some renegade dreams.

Chances are, you know this story - it was one of the most popular of the early episodes of Neil Gaiman's extraordinary Sandman series, back during the book's first year of publication, 1989 - about seven years ago. In fact, it was the story ("The Sound of Her Wings," Issue Eight) in which Gaiman later said he had finally found his voice for the series. I would argue that he found it a couple of issues earlier, in a pair of genuinely unhinging tales, "Passengers" and "24 Hours." It was in those pages, I think, that Gaiman first truly closed in on the possibilities of the eerie and wonderful chronicle that he was fast inventing. With "Passengers" and "24 Hours," Gaiman made plain that Sandman was a book that would take us on a tour of horror and hope that was at times frighteningly otherworldly, though also as familiar and profound and surprising as the depths of the human heart itself - and without those two prior unflinching terror-tales, with their truly awful, spellbinding revelations, the introduction of the Dream Lord's cutie-pie older sister, Death, might not have counted for as much.

In any event, as I say, it was 1989: all in all, a damn good season to dream of doing something ambitious and substantial in the world of comics. Indeed, comic books were enjoying more hip credibility than at any time since the 1960s. Mid 1980s breakthrough ventures like Alan Moore's Watchmen and Frank Miller's The Dark Knight Returns - super-hero fantasias, imbued with horrific social realism - brought a massive new readership to the idiom. In addition, Art Spiegelman (Maus), Dave Sim (Cerebus), Chester Brown (Yummy Fur), Jaime and Gilberto Hernandez (Love and Rockets) and Jamie Delano (Hellblazer) were writing smart and compelling tales about rapture, fear, carnality, desperation, doom, history, spirit and (occasionally) salvation, that proved some of the most imaginative and rewarding works in comics' 50-year-plus history.

It was in this time and atmosphere that The Sandman emerged. British author and journalist Neil Gaiman had already written three decidedly offbeat comics projects, Signal to Noise, Violent Cases and Black Orchid (all illustrated by Gaiman's longtime friend and partner, Dave McKean, who would also produce the strangely beautiful, form-breaking art for the entire run of Sandman's covers). In those earlier titles, Gaiman had demonstrated powerful knacks for mood, language and characterization, but with Sandman, his verve went deeper, turning wildly imaginative and downright radical. There had been an earlier Sandman in DC's pantheon - a war-era crime fighter - but he bore little resemblance to the dark magus that Gaiman would conjure. In Gaiman's hands, Sandman became the story of the Lord of Dreams, Morpheus (as Neil described him, "an anthropomorphic personification of dreams"), and his encounters with other gods, demons, renegade dreams and frail humans. By entering the realms where these characters dream or rule, Morpheus was forced to wrestle with their most secret hurts and hopes. Sometimes - as in the aforementioned "The Sound of Her Wings," the book proved simply loopy and lyrical. At other times - for example, in "Passengers" and "24 Hours," or in "Collectors," in which Morpheus intruded on a convention of serial killers and turned their horror back on them - Sandman could be so creepy, so unhinging, it was astonishing (and heartening) that the book continued to be published. "Sandman won't always be a horror book," Gaiman told me in 1989, "though horror is very often the lie that tells the truth about our lives - and in that sense, it's ultimately an optimistic genre. But actually, I'd like the stories to be as varied and unpredictable as dreams themselves - which means that the Sandman should be willing to follow the human subconscious wherever it may go, even into the darker realm of internal mythologies. At the same time, I keep expecting for DC to call at some point and say, 'Sorry, we're not going to print this anymore.' Instead, they've been very supportive. And for my part, I'd like to turn out a good book once a month. I mean, why shouldn't there be good mainstream comics?"

In time, it became apparent that Gaiman was doing something more than simply producing good comics stories on a monthly basis: he was also creating a work that aspired to stand as genuine, full-fledged mythology. In and of itself, the use of myth was nothing new in comic-book narratives. Winsor McCay (with his form-setting 1920s Little Nemo tales), Carl Barks (with his 1950s Uncle Scrooge and Donald Duck books), Will Eisner (with his spooky Spirit comics), Jerry Siegel and Joe Shuster (with the original 1930s Superman yarns), Herge (with his many Tin Tin books), and Jack Kirby and Stan Lee (with their 1960s Marvel wonders) had all brought mythological plots, devices and characters to their splendid examples of graphic storytelling. But with Sandman, Gaiman aimed to use a comics-based mythos to expand on, interact with, and **deepen** classical legends of mythology and popular history. On one hand, this approach might seem like merely another clever postmodern ruse, taking old Greek and Norse myths, European and Asian and Islamic folk tales, plus scenarios from Dante, Blake, Milton and Dore, and mixing them with 20th-century comics and horror elements. Still, Gaiman made it all work, and on his own terms. His tales of the Endless - the lords of Death, Despair, Delight, Delirium, Destruction and Destiny who made up Dream's family - resounded as works of both grand invention and wondrous apocrypha. Which is to say, sure, you could see the modern-day sensibility in it all - the fun subterfuge of deities and comics characters sharing the same space, the same dilemmas. At the same time, it was as if you had discovered a timeless trove of fascinating lost legends and mysteries: missing vellums that revealed how so many different peoples shared so many similar patterns of fable and providence in their disparate histories of storytelling. In its best (frequent) moments, The Sandman was like a secret history of the unconscious: a panorama of the many hidden connections between gods and devils, monsters and humans, the living and the dead, and the shadowy dreams and fears that construct and animate mythical beings in the first place. In this way, The Sandman managed to add as much to any real understanding of mankind's myths as the works of Thomas Bulfinch, Sir James Frazer, Edith Hamilton or Joseph Campbell. But don't take my word for it. Read it, and decide for yourself.

THERE HAVE BEEN MANY PLEASURES that have come from following Sandman's saga, as it unfolded from 1988 to 1996. Among them: the inventive way that Neil told stories about the real world and fantastic realms, so that both the narratives and their provinces circled around and within one another, each changing the other's fates and setting off events and probabilities that would reverberate years later at unexpected junctures in the overall tale. Some might view this as the comic book's equivalent of magic realism, but Neil himself has never disguised the real source for his surreal-existential brand of storytelling: it springs from a deep affection for William Shakespeare's "A Midsummer Night's Dream," and a desire to translate that play's mix of horror and playfulness into modern forms. Another Sandman delight: Gaiman's deft manipulation of a large gallery of wildly diverse, indelible characters, who often turn out to have greater depth, consequence and, in some cases, deadliness than might first seem apparent. I'm thinking here chiefly of Lyta - the demented, damaged wannabe super-heroine who is terribly mistreated by Dream early in the series, and who pays him back in kind at the end - and Thessaly, the smart, murderous witch from A Game of You, whose lack of love for Morpheus helps launch him on his path to self-ruin in Brief Lives. (Just what the fuck was the Dream Lord thinking, taking **her** as a lover?)

But there are two pleasures about Sandman that, I think, beat the others. One comes from tracking the development of Morpheus himself. It's an evolvement that proves as subtle as it is complex, and it demands some real liberality and compassion from the reader. Certainly, the Dream Lord is not an easy man to fathom, nor is he the most sympathetic or likable of the characters that you will come across in this epic. (Save that tribute for Morpheus's two most humane siblings - his sisters Delirium and Death - plus two strong-willed yet constantly perplexed talking animals, Matthew the smart-assed raven, and Barnabas, the smart-assed dog. Thank God for talking animals, I say - especially smart-assed ones). In comparison to some of the others who populate the Sandman mythos, Morpheus is, at times, a plain and simple pill or prick. He is haughty, cold and callous. He woos then abandons lovers, or worse: Nada (whose tale was told during The Doll's House series) found herself cast into the abyss of Hell, her soul consigned to infinite suffering, for offending the Dream Lord's pride. Dream also fathers a son, Orpheus, that he does not attend to enough, and then later, when Orpheus is at his most bereft and helpless, Morpheus leaves him to an eternity of unspeakable torment. And early in the series, he comes upon Orpheus's mother, Calliope, in an unexpected and barbarous place, and must face the truth that some of the abuse and devastation that is now her life is a result of his own bad faith.

But Dream also has twinges of conscience, and gradually and reluctantly he comes to examine his actions. Maybe he even comes to know himself. In an early storyline, The Doll's House, Morpheus comes to see how his own creations - the dreams he fashions to stalk our darkness, to reflect and sometimes inspire our deepest longings or cruelties - can do great damage beyond their lives in dreams: damage that never stops spilling into the world's already boundless pain and terror. In Season of Mists, Dream sets out to free, at long last, Nada, the lover he sent to Hell. When he finally encounters Nada, he must learn that his regret for wronging her can never be payment enough for his sin. In Brief Lives (for my money, the best of the individual Sandman novels), Dream is obliged to make right the horrible fate he left his son Orpheus to - in the only way he can. The epiphany of despair that Morpheus faces after he slays his son is the single most affecting and consequential moment in the entire series. Finally in The Kindly Ones - the book that immediately precedes the stories collected in this present volume - Dream comes to understand how his obsessions with his powers and responsibilities, with the noble rules of authority, were simply an echo of his own emptiness. Worse than that, these things worked as excuses for failing to provide the sort of risky real love and protection that those who loved and depended on him deserved. And then, he understands what he must do to redeem himself: At the end of The Kindly Ones, Morpheus gives his hand to his closest sister, Death; she takes his hand and he is no more. You may come to your own conclusions about why Dream chose this end. Perhaps, as one character implies, he wanted to pay for his neglect and destruction of Orpheus. But here is my verdict: Morpheus died for love. This isn't to say that love simply broke his heart - that an uncaring lover finally shredded his spirit and will - though that's a part of it. (Let me repeat: Thessaly, who is called Larissa at this point in the story, should clearly have been seen as walking-talking bad news.) But it isn't just a matter of hard luck. Morpheus made bad choices: bad for himself, bad for others. He could not understand how to care for his own heart - he could not grasp its limitations or vanities or real needs - nor could he understand or respect the true patterns in the hearts of others. He was great, but he was also terrible - and while each of those aspects of his heart and being might comprehend one another, neither could subdue or transform the other. Until, that is, the end.

I realize that everything I'm saying here may not seem an especially flattering portrayal of the primary character who has carried The Sandman for several years and myriad pages. (I also realize that my ideas might run strongly contrary to Gaiman's own view of Dream, but that's only a further testament to how well Neil has done his job: when you create characters and a storyscape that occupy somebody else's imagination, you lose the sole authority to determine how that work resounds in others' dreams.) At the same time, it's Morpheus's flaws that, I think, make him truly worthy of the mythic dimension that Gaiman has placed him in, and it's Dream's recognition of his shortcomings that finally allows him to win whatever redemption he pulls off - that makes him, finally, a real hero. Heroes, remember, weren't always very nice folks. In fact, many of the classical ones - not to mention quite a few of the real-life historical ones - were vain, murderous or otherwise interestingly fucked-up. The idea of the uncomplicated hero - like our current obsession with "moral" character - is a fairly modern-day work of misfortune.

I noted before that the episode in which Morpheus slays his son Orpheus is the single most heartaching and eventful scene in the saga - but it is also Sandman's single kindest moment. It is a necessary work of mercy - but even as Morpheus accomplishes it, he must realize that he is also, in effect, killing himself (which may be part of his motivation). There are, after all, punishments for shedding blood, and few acts are worse than spilling the blood of family. Later, when Morpheus pays the price for his deed, he also completes his final, kindly act of mercy. (You didn't think the "kindly ones" were really those nasty old Furies, did you? Actually, they're Dream and Death, and in their own tragic and unintentional ways, Lyta, Larissa and Nuala.) In the end, Morpheus's heart could not be fixed or healed; it could not simply be set right by his own will, or by therapy and medication (gods - or their equals - don't get to opt for therapy or medication, though one can see how such things might do wonders for the Judeo-Christian god), and Morpheus, in these tales, has come to understand the futility of living with a heart that cannot be fixed - especially living endlessly with such a heart.

So Morpheus dies. It's all, really, he can do - it is, if you need to see it this way, the "right" thing to do.

As the writer and activist John Perry Barlow once said, in speaking about the death of his friend Jerry Garcia, it is "a big death." It resonates back through the structure of everything that has occurred in the story before. It isn't just a god or an endless being who dies. Far worse (and far better), it is a man, who has finally delivered his own troubled heart, and saved others in the process.

There will be another Dream Lord - you will see him in the pages of this present book - and likely, he will be a better Dream. But there will never again be a Morpheus.

I MENTIONED A FEW PARAGRAPHS BACK that there are two exceptional pleasures that come from a reading of The Sandman. The other - like following the growth of the central character, Morpheus - has been watching the growth of Neil Gaiman's talents. It's not unlike the delight that came from viewing the development of rock & roll forces like the Beatles or the Clash over the stretch of their careers: it is the joy of witnessing extraordinary artistry become even more extraordinary, as the mind (or minds) behind that art meets the challenge of its own promise.

I can't say for sure (and don't plan to ask) whether Gaiman envisioned the whole intricate sweep of what he eventually accomplished with The Sandman (which stretched over 76 monthly issues, making for roughly 2000 pages of graphics and text), or if he ended up concocting a lot of it as he went along. (I suspect - hope, in fact - that it's more the latter than the former. Years ago, in the early seasons of Sandman's run, Neil told me he planned to stay on the book until about Issue 40. "I've always known where this story is going," he said, "what its last panel will be." A short time later, I related this disclosure to another British comics author, who at first grew wide-eyed, then snorted and laughed. "He actually thinks he knows where he's going with this - where it will all end? More power to him, the cheeky bastard, but I think he's in for a surprise.") Anyway, no matter the method. Gaiman has pulled off a coherent, rich and transfixing long-range narrative, and I imagine that anybody who has read the whole series is grateful that it took him nearly twice as long to accomplish as he first envisioned.

In addition to the 76 issues of The Sandman that Gaiman wrote these last several years, he also authored several other single-volume and multi-issue works, including The Books of Magic; two miniseries featuring Death, Morpheus's cooler-than-life big sister; Mr. Punch, a terrific tale about youth and its necessary lessons of disillusion, featuring the mind-blazing and inventive illustrations of longtime friend and partner Dave McKean (who has produced his own fine series these last few years, Cages, published by Tundra); a BBC-TV miniseries, Neverwhere, that should make its debut around the time this volume sees print; and has co-authored a dark religious fantasy novel with Terry Pratchett, Good Omens. It's a prodigious amount of work, of course, and what makes its output even more notable (or insane) is that Neil has also toured and made personal appearances to support nearly all these works. In addition, Gaiman's personal life went through some upheaval during this period: a little over halfway through Sandman's run, he found himself uprooted from his native England and dropped down into the middle of America (trading one deeply weird country for another, maybe even deeply **weirder** land), and also became the father of his third child. Much of all this work and transformation had no doubt proved heady and rewarding for Neil, but I'd bet there were also times when he felt lost in all the commotion, and perhaps those occasions have informed some of Sandman's most eloquent and impassioned writing. I wouldn't be surprised at all.

Anyway, a major element of Gaiman's work is now finished. The Sandman saga closes with the volume you are holding.

To be more accurate, it actually closed with the previous book, The Kindly Ones; if anything, The Wake is a story of the strange limbo-gulf zone that exists between death and renewal, between the horror of grief and the sometimes even greater horror of possible hope. But while Gaiman has said he will write shorter works about the other members of the Endless - and maybe even fill in one or two of the missing chapters in Morpheus's tale - it is unlikely that he will ever tell us the story of the new Dream Lord's reign.

I admit, I'll miss this monthly treat (though I'm quite happy to have Garth Ennis's Preacher, Jeff Smith's Bone and David Lapham's Stray Bullets to look forward to). For me, The Sandman has been the most exciting and involving literary adventure of the last decade, and it has been vastly better than most of the storytelling that film and television have had to offer. At the same time, it was necessary for The Sandman, like Morpheus himself, to finish. As a favorite poet of mine once wrote: "A story can't be told/Until a story's done." With this final volume, we can now look back and measure what Gaiman has created: nothing less than a popular culture masterpiece, and a work that is braver, smarter and more meaningful than just about anything "high culture" has produced during the same period. It doesn't matter that most mainstream literary critics or taste-arbiters haven't also declared this truth - they necessarily lag far behind the edge that an artist like Gaiman inhabits. What **does** matter is that The Sandman happened, that it is here, and that Gaiman and the several outstanding graphics artists that he has worked with these last few years have fashioned such an imaginative and vital work of renegade art.

My favorite character in Sandman, the soft-hearted, broken Delirium, asks Morpheus at one point: "What's the word for things not being the same always. You know. I'm sure there is one. Isn't there?" Dream names the word for her. "Change," he says. She also asks him: "What's the name for the precise moment when you've actually forgotten how it felt to make love to somebody you really liked a long time ago?" Dream replies: "There isn't one." Says Delirium: "Oh. I thought maybe there was." Delirium's right, of course: there is one, and I think that in his heart, Dream knew it - but he wasn't yet ready to speak it. That word is: "Mercy," and it stands for an attribute that does not always fare well in the hard realities of waking life. It is only readily available, in fact, in that odd realm known as dreaming, and even there its blessings are ephemeral.

That's how The Sandman works: It opens some truths and conceivabilities for the reader, then lets you figure out the others - the best ones - for yourself. It is a work that engages the mind and the heart without trying to manipulate either. That's a neat trick, in this - or any - time.

And that's all I wanted to say, except for this: Thanks, Neil, for giving us such a memorable and enduring gift. Can't wait for the next one.

MIKAL GILMORE HAS BEEN A FREQUENT CONTRIBUTOR TO ROLLING STONE MAGAZINE SINCE 1977. AND IS THE AUTHOR OF AN AWARD WINNING NON FICTION WORK, SHOT IN THE HEART (DOUBLEDAY). IN 1994.

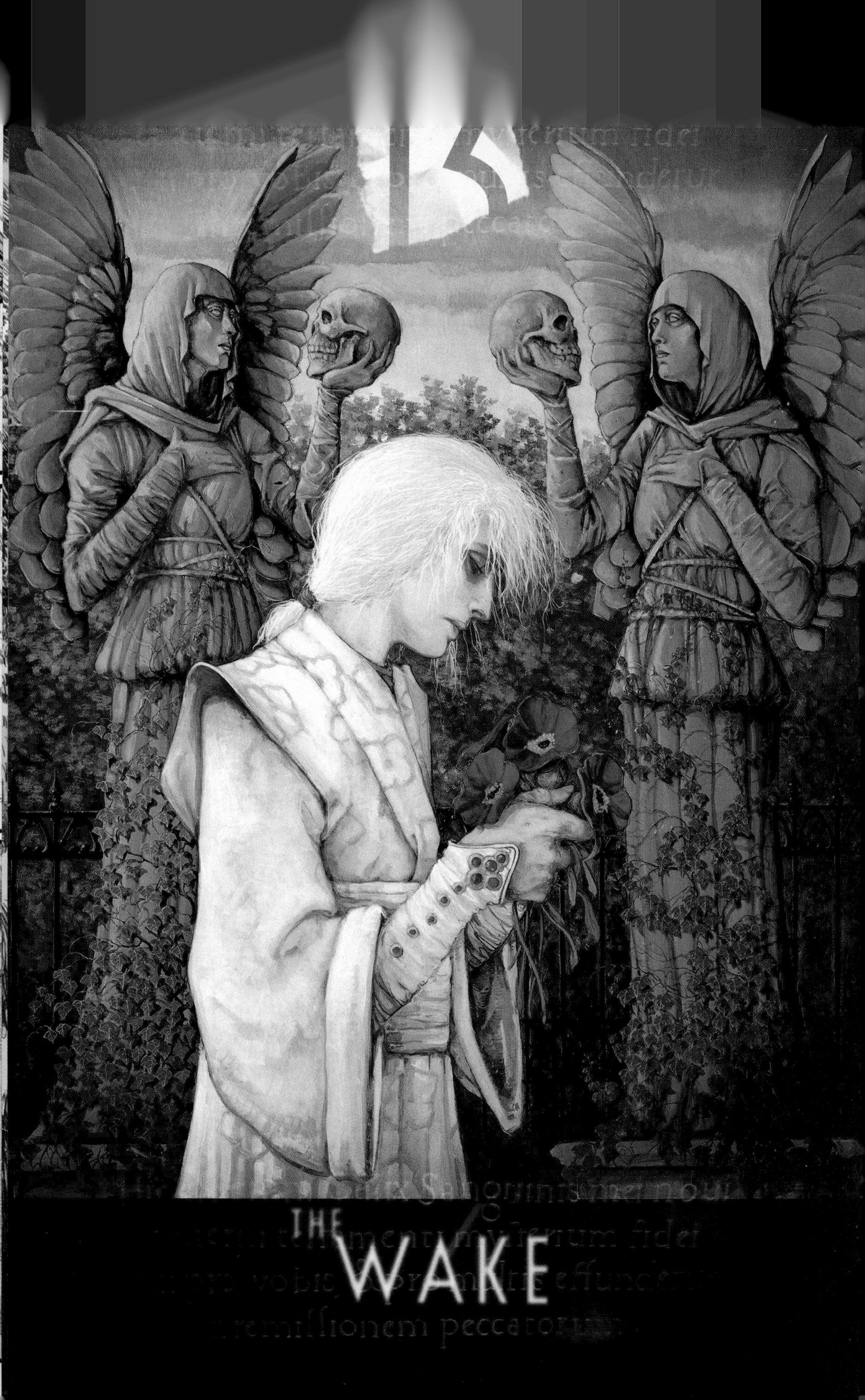
13
THE
WAKE

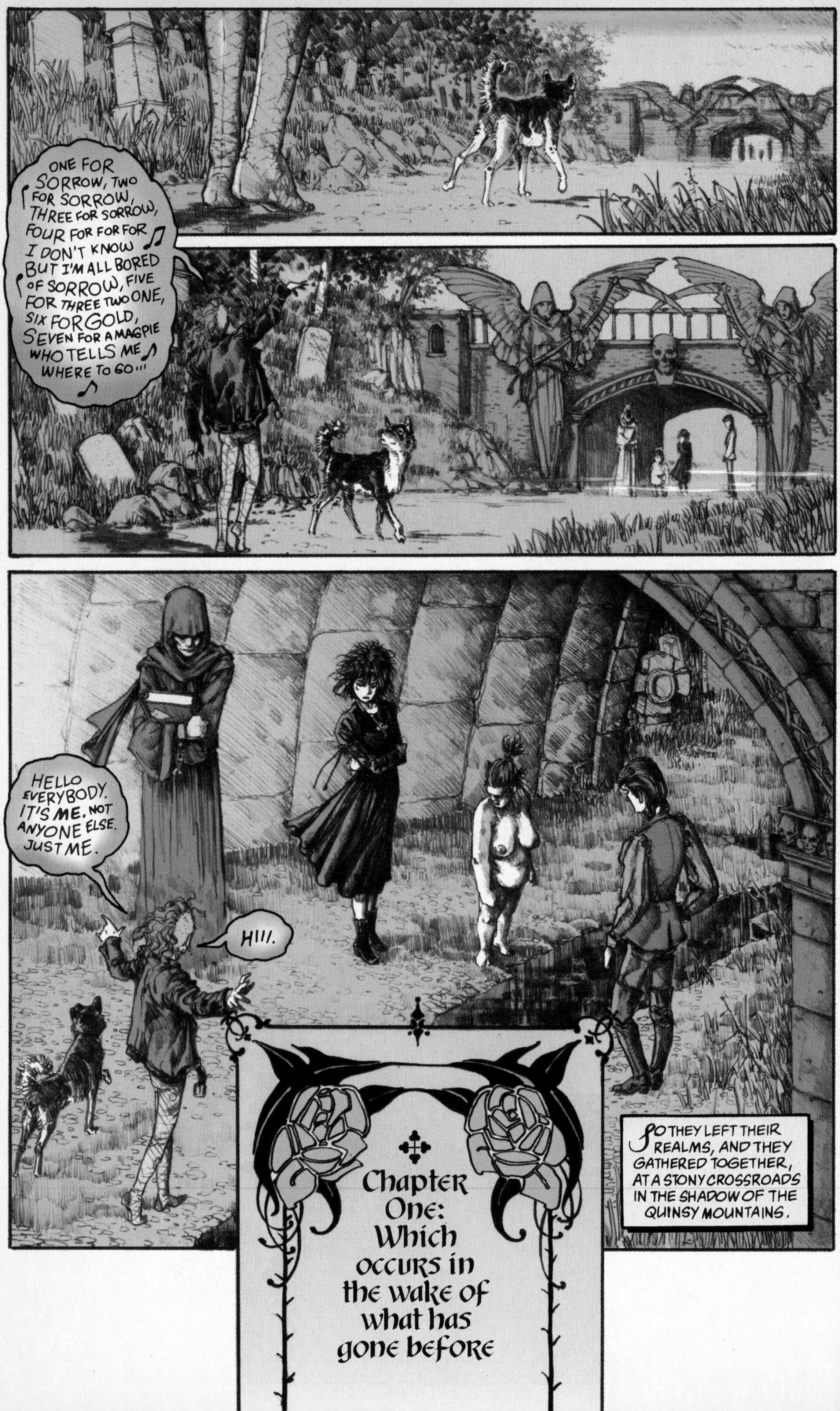
ONE FOR SORROW, TWO FOR SORROW, THREE FOR SORROW, FOUR FOR FOR FOR I DON'T KNOW BUT I'M ALL BORED OF SORROW, FIVE FOR THREE TWO ONE, SIX FOR GOLD, SEVEN FOR A MAGPIE WHO TELLS ME WHERE TO GO!!!
HELLO EVERYBODY. IT'S **ME.** NOT ANYONE ELSE. JUST ME.
HI!!.
SO THEY LEFT THEIR REALMS, AND THEY GATHERED TOGETHER, AT A STONY CROSSROADS IN THE SHADOW OF THE QUINSY MOUNTAINS.
Chapter One: Which occurs in the wake of what has gone before

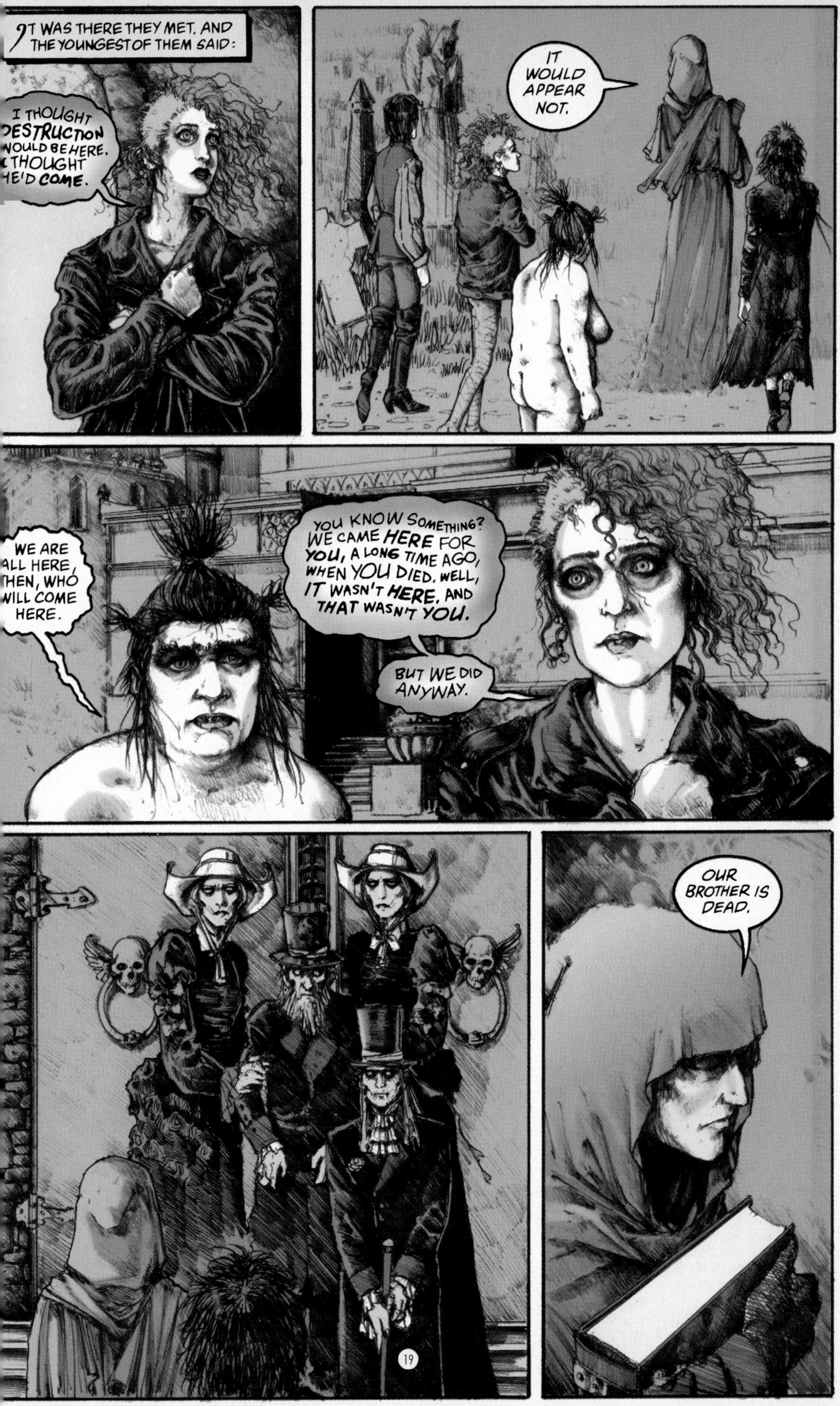
IT WAS THERE THEY MET, AND THE YOUNGEST OF THEM SAID:
I THOUGHT DESTRUCTION WOULD BE HERE. I THOUGHT HE'D COME.
IT WOULD APPEAR NOT.
WE ARE ALL HERE, THEN, WHO WILL COME HERE.
YOU KNOW SOMETHING? WE CAME HERE FOR YOU, A LONG TIME AGO, WHEN YOU DIED. WELL, IT WASN'T HERE. AND THAT WASN'T YOU.
BUT WE DID ANYWAY.
OUR BROTHER IS DEAD.

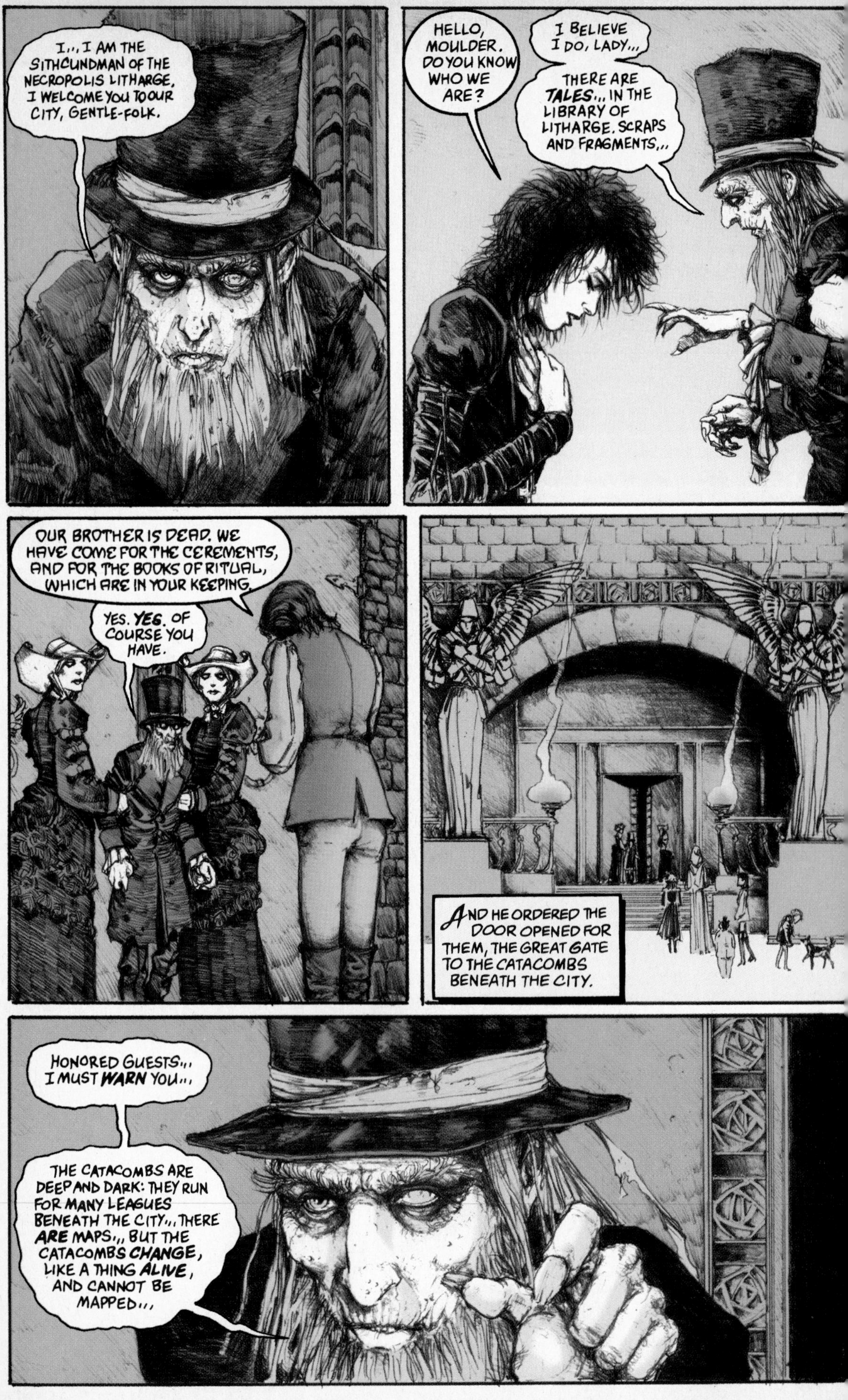
I... I AM THE SITHCUNDMAN OF THE NECROPOLIS LITHARGE. I WELCOME YOU TO OUR CITY, GENTLE-FOLK.
HELLO, MOULDER. DO YOU KNOW WHO WE ARE?
I BELIEVE I DO, LADY...
THERE ARE TALES... IN THE LIBRARY OF LITHARGE. SCRAPS AND FRAGMENTS...
OUR BROTHER IS DEAD. WE HAVE COME FOR THE CEREMENTS, AND FOR THE BOOKS OF RITUAL, WHICH ARE IN YOUR KEEPING.
YES. YES. OF COURSE YOU HAVE.
AND HE ORDERED THE DOOR OPENED FOR THEM, THE GREAT GATE TO THE CATACOMBS BENEATH THE CITY.
HONORED GUESTS... I MUST WARN YOU...
THE CATACOMBS ARE DEEP AND DARK: THEY RUN FOR MANY LEAGUES BENEATH THE CITY... THERE ARE MAPS... BUT THE CATACOMBS CHANGE, LIKE A THING ALIVE, AND CANNOT BE MAPPED...

WE APPRECIATE THE ADVICE; BUT IT IS NOT NEEDED, MOULDER.

WHICH OF US MUST GO TO THE ROOM?

NONE OF US CAN GO INSIDE, NOT EVEN OUR SISTER. WE NEED AN ENVOY.

AND WHERE DO WE FIND AN ENVOY?

WE DON'T FIND ONE, SILLY-OLD-LADY-SISTER...

WE MAKE ONE.

OUT! OF! MUD!

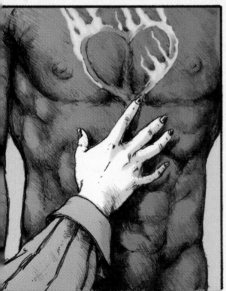

HE IS YOURS, NOW, MY SISTER.

21

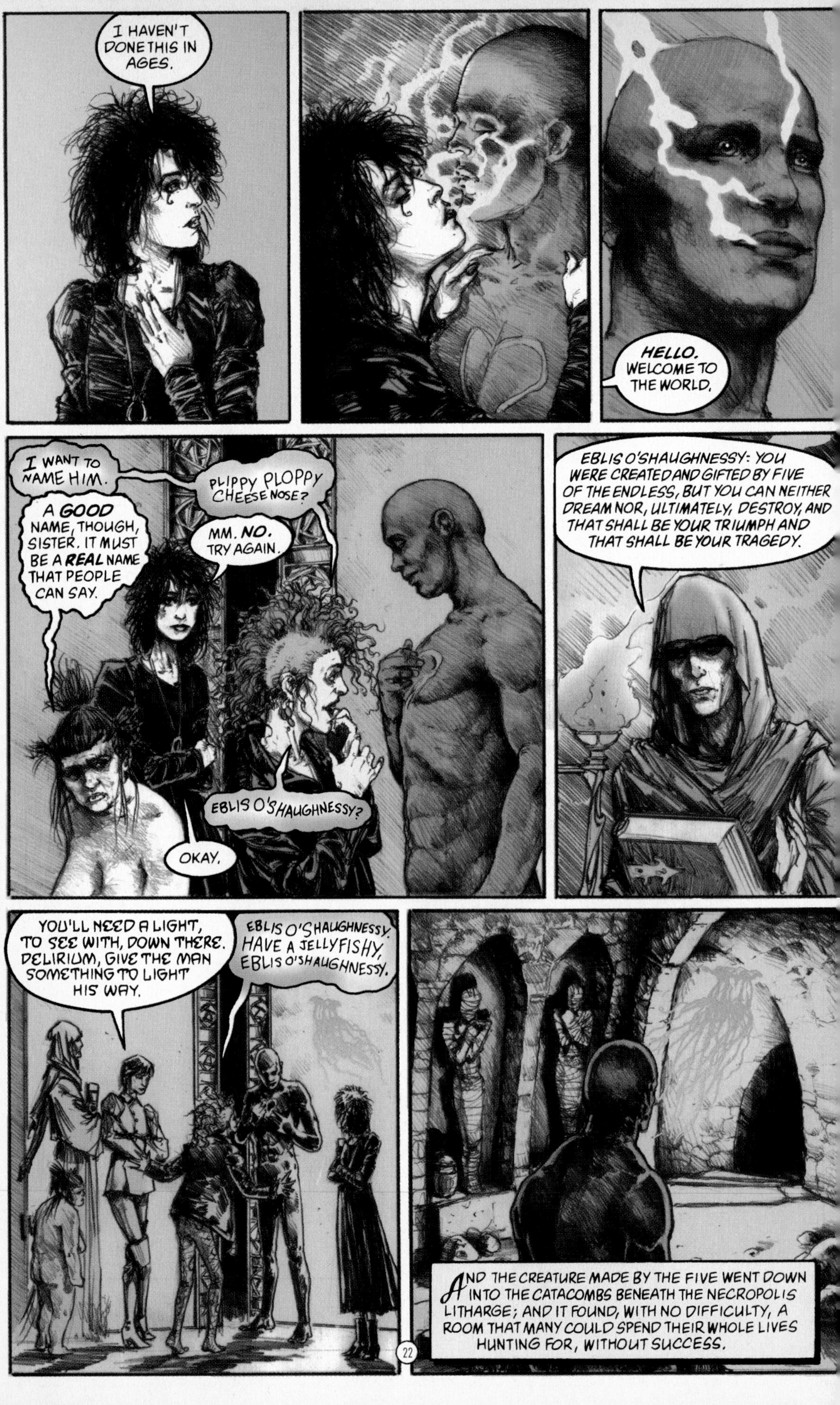

I HAVEN'T DONE THIS IN AGES.
HELLO. WELCOME TO THE WORLD.
I WANT TO NAME HIM.
PLIPPY PLOPPY CHEESE NOSE?
A GOOD NAME, THOUGH, SISTER. IT MUST BE A REAL NAME THAT PEOPLE CAN SAY.
MM. NO. TRY AGAIN.
EBLIS O'SHAUGHNESSY?
OKAY.
EBLIS O'SHAUGHNESSY: YOU WERE CREATED AND GIFTED BY FIVE OF THE ENDLESS, BUT YOU CAN NEITHER DREAM NOR, ULTIMATELY, DESTROY, AND THAT SHALL BE YOUR TRIUMPH AND THAT SHALL BE YOUR TRAGEDY.
YOU'LL NEED A LIGHT, TO SEE WITH, DOWN THERE. DELIRIUM, GIVE THE MAN SOMETHING TO LIGHT HIS WAY.
EBLIS O'SHAUGHNESSY. HAVE A JELLYFISHY, EBLIS O'SHAUGHNESSY.
AND THE CREATURE MADE BY THE FIVE WENT DOWN INTO THE CATACOMBS BENEATH THE NECROPOLIS LITHARGE; AND IT FOUND, WITH NO DIFFICULTY, A ROOM THAT MANY COULD SPEND THEIR WHOLE LIVES HUNTING FOR, WITHOUT SUCCESS.

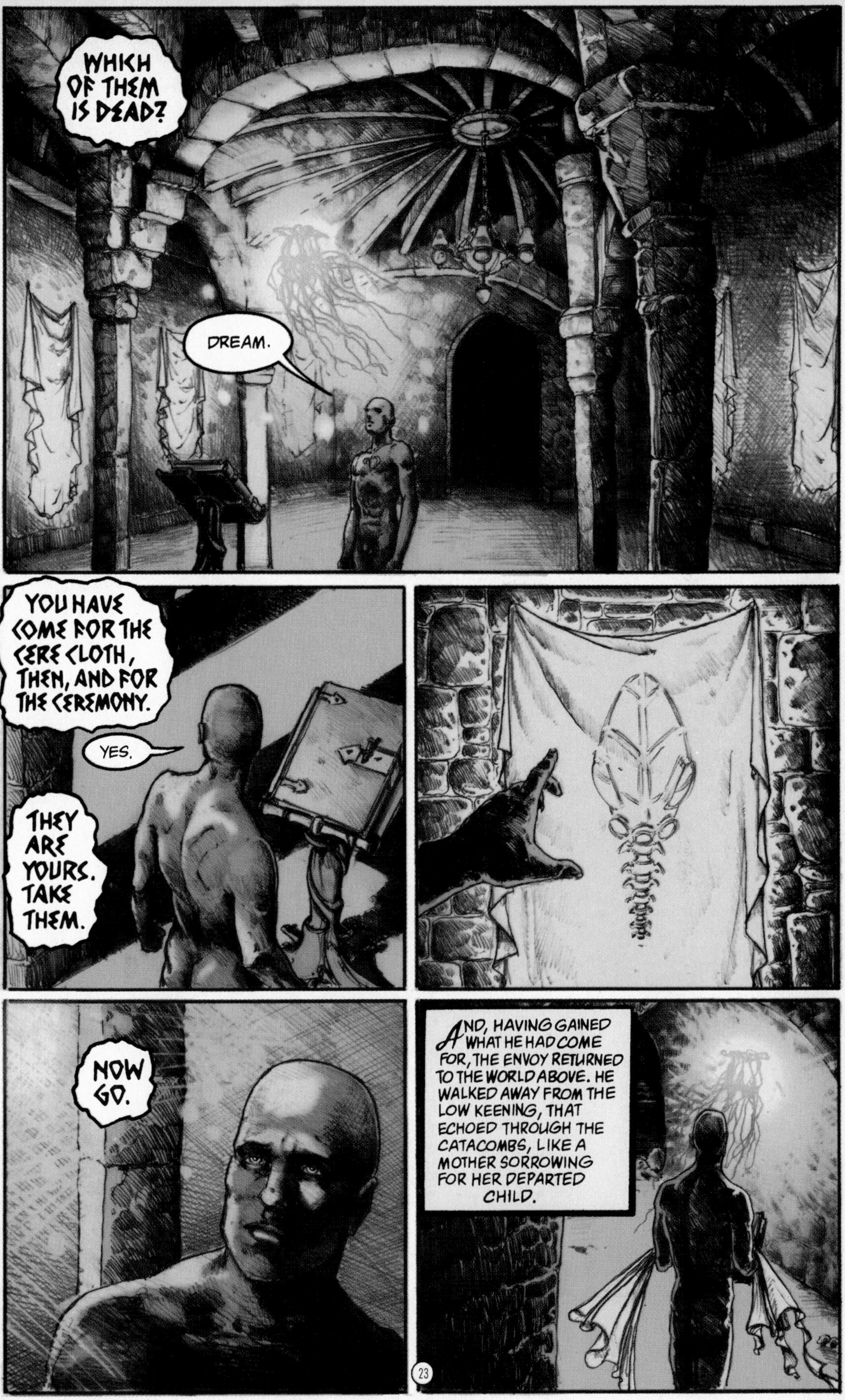
WHICH OF THEM IS DEAD?
DREAM.
YOU HAVE COME FOR THE CERE CLOTH, THEN, AND FOR THE CEREMONY.
YES.
THEY ARE YOURS. TAKE THEM.
NOW GO.
AND, HAVING GAINED WHAT HE HAD COME FOR, THE ENVOY RETURNED TO THE WORLD ABOVE. HE WALKED AWAY FROM THE LOW KEENING, THAT ECHOED THROUGH THE CATACOMBS, LIKE A MOTHER SORROWING FOR HER DEPARTED CHILD.

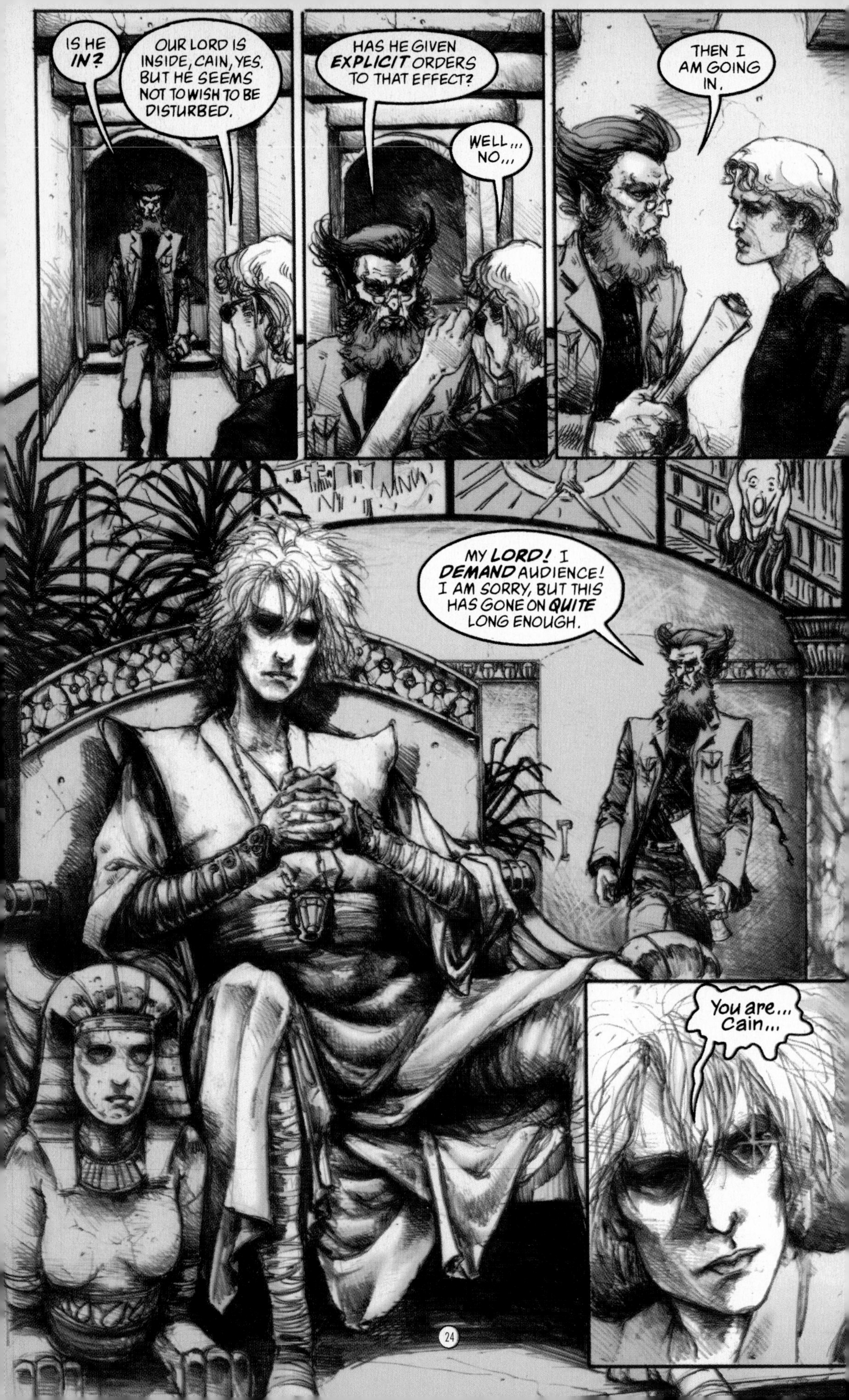
IS HE IN?
OUR LORD IS INSIDE, CAIN, YES. BUT HE SEEMS NOT TO WISH TO BE DISTURBED.
HAS HE GIVEN EXPLICIT ORDERS TO THAT EFFECT?
WELL... NO...
THEN I AM GOING IN.
MY LORD! I DEMAND AUDIENCE! I AM SORRY, BUT THIS HAS GONE ON QUITE LONG ENOUGH.
You are... Cain...

PRECISELY SO,

I AM CAIN, AND THIS IS MY *CONTRACT* WITH YOUR PREDECESSOR,,,

With me, Cain.

I am Dream of the Endless. Your contract is with me.

MY LETTER OF COMMISSION -- ORIGINALLY DRAWN UP BEFORE THE DAWN OF TIME AND REISSUED AND AMENDED IN APRIL OF 1989--STATES *QUITE* EXPLICITLY THAT I AM PART OF A DOUBLE ACT: CAIN AND ABEL. SECRETS AND MYSTERIES. THE THIN ONE AND THE FAT ONE. VICTIM AND VICTOR. IT'S *ALL* HERE.

And...?

AND I DE*MAND*-- I IN*SIST*-- UNDER MY *CON*TRACT--THAT YOU RECREATE MY BROTHER.

OTHERWISE I SHALL BE *FORCED* TO TAKE ACTION OF AN IM*MED*IATE AND *SUMM*ARY NATURE.

Cain. Do not presume.

I do not believe,,, that I take well to threats, inferred or otherwise...

...Nor to an excess of unwarranted familiarity...

AH.

I am not impressed by your behavior.

I AM,,, I AM SORRY.

BUT, MY LORD, MY *BROTHER*,,, PLEASE?

There are ...others... hurt, Cain.

YES, YES, *MANY* OF THEM. BUT MY BROTHER,,,

Abel.

THAT'S EXACTLY IT. *ABEL*.

Describe him for me.

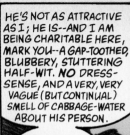

HE'S NOT AS ATTRACTIVE AS I; HE IS--AND I AM BEING CHARITABLE HERE, MARK YOU--A GAP-TOOTHED, BLUBBERY, STUTTERING HALF-WIT. *NO* DRESS-SENSE, AND A VERY, VERY VAGUE (BUT CONTINUAL) SMELL OF CABBAGE-WATER ABOUT HIS PERSON.

CHEWS WITH HIS MOUTH OPEN.

AND THE *STATE* OF HIS *BATH*ROOM -- I'M *NOT* ONE TO GOSSIP, BUT THERE ARE THINGS CRUSTED ON HIS SINK THAT HAVE NOT SIMPLY DEVELOPED INTELLIGENT LIFE BUT HAVE IN ALL PROBABILITY BY NOW EVOLVED THEIR OWN POLITICAL SYSTEMS.

Hush, Cain...

Enough...

I-uh-I-uh-I-I-I-uh- I *THOUGHT* I WAS-*hmn*-- OVER AND, mm, DUH *DONE* WITH.

NONSENSE. LORD MORPHEUS BROUGHT YOU BACK, RIGHT AS RAIN...

Not Morpheus. I have no right to that name. I am Dream of the Endless: it is enough.

26

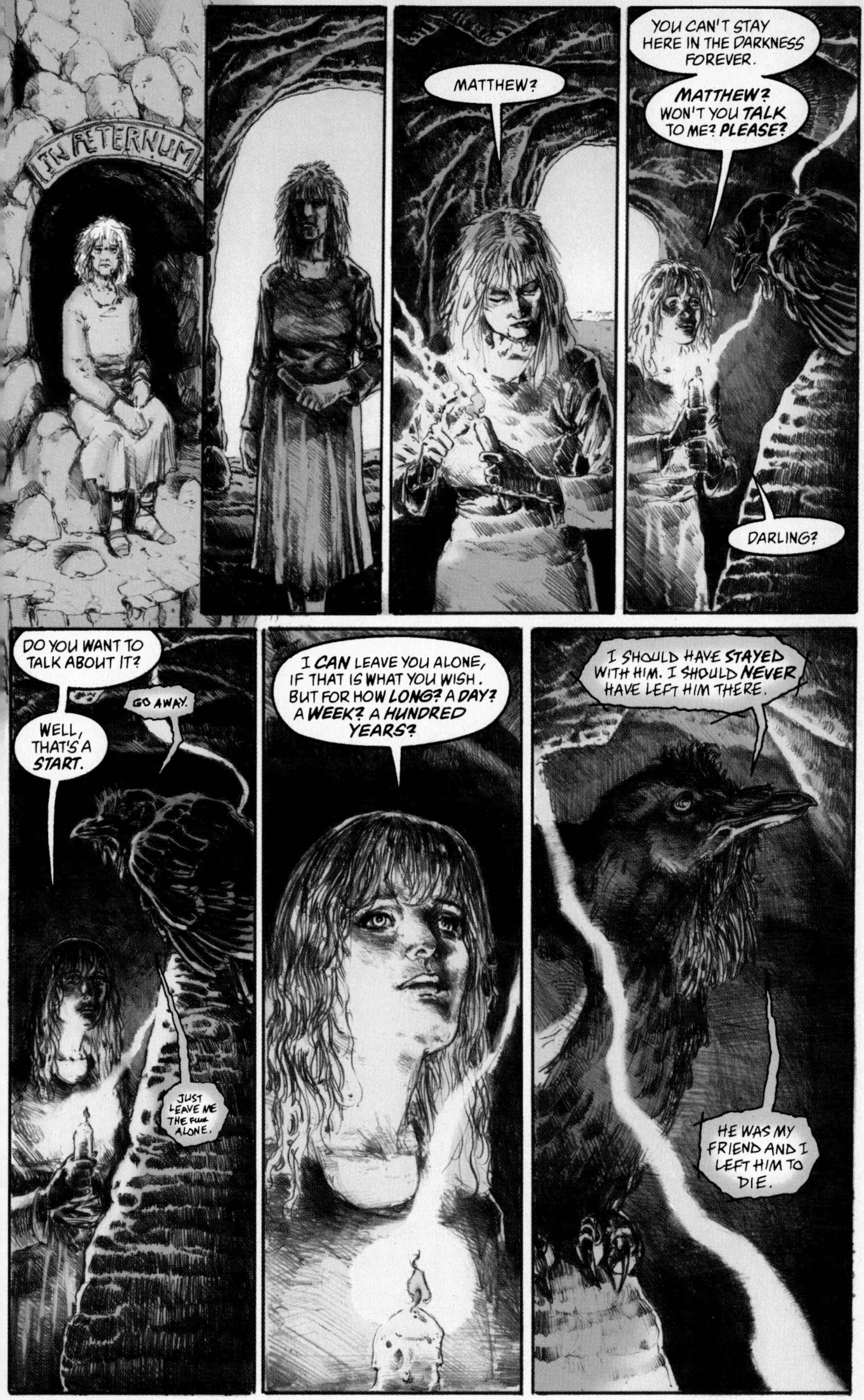
IN AETERNUM
MATTHEW?
YOU CAN'T STAY HERE IN THE DARKNESS FOREVER.
MATTHEW? WON'T YOU TALK TO ME? PLEASE?
DARLING?
DO YOU WANT TO TALK ABOUT IT?
GO AWAY.
WELL, THAT'S A START.
JUST LEAVE ME THE FUCK ALONE.
I CAN LEAVE YOU ALONE, IF THAT IS WHAT YOU WISH. BUT FOR HOW LONG? A DAY? A WEEK? A HUNDRED YEARS?
I SHOULD HAVE STAYED WITH HIM. I SHOULD NEVER HAVE LEFT HIM THERE.
HE WAS MY FRIEND AND I LEFT HIM TO DIE.

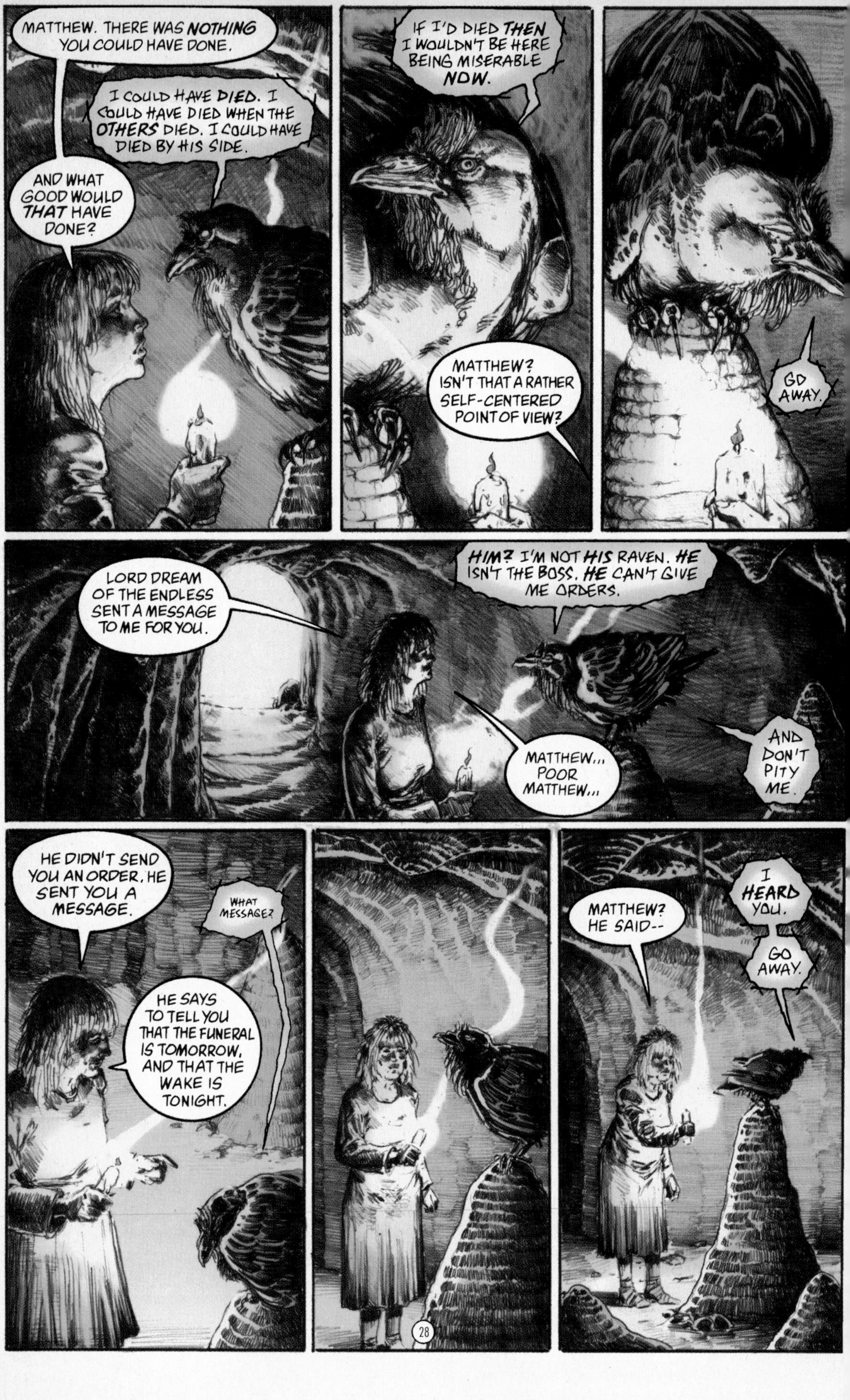
MATTHEW. THERE WAS NOTHING YOU COULD HAVE DONE.
I COULD HAVE DIED. I COULD HAVE DIED WHEN THE OTHERS DIED. I COULD HAVE DIED BY HIS SIDE.
AND WHAT GOOD WOULD THAT HAVE DONE?
IF I'D DIED THEN I WOULDN'T BE HERE BEING MISERABLE NOW.
MATTHEW? ISN'T THAT A RATHER SELF-CENTERED POINT OF VIEW?
GO AWAY.
LORD DREAM OF THE ENDLESS SENT A MESSAGE TO ME FOR YOU.
HIM? I'M NOT HIS RAVEN. HE ISN'T THE BOSS. HE CAN'T GIVE ME ORDERS.
MATTHEW... POOR MATTHEW...
AND DON'T PITY ME.
HE DIDN'T SEND YOU AN ORDER. HE SENT YOU A MESSAGE.
WHAT MESSAGE?
HE SAYS TO TELL YOU THAT THE FUNERAL IS TOMORROW, AND THAT THE WAKE IS TONIGHT.
MATTHEW? HE SAID--
I HEARD YOU.
GO AWAY.

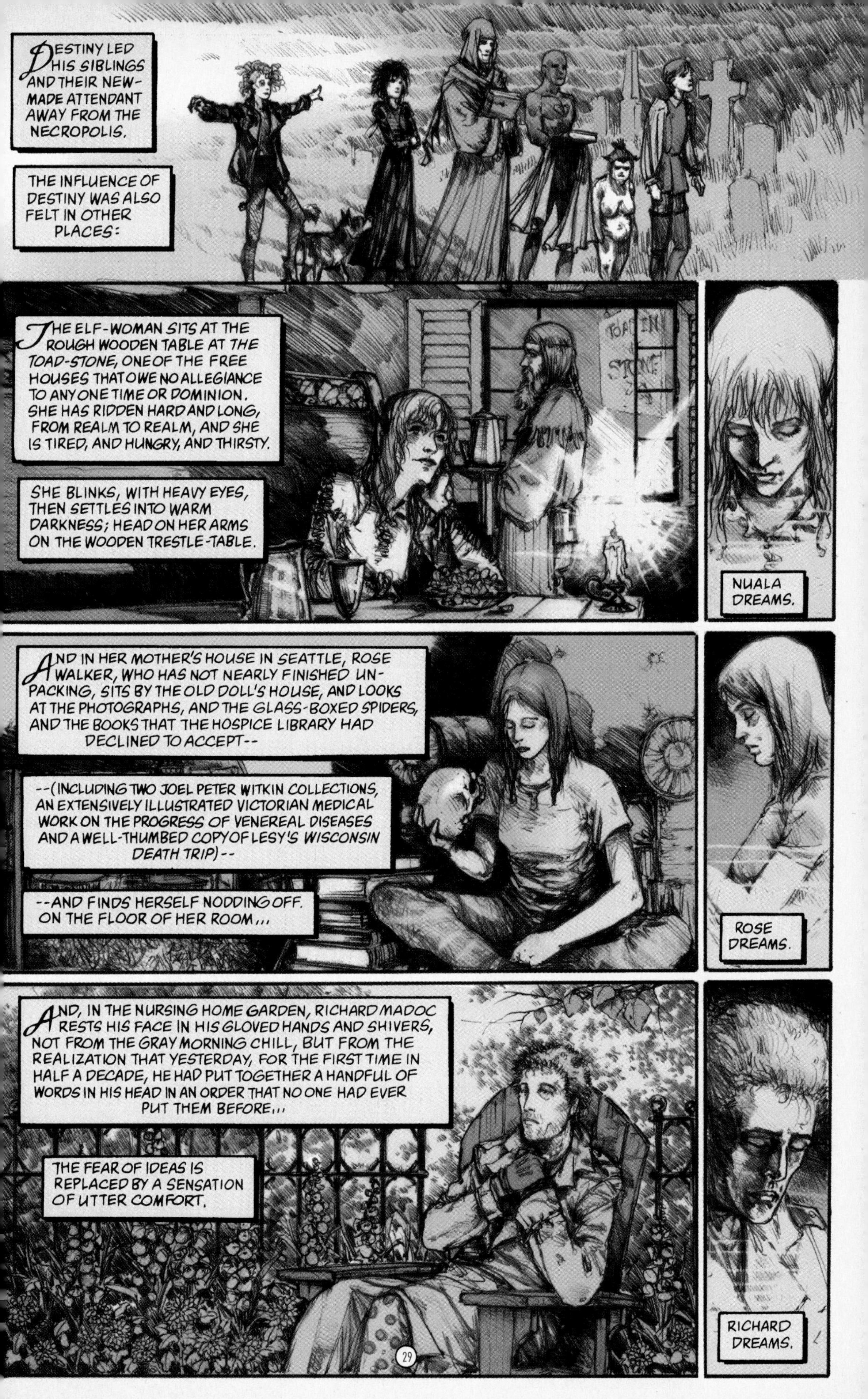
DESTINY LED HIS SIBLINGS AND THEIR NEW-MADE ATTENDANT AWAY FROM THE NECROPOLIS.
THE INFLUENCE OF DESTINY WAS ALSO FELT IN OTHER PLACES:
THE ELF-WOMAN SITS AT THE ROUGH WOODEN TABLE AT THE TOAD-STONE, ONE OF THE FREE HOUSES THAT OWE NO ALLEGIANCE TO ANY ONE TIME OR DOMINION. SHE HAS RIDDEN HARD AND LONG, FROM REALM TO REALM, AND SHE IS TIRED, AND HUNGRY, AND THIRSTY.
SHE BLINKS, WITH HEAVY EYES, THEN SETTLES INTO WARM DARKNESS; HEAD ON HER ARMS ON THE WOODEN TRESTLE-TABLE.
TOAD IN STONE
NUALA DREAMS.
AND IN HER MOTHER'S HOUSE IN SEATTLE, ROSE WALKER, WHO HAS NOT NEARLY FINISHED UNPACKING, SITS BY THE OLD DOLL'S HOUSE, AND LOOKS AT THE PHOTOGRAPHS, AND THE GLASS-BOXED SPIDERS, AND THE BOOKS THAT THE HOSPICE LIBRARY HAD DECLINED TO ACCEPT--
--(INCLUDING TWO JOEL PETER WITKIN COLLECTIONS, AN EXTENSIVELY ILLUSTRATED VICTORIAN MEDICAL WORK ON THE PROGRESS OF VENEREAL DISEASES AND A WELL-THUMBED COPY OF LESY'S WISCONSIN DEATH TRIP)--
--AND FINDS HERSELF NODDING OFF. ON THE FLOOR OF HER ROOM...
ROSE DREAMS.
AND, IN THE NURSING HOME GARDEN, RICHARD MADOC RESTS HIS FACE IN HIS GLOVED HANDS AND SHIVERS, NOT FROM THE GRAY MORNING CHILL, BUT FROM THE REALIZATION THAT YESTERDAY, FOR THE FIRST TIME IN HALF A DECADE, HE HAD PUT TOGETHER A HANDFUL OF WORDS IN HIS HEAD IN AN ORDER THAT NO ONE HAD EVER PUT THEM BEFORE...
THE FEAR OF IDEAS IS REPLACED BY A SENSATION OF UTTER COMFORT.
RICHARD DREAMS.

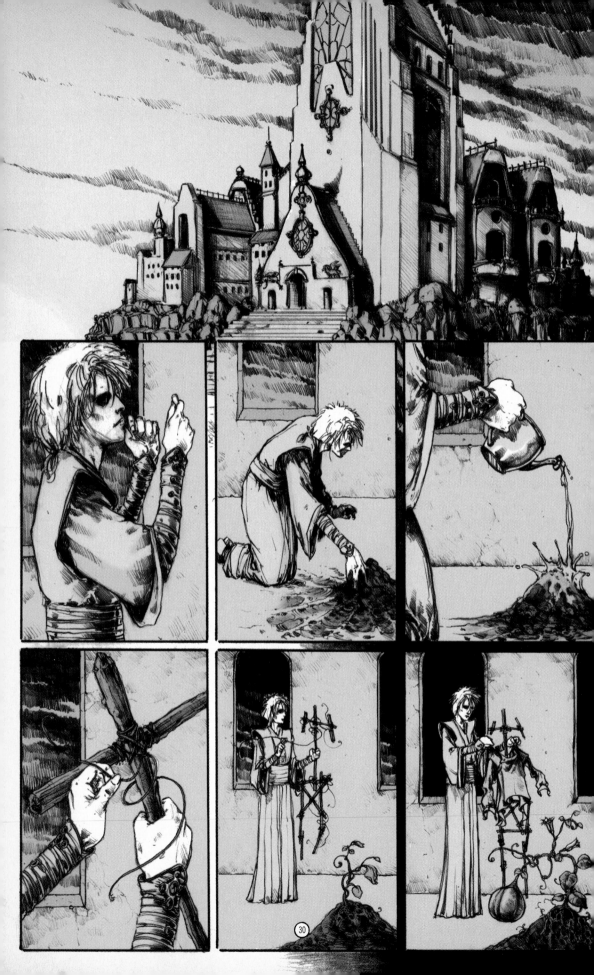

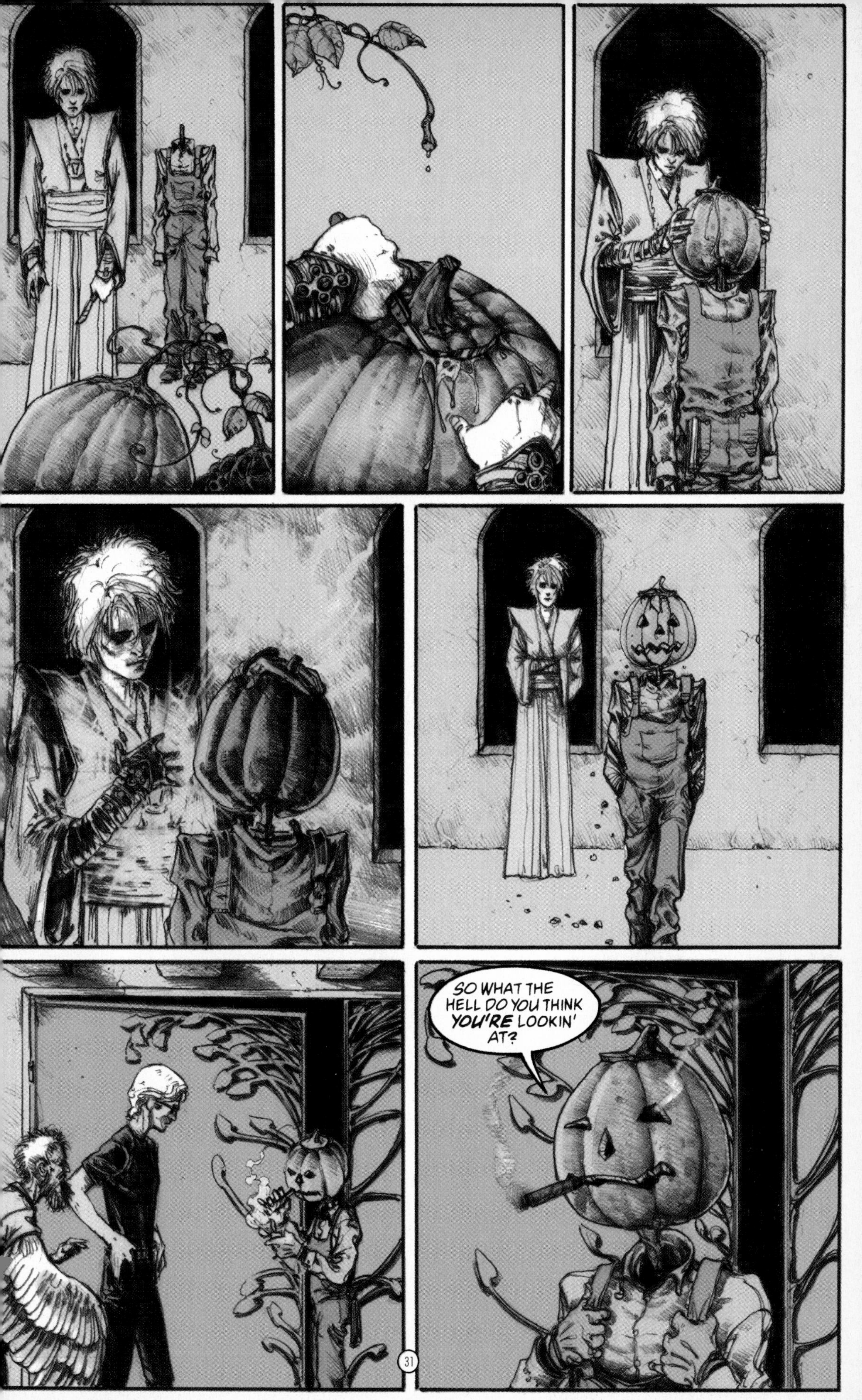
SO WHAT THE HELL DO YOU THINK YOU'RE LOOKIN' AT?

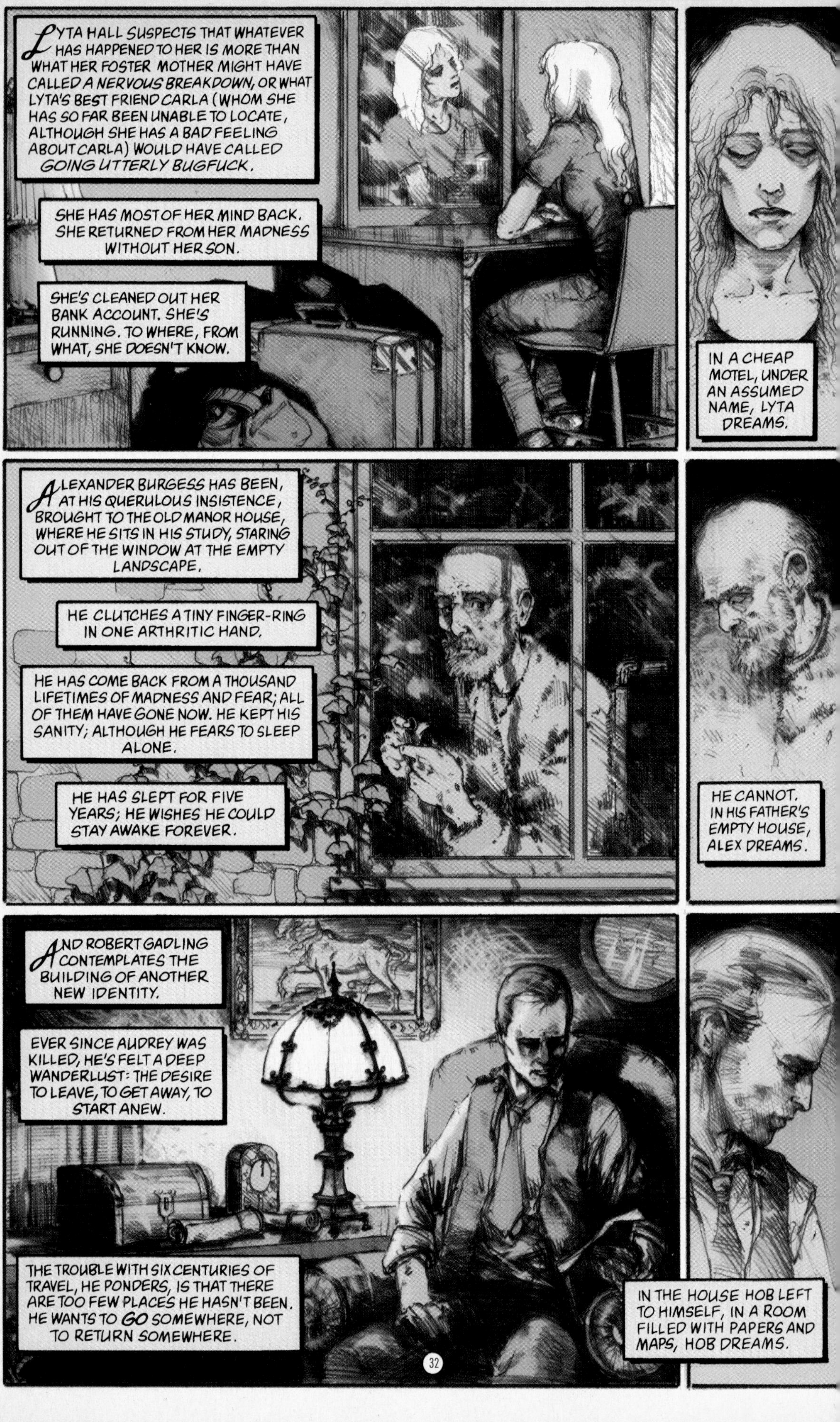
LYTA HALL SUSPECTS THAT WHATEVER HAS HAPPENED TO HER IS MORE THAN WHAT HER FOSTER MOTHER MIGHT HAVE CALLED A *NERVOUS BREAKDOWN*; OR WHAT LYTA'S BEST FRIEND CARLA (WHOM SHE HAS SO FAR BEEN UNABLE TO LOCATE, ALTHOUGH SHE HAS A BAD FEELING ABOUT CARLA) WOULD HAVE CALLED *GOING UTTERLY BUGFUCK*.
SHE HAS MOST OF HER MIND BACK. SHE RETURNED FROM HER MADNESS WITHOUT HER SON.
SHE'S CLEANED OUT HER BANK ACCOUNT. SHE'S RUNNING. TO WHERE, FROM WHAT, SHE DOESN'T KNOW.
IN A CHEAP MOTEL, UNDER AN ASSUMED NAME, LYTA DREAMS.
ALEXANDER BURGESS HAS BEEN, AT HIS QUERULOUS INSISTENCE, BROUGHT TO THE OLD MANOR HOUSE, WHERE HE SITS IN HIS STUDY, STARING OUT OF THE WINDOW AT THE EMPTY LANDSCAPE.
HE CLUTCHES A TINY FINGER-RING IN ONE ARTHRITIC HAND.
HE HAS COME BACK FROM A THOUSAND LIFETIMES OF MADNESS AND FEAR; ALL OF THEM HAVE GONE NOW. HE KEPT HIS SANITY; ALTHOUGH HE FEARS TO SLEEP ALONE.
HE HAS SLEPT FOR FIVE YEARS; HE WISHES HE COULD STAY AWAKE FOREVER.
HE CANNOT. IN HIS FATHER'S EMPTY HOUSE, ALEX DREAMS.
AND ROBERT GADLING CONTEMPLATES THE BUILDING OF ANOTHER NEW IDENTITY.
EVER SINCE AUDREY WAS KILLED, HE'S FELT A DEEP WANDERLUST: THE DESIRE TO LEAVE, TO GET AWAY, TO START ANEW.
THE TROUBLE WITH SIX CENTURIES OF TRAVEL, HE PONDERS, IS THAT THERE ARE TOO FEW PLACES HE HASN'T BEEN. HE WANTS TO *GO* SOMEWHERE, NOT TO RETURN SOMEWHERE.
IN THE HOUSE HOB LEFT TO HIMSELF, IN A ROOM FILLED WITH PAPERS AND MAPS, HOB DREAMS.

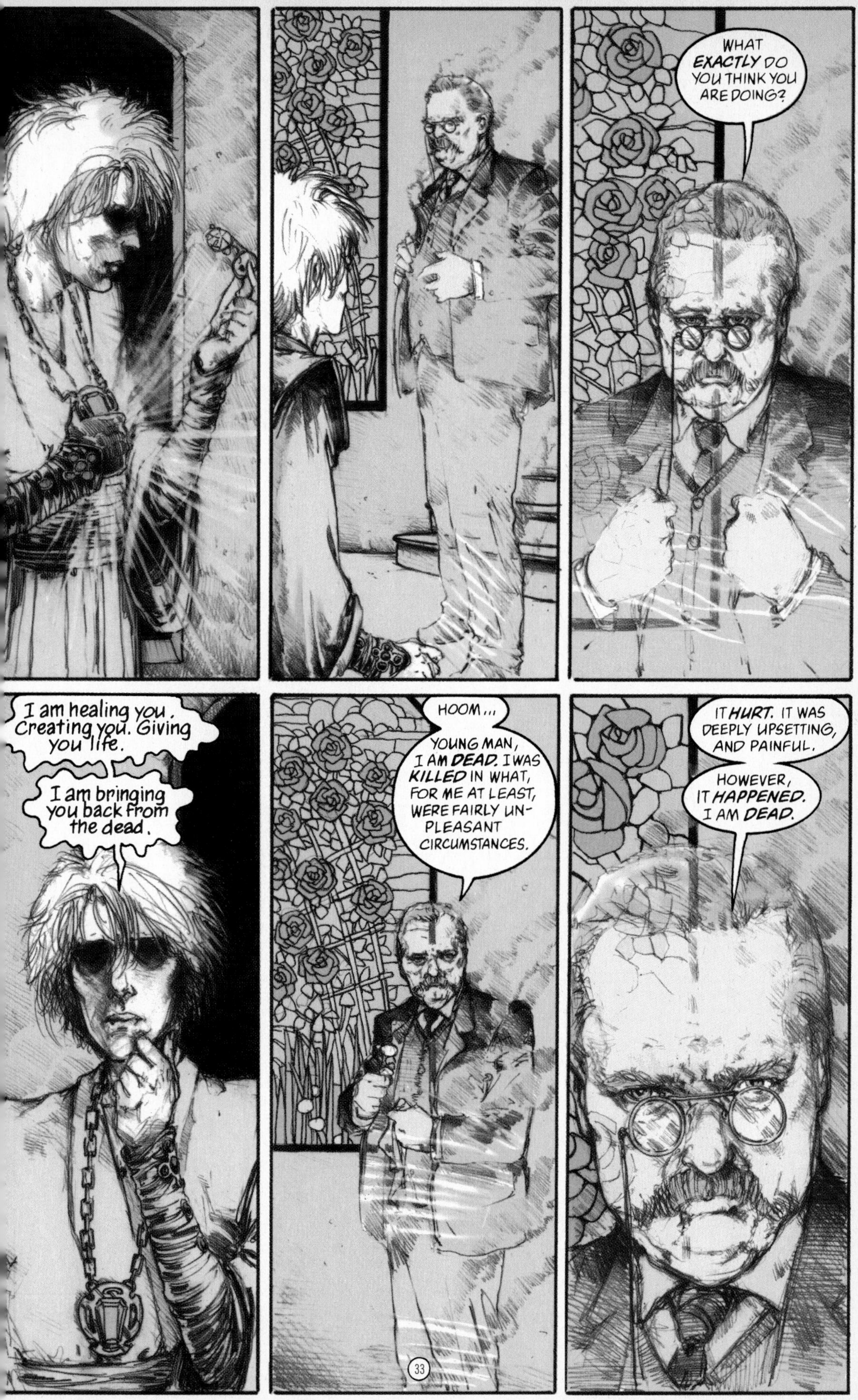
WHAT EXACTLY DO YOU THINK YOU ARE DOING?
I am healing you. Creating you. Giving you life.
I am bringing you back from the dead.
HOOM...
YOUNG MAN, I AM DEAD. I WAS KILLED IN WHAT, FOR ME AT LEAST, WERE FAIRLY UN-PLEASANT CIRCUMSTANCES.
IT HURT. IT WAS DEEPLY UPSETTING, AND PAINFUL.
HOWEVER, IT HAPPENED. I AM DEAD.

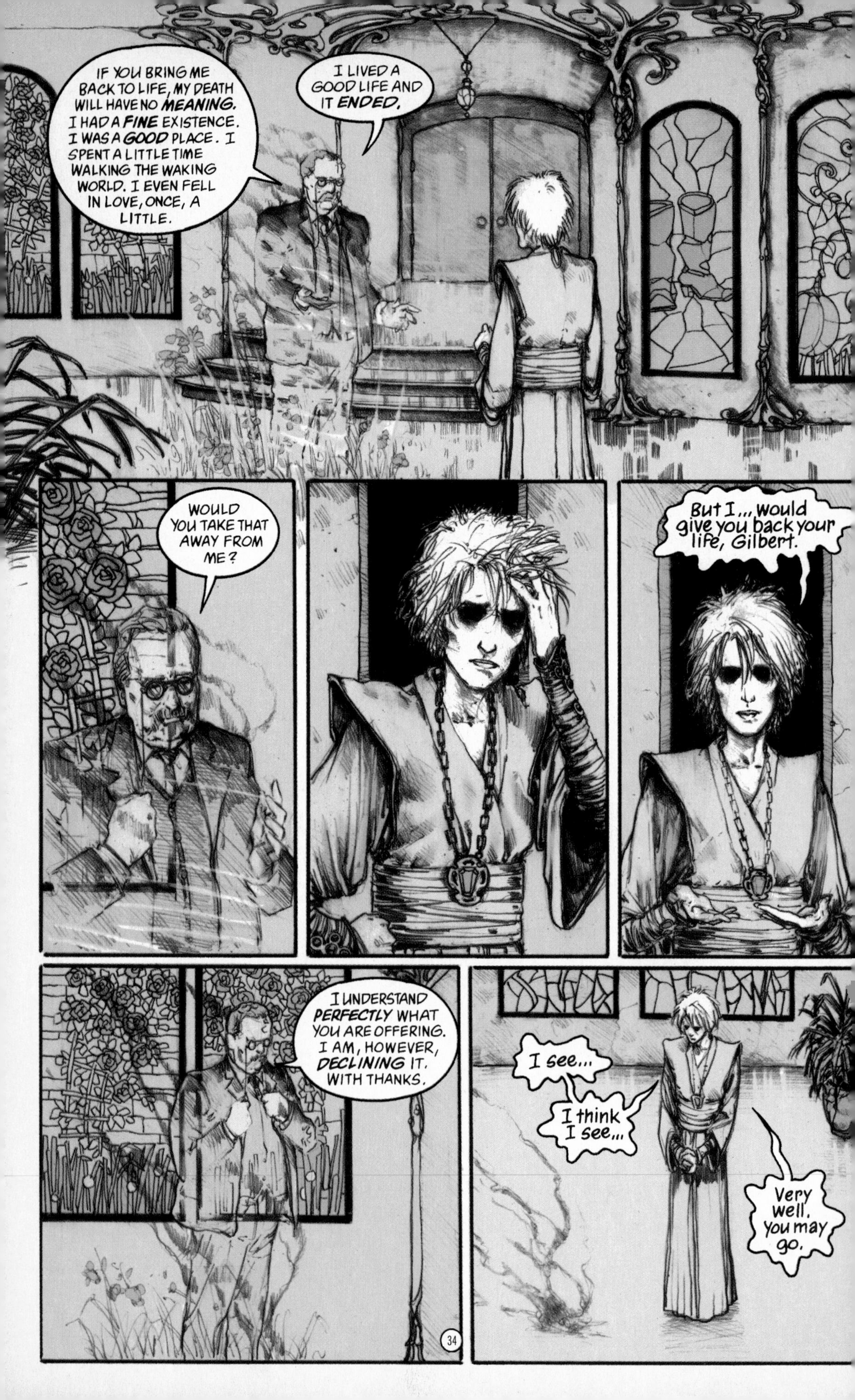
IF YOU BRING ME BACK TO LIFE, MY DEATH WILL HAVE NO MEANING. I HAD A FINE EXISTENCE. I WAS A GOOD PLACE. I SPENT A LITTLE TIME WALKING THE WAKING WORLD. I EVEN FELL IN LOVE, ONCE, A LITTLE.
I LIVED A GOOD LIFE AND IT ENDED.
WOULD YOU TAKE THAT AWAY FROM ME?
But I... would give you back your life, Gilbert.
I UNDERSTAND PERFECTLY WHAT YOU ARE OFFERING. I AM, HOWEVER, DECLINING IT. WITH THANKS.
I see...
I think I see...
Very well. You may go.

SO TITANIA, THE QUEEN OF ALL FAERIE, HAS RAISED HER HORSE AND, DRESSED IN DEEPEST BLACK, SHE RIDES FOR THE NEAREST PORTAL TO THE DREAMING.

AND THE ANGEL DUMA (WHO IS NOT EXACTLY FALLEN, MORE TOPPLED, PERHAPS, OR EVEN TUMBLED), INVOKES A DOOR TO THE DREAMING, AND WALKS THROUGH IT. DUMA'S FEET MAY, OR MAY NOT, QUITE TOUCH THE GROUND.

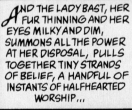

AND THE LADY BAST, HER FUR THINNING AND HER EYES MILKY AND DIM, SUMMONS ALL THE POWER AT HER DISPOSAL, PULLS TOGETHER TINY STRANDS OF BELIEF, A HANDFUL OF INSTANTS OF HALFHEARTED WORSHIP...

AT A CAT SHOW IN GLASGOW, A TEENAGE BOY STARES AT A ONE-YEAR-OLD ABYSSINIAN AND, FOR A MOMENT, HE SEES A GODDESS...

HEAD HELD HIGH, EYES CLEAR, FUR SLEEK, SHE WALKS TO THE DREAMING.

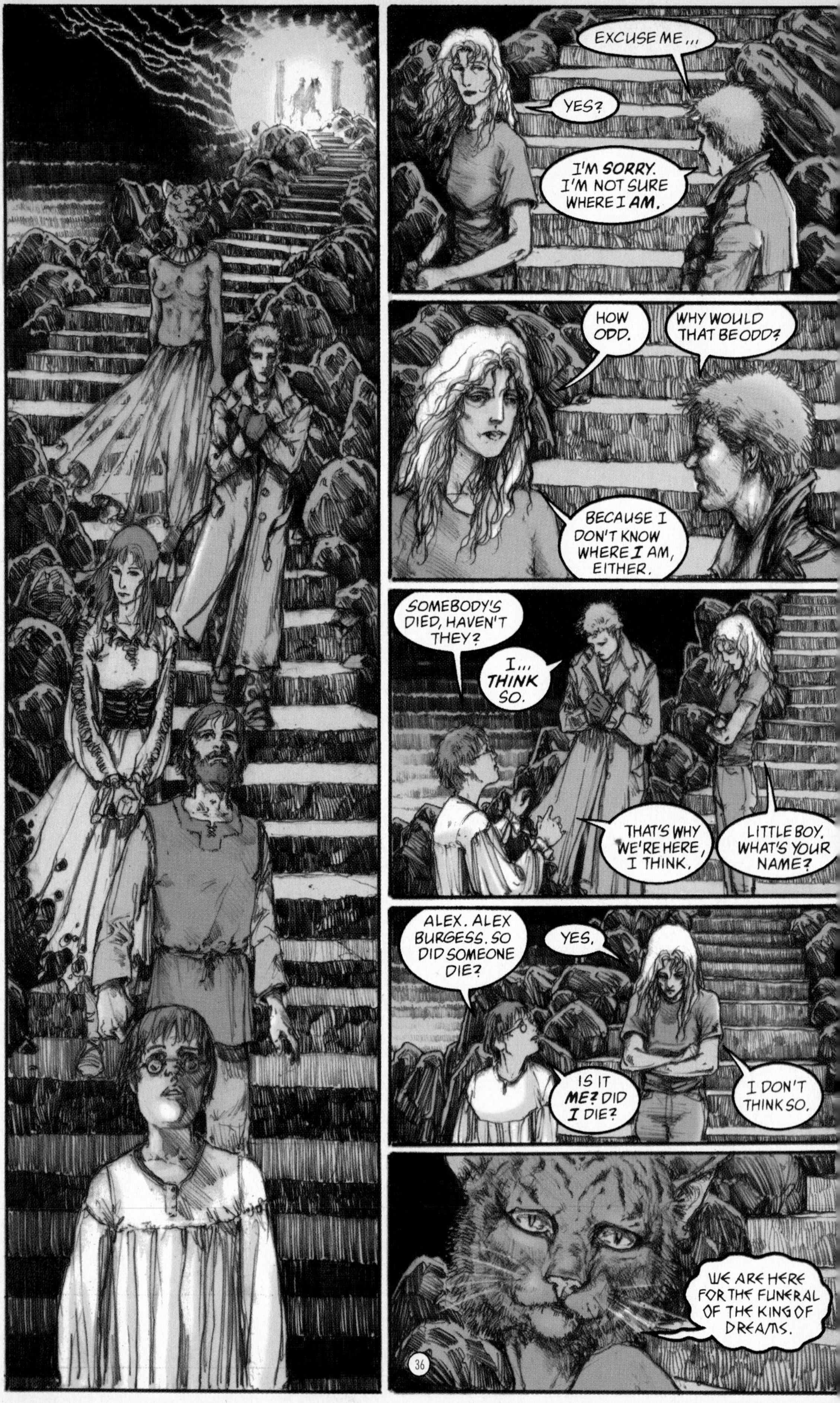
EXCUSE ME...
YES?
I'M SORRY. I'M NOT SURE WHERE I AM.
HOW ODD.
WHY WOULD THAT BE ODD?
BECAUSE I DON'T KNOW WHERE I AM, EITHER.
SOMEBODY'S DIED, HAVEN'T THEY?
I... THINK SO.
THAT'S WHY WE'RE HERE, I THINK.
LITTLE BOY. WHAT'S YOUR NAME?
ALEX. ALEX BURGESS. SO DID SOMEONE DIE?
YES.
IS IT ME? DID I DIE?
I DON'T THINK SO.
WE ARE HERE FOR THE FUNERAL OF THE KING OF DREAMS.

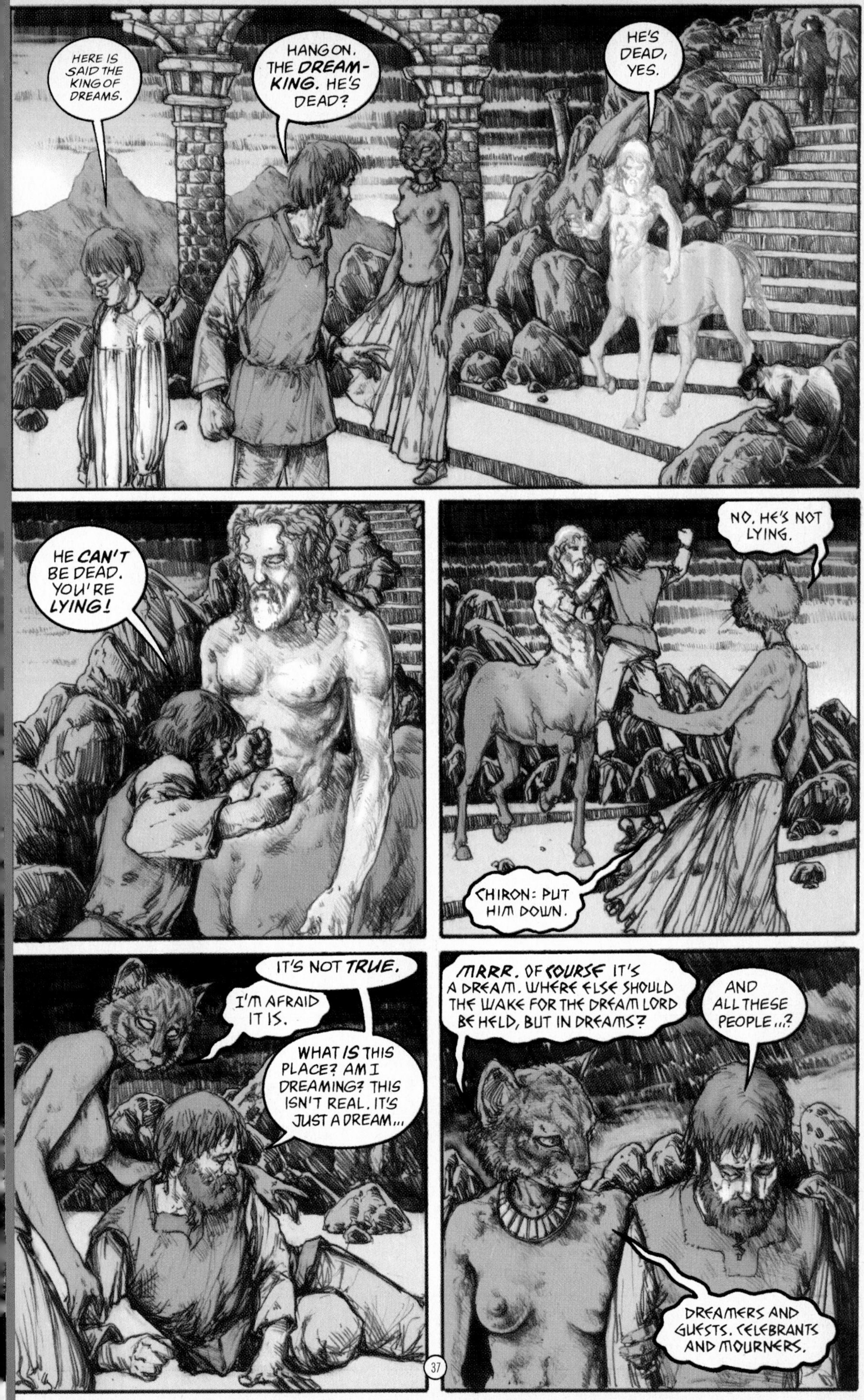
HERE IS SAID THE KING OF DREAMS.
HANG ON. THE DREAM-KING. HE'S DEAD?
HE'S DEAD, YES.
HE CAN'T BE DEAD. YOU'RE LYING!
NO, HE'S NOT LYING.
CHIRON: PUT HIM DOWN.
IT'S NOT TRUE.
I'M AFRAID IT IS.
WHAT IS THIS PLACE? AM I DREAMING? THIS ISN'T REAL. IT'S JUST A DREAM...
MRRR. OF COURSE IT'S A DREAM. WHERE ELSE SHOULD THE WAKE FOR THE DREAM LORD BE HELD, BUT IN DREAMS?
AND ALL THESE PEOPLE...?
DREAMERS AND GUESTS. CELEBRANTS AND MOURNERS.

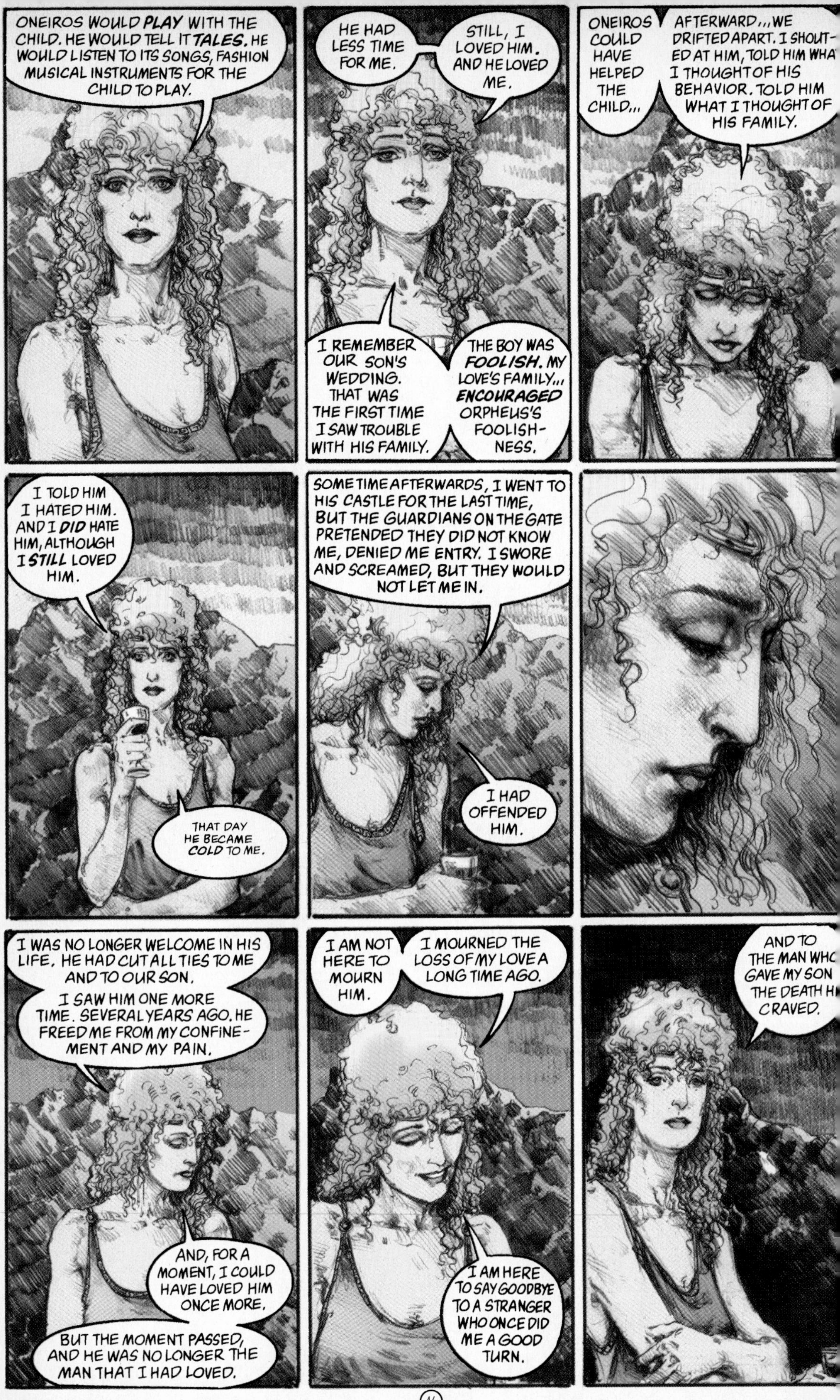
ONEIROS WOULD PLAY WITH THE CHILD. HE WOULD TELL IT TALES. HE WOULD LISTEN TO ITS SONGS, FASHION MUSICAL INSTRUMENTS FOR THE CHILD TO PLAY.
HE HAD LESS TIME FOR ME.
STILL, I LOVED HIM. AND HE LOVED ME.
I REMEMBER OUR SON'S WEDDING. THAT WAS THE FIRST TIME I SAW TROUBLE WITH HIS FAMILY.
THE BOY WAS FOOLISH. MY LOVE'S FAMILY... ENCOURAGED ORPHEUS'S FOOLISHNESS.
ONEIROS COULD HAVE HELPED THE CHILD...
AFTERWARD... WE DRIFTED APART. I SHOUTED AT HIM, TOLD HIM WHA I THOUGHT OF HIS BEHAVIOR. TOLD HIM WHAT I THOUGHT OF HIS FAMILY.
I TOLD HIM I HATED HIM. AND I DID HATE HIM, ALTHOUGH I STILL LOVED HIM.
THAT DAY HE BECAME COLD TO ME.
SOME TIME AFTERWARDS, I WENT TO HIS CASTLE FOR THE LAST TIME, BUT THE GUARDIANS ON THE GATE PRETENDED THEY DID NOT KNOW ME, DENIED ME ENTRY. I SWORE AND SCREAMED, BUT THEY WOULD NOT LET ME IN.
I HAD OFFENDED HIM.
I WAS NO LONGER WELCOME IN HIS LIFE. HE HAD CUT ALL TIES TO ME AND TO OUR SON.
I SAW HIM ONE MORE TIME. SEVERAL YEARS AGO. HE FREED ME FROM MY CONFINEMENT AND MY PAIN.
AND, FOR A MOMENT, I COULD HAVE LOVED HIM ONCE MORE.
BUT THE MOMENT PASSED, AND HE WAS NO LONGER THE MAN THAT I HAD LOVED.
I AM NOT HERE TO MOURN HIM.
I MOURNED THE LOSS OF MY LOVE A LONG TIME AGO.
I AM HERE TO SAY GOODBYE TO A STRANGER WHO ONCE DID ME A GOOD TURN.
AND TO THE MAN WHC GAVE MY SON THE DEATH H CRAVED.

WHAT THE **HELL** IS GOING ON HERE?

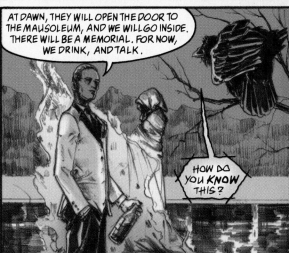

AT DAWN, THEY WILL OPEN THE DOOR TO THE MAUSOLEUM, AND WE WILL GO INSIDE. THERE WILL BE A MEMORIAL. FOR NOW, WE DRINK, AND TALK.

HOW DO YOU **KNOW** THIS?

I... I KNEW IT WHEN I **CAME** TO THIS PLACE.

IT WAS LIKE THE WAY ONE KNOWS THINGS IN DREAMS...

...WHERE YOU KNOW THAT YOU'RE A SECRET AGENT, OR THAT YOUR BROTHER IS TRYING TO KILL YOU, OR THAT THE EGG IN YOUR HAND WILL SOON HATCH INTO A PHOTOGRAPH OF YOUR TRUE LOVE...

Y'**KNOW**, BIRDIE, TALKIN' TO DREAMERS IS LIKE TALKIN' TO ZOMBIES OR SUMP'N. I DON'T KNOW WHY YA EVEN **TRY.**

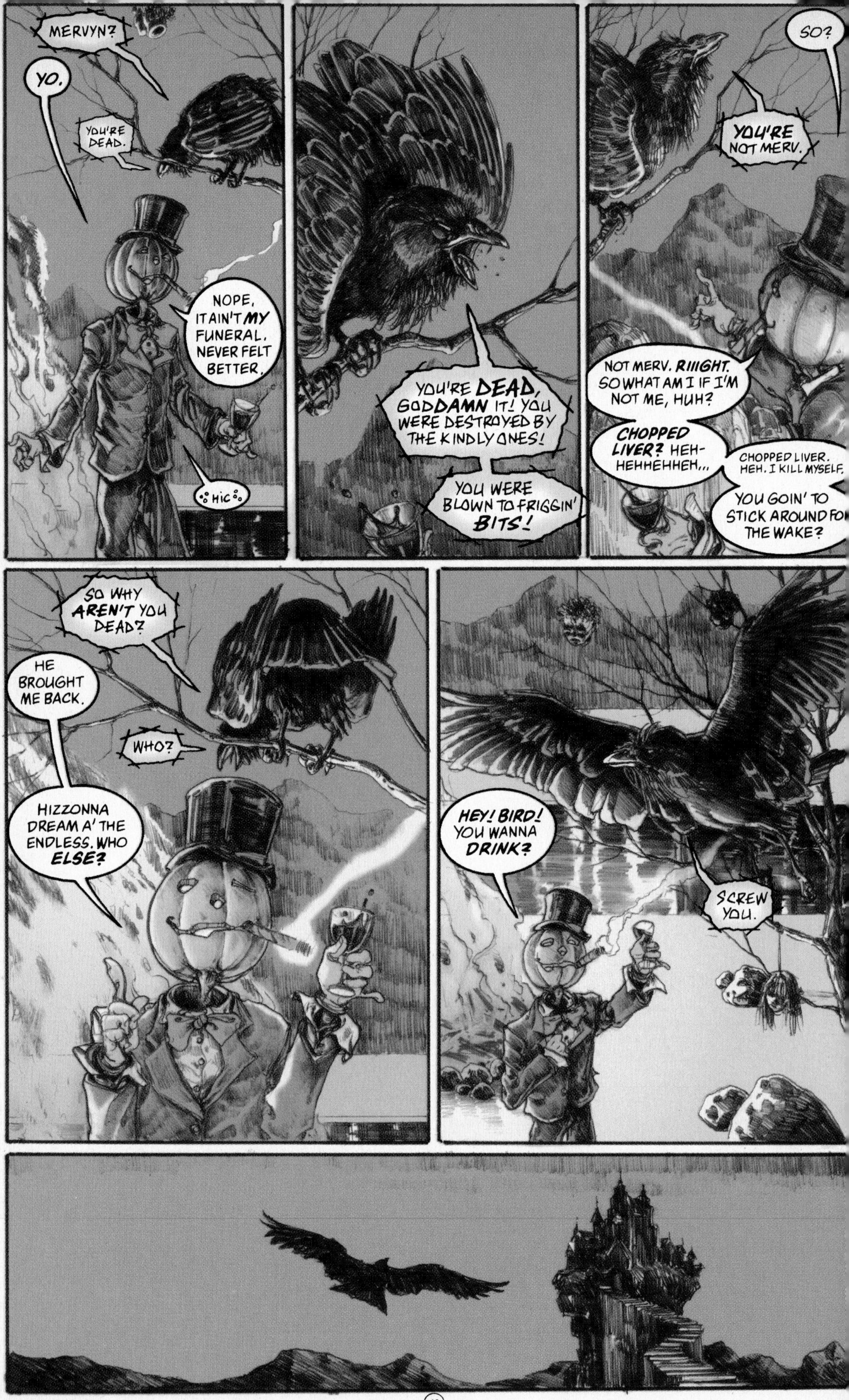
MERVYN?
YO.
YOU'RE DEAD.
NOPE, IT AIN'T MY FUNERAL. NEVER FELT BETTER.
HIC
YOU'RE DEAD, GODDAMN IT! YOU WERE DESTROYED BY THE KINDLY ONES!
YOU WERE BLOWN TO FRIGGIN' BITS!
SO?
YOU'RE NOT MERV.
NOT MERV. RIIIGHT. SO WHAT AM I IF I'M NOT ME, HUH?
CHOPPED LIVER? HEH-HEHHEHHEH...
CHOPPED LIVER. HEH. I KILL MYSELF.
YOU GOIN' TO STICK AROUND FOR THE WAKE?
SO WHY AREN'T YOU DEAD?
HE BROUGHT ME BACK.
WHO?
HIZZONNA DREAM A' THE ENDLESS. WHO ELSE?
HEY! BIRD! YOU WANNA DRINK?
SCREW YOU.

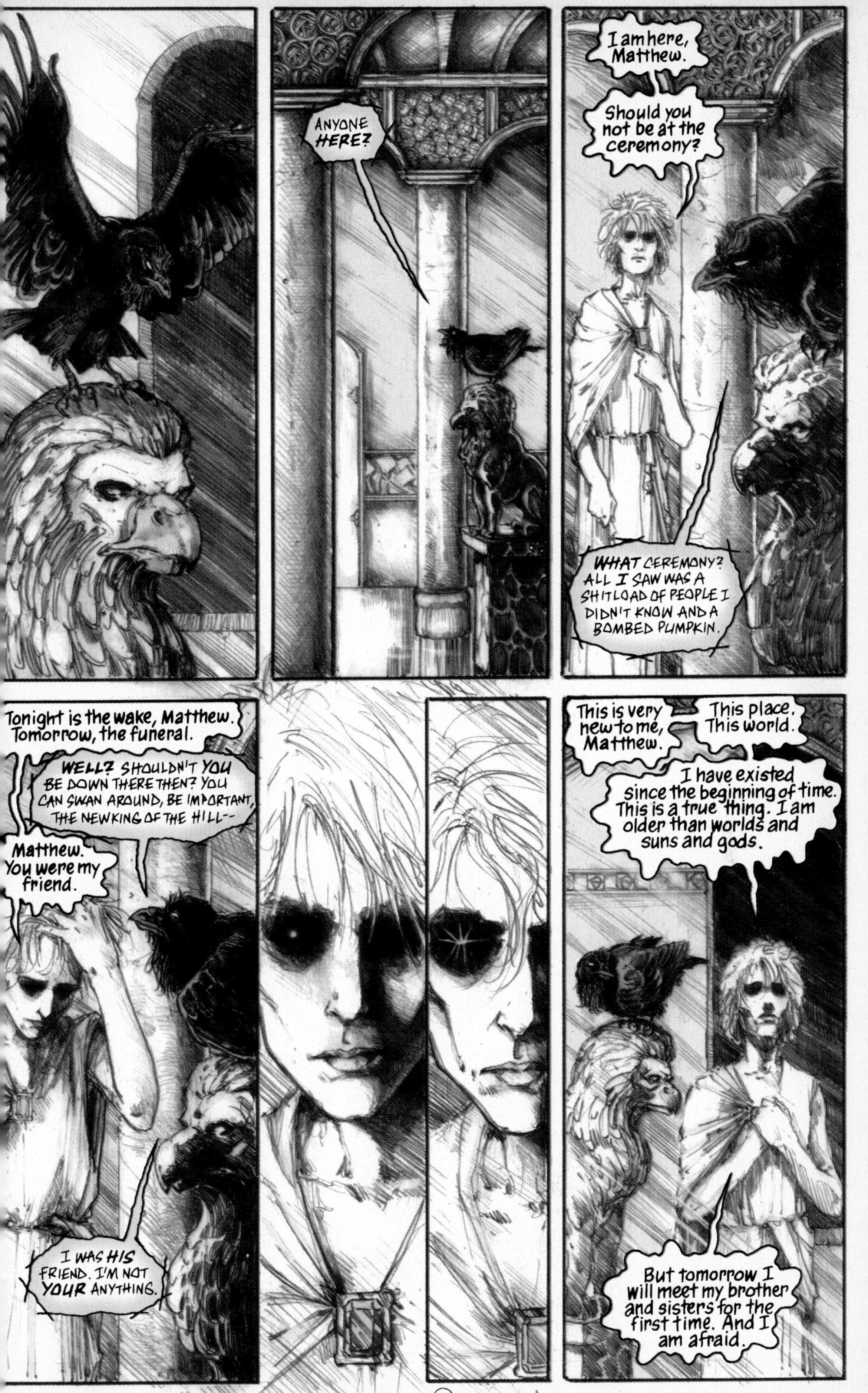
ANYONE HERE?
I am here, Matthew.
Should you not be at the ceremony?
WHAT CEREMONY? ALL I SAW WAS A SHITLOAD OF PEOPLE I DIDN'T KNOW AND A BOMBED PUMPKIN.
Tonight is the wake, Matthew. Tomorrow, the funeral.
WELL? SHOULDN'T YOU BE DOWN THERE THEN? YOU CAN SWAN AROUND, BE IMPORTANT, THE NEW KING OF THE HILL--
Matthew. You were my friend.
I WAS HIS FRIEND. I'M NOT YOUR ANYTHING.
This is very new to me, Matthew.
This place. This world.
I have existed since the beginning of time. This is a true thing. I am older than worlds and suns and gods.
But tomorrow I will meet my brother and sisters for the first time. And I am afraid.

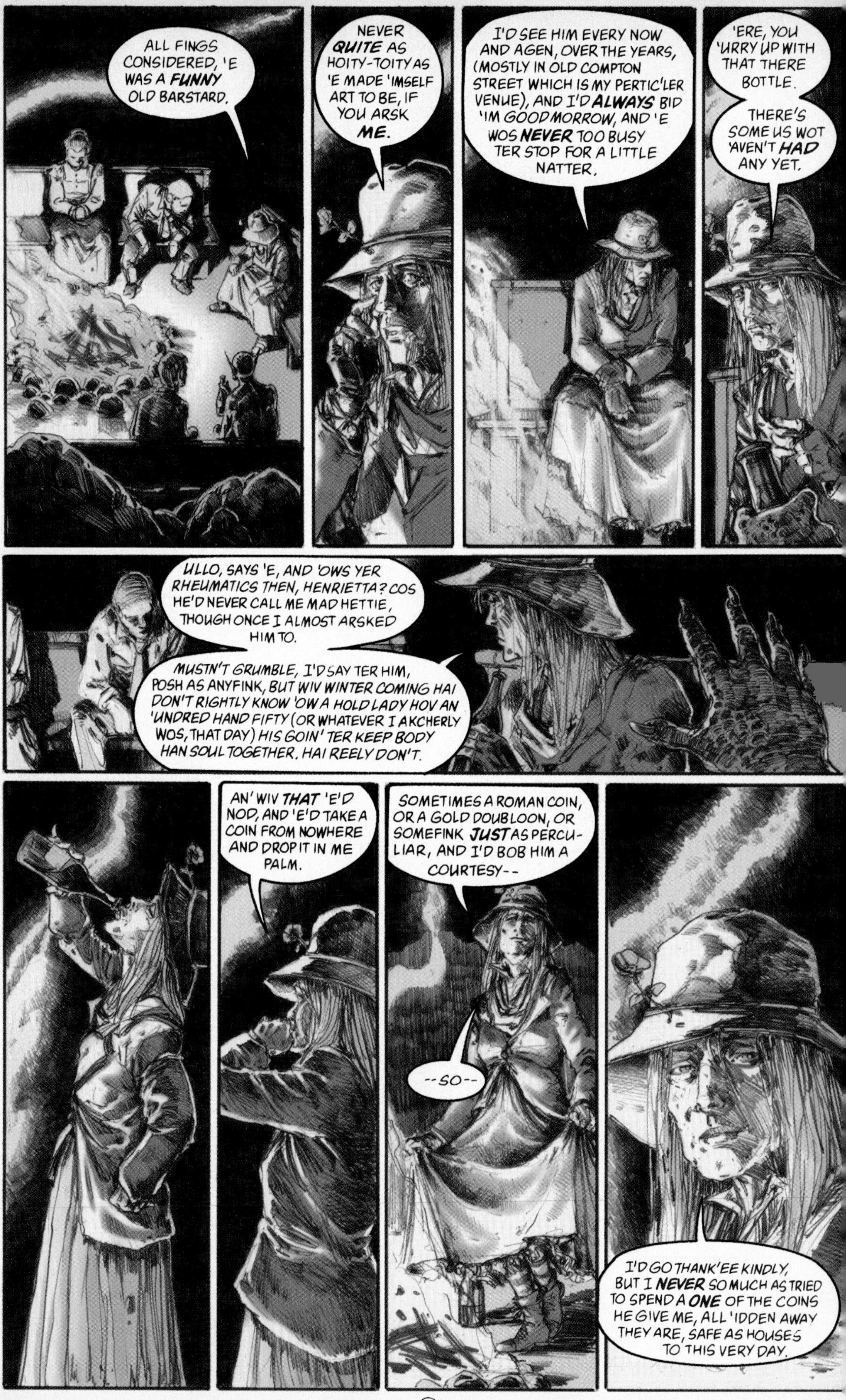
ALL FINGS CONSIDERED, 'E WAS A FUNNY OLD BARSTARD.
NEVER QUITE AS HOITY-TOITY AS 'E MADE 'IMSELF ART TO BE, IF YOU ARSK ME.
I'D SEE HIM EVERY NOW AND AGEN, OVER THE YEARS, (MOSTLY IN OLD COMPTON STREET WHICH IS MY PERTIC'LER VENUE), AND I'D ALWAYS BID 'IM GOOD MORROW, AND 'E WOS NEVER TOO BUSY TER STOP FOR A LITTLE NATTER.
'ERE, YOU 'URRY UP WITH THAT THERE BOTTLE.
THERE'S SOME US WOT 'AVEN'T HAD ANY YET.
ULLO, SAYS 'E, AND 'OWS YER RHEUMATICS THEN, HENRIETTA? COS HE'D NEVER CALL ME MAD HETTIE, THOUGH ONCE I ALMOST ARSKED HIM TO.
MUSTN'T GRUMBLE, I'D SAY TER HIM, POSH AS ANYFINK, BUT WIV WINTER COMING HAI DON'T RIGHTLY KNOW 'OW A HOLD LADY HOV AN 'UNDRED HAND FIFTY (OR WHATEVER I AKCHERLY WOS, THAT DAY) HIS GOIN' TER KEEP BODY HAN SOUL TOGETHER. HAI REELY DON'T.
AN' WIV THAT 'E'D NOD, AND 'E'D TAKE A COIN FROM NOWHERE AND DROP IT IN ME PALM.
SOMETIMES A ROMAN COIN, OR A GOLD DOUBLOON, OR SOMEFINK JUST AS PERCULIAR, AND I'D BOB HIM A COURTESY--
--SO--
I'D GO THANK'EE KINDLY, BUT I NEVER SO MUCH AS TRIED TO SPEND A ONE OF THE COINS HE GIVE ME, ALL 'IDDEN AWAY THEY ARE, SAFE AS HOUSES TO THIS VERY DAY.

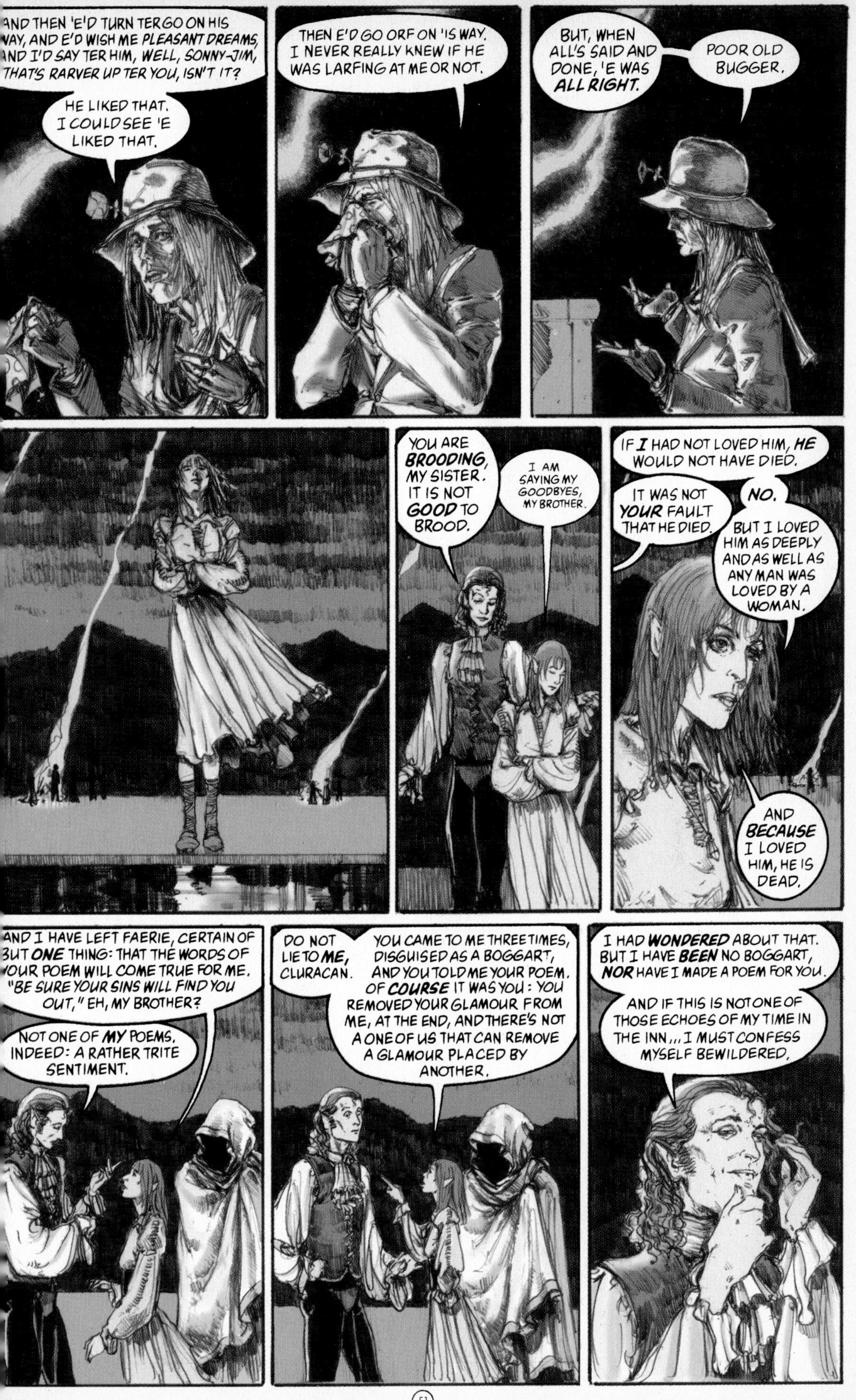
AND THEN 'E'D TURN TER GO ON HIS WAY, AND E'D WISH ME PLEASANT DREAMS, AND I'D SAY TER HIM, WELL, SONNY-JIM, THAT'S RARVER UP TER YOU, ISN'T IT?
HE LIKED THAT. I COULD SEE 'E LIKED THAT.
THEN E'D GO ORF ON 'IS WAY. I NEVER REALLY KNEW IF HE WAS LARFING AT ME OR NOT.
BUT, WHEN ALL'S SAID AND DONE, 'E WAS ALL RIGHT.
POOR OLD BUGGER.
YOU ARE BROODING, MY SISTER. IT IS NOT GOOD TO BROOD.
I AM SAYING MY GOODBYES, MY BROTHER.
IF I HAD NOT LOVED HIM, HE WOULD NOT HAVE DIED.
IT WAS NOT YOUR FAULT THAT HE DIED.
NO.
BUT I LOVED HIM AS DEEPLY AND AS WELL AS ANY MAN WAS LOVED BY A WOMAN.
AND BECAUSE I LOVED HIM, HE IS DEAD.
AND I HAVE LEFT FAERIE, CERTAIN OF BUT ONE THING: THAT THE WORDS OF YOUR POEM WILL COME TRUE FOR ME. "BE SURE YOUR SINS WILL FIND YOU OUT," EH, MY BROTHER?
NOT ONE OF MY POEMS, INDEED: A RATHER TRITE SENTIMENT.
DO NOT LIE TO ME, CLURACAN.
YOU CAME TO ME THREE TIMES, DISGUISED AS A BOGGART, AND YOU TOLD ME YOUR POEM. OF COURSE IT WAS YOU: YOU REMOVED YOUR GLAMOUR FROM ME, AT THE END, AND THERE'S NOT A ONE OF US THAT CAN REMOVE A GLAMOUR PLACED BY ANOTHER.
I HAD WONDERED ABOUT THAT. BUT I HAVE BEEN NO BOGGART, NOR HAVE I MADE A POEM FOR YOU.
AND IF THIS IS NOT ONE OF THOSE ECHOES OF MY TIME IN THE INN,,, I MUST CONFESS MYSELF BEWILDERED.

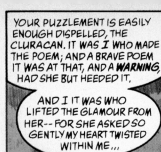

YOUR PUZZLEMENT IS EASILY ENOUGH DISPELLED, THE CLURACAN. IT WAS *I* WHO MADE THE POEM; AND A BRAVE POEM IT *WAS* AT THAT, AND A *WARNING*, HAD SHE BUT HEEDED IT.

AND *I* IT WAS WHO LIFTED THE GLAMOUR FROM HER-- FOR SHE ASKED SO *GENTLY* MY HEART TWISTED WITHIN ME...

WHAT *ARE* YOU?

PERHAPS YOU'D KNOW ME BETTER WITH *THESE*, MY *BROTHER.*

UM. *NO.* NOT REALLY. YOU *LOOK* LIKE ME-- *NOT* AS GOOD-LOOKING, AND THERE'S SOMETHING A LITTLE ODD ABOUT THE NOSE, BUT ENOUG LIKE ME TO FOOL THOSE WHO HADN'T MADE SUCH A STUDY OF MY FACE AS I HAVE-- ONI WITH THE HORNS OF A STAG.

I'VE NOT WORN ANTLERS SINCE TH' ELEVENTH CENTURY, AND I'M NO CUCKOLD...

I SUPPOSE, WITH TOO MUCH WINE, *ALL* THINGS ARE POSSIBLE, THOUGH THE THOUGHT OF IT MAKES ME A LITTLE UNEASY TO ME STOMACH: YE'D NOT BE MY *SON*, WOULD YE?

CLOSE, THE CLURACAN, BUT ONLY IN A MANNER OF SPEAKING. IT WAS HERE YOU SPAWNED ME. *I* AM YOUR NEMESIS.

OH.

AREN'T YOU MEANT TO BE BUSILY TRYING TO DESTROY ME, OR SOMETHING?

AT A *WAKE? WHERE* WOULD BE THE MANNERS IN ME IF I TRIED SUCH A THING? NO, IT'S MY OWN SWEET TIME ABOUT THE TASK I'LL BE TAKING.

AND IT *WON'T* BE IN THE DREAMING, WHERE *I* WAS BORN, NOR IN *FAERIE*, WHERE *YOU* BEGAN, BUT IN THE WIDE WORLDS BETWEEN I'LL COME FOR YOU, HIDE AND RUN HOW YOU MAY.

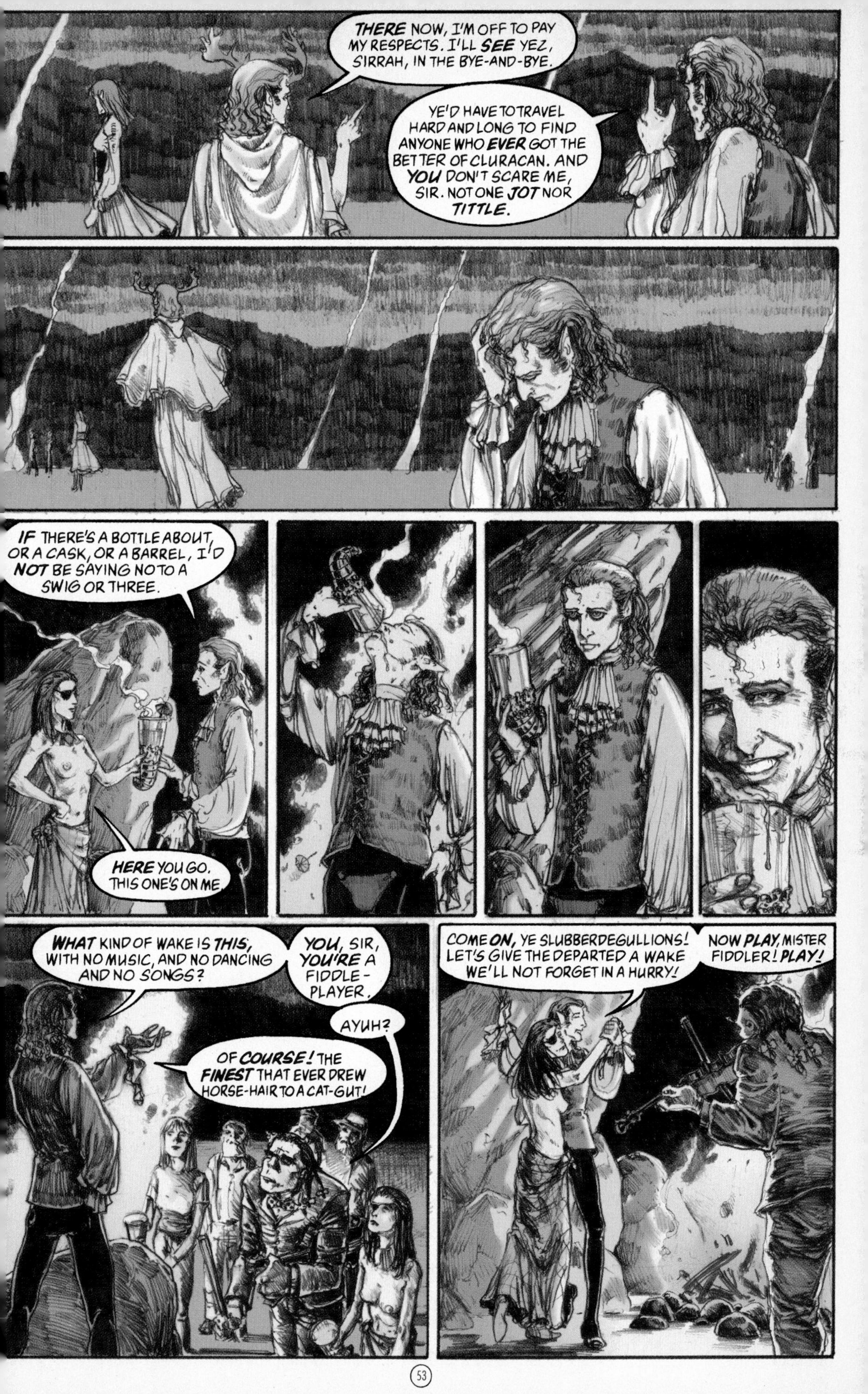
THERE NOW, I'M OFF TO PAY MY RESPECTS. I'LL SEE YEZ, SIRRAH, IN THE BYE-AND-BYE.
YE'D HAVE TO TRAVEL HARD AND LONG TO FIND ANYONE WHO EVER GOT THE BETTER OF CLURACAN. AND YOU DON'T SCARE ME, SIR. NOT ONE JOT NOR TITTLE.
IF THERE'S A BOTTLE ABOUT, OR A CASK, OR A BARREL, I'D NOT BE SAYING NO TO A SWIG OR THREE.
HERE YOU GO. THIS ONE'S ON ME.
WHAT KIND OF WAKE IS THIS, WITH NO MUSIC, AND NO DANCING AND NO SONGS?
YOU, SIR, YOU'RE A FIDDLE-PLAYER.
AYUH?
OF COURSE! THE FINEST THAT EVER DREW HORSE-HAIR TO A CAT-GUT!
COME ON, YE SLUBBERDEGULLIONS! LET'S GIVE THE DEPARTED A WAKE WE'LL NOT FORGET IN A HURRY!
NOW PLAY, MISTER FIDDLER! PLAY!

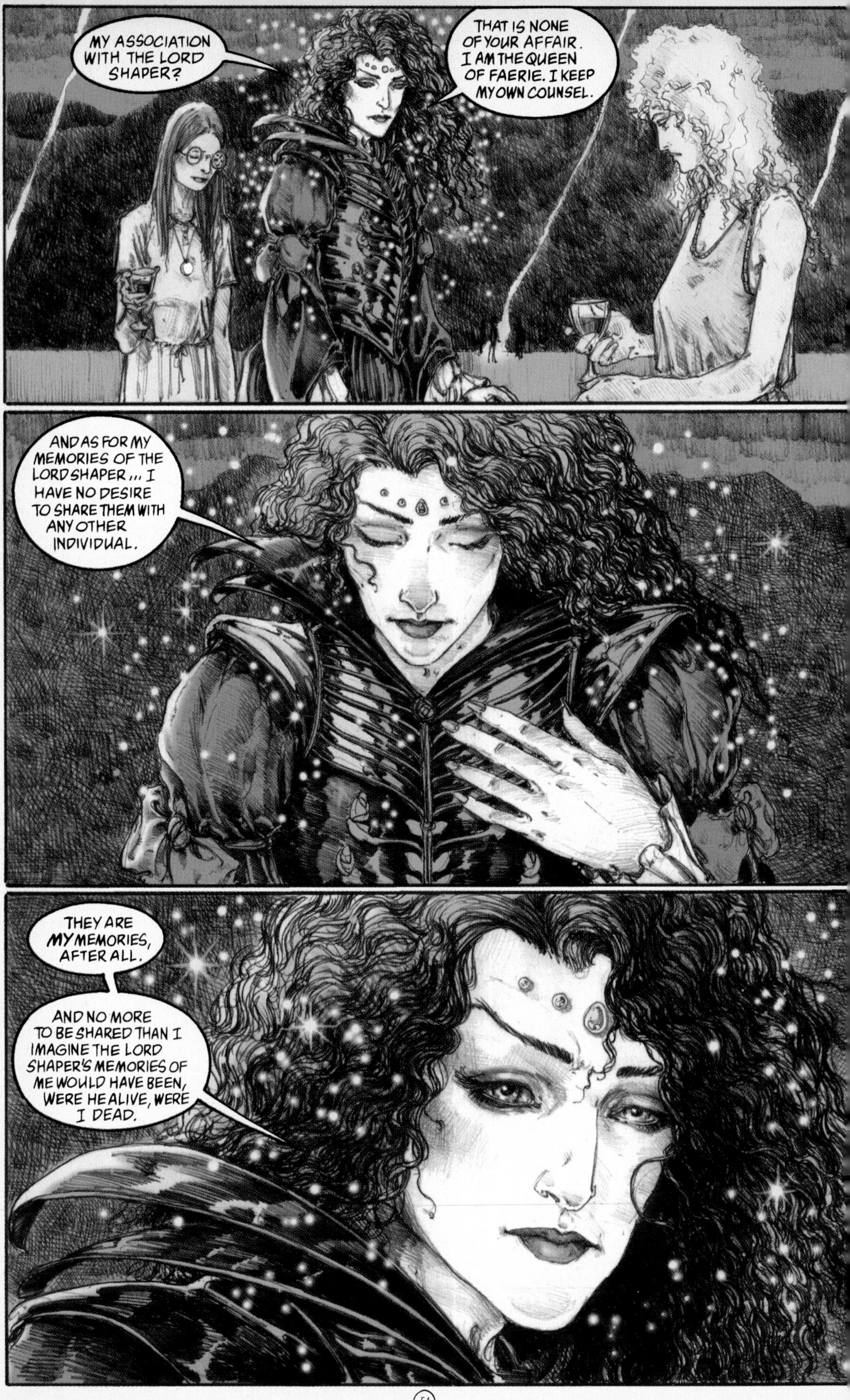

MY ASSOCIATION WITH THE LORD SHAPER?
THAT IS NONE OF YOUR AFFAIR. I AM THE QUEEN OF FAERIE. I KEEP MY OWN COUNSEL.
AND AS FOR MY MEMORIES OF THE LORD SHAPER ... I HAVE NO DESIRE TO SHARE THEM WITH ANY OTHER INDIVIDUAL.
THEY ARE *MY* MEMORIES, AFTER ALL.
AND NO MORE TO BE SHARED THAN I IMAGINE THE LORD SHAPER'S MEMORIES OF ME WOULD HAVE BEEN, WERE HE ALIVE, WERE I DEAD.

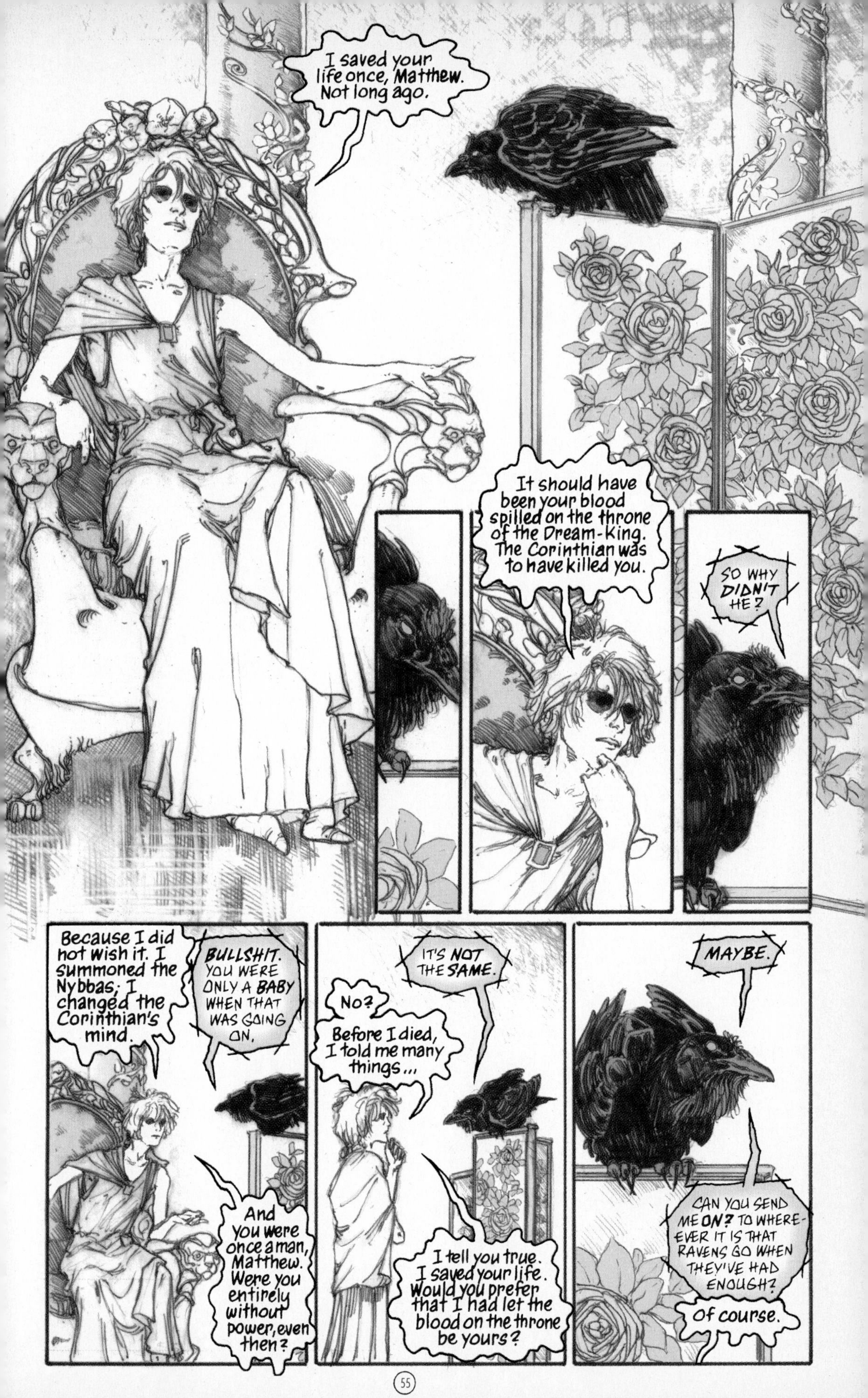

I saved your life once, Matthew. Not long ago.
It should have been your blood spilled on the throne of the Dream-King. The Corinthian was to have killed you.
SO WHY DIDN'T HE?
Because I did not wish it. I summoned the Nybbas; I changed the Corinthian's mind.
BULLSHIT. YOU WERE ONLY A BABY WHEN THAT WAS GOING ON.
And you were once a man, Matthew. Were you entirely without power, even then?
IT'S NOT THE SAME.
No?
Before I died, I told me many things...
I tell you true. I saved your life. Would you prefer that I had let the blood on the throne be yours?
MAYBE.
CAN YOU SEND ME ON? TO WHERE-EVER IT IS THAT RAVENS GO WHEN THEY'VE HAD ENOUGH?
Of course.

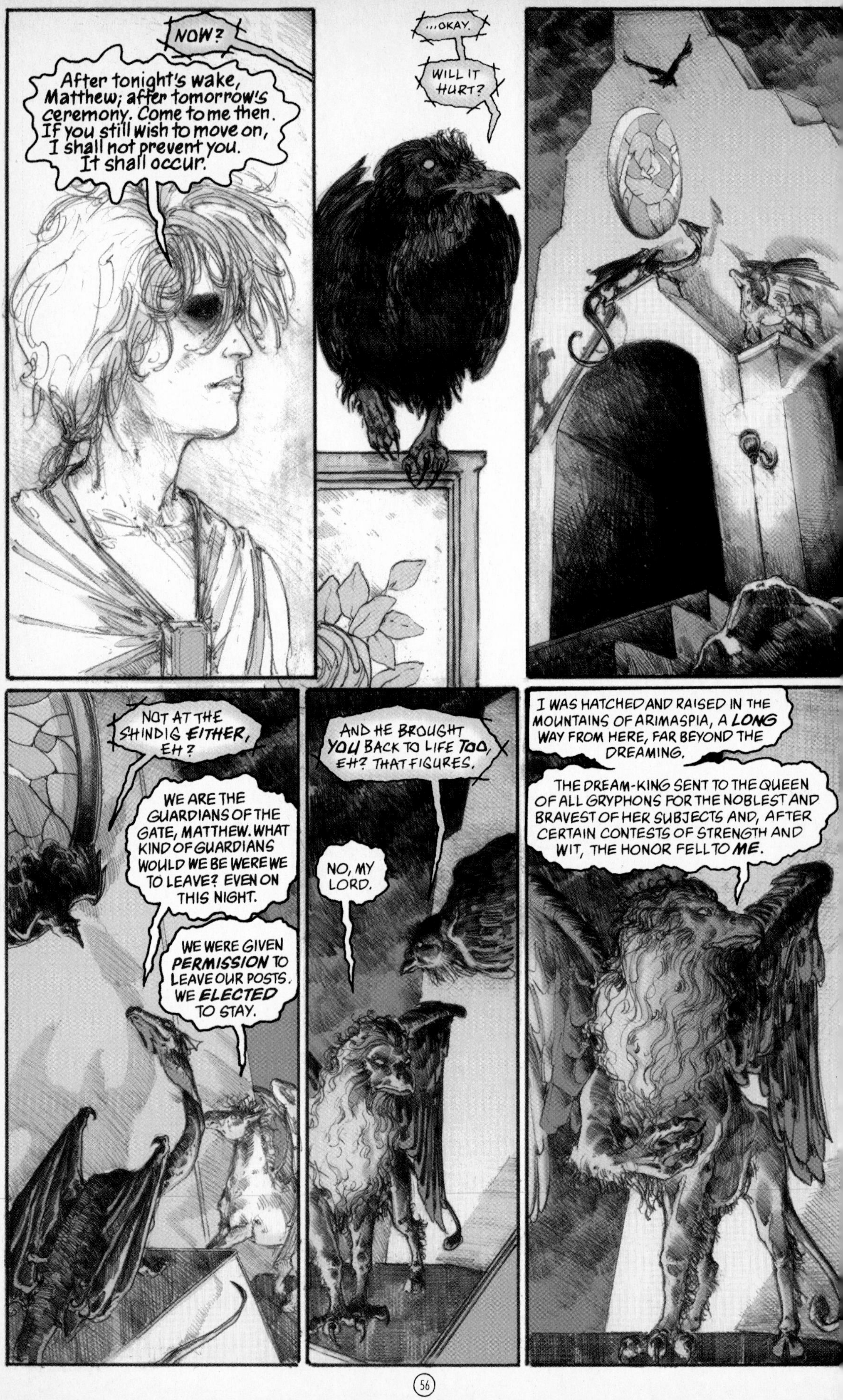
NOW?
After tonight's wake, Matthew; after tomorrow's ceremony. Come to me then. If you still wish to move on, I shall not prevent you. It shall occur.
...OKAY.
WILL IT HURT?
NOT AT THE SHINDIG EITHER, EH?
WE ARE THE GUARDIANS OF THE GATE, MATTHEW. WHAT KIND OF GUARDIANS WOULD WE BE WERE WE TO LEAVE? EVEN ON THIS NIGHT.
WE WERE GIVEN PERMISSION TO LEAVE OUR POSTS. WE ELECTED TO STAY.
AND HE BROUGHT YOU BACK TO LIFE TOO, EH? THAT FIGURES.
NO, MY LORD.
I WAS HATCHED AND RAISED IN THE MOUNTAINS OF ARIMASPIA, A LONG WAY FROM HERE, FAR BEYOND THE DREAMING.
THE DREAM-KING SENT TO THE QUEEN OF ALL GRYPHONS FOR THE NOBLEST AND BRAVEST OF HER SUBJECTS AND, AFTER CERTAIN CONTESTS OF STRENGTH AND WIT, THE HONOR FELL TO ME.

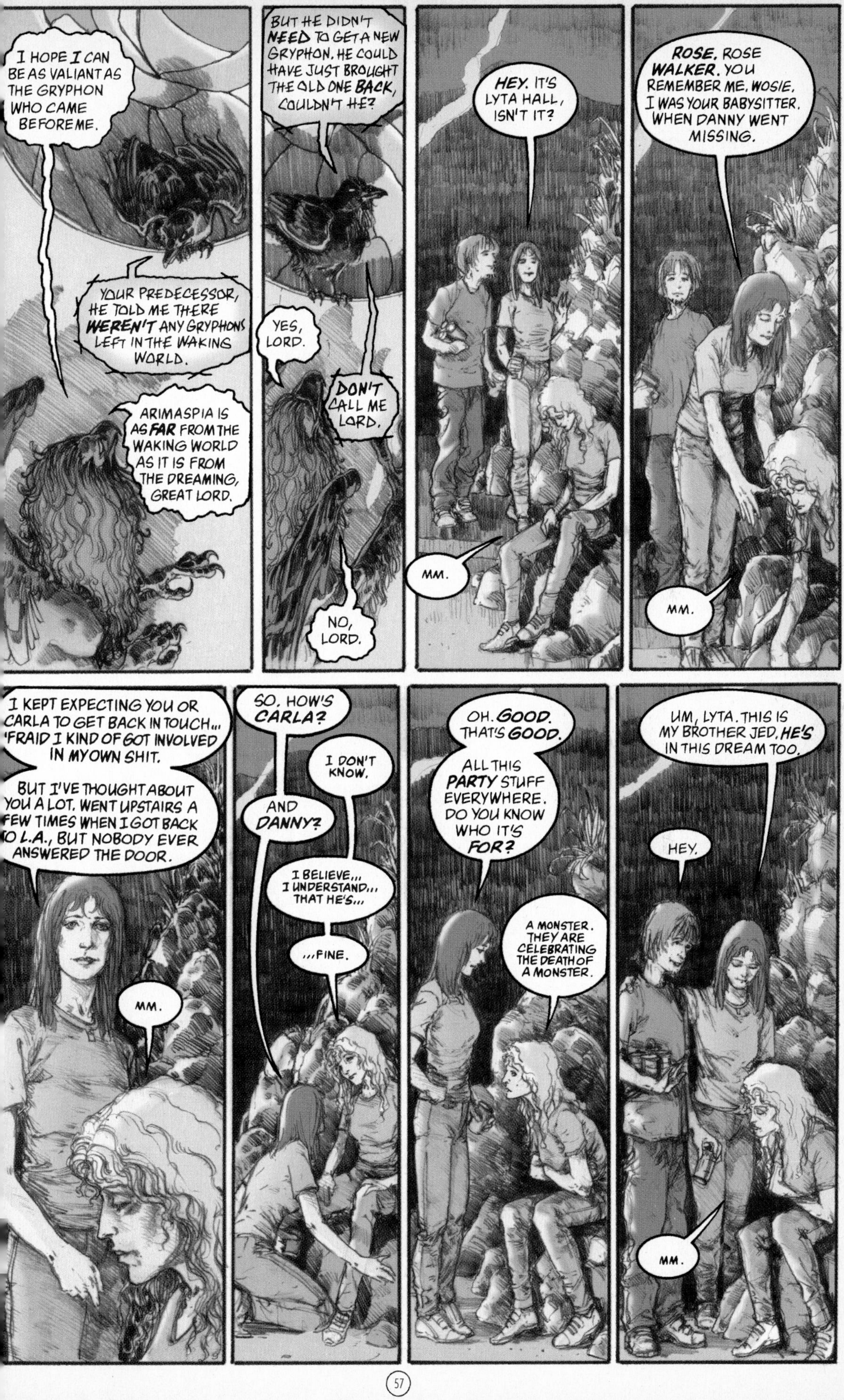
I HOPE I CAN BE AS VALIANT AS THE GRYPHON WHO CAME BEFORE ME.
YOUR PREDECESSOR, HE TOLD ME THERE WEREN'T ANY GRYPHONS LEFT IN THE WAKING WORLD.
ARIMASPIA IS AS FAR FROM THE WAKING WORLD AS IT IS FROM THE DREAMING, GREAT LORD.
BUT HE DIDN'T NEED TO GET A NEW GRYPHON. HE COULD HAVE JUST BROUGHT THE OLD ONE BACK, COULDN'T HE?
YES, LORD.
DON'T CALL ME LORD.
NO, LORD.
HEY. IT'S LYTA HALL, ISN'T IT?
MM.
ROSE. ROSE WALKER. YOU REMEMBER ME. WOSIE. I WAS YOUR BABYSITTER. WHEN DANNY WENT MISSING.
MM.
I KEPT EXPECTING YOU OR CARLA TO GET BACK IN TOUCH... 'FRAID I KIND OF GOT INVOLVED IN MY OWN SHIT.
BUT I'VE THOUGHT ABOUT YOU A LOT. WENT UPSTAIRS A FEW TIMES WHEN I GOT BACK TO L.A., BUT NOBODY EVER ANSWERED THE DOOR.
MM.
SO, HOW'S CARLA?
I DON'T KNOW.
AND DANNY?
I BELIEVE... I UNDERSTAND... THAT HE'S...
...FINE.
OH. GOOD. THAT'S GOOD.
ALL THIS PARTY STUFF EVERYWHERE. DO YOU KNOW WHO IT'S FOR?
A MONSTER. THEY ARE CELEBRATING THE DEATH OF A MONSTER.
UM, LYTA. THIS IS MY BROTHER JED. HE'S IN THIS DREAM TOO.
HEY.
MM.

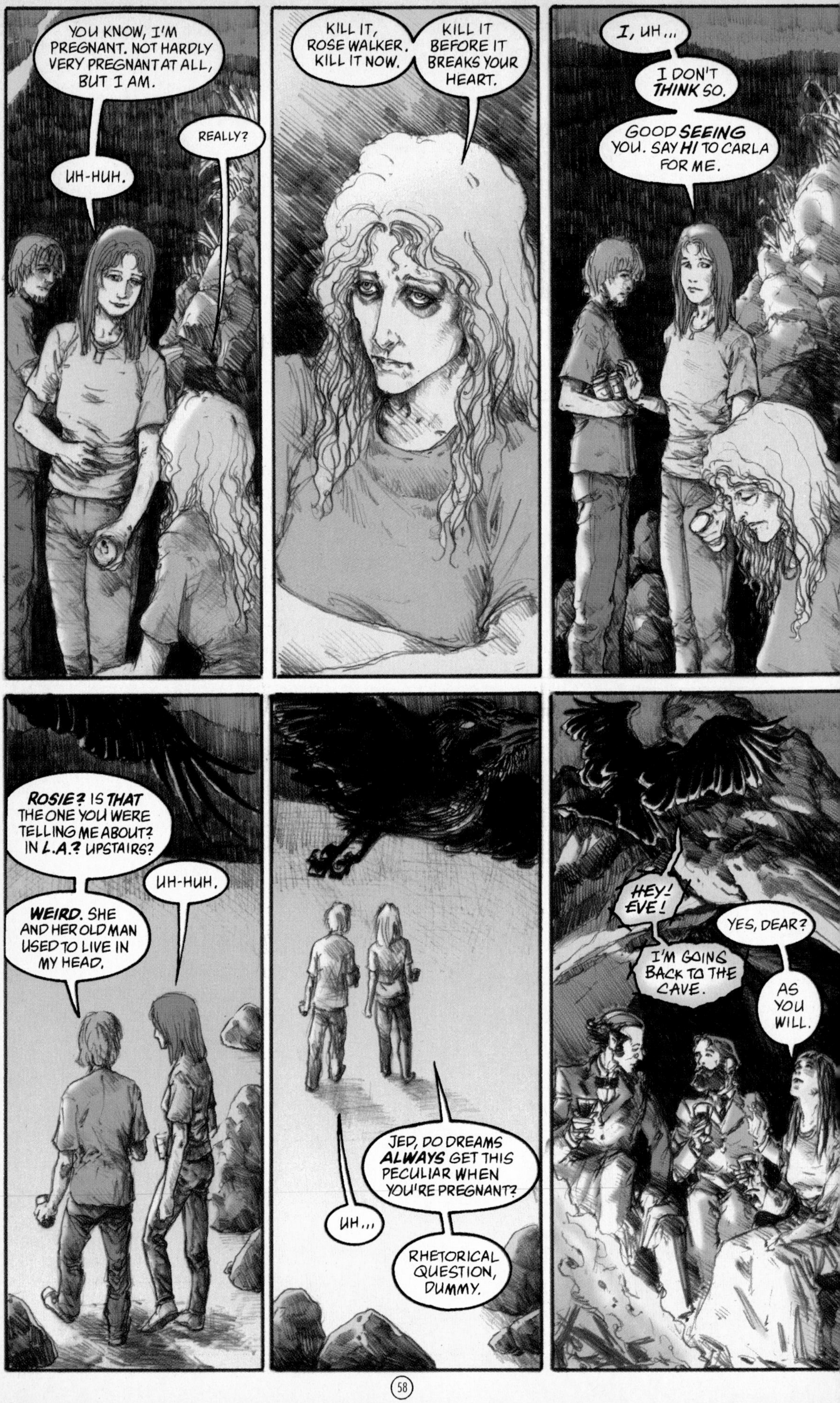
YOU KNOW, I'M PREGNANT. NOT HARDLY VERY PREGNANT AT ALL, BUT I AM.
REALLY?
UH-HUH.
KILL IT, ROSE WALKER. KILL IT NOW.
KILL IT BEFORE IT BREAKS YOUR HEART.
I, UH...
I DON'T THINK SO.
GOOD SEEING YOU. SAY HI TO CARLA FOR ME.
ROSIE? IS THAT THE ONE YOU WERE TELLING ME ABOUT? IN L.A.? UPSTAIRS?
UH-HUH.
WEIRD. SHE AND HER OLD MAN USED TO LIVE IN MY HEAD.
JED, DO DREAMS ALWAYS GET THIS PECULIAR WHEN YOU'RE PREGNANT?
UH...
RHETORICAL QUESTION, DUMMY.
HEY! EVE!
YES, DEAR?
I'M GOING BACK TO THE CAVE.
AS YOU WILL.

HE SAYS HE SAVED MY LIFE. THAT THE CORINTHIAN WAS GOING TO KILL ME, AND HE MADE IT SO THAT IT WAS THE NYBASS-THING INSTEAD.

THEN I'M SURE HE DID. HE HAS NO REASON TO *LIE* TO YOU.

MATTHEW? *DEAR* FELLOW. WILL YOU *JOIN* US IN A SMALL LIBATION?

YOU *KNOW* I DON'T DRINK, LUCIEN.

NEITHER DO I, ON ANY NORMAL OCCASION. BUT TONIGHT IS FAR FROM NORMAL.

DO YOU KNOW BHARTARI RAJA? THIS IS THE BHARTARI RAJA. OLD *OLD* FRIEND OF MINE. BHARTARI, MATTHEW.

PLEASE, NO. *NOT* BHARTARI, LUCIEN. I AM *PRESENTLY* LIVING UNDER THE NAME OF SILAS TOMKEN CUMBERBATCH, LIKE WINNIE THE POOH AND MISTER SAUNDERS.

HERE, SIR RAVEN, WET YOUR *BLACK BEAK* ON THIS.

I DON'T DRINK.

I STOPPED DRINKING THE HARD WAY.

"THE NIGHT CAN MAKE A MAN MORE BRAVE..."

"...BUT NOT MORE SOBER." I TAKE YOUR POINT.

LUCIEN?

WHY DID IT *HAPPEN*? WHY DID HE *LET* IT HAPPEN?

LET IT, MATTHEW? I THINK HE DID A LITTLE MORE THAN *LET* IT HAPPEN...

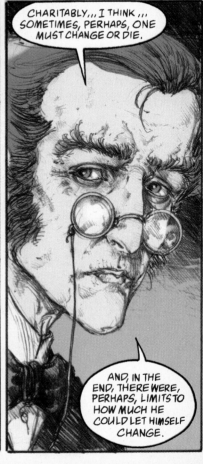

CHARITABLY... I THINK... SOMETIMES, PERHAPS, ONE MUST CHANGE OR DIE.

AND, IN THE END, THERE WERE, PERHAPS, LIMITS TO HOW MUCH HE COULD LET HIMSELF CHANGE.

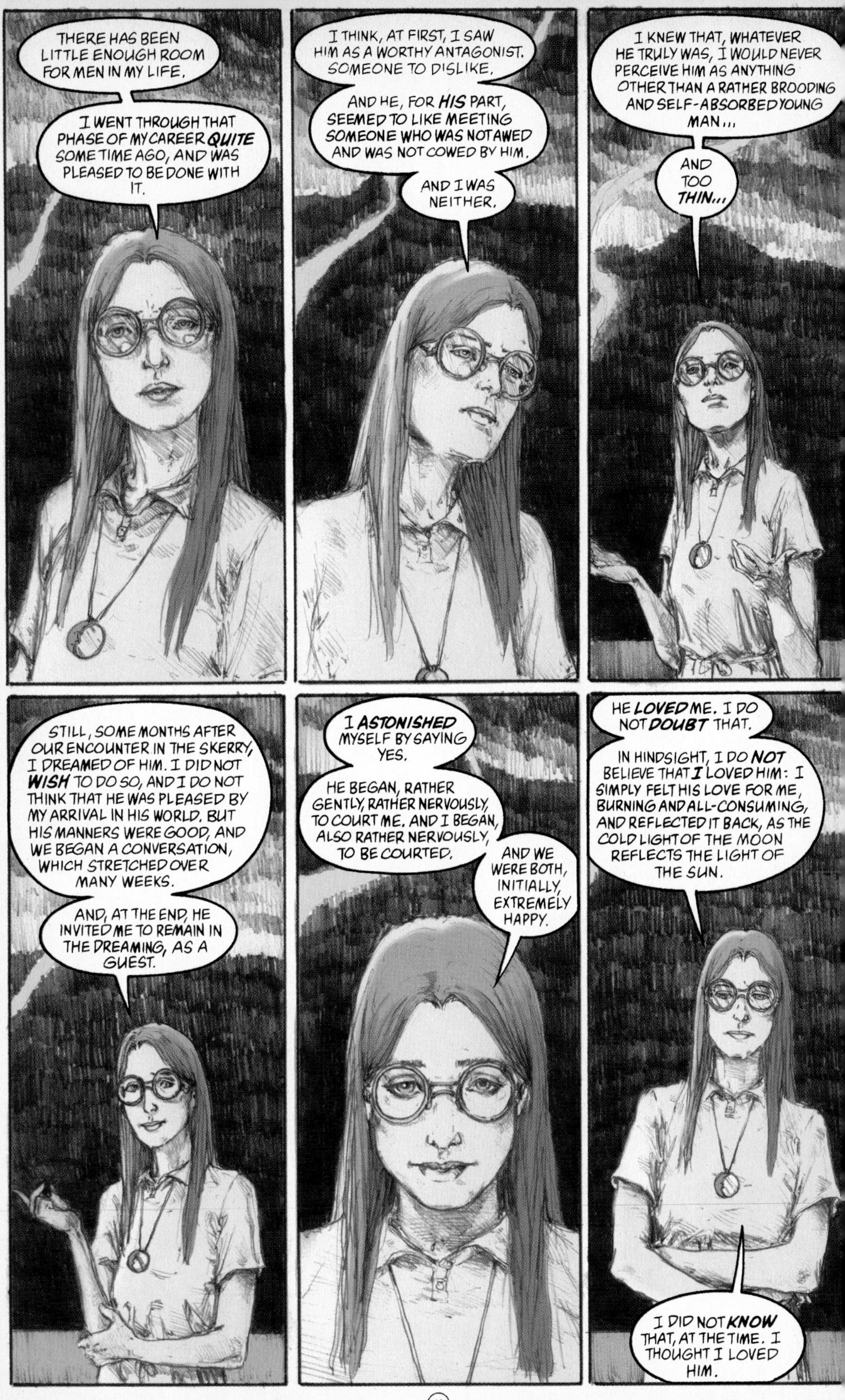

THERE HAS BEEN LITTLE ENOUGH ROOM FOR MEN IN MY LIFE.
I WENT THROUGH THAT PHASE OF MY CAREER **QUITE** SOME TIME AGO, AND WAS PLEASED TO BE DONE WITH IT.
I THINK, AT FIRST, I SAW HIM AS A WORTHY ANTAGONIST. SOMEONE TO DISLIKE.
AND HE, FOR **HIS** PART, SEEMED TO LIKE MEETING SOMEONE WHO WAS NOT AWED AND WAS NOT COWED BY HIM.
AND I WAS NEITHER.
I KNEW THAT, WHATEVER HE TRULY WAS, I WOULD NEVER PERCEIVE HIM AS ANYTHING OTHER THAN A RATHER BROODING AND SELF-ABSORBED YOUNG MAN...
AND TOO **THIN...**
STILL, SOME MONTHS AFTER OUR ENCOUNTER IN THE SKERRY, I DREAMED OF HIM. I DID NOT **WISH** TO DO SO, AND I DO NOT THINK THAT HE WAS PLEASED BY MY ARRIVAL IN HIS WORLD. BUT HIS MANNERS WERE GOOD, AND WE BEGAN A CONVERSATION, WHICH STRETCHED OVER MANY WEEKS.
AND, AT THE END, HE INVITED ME TO REMAIN IN THE DREAMING, AS A GUEST.
I **ASTONISHED** MYSELF BY SAYING YES.
HE BEGAN, RATHER GENTLY, RATHER NERVOUSLY, TO COURT ME. AND I BEGAN, ALSO RATHER NERVOUSLY, TO BE COURTED.
AND WE WERE BOTH, INITIALLY, EXTREMELY HAPPY.
HE **LOVED** ME. I DO NOT **DOUBT** THAT.
IN HINDSIGHT, I DO **NOT** BELIEVE THAT **I** LOVED HIM: I SIMPLY FELT HIS LOVE FOR ME, BURNING AND ALL-CONSUMING, AND REFLECTED IT BACK, AS THE COLD LIGHT OF THE MOON REFLECTS THE LIGHT OF THE SUN.
I DID NOT **KNOW** THAT, AT THE TIME. I THOUGHT I LOVED HIM.

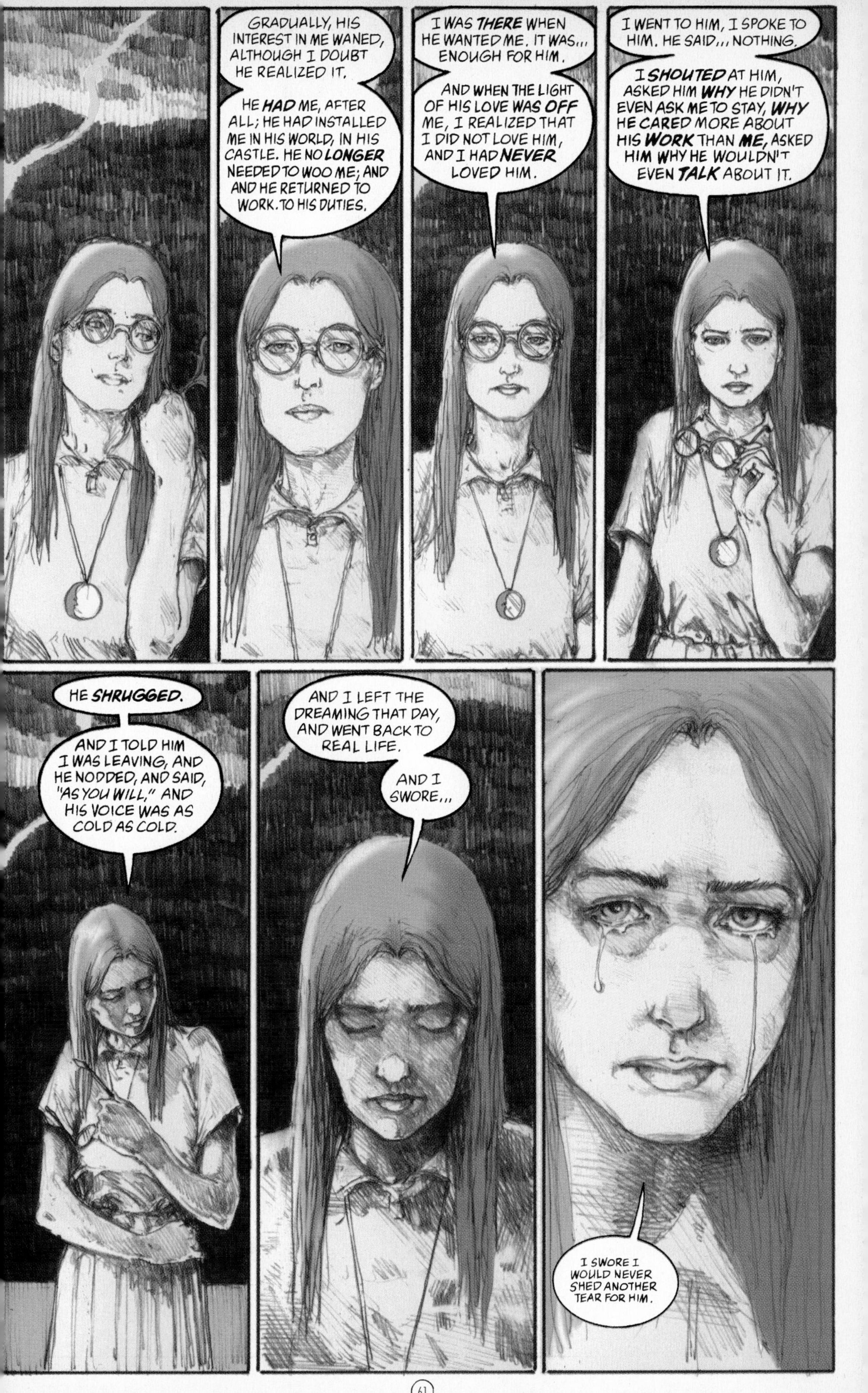
GRADUALLY, HIS INTEREST IN ME WANED, ALTHOUGH I DOUBT HE REALIZED IT.
HE HAD ME, AFTER ALL; HE HAD INSTALLED ME IN HIS WORLD, IN HIS CASTLE. HE NO LONGER NEEDED TO WOO ME; AND AND HE RETURNED TO WORK. TO HIS DUTIES.
I WAS THERE WHEN HE WANTED ME. IT WAS... ENOUGH FOR HIM.
AND WHEN THE LIGHT OF HIS LOVE WAS OFF ME, I REALIZED THAT I DID NOT LOVE HIM, AND I HAD NEVER LOVED HIM.
I WENT TO HIM, I SPOKE TO HIM. HE SAID... NOTHING.
I SHOUTED AT HIM, ASKED HIM WHY HE DIDN'T EVEN ASK ME TO STAY, WHY HE CARED MORE ABOUT HIS WORK THAN ME, ASKED HIM WHY HE WOULDN'T EVEN TALK ABOUT IT.
HE SHRUGGED.
AND I TOLD HIM I WAS LEAVING, AND HE NODDED, AND SAID, "AS YOU WILL," AND HIS VOICE WAS AS COLD AS COLD.
AND I LEFT THE DREAMING THAT DAY, AND WENT BACK TO REAL LIFE.
AND I SWORE...
I SWORE I WOULD NEVER SHED ANOTHER TEAR FOR HIM.

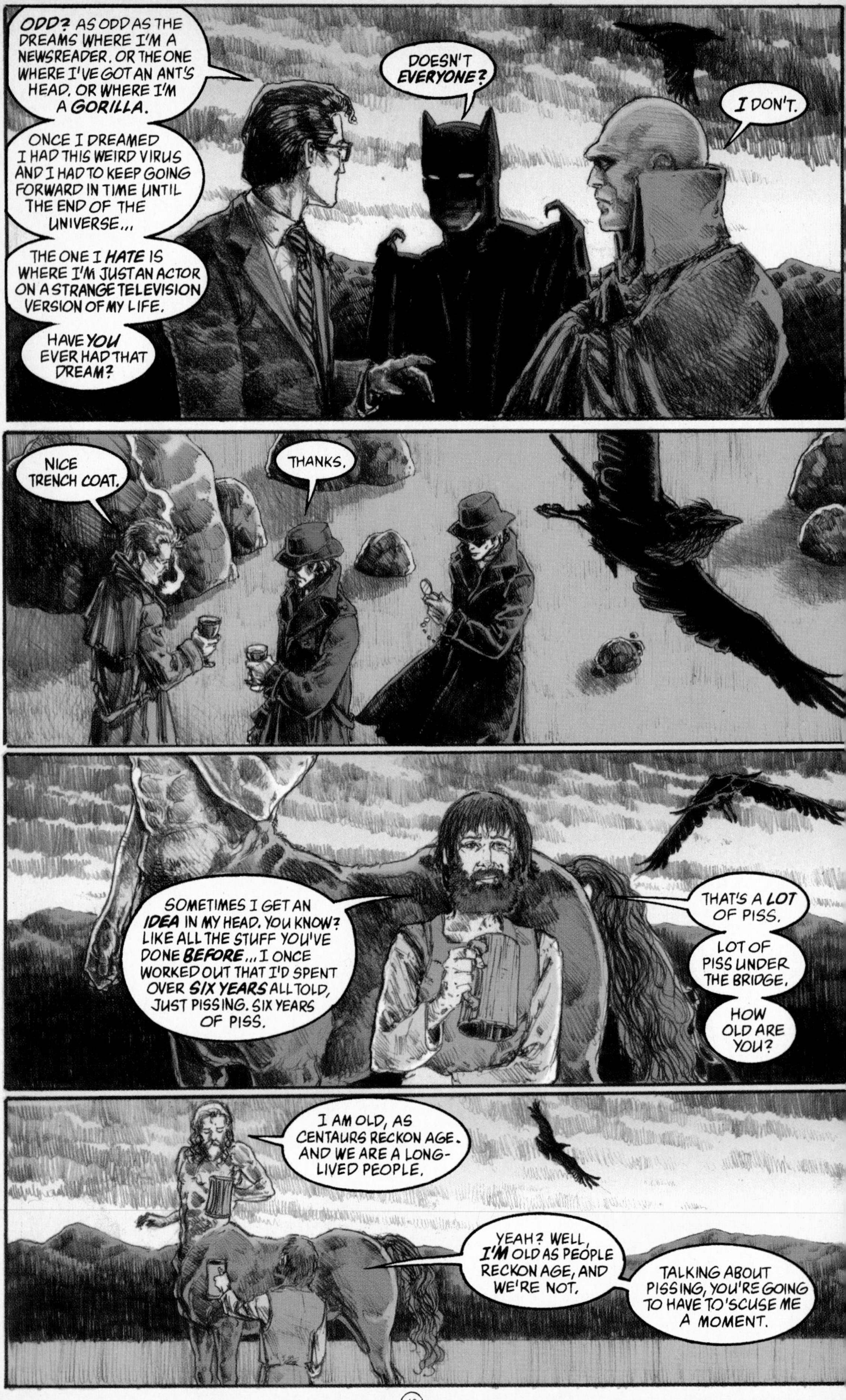
ODD? AS ODD AS THE DREAMS WHERE I'M A NEWSREADER. OR THE ONE WHERE I'VE GOT AN ANT'S HEAD. OR WHERE I'M A GORILLA.
ONCE I DREAMED I HAD THIS WEIRD VIRUS AND I HAD TO KEEP GOING FORWARD IN TIME UNTIL THE END OF THE UNIVERSE...
THE ONE I HATE IS WHERE I'M JUST AN ACTOR ON A STRANGE TELEVISION VERSION OF MY LIFE.
HAVE YOU EVER HAD THAT DREAM?
DOESN'T EVERYONE?
I DON'T.
NICE TRENCH COAT.
THANKS.
SOMETIMES I GET AN IDEA IN MY HEAD. YOU KNOW? LIKE ALL THE STUFF YOU'VE DONE BEFORE... I ONCE WORKED OUT THAT I'D SPENT OVER SIX YEARS ALL TOLD, JUST PISSING. SIX YEARS OF PISS.
THAT'S A LOT OF PISS.
LOT OF PISS UNDER THE BRIDGE.
HOW OLD ARE YOU?
I AM OLD, AS CENTAURS RECKON AGE. AND WE ARE A LONG-LIVED PEOPLE.
YEAH? WELL, I'M OLD AS PEOPLE RECKON AGE, AND WE'RE NOT.
TALKING ABOUT PISSING, YOU'RE GOING TO HAVE TO 'SCUSE ME A MOMENT.

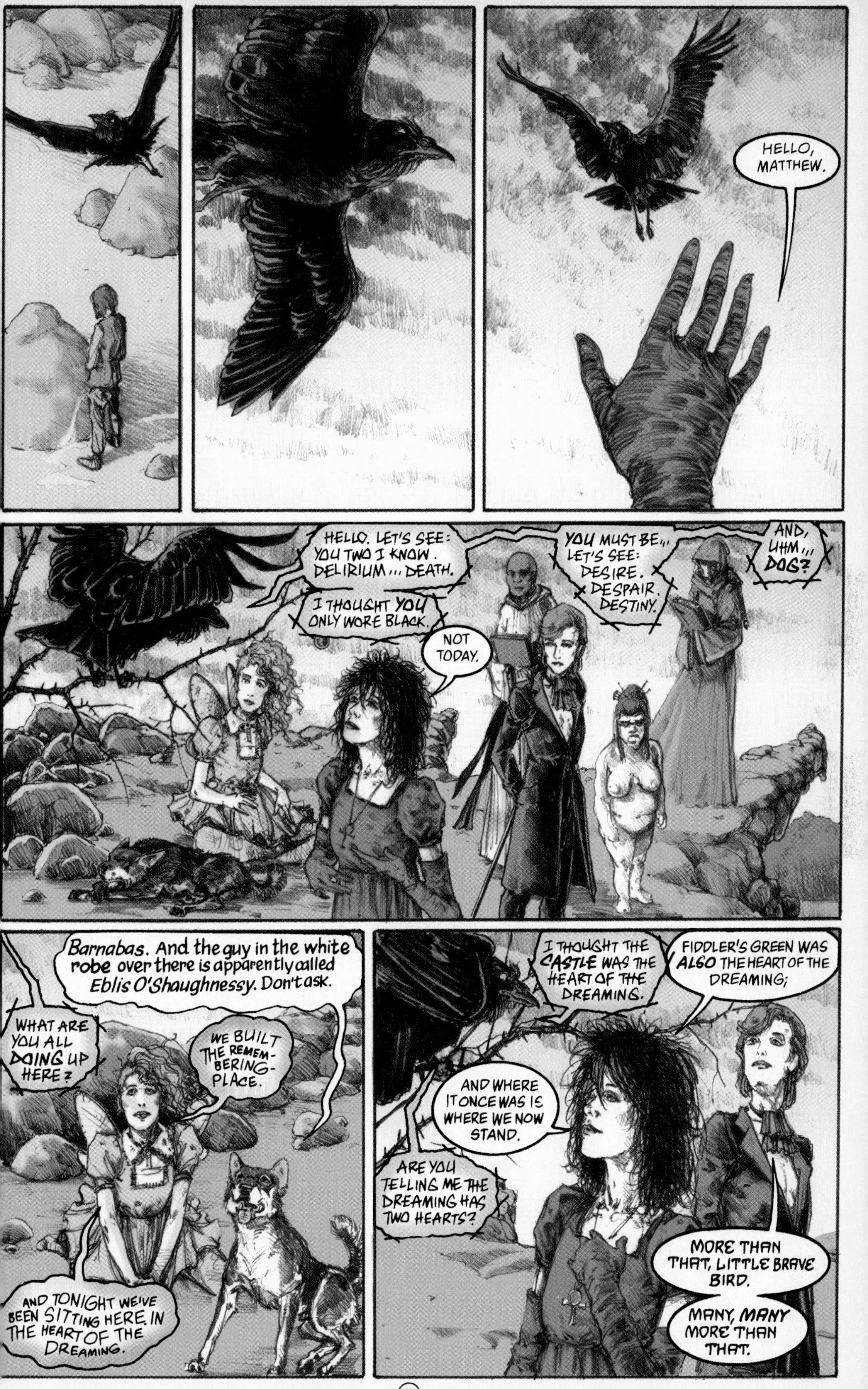
HELLO, MATTHEW.
HELLO. LET'S SEE: YOU TWO I KNOW. DELIRIUM... DEATH.
I THOUGHT YOU ONLY WORE BLACK.
NOT TODAY.
YOU MUST BE... LET'S SEE: DESIRE. DESPAIR. DESTINY.
AND, UHM... DOG?
Barnabas. And the guy in the white robe over there is apparently called Eblis O'Shaughnessy. Don't ask.
WHAT ARE YOU ALL DOING UP HERE?
WE BUILT THE REMEMBERING-PLACE.
AND TONIGHT WE'VE BEEN SITTING HERE, IN THE HEART OF THE DREAMING.
I THOUGHT THE CASTLE WAS THE HEART OF THE DREAMING.
FIDDLER'S GREEN WAS ALSO THE HEART OF THE DREAMING;
AND WHERE IT ONCE WAS IS WHERE WE NOW STAND.
ARE YOU TELLING ME THE DREAMING HAS TWO HEARTS?
MORE THAN THAT, LITTLE BRAVE BIRD.
MANY, MANY MORE THAN THAT.

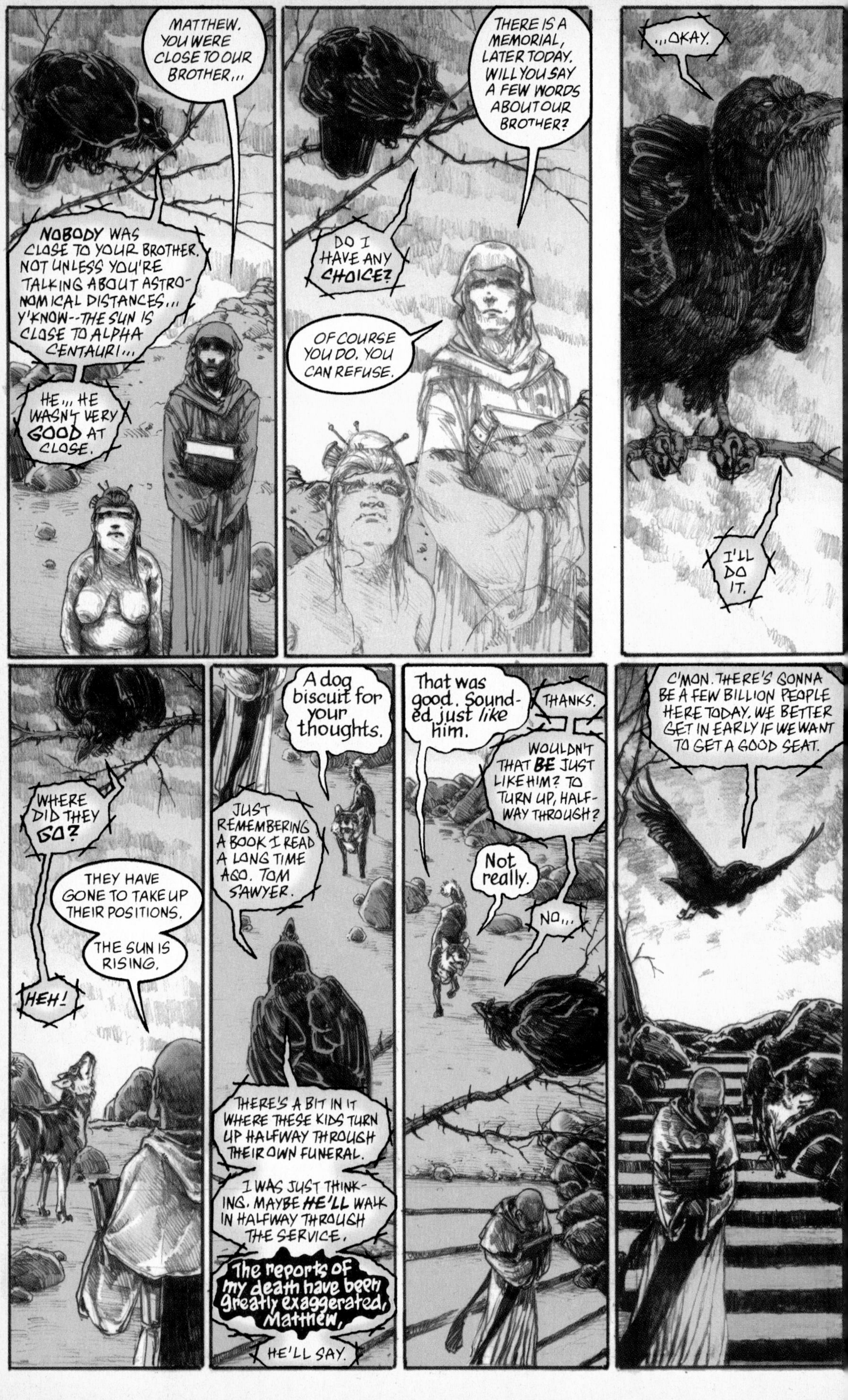
MATTHEW. YOU WERE CLOSE TO OUR BROTHER...
NOBODY WAS CLOSE TO YOUR BROTHER. NOT UNLESS YOU'RE TALKING ABOUT ASTRONOMICAL DISTANCES... Y'KNOW--THE SUN IS CLOSE TO ALPHA CENTAURI...
HE... HE WASN'T VERY GOOD AT CLOSE.
THERE IS A MEMORIAL, LATER TODAY. WILL YOU SAY A FEW WORDS ABOUT OUR BROTHER?
DO I HAVE ANY CHOICE?
OF COURSE YOU DO. YOU CAN REFUSE.
...OKAY.
I'LL DO IT.
WHERE DID THEY GO?
THEY HAVE GONE TO TAKE UP THEIR POSITIONS.
THE SUN IS RISING.
HEH!
A dog biscuit for your thoughts.
JUST REMEMBERING A BOOK I READ A LONG TIME AGO. TOM SAWYER.
THERE'S A BIT IN IT WHERE THESE KIDS TURN UP HALFWAY THROUGH THEIR OWN FUNERAL.
I WAS JUST THINKING. MAYBE HE'LL WALK IN HALFWAY THROUGH THE SERVICE.
The reports of my death have been greatly exaggerated, Matthew,
HE'LL SAY.
That was good. Sounded just like him.
THANKS.
WOULDN'T THAT BE JUST LIKE HIM? TO TURN UP, HALFWAY THROUGH?
Not really.
NO...
C'MON. THERE'S GONNA BE A FEW BILLION PEOPLE HERE TODAY. WE BETTER GET IN EARLY IF WE WANT TO GET A GOOD SEAT.

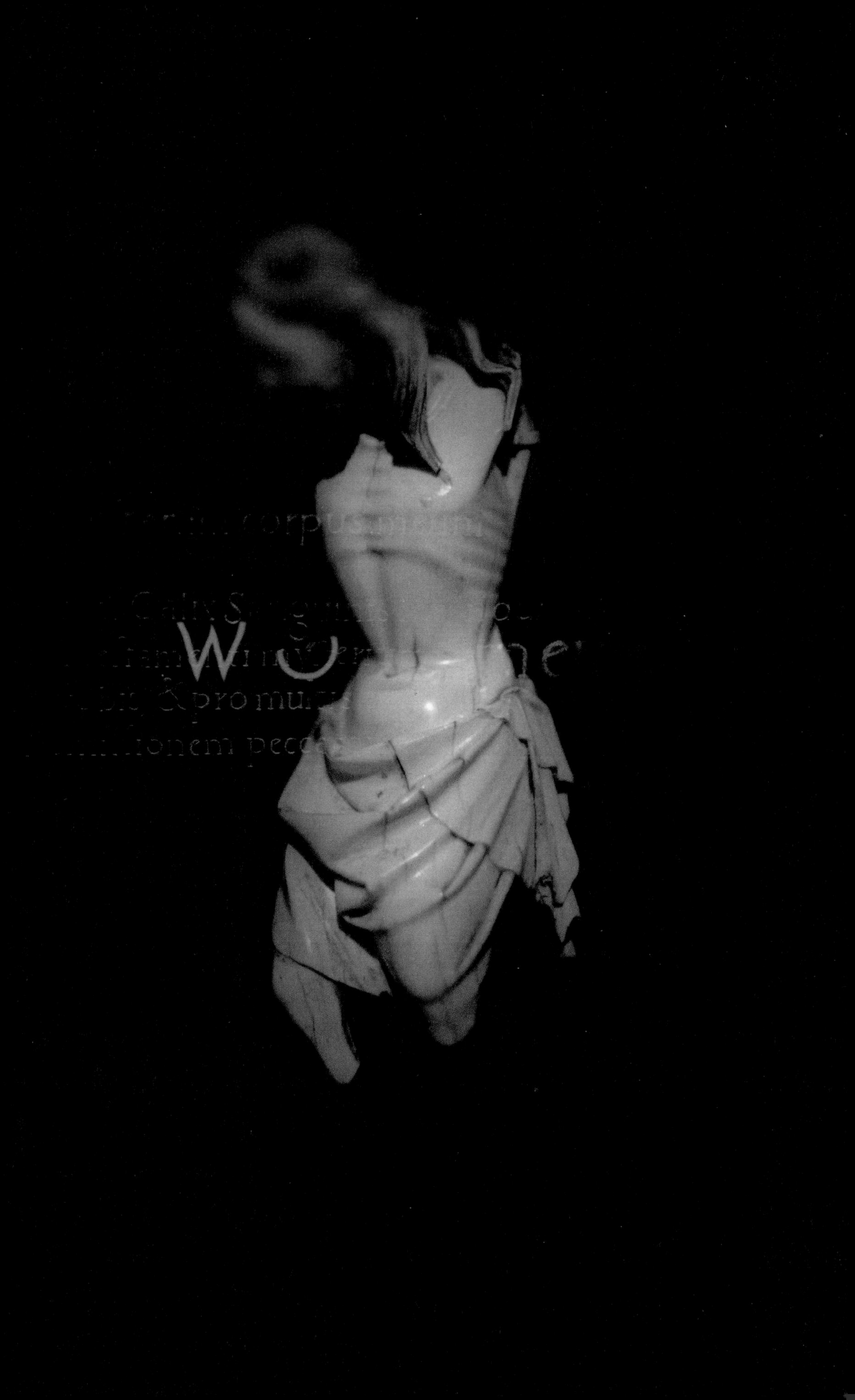

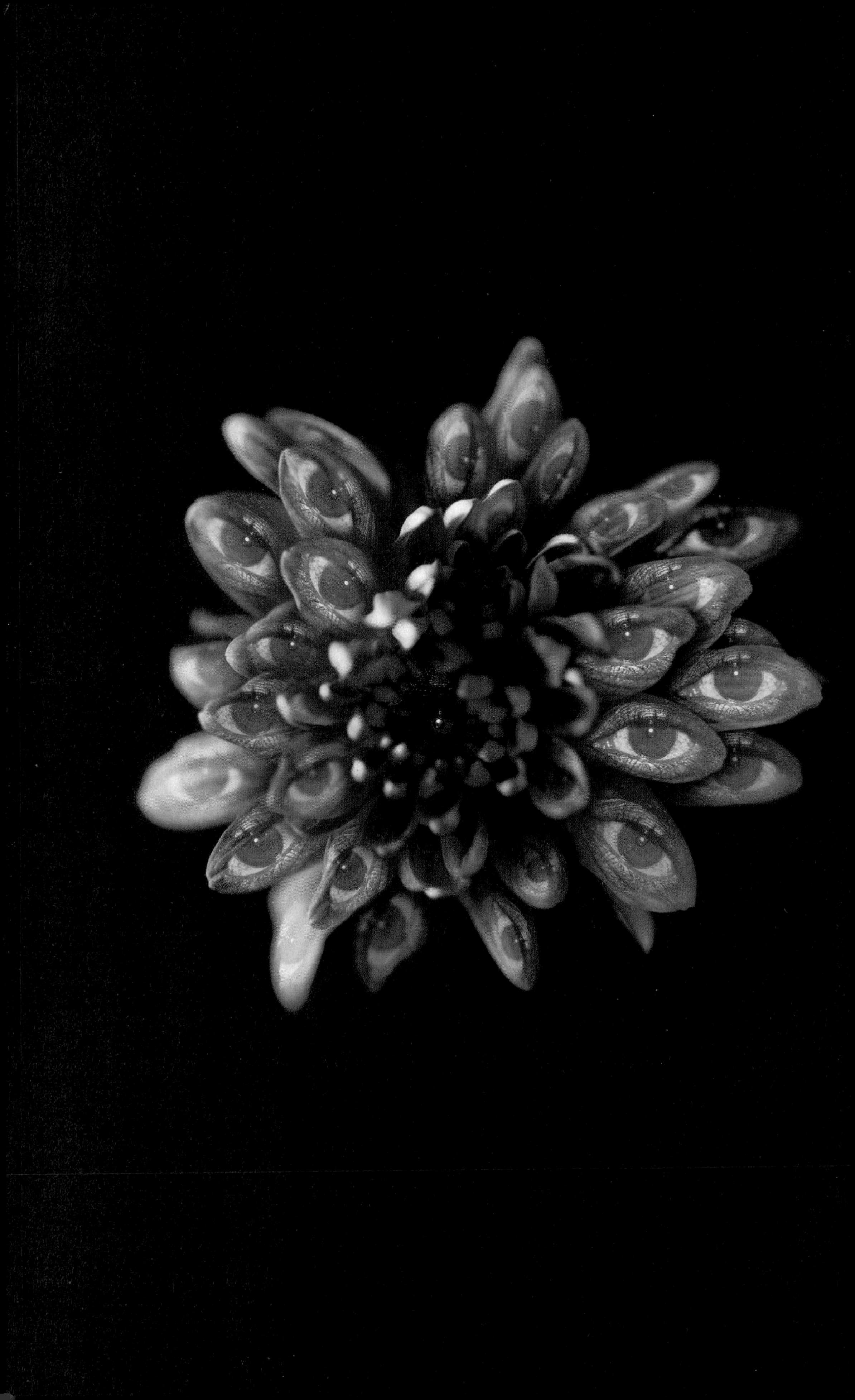

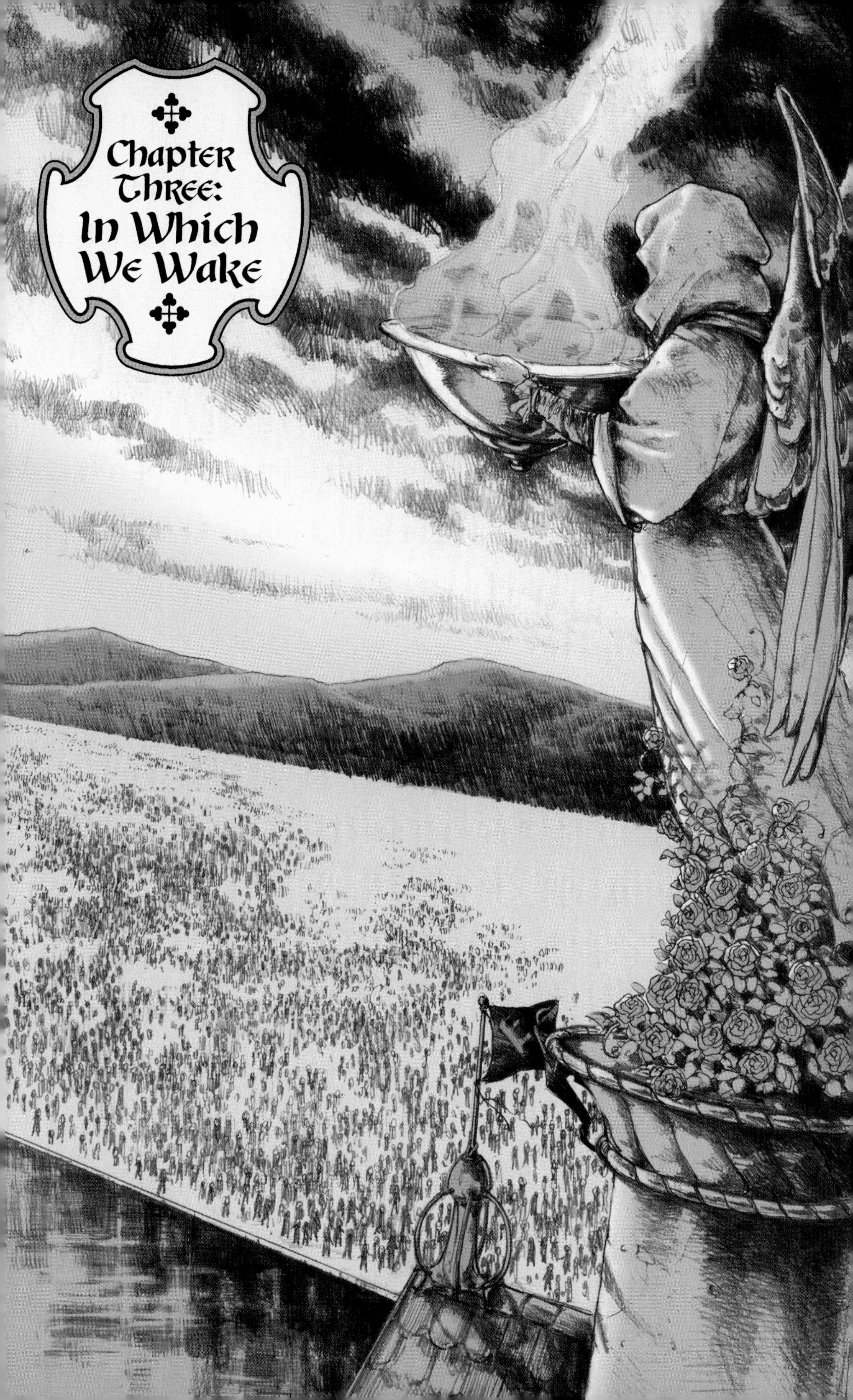
Chapter Three:
In Which We Wake

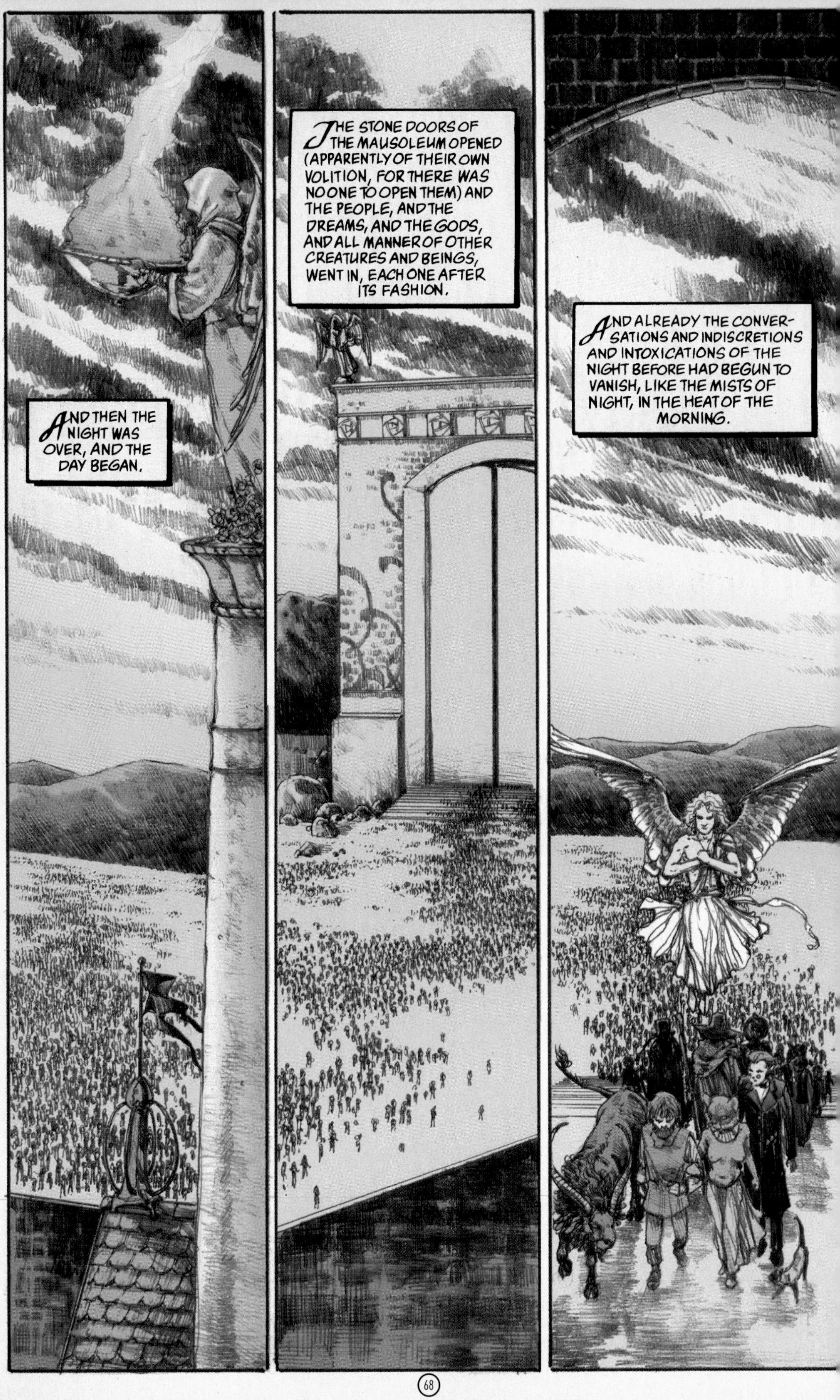
AND THEN THE NIGHT WAS OVER, AND THE DAY BEGAN.
THE STONE DOORS OF THE MAUSOLEUM OPENED (APPARENTLY OF THEIR OWN VOLITION, FOR THERE WAS NO ONE TO OPEN THEM) AND THE PEOPLE, AND THE DREAMS, AND THE GODS, AND ALL MANNER OF OTHER CREATURES AND BEINGS, WENT IN, EACH ONE AFTER ITS FASHION.
AND ALREADY THE CONVERSATIONS AND INDISCRETIONS AND INTOXICATIONS OF THE NIGHT BEFORE HAD BEGUN TO VANISH, LIKE THE MISTS OF NIGHT, IN THE HEAT OF THE MORNING.

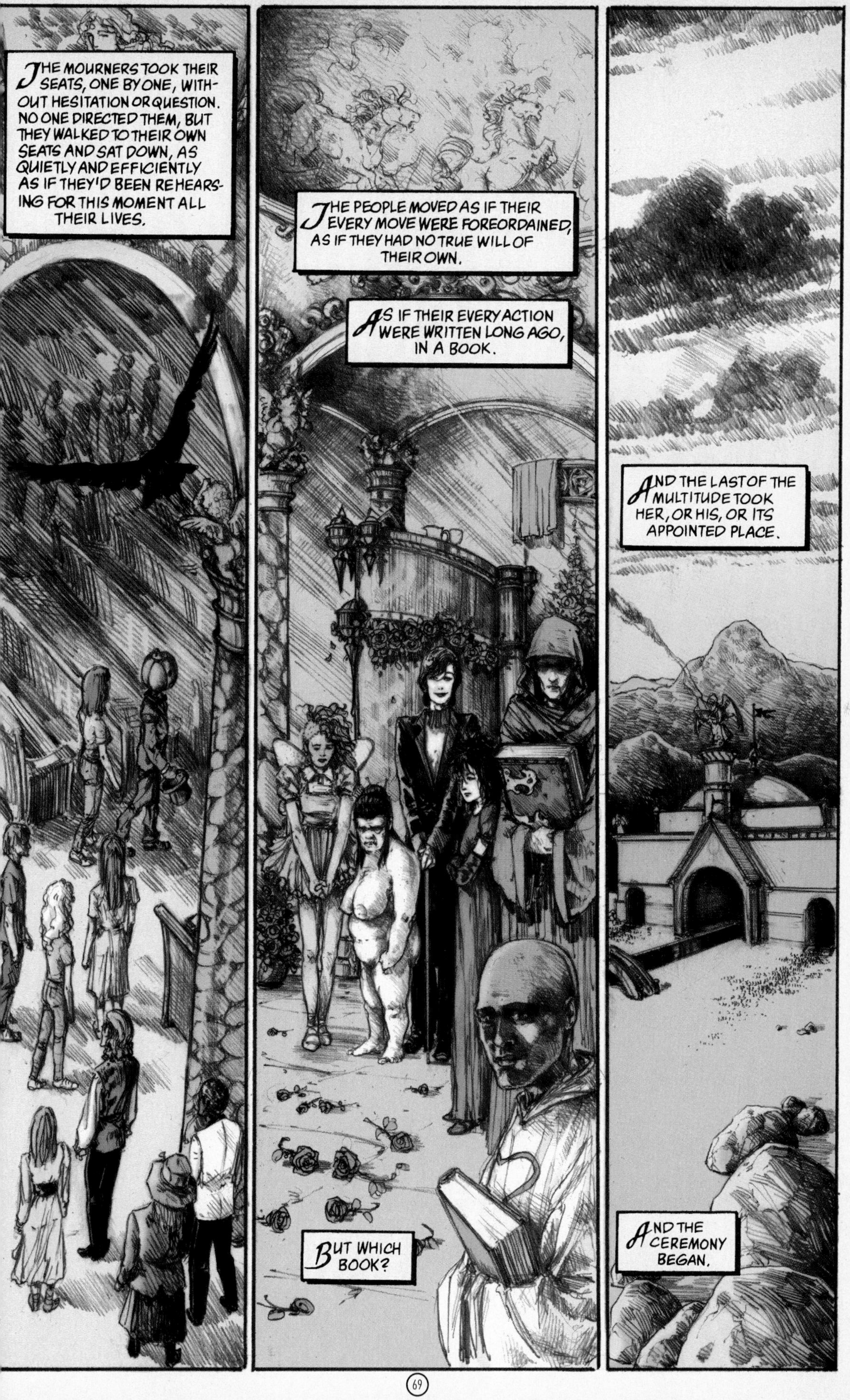
THE MOURNERS TOOK THEIR SEATS, ONE BY ONE, WITHOUT HESITATION OR QUESTION. NO ONE DIRECTED THEM, BUT THEY WALKED TO THEIR OWN SEATS AND SAT DOWN, AS QUIETLY AND EFFICIENTLY AS IF THEY'D BEEN REHEARSING FOR THIS MOMENT ALL THEIR LIVES.
THE PEOPLE MOVED AS IF THEIR EVERY MOVE WERE FOREORDAINED, AS IF THEY HAD NO TRUE WILL OF THEIR OWN.
AS IF THEIR EVERY ACTION WERE WRITTEN LONG AGO, IN A BOOK.
BUT WHICH BOOK?
AND THE LAST OF THE MULTITUDE TOOK HER, OR HIS, OR ITS APPOINTED PLACE.
AND THE CEREMONY BEGAN.

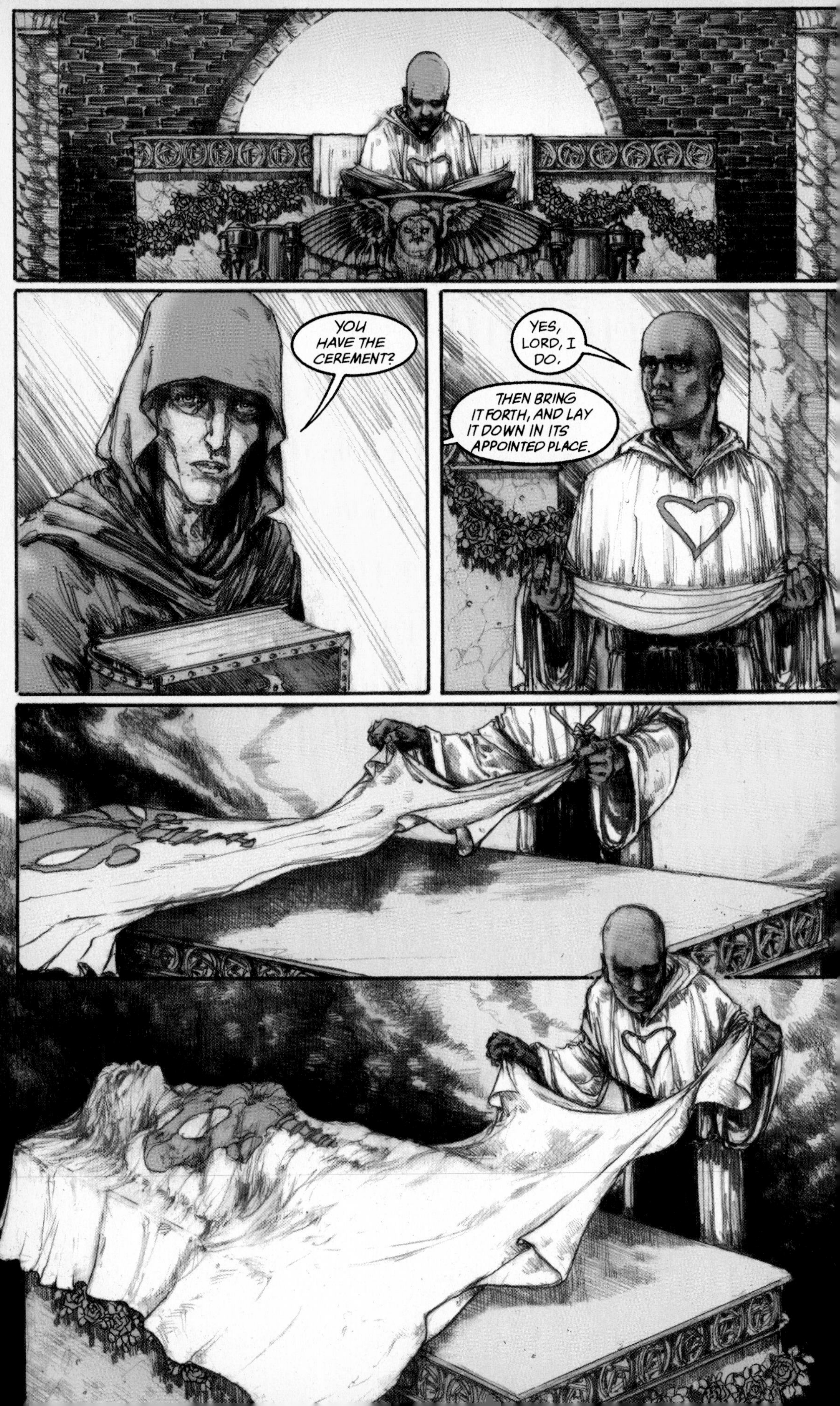
YOU HAVE THE CEREMENT?
YES, LORD, I DO.
THEN BRING IT FORTH, AND LAY IT DOWN IN ITS APPOINTED PLACE.

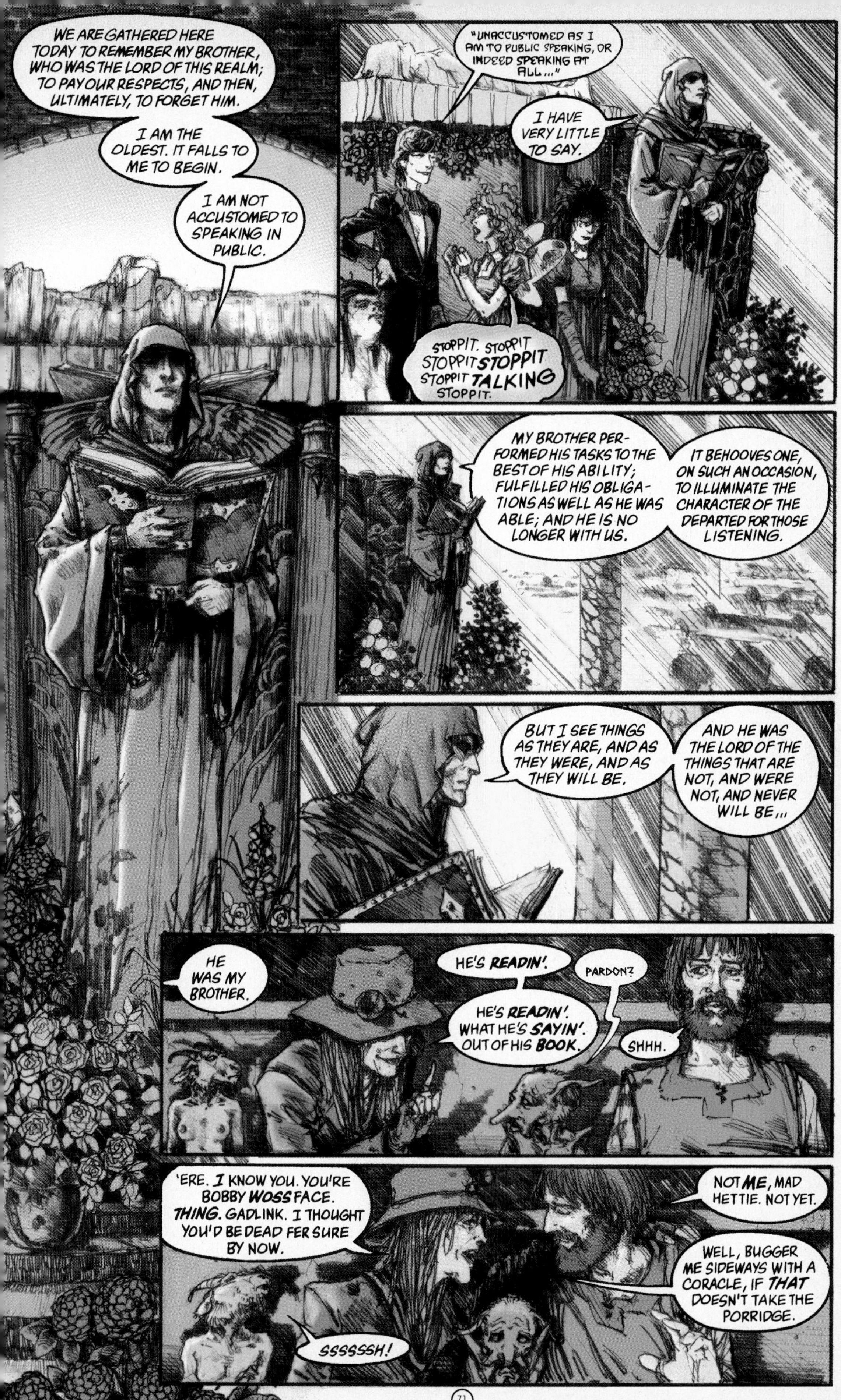

WE ARE GATHERED HERE TODAY TO REMEMBER MY BROTHER, WHO WAS THE LORD OF THIS REALM; TO PAY OUR RESPECTS, AND THEN, ULTIMATELY, TO FORGET HIM.
I AM THE OLDEST. IT FALLS TO ME TO BEGIN.
I AM NOT ACCUSTOMED TO SPEAKING IN PUBLIC.
"UNACCUSTOMED AS I AM TO PUBLIC SPEAKING, OR INDEED SPEAKING AT ALL..."
I HAVE VERY LITTLE TO SAY.
STOPPIT. STOPPIT STOPPIT STOPPIT STOPPIT TALKING STOPPIT.
MY BROTHER PERFORMED HIS TASKS TO THE BEST OF HIS ABILITY; FULFILLED HIS OBLIGATIONS AS WELL AS HE WAS ABLE; AND HE IS NO LONGER WITH US.
IT BEHOOVES ONE, ON SUCH AN OCCASION, TO ILLUMINATE THE CHARACTER OF THE DEPARTED FOR THOSE LISTENING.
BUT I SEE THINGS AS THEY ARE, AND AS THEY WERE, AND AS THEY WILL BE.
AND HE WAS THE LORD OF THE THINGS THAT ARE NOT, AND WERE NOT, AND NEVER WILL BE...
HE WAS MY BROTHER.
HE'S READIN'.
PARDON?
HE'S READIN'. WHAT HE'S SAYIN'. OUT OF HIS BOOK.
SHHH.
'ERE. I KNOW YOU. YOU'RE BOBBY WOSS FACE. THING. GADLINK. I THOUGHT YOU'D BE DEAD FER SURE BY NOW.
NOT ME, MAD HETTIE. NOT YET.
WELL, BUGGER ME SIDEWAYS WITH A CORACLE, IF THAT DOESN'T TAKE THE PORRIDGE.
SSSSSSH!

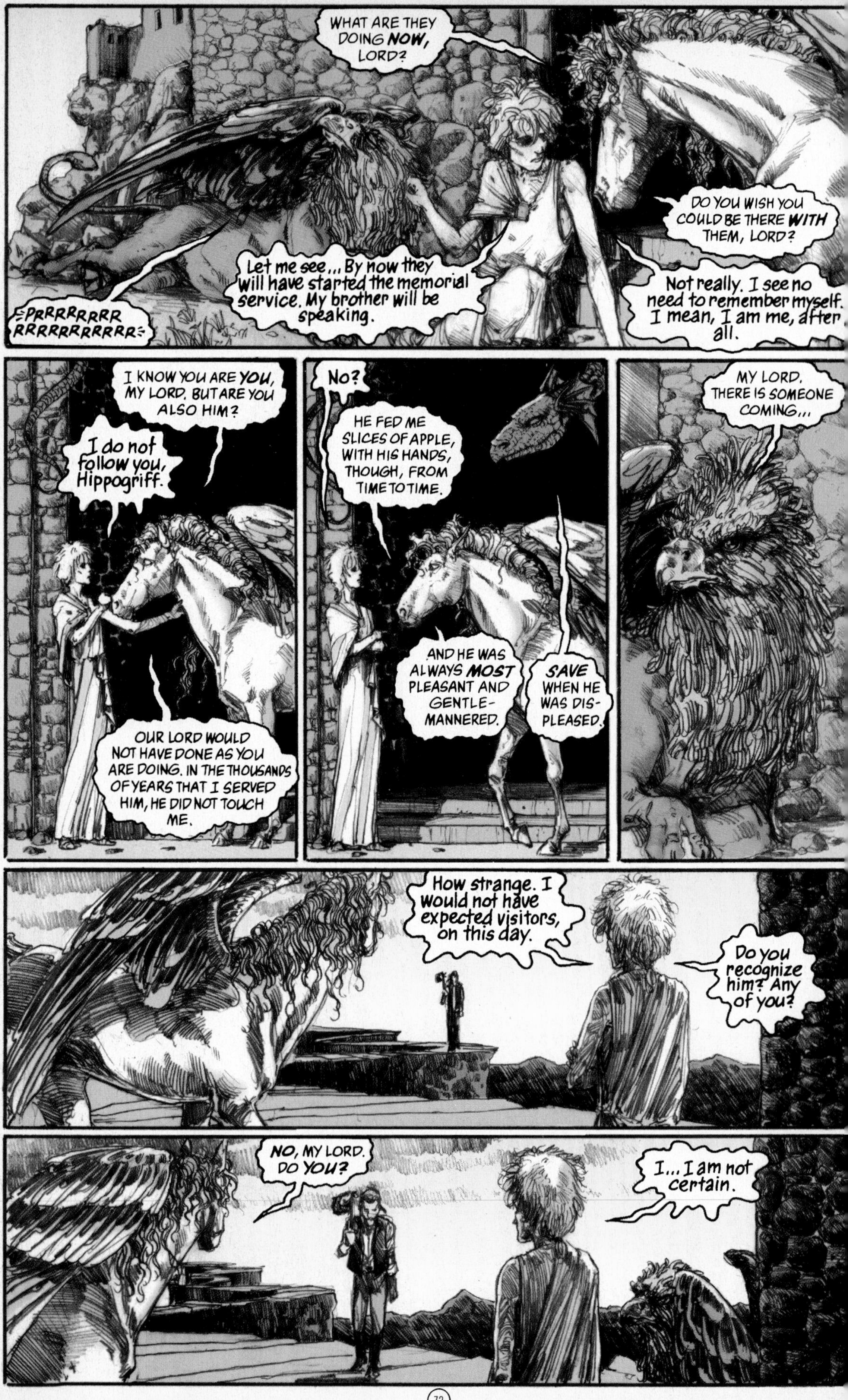
WHAT ARE THEY DOING NOW, LORD?
DO YOU WISH YOU COULD BE THERE WITH THEM, LORD?
Let me see... By now they will have started the memorial service. My brother will be speaking.
Not really. I see no need to remember myself. I mean, I am me, after all.
PRRRRRRRR RRRRRRRRRR
I KNOW YOU ARE YOU, MY LORD. BUT ARE YOU ALSO HIM?
I do not follow you, Hippogriff.
OUR LORD WOULD NOT HAVE DONE AS YOU ARE DOING. IN THE THOUSANDS OF YEARS THAT I SERVED HIM, HE DID NOT TOUCH ME.
No?
HE FED ME SLICES OF APPLE, WITH HIS HANDS, THOUGH, FROM TIME TO TIME.
AND HE WAS ALWAYS MOST PLEASANT AND GENTLE-MANNERED.
SAVE WHEN HE WAS DIS-PLEASED.
MY LORD. THERE IS SOMEONE COMING...
How strange. I would not have expected visitors, on this day.
Do you recognize him? Any of you?
NO, MY LORD. DO YOU?
I... I am not certain.

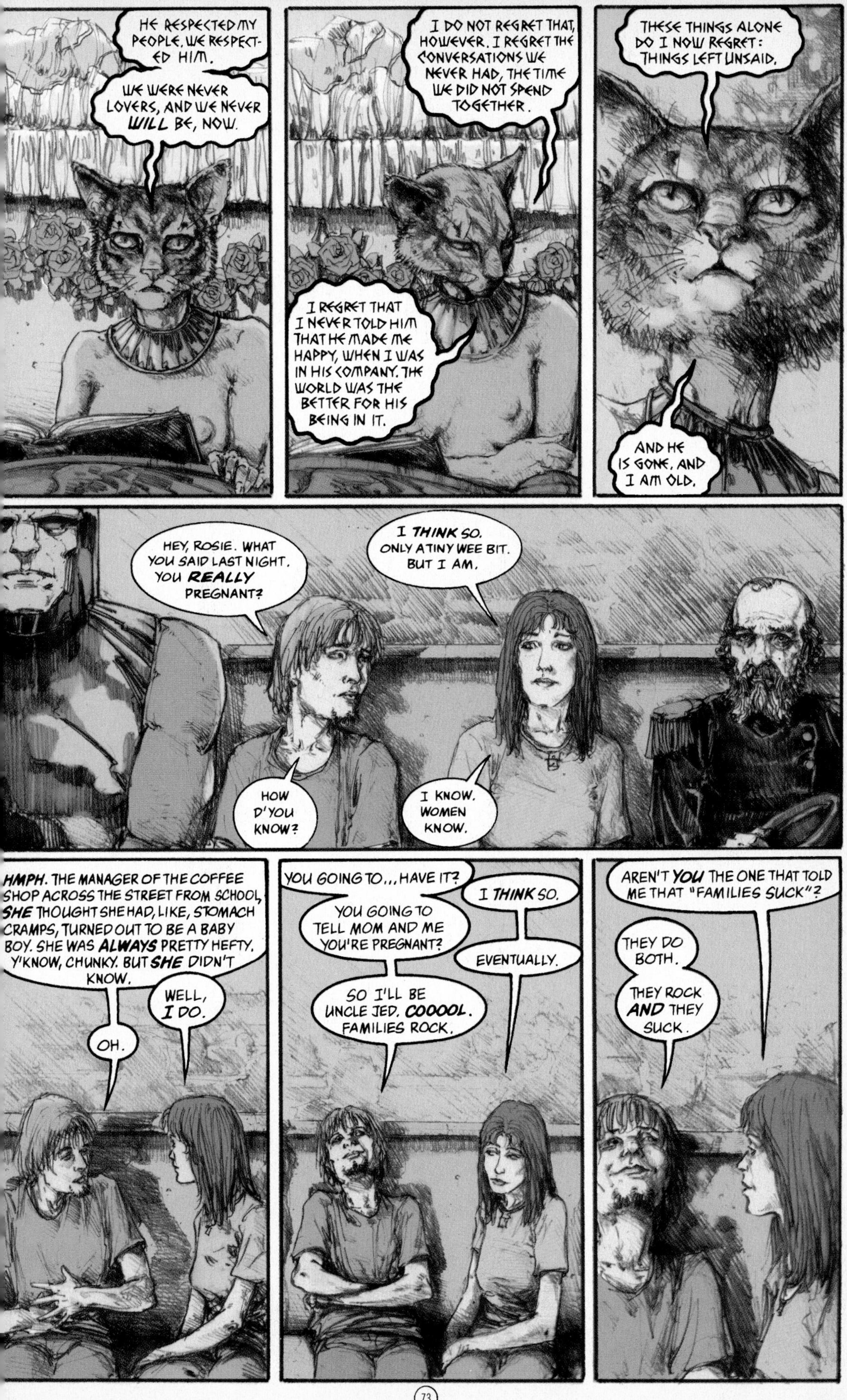

HE RESPECTED MY PEOPLE, WE RESPECTED HIM.
WE WERE NEVER LOVERS, AND WE NEVER WILL BE, NOW.
I DO NOT REGRET THAT, HOWEVER. I REGRET THE CONVERSATIONS WE NEVER HAD, THE TIME WE DID NOT SPEND TOGETHER.
I REGRET THAT I NEVER TOLD HIM THAT HE MADE ME HAPPY, WHEN I WAS IN HIS COMPANY. THE WORLD WAS THE BETTER FOR HIS BEING IN IT.
THESE THINGS ALONE DO I NOW REGRET: THINGS LEFT UNSAID.
AND HE IS GONE. AND I AM OLD.
HEY, ROSIE. WHAT YOU SAID LAST NIGHT. YOU REALLY PREGNANT?
I THINK SO. ONLY A TINY WEE BIT. BUT I AM.
HOW D'YOU KNOW?
I KNOW. WOMEN KNOW.
HMPH. THE MANAGER OF THE COFFEE SHOP ACROSS THE STREET FROM SCHOOL, SHE THOUGHT SHE HAD, LIKE, STOMACH CRAMPS, TURNED OUT TO BE A BABY BOY. SHE WAS ALWAYS PRETTY HEFTY. Y'KNOW, CHUNKY. BUT SHE DIDN'T KNOW.
WELL, I DO.
OH.
YOU GOING TO... HAVE IT?
I THINK SO.
YOU GOING TO TELL MOM AND ME YOU'RE PREGNANT?
EVENTUALLY.
SO I'LL BE UNCLE JED. COOOOL. FAMILIES ROCK.
AREN'T YOU THE ONE THAT TOLD ME THAT "FAMILIES SUCK"?
THEY DO BOTH.
THEY ROCK AND THEY SUCK.

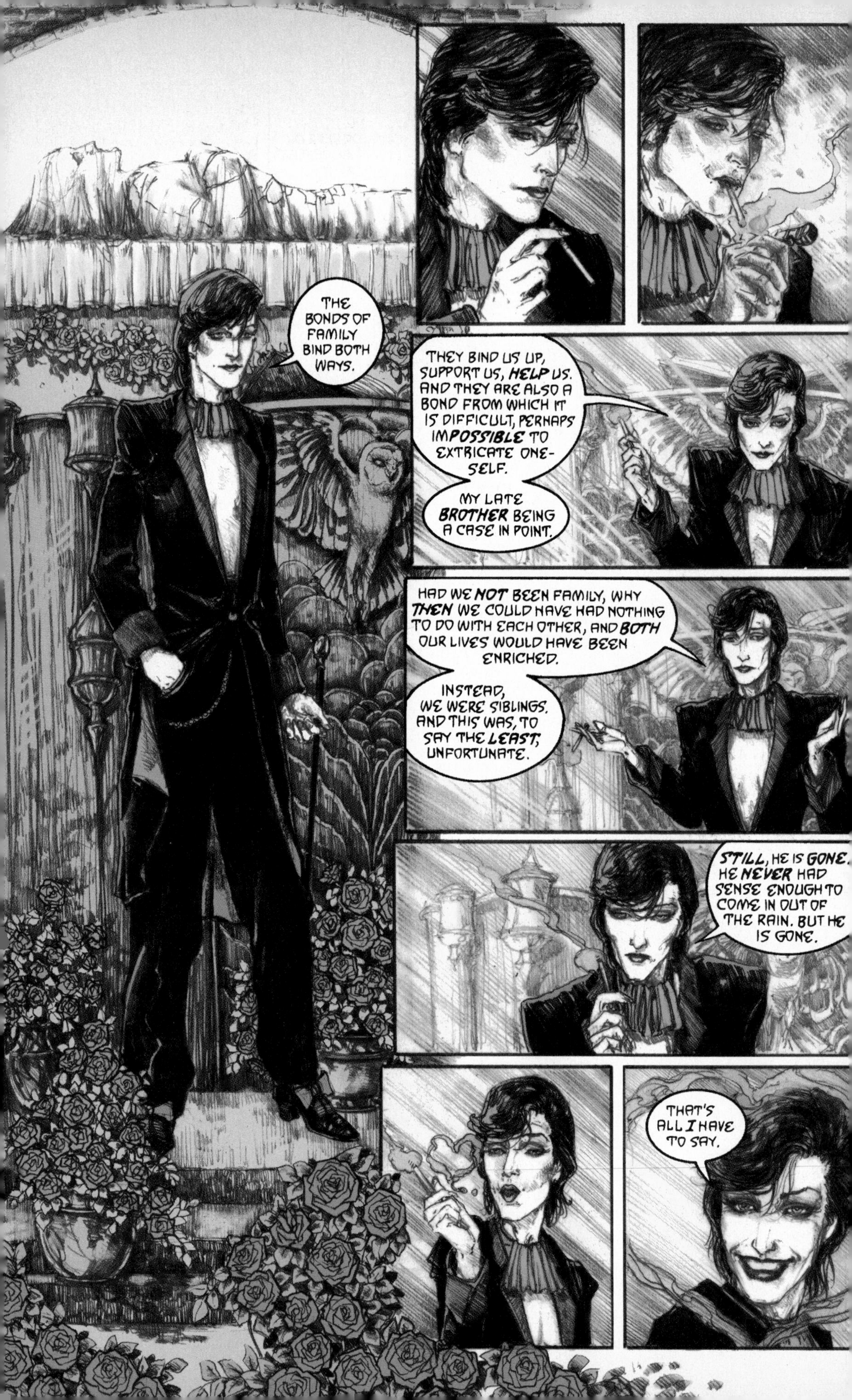
THE BONDS OF FAMILY BIND BOTH WAYS.
THEY BIND US UP, SUPPORT US, HELP US. AND THEY ARE ALSO A BOND FROM WHICH IT IS DIFFICULT, PERHAPS IMPOSSIBLE TO EXTRICATE ONE-SELF.
MY LATE BROTHER BEING A CASE IN POINT.
HAD WE NOT BEEN FAMILY, WHY THEN WE COULD HAVE HAD NOTHING TO DO WITH EACH OTHER, AND BOTH OUR LIVES WOULD HAVE BEEN ENRICHED.
INSTEAD, WE WERE SIBLINGS. AND THIS WAS, TO SAY THE LEAST, UNFORTUNATE.
STILL, HE IS GONE. HE NEVER HAD SENSE ENOUGH TO COME IN OUT OF THE RAIN. BUT HE IS GONE.
THAT'S ALL I HAVE TO SAY.

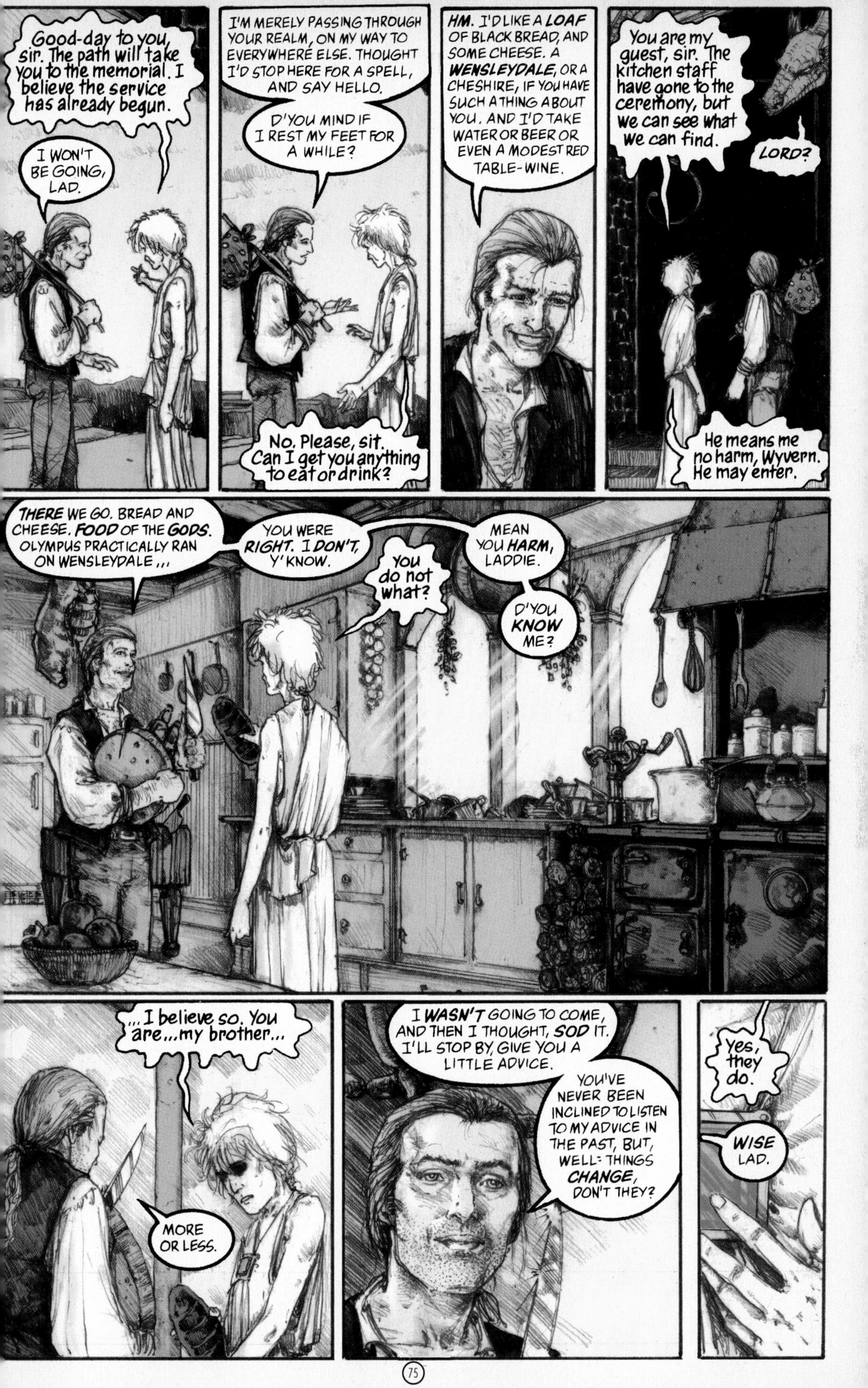
Good-day to you, sir. The path will take you to the memorial. I believe the service has already begun.
I WON'T BE GOING, LAD.
I'M MERELY PASSING THROUGH YOUR REALM, ON MY WAY TO EVERYWHERE ELSE. THOUGHT I'D STOP HERE FOR A SPELL, AND SAY HELLO.
D'YOU MIND IF I REST MY FEET FOR A WHILE?
No. Please, sit. Can I get you anything to eat or drink?
HM. I'D LIKE A LOAF OF BLACK BREAD, AND SOME CHEESE. A WENSLEYDALE, OR A CHESHIRE, IF YOU HAVE SUCH A THING ABOUT YOU. AND I'D TAKE WATER OR BEER OR EVEN A MODEST RED TABLE-WINE.
You are my guest, sir. The kitchen staff have gone to the ceremony, but we can see what we can find.
LORD?
He means me no harm, Wyvern. He may enter.
THERE WE GO. BREAD AND CHEESE. FOOD OF THE GODS. OLYMPUS PRACTICALLY RAN ON WENSLEYDALE...
YOU WERE RIGHT. I DON'T, Y'KNOW.
You do not what?
MEAN YOU HARM, LADDIE.
D'YOU KNOW ME?
...I believe so. You are...my brother...
MORE OR LESS.
I WASN'T GOING TO COME, AND THEN I THOUGHT, SOD IT. I'LL STOP BY, GIVE YOU A LITTLE ADVICE.
YOU'VE NEVER BEEN INCLINED TO LISTEN TO MY ADVICE IN THE PAST, BUT, WELL: THINGS CHANGE, DON'T THEY?
Yes, they do.
WISE LAD.

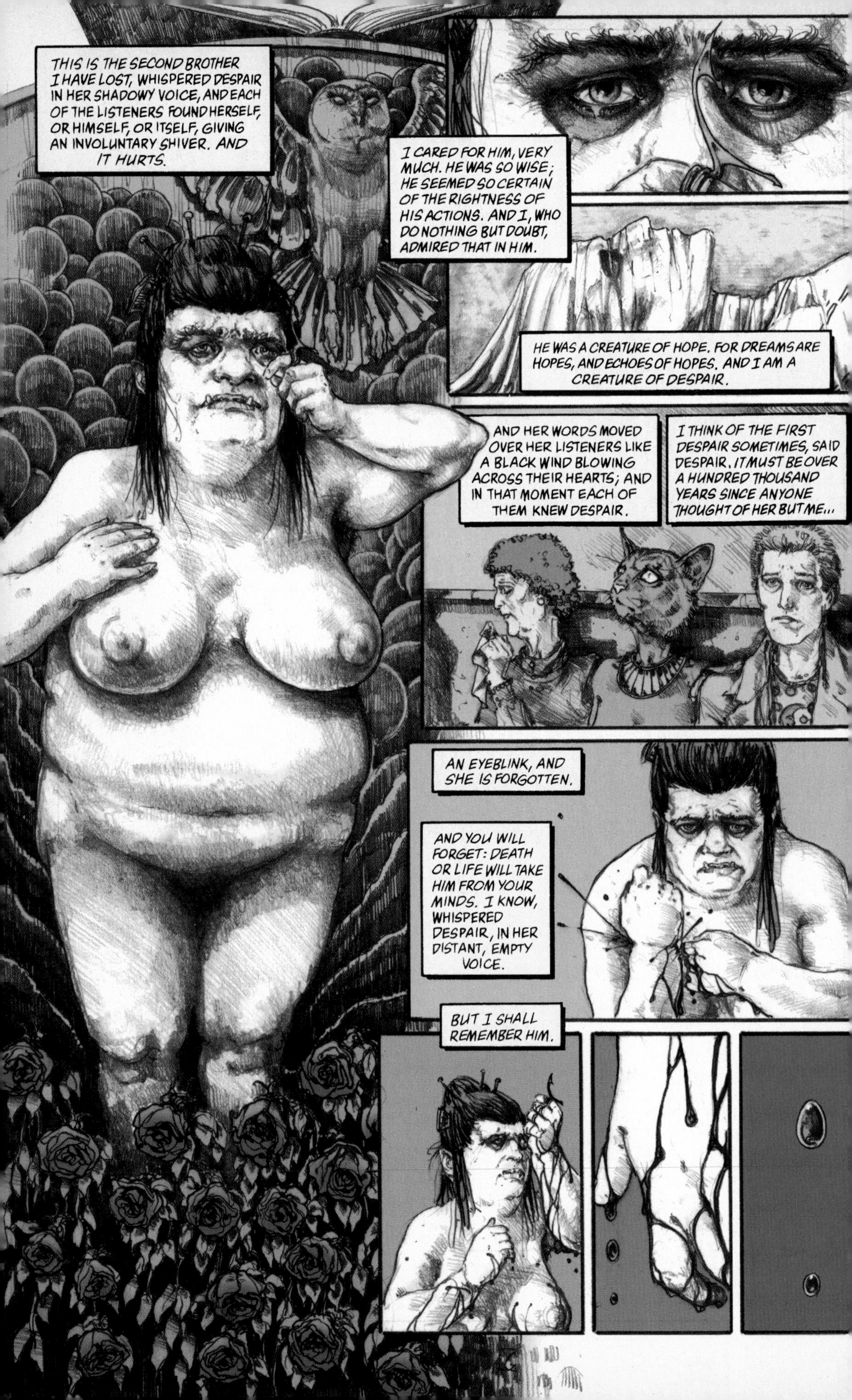
THIS IS THE SECOND BROTHER I HAVE LOST, WHISPERED DESPAIR IN HER SHADOWY VOICE, AND EACH OF THE LISTENERS FOUND HERSELF, OR HIMSELF, OR ITSELF, GIVING AN INVOLUNTARY SHIVER. AND IT HURTS.
I CARED FOR HIM, VERY MUCH. HE WAS SO WISE; HE SEEMED SO CERTAIN OF THE RIGHTNESS OF HIS ACTIONS. AND I, WHO DO NOTHING BUT DOUBT, ADMIRED THAT IN HIM.
HE WAS A CREATURE OF HOPE. FOR DREAMS ARE HOPES, AND ECHOES OF HOPES. AND I AM A CREATURE OF DESPAIR.
AND HER WORDS MOVED OVER HER LISTENERS LIKE A BLACK WIND BLOWING ACROSS THEIR HEARTS; AND IN THAT MOMENT EACH OF THEM KNEW DESPAIR.
I THINK OF THE FIRST DESPAIR SOMETIMES, SAID DESPAIR. IT MUST BE OVER A HUNDRED THOUSAND YEARS SINCE ANYONE THOUGHT OF HER BUT ME...
AN EYEBLINK, AND SHE IS FORGOTTEN.
AND YOU WILL FORGET: DEATH OR LIFE WILL TAKE HIM FROM YOUR MINDS. I KNOW, WHISPERED DESPAIR, IN HER DISTANT, EMPTY VOICE.
BUT I SHALL REMEMBER HIM.

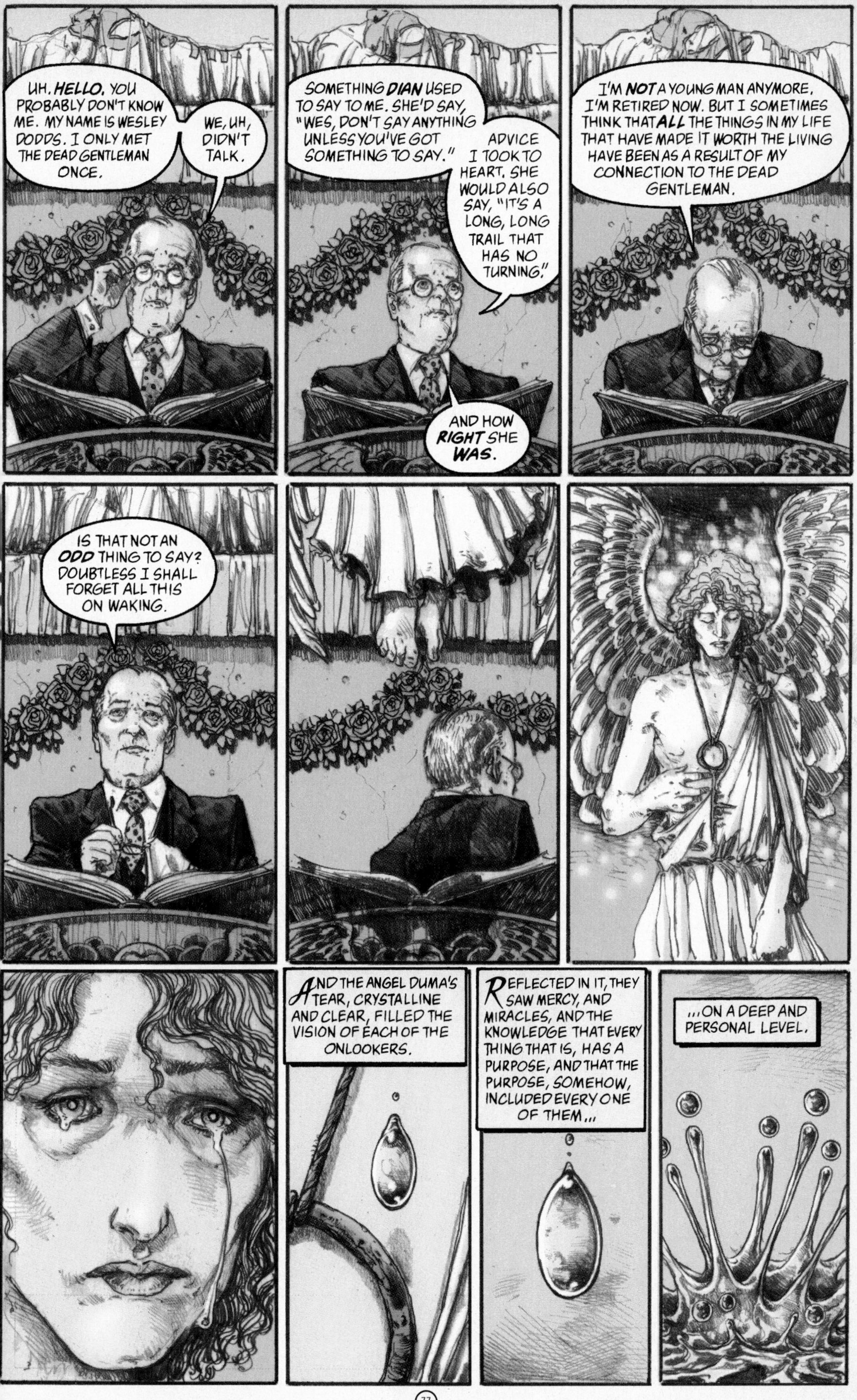
UH. **HELLO.** YOU PROBABLY DON'T KNOW ME. MY NAME IS WESLEY DODDS. I ONLY MET THE DEAD GENTLEMAN ONCE.
WE, UH, DIDN'T TALK.
SOMETHING **DIAN** USED TO SAY TO ME. SHE'D SAY, "WES, DON'T SAY ANYTHING UNLESS YOU'VE GOT SOMETHING TO SAY."
ADVICE I TOOK TO HEART. SHE WOULD ALSO SAY, "IT'S A LONG, LONG TRAIL THAT HAS NO TURNING."
AND HOW **RIGHT** SHE **WAS.**
I'M **NOT** A YOUNG MAN ANYMORE. I'M RETIRED NOW. BUT I SOMETIMES THINK THAT **ALL** THE THINGS IN MY LIFE THAT HAVE MADE IT WORTH THE LIVING HAVE BEEN AS A RESULT OF MY CONNECTION TO THE DEAD GENTLEMAN.
IS THAT NOT AN **ODD** THING TO SAY? DOUBTLESS I SHALL FORGET ALL THIS ON WAKING.
AND THE ANGEL DUMA'S TEAR, CRYSTALLINE AND CLEAR, FILLED THE VISION OF EACH OF THE ONLOOKERS.
REFLECTED IN IT, THEY SAW MERCY, AND MIRACLES, AND THE KNOWLEDGE THAT EVERY THING THAT IS, HAS A PURPOSE, AND THAT THE PURPOSE, SOMEHOW, INCLUDED EVERY ONE OF THEM...
...ON A DEEP AND PERSONAL LEVEL.

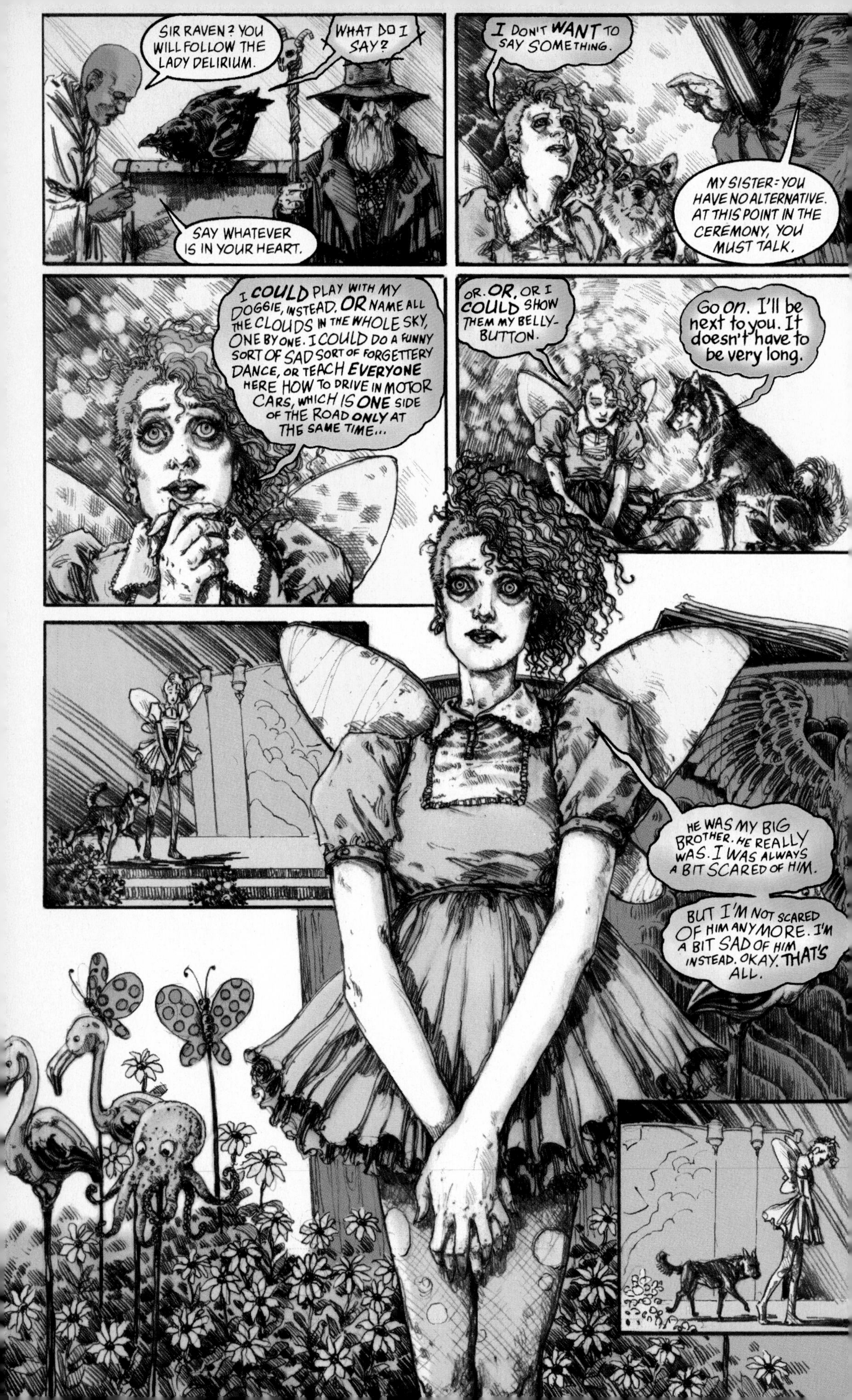
SIR RAVEN? YOU WILL FOLLOW THE LADY DELIRIUM.
WHAT DO I SAY?
SAY WHATEVER IS IN YOUR HEART.
I DON'T WANT TO SAY SOMETHING.
MY SISTER: YOU HAVE NO ALTERNATIVE. AT THIS POINT IN THE CEREMONY, YOU MUST TALK.
I COULD PLAY WITH MY DOGGIE, INSTEAD. OR NAME ALL THE CLOUDS IN THE WHOLE SKY, ONE BY ONE. I COULD DO A FUNNY SORT OF SAD SORT OF FORGETTERY DANCE, OR TEACH EVERYONE HERE HOW TO DRIVE IN MOTOR CARS, WHICH IS ONE SIDE OF THE ROAD ONLY AT THE SAME TIME...
OR. OR. OR I COULD SHOW THEM MY BELLY-BUTTON.
Go on. I'll be next to you. It doesn't have to be very long.
HE WAS MY BIG BROTHER. HE REALLY WAS. I WAS ALWAYS A BIT SCARED OF HIM.
BUT I'M NOT SCARED OF HIM ANYMORE. I'M A BIT SAD OF HIM INSTEAD. OKAY. THAT'S ALL.

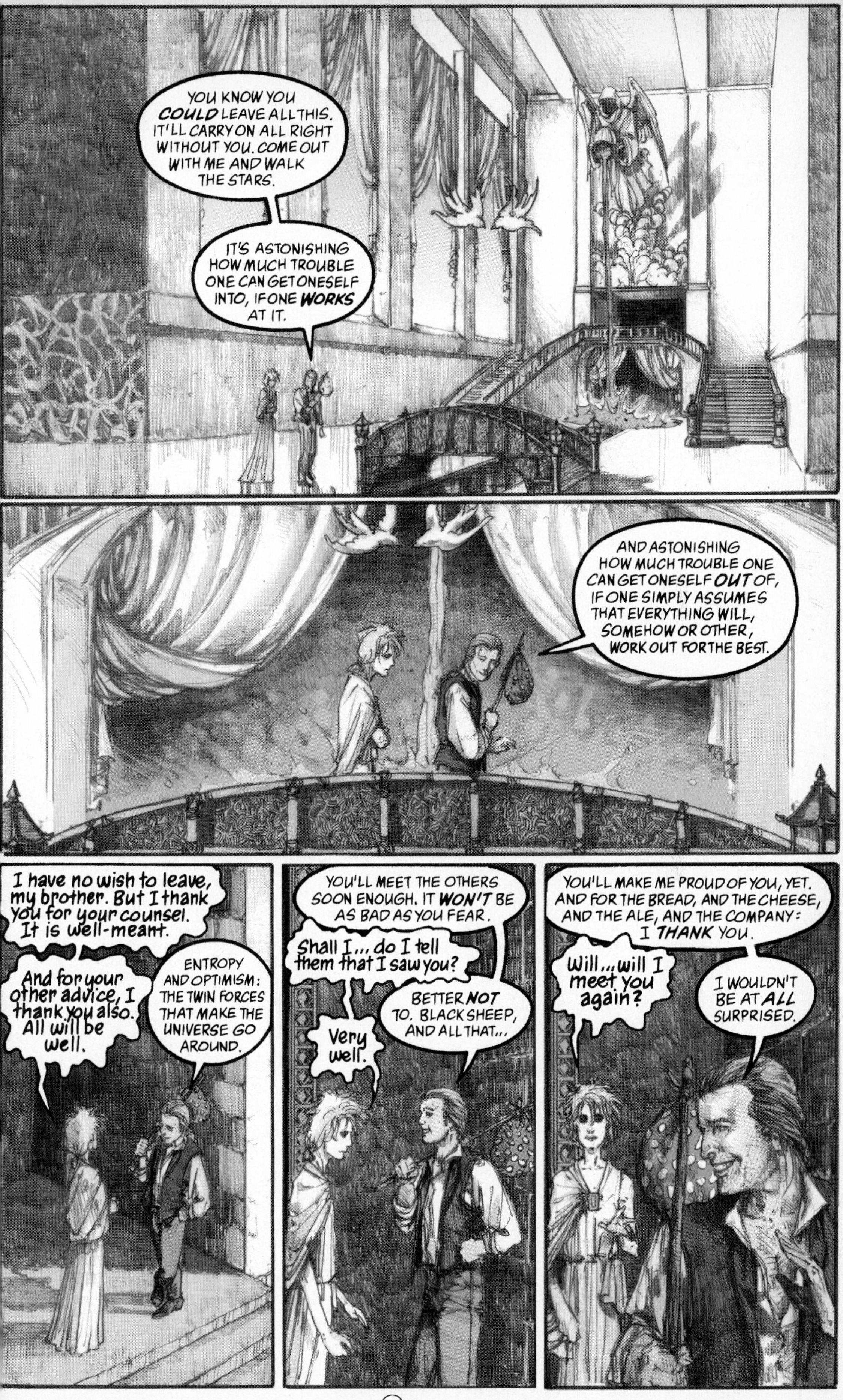
YOU KNOW YOU COULD LEAVE ALL THIS. IT'LL CARRY ON ALL RIGHT WITHOUT YOU. COME OUT WITH ME AND WALK THE STARS.
IT'S ASTONISHING HOW MUCH TROUBLE ONE CAN GET ONESELF INTO, IF ONE WORKS AT IT.
AND ASTONISHING HOW MUCH TROUBLE ONE CAN GET ONESELF OUT OF, IF ONE SIMPLY ASSUMES THAT EVERYTHING WILL, SOMEHOW OR OTHER, WORK OUT FOR THE BEST.
I have no wish to leave, my brother. But I thank you for your counsel. It is well-meant.
And for your other advice, I thank you also. All will be well.
ENTROPY AND OPTIMISM: THE TWIN FORCES THAT MAKE THE UNIVERSE GO AROUND.
YOU'LL MEET THE OTHERS SOON ENOUGH. IT WON'T BE AS BAD AS YOU FEAR.
Shall I... do I tell them that I saw you?
BETTER NOT TO. BLACK SHEEP, AND ALL THAT...
Very well.
YOU'LL MAKE ME PROUD OF YOU, YET. AND FOR THE BREAD, AND THE CHEESE, AND THE ALE, AND THE COMPANY: I THANK YOU.
Will... will I meet you again?
I WOULDN'T BE AT ALL SURPRISED.

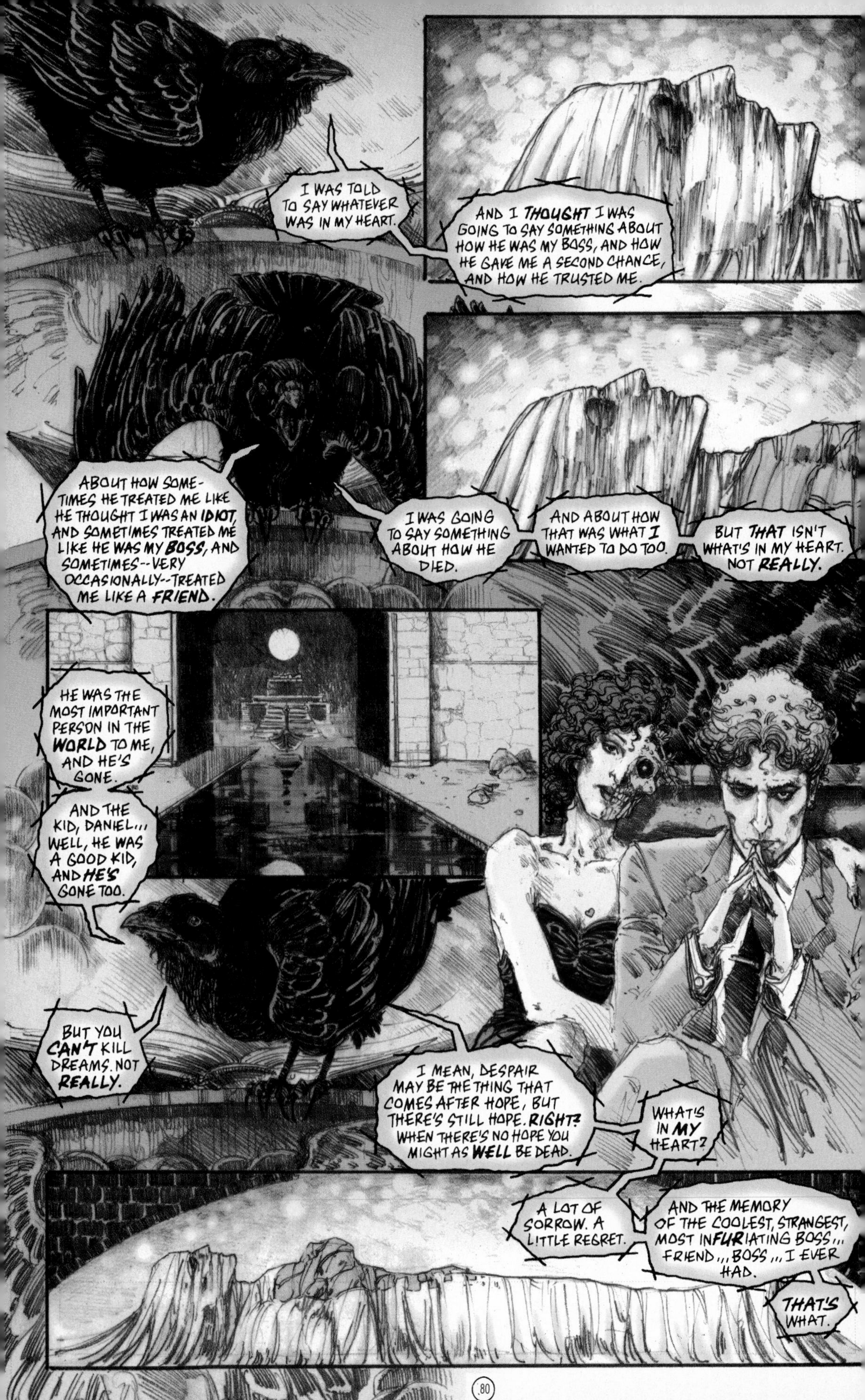
I WAS TOLD TO SAY WHATEVER WAS IN MY HEART.
AND I THOUGHT I WAS GOING TO SAY SOMETHING ABOUT HOW HE WAS MY BOSS, AND HOW HE GAVE ME A SECOND CHANCE, AND HOW HE TRUSTED ME.
ABOUT HOW SOME-TIMES HE TREATED ME LIKE HE THOUGHT I WAS AN IDIOT, AND SOMETIMES TREATED ME LIKE HE WAS MY BOSS, AND SOMETIMES--VERY OCCASIONALLY--TREATED ME LIKE A FRIEND.
I WAS GOING TO SAY SOMETHING ABOUT HOW HE DIED.
AND ABOUT HOW THAT WAS WHAT I WANTED TO DO TOO.
BUT THAT ISN'T WHAT'S IN MY HEART. NOT REALLY.
HE WAS THE MOST IMPORTANT PERSON IN THE WORLD TO ME, AND HE'S GONE.
AND THE KID, DANIEL... WELL, HE WAS A GOOD KID, AND HE'S GONE TOO.
BUT YOU CAN'T KILL DREAMS. NOT REALLY.
I MEAN, DESPAIR MAY BE THE THING THAT COMES AFTER HOPE, BUT THERE'S STILL HOPE. RIGHT? WHEN THERE'S NO HOPE YOU MIGHT AS WELL BE DEAD.
WHAT'S IN MY HEART?
A LOT OF SORROW. A LITTLE REGRET.
AND THE MEMORY OF THE COOLEST, STRANGEST, MOST INFURIATING BOSS... FRIEND... BOSS... I EVER HAD.
THAT'S WHAT.

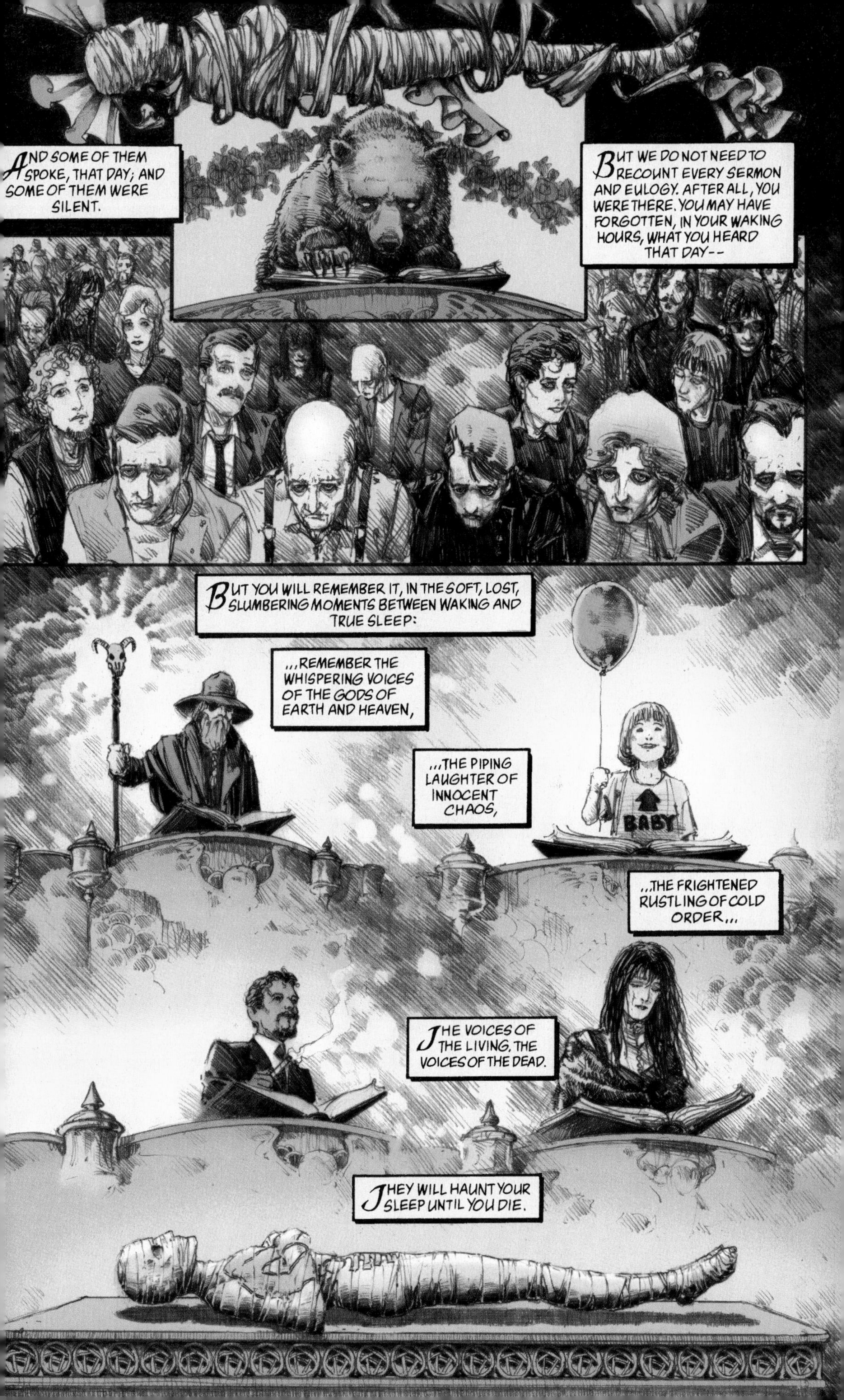
AND SOME OF THEM SPOKE, THAT DAY; AND SOME OF THEM WERE SILENT.
BUT WE DO NOT NEED TO RECOUNT EVERY SERMON AND EULOGY. AFTER ALL, YOU WERE THERE. YOU MAY HAVE FORGOTTEN, IN YOUR WAKING HOURS, WHAT YOU HEARD THAT DAY--
BUT YOU WILL REMEMBER IT, IN THE SOFT, LOST, SLUMBERING MOMENTS BETWEEN WAKING AND TRUE SLEEP:
...REMEMBER THE WHISPERING VOICES OF THE GODS OF EARTH AND HEAVEN,
...THE PIPING LAUGHTER OF INNOCENT CHAOS,
BABY
...THE FRIGHTENED RUSTLING OF COLD ORDER...
THE VOICES OF THE LIVING, THE VOICES OF THE DEAD.
THEY WILL HAUNT YOUR SLEEP UNTIL YOU DIE.

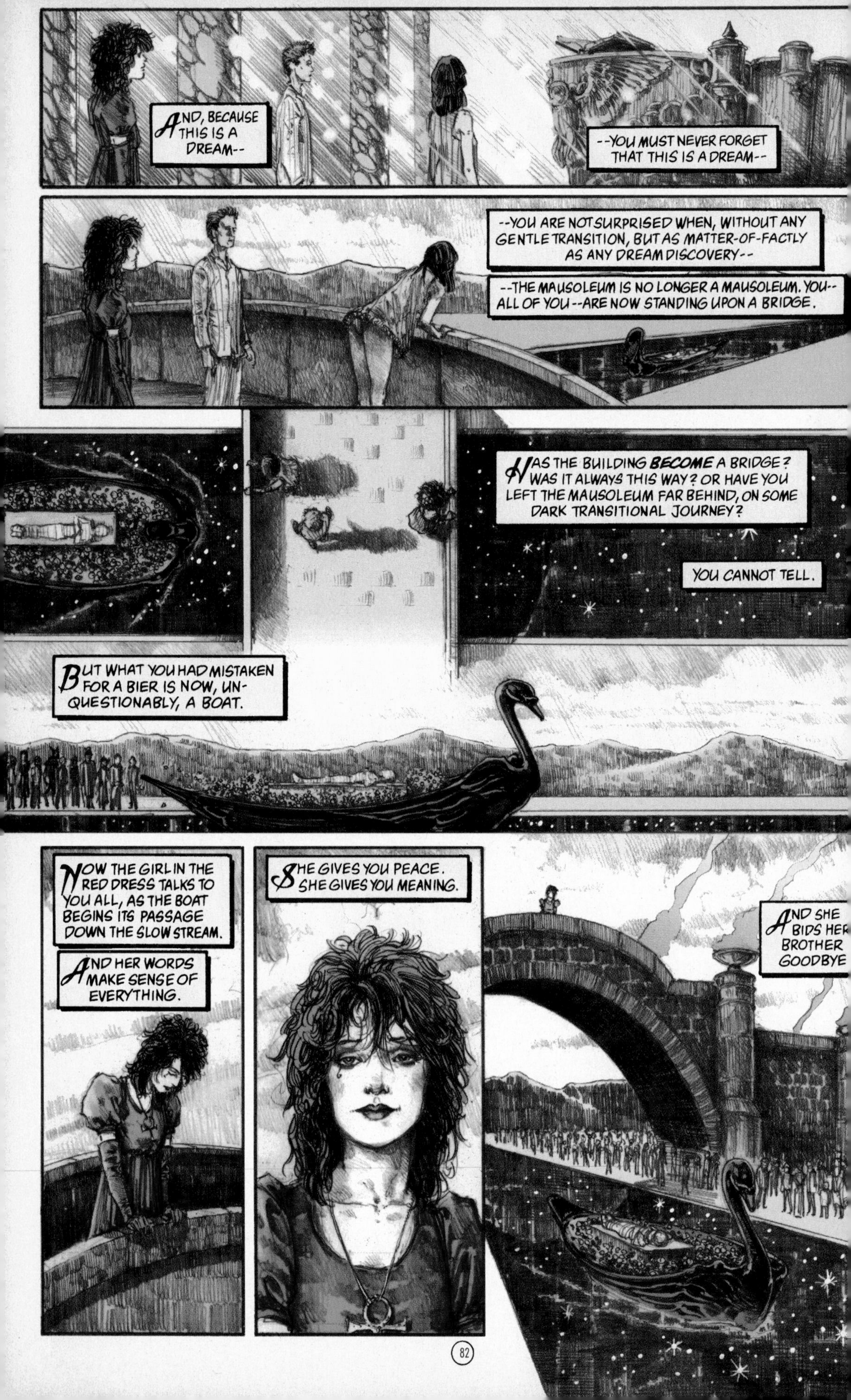
AND, BECAUSE THIS IS A DREAM--
--YOU MUST NEVER FORGET THAT THIS IS A DREAM--
--YOU ARE NOT SURPRISED WHEN, WITHOUT ANY GENTLE TRANSITION, BUT AS MATTER-OF-FACTLY AS ANY DREAM DISCOVERY--
--THE MAUSOLEUM IS NO LONGER A MAUSOLEUM. YOU--ALL OF YOU--ARE NOW STANDING UPON A BRIDGE.
HAS THE BUILDING BECOME A BRIDGE? WAS IT ALWAYS THIS WAY? OR HAVE YOU LEFT THE MAUSOLEUM FAR BEHIND, ON SOME DARK TRANSITIONAL JOURNEY?
YOU CANNOT TELL.
BUT WHAT YOU HAD MISTAKEN FOR A BIER IS NOW, UN-QUESTIONABLY, A BOAT.
NOW THE GIRL IN THE RED DRESS TALKS TO YOU ALL, AS THE BOAT BEGINS ITS PASSAGE DOWN THE SLOW STREAM.
AND HER WORDS MAKE SENSE OF EVERYTHING.
SHE GIVES YOU PEACE. SHE GIVES YOU MEANING.
AND SHE BIDS HER BROTHER GOODBYE

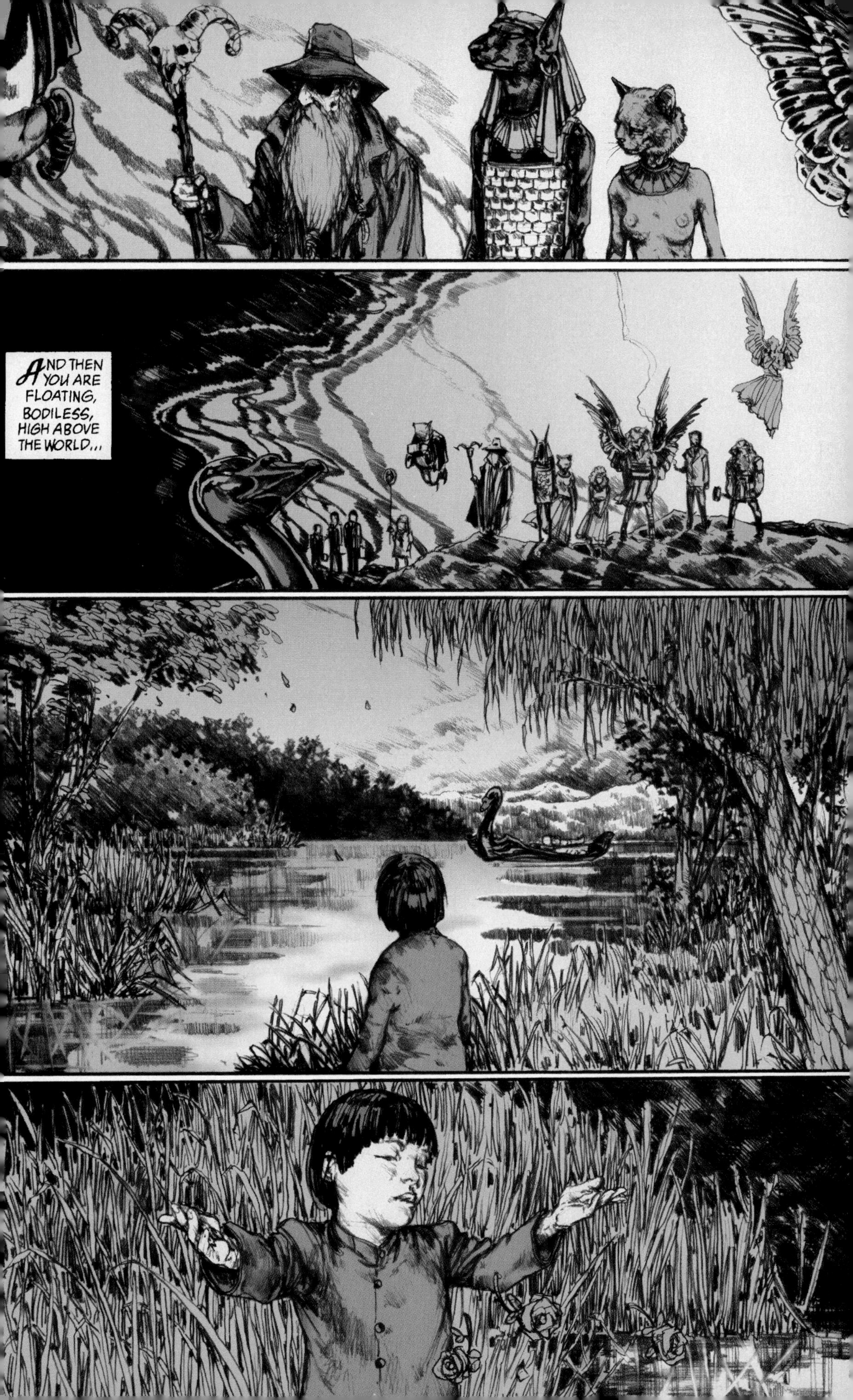
AND THEN YOU ARE FLOATING, BODILESS, HIGH ABOVE THE WORLD...

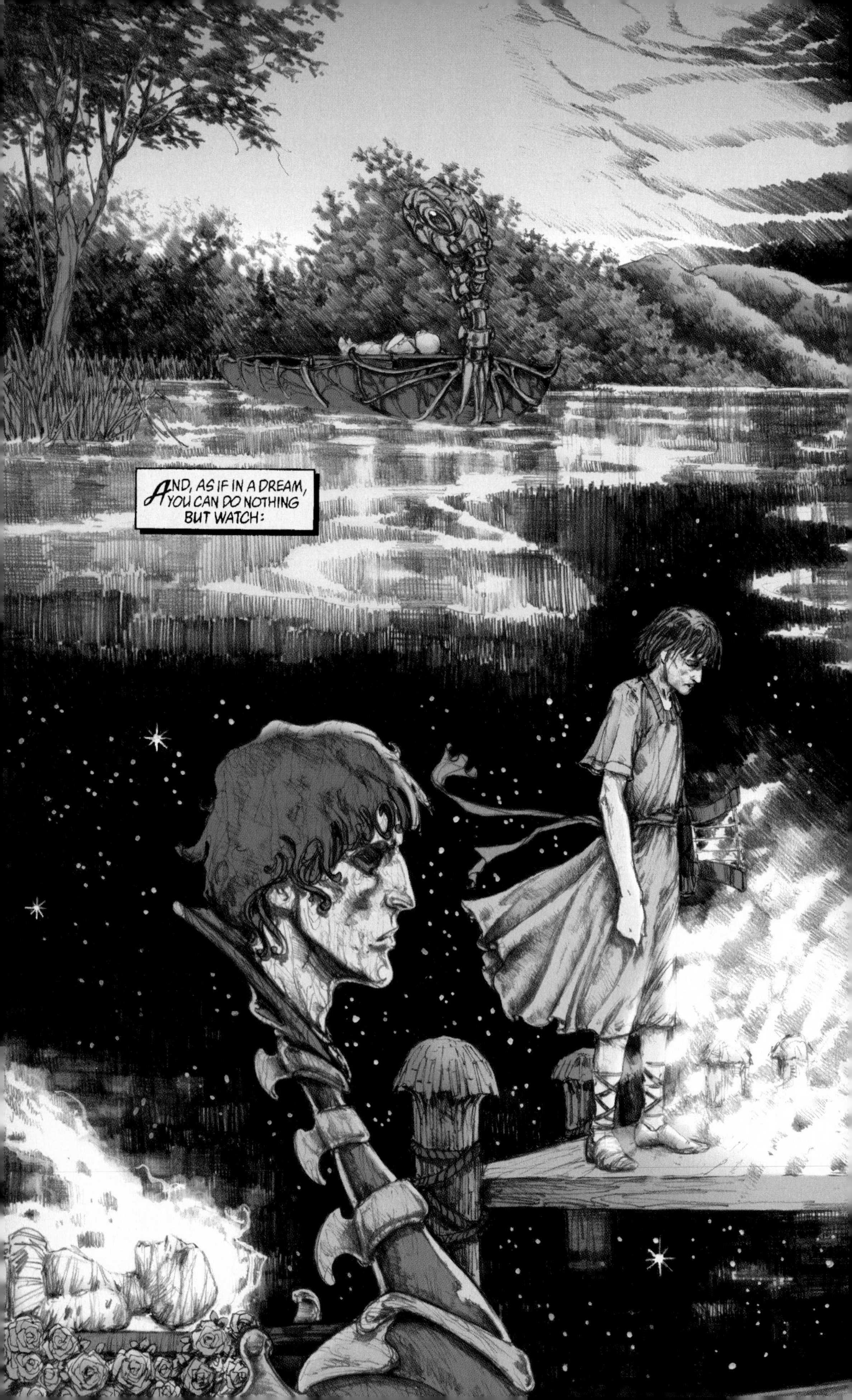
AND, AS IF IN A DREAM, YOU CAN DO NOTHING BUT WATCH:

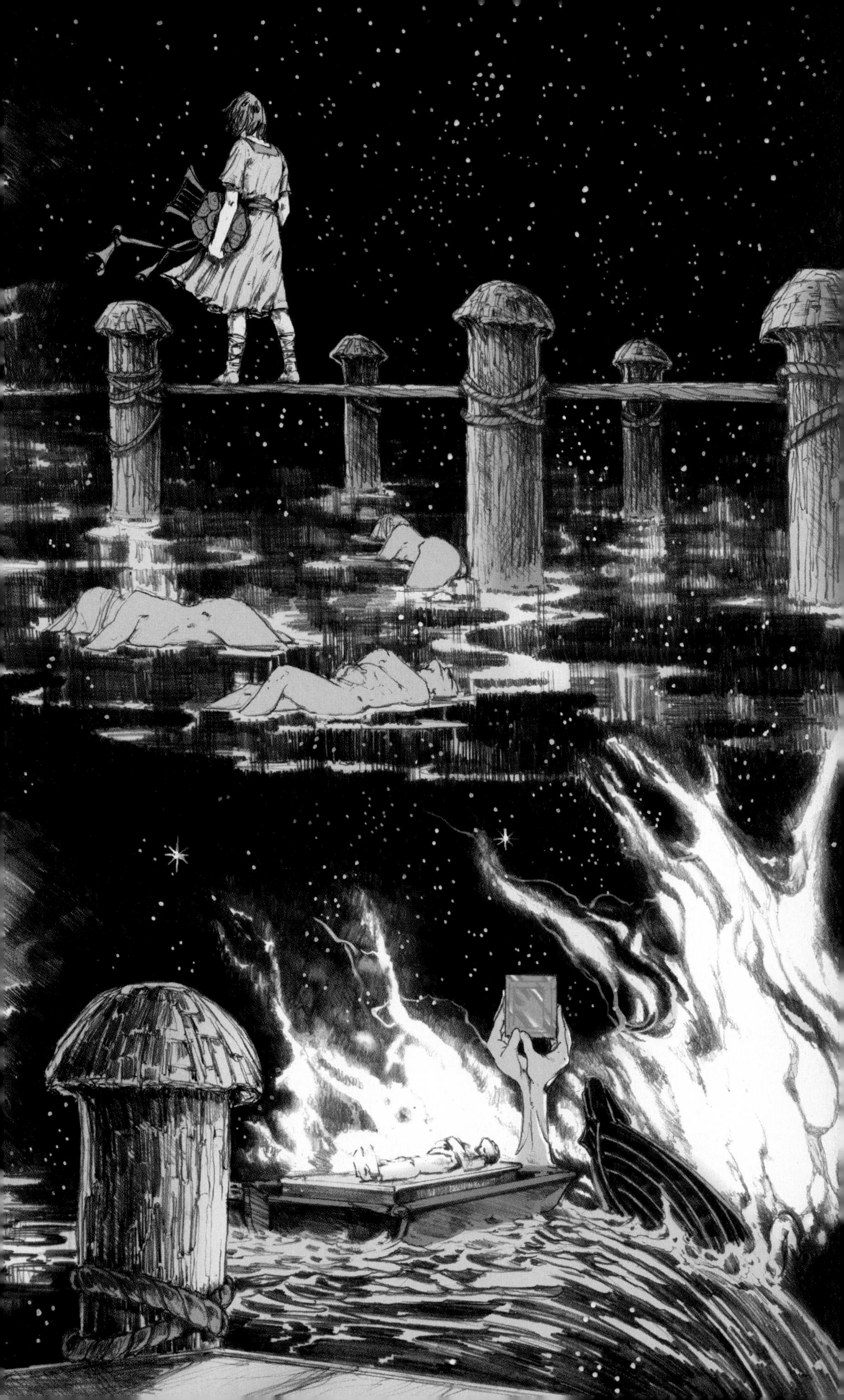

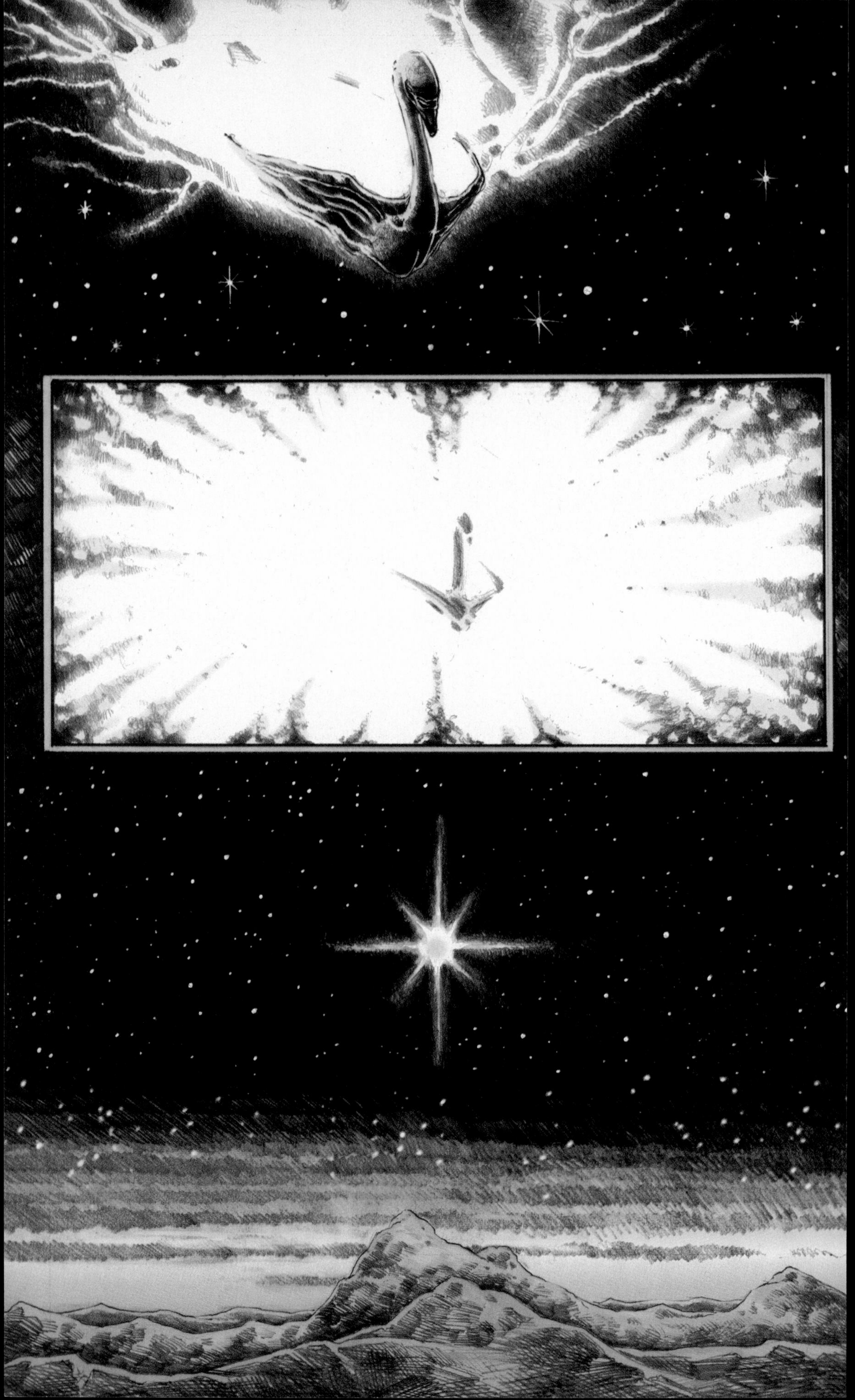

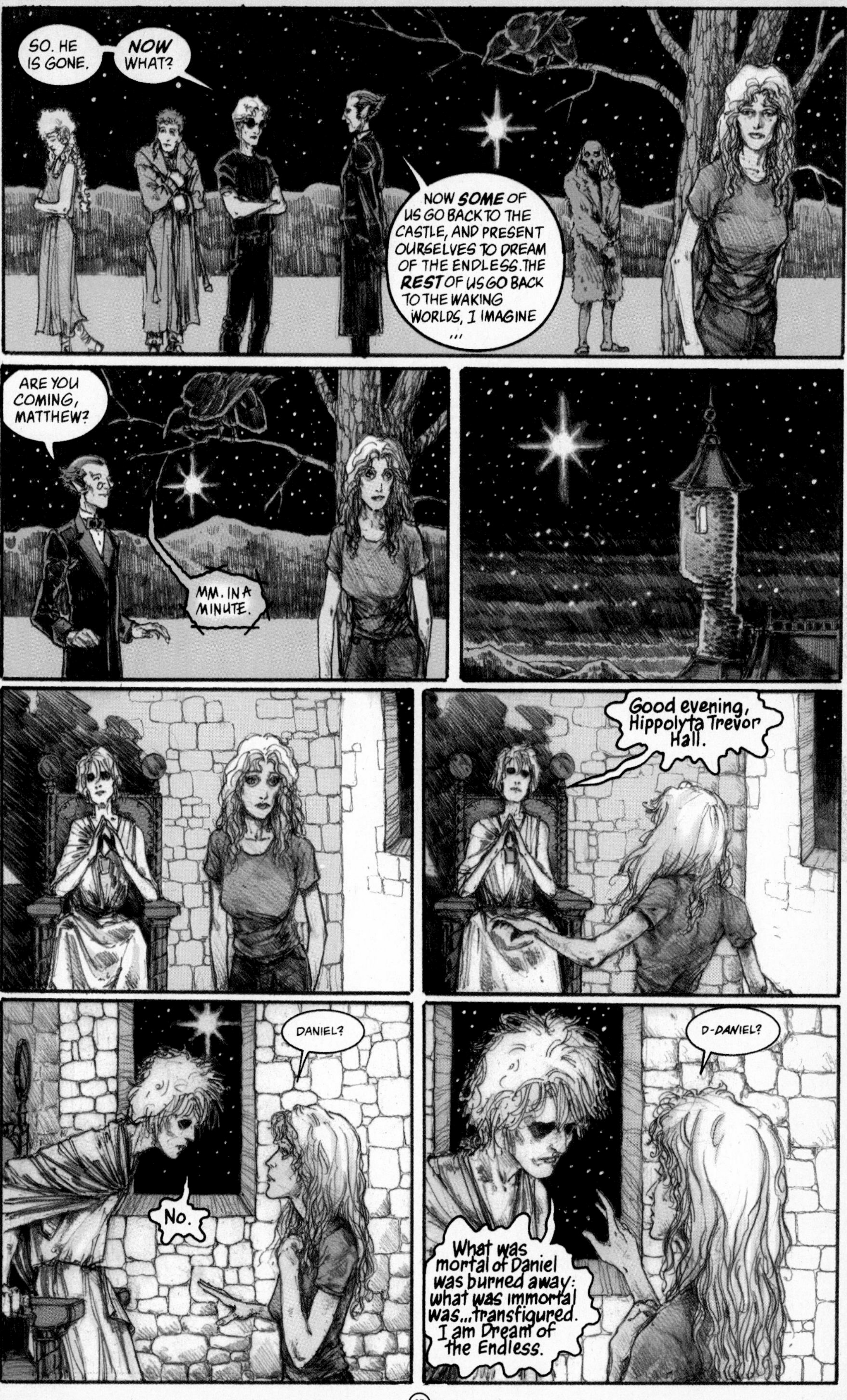
SO. HE IS GONE.
NOW WHAT?
NOW SOME OF US GO BACK TO THE CASTLE, AND PRESENT OURSELVES TO DREAM OF THE ENDLESS. THE REST OF US GO BACK TO THE WAKING WORLDS, I IMAGINE ...
ARE YOU COMING, MATTHEW?
MM. IN A MINUTE.
Good evening, Hippolyta Trevor Hall.
DANIEL?
No.
D-DANIEL?
What was mortal of Daniel was burned away: what was immortal was... transfigured. I am Dream of the Endless.

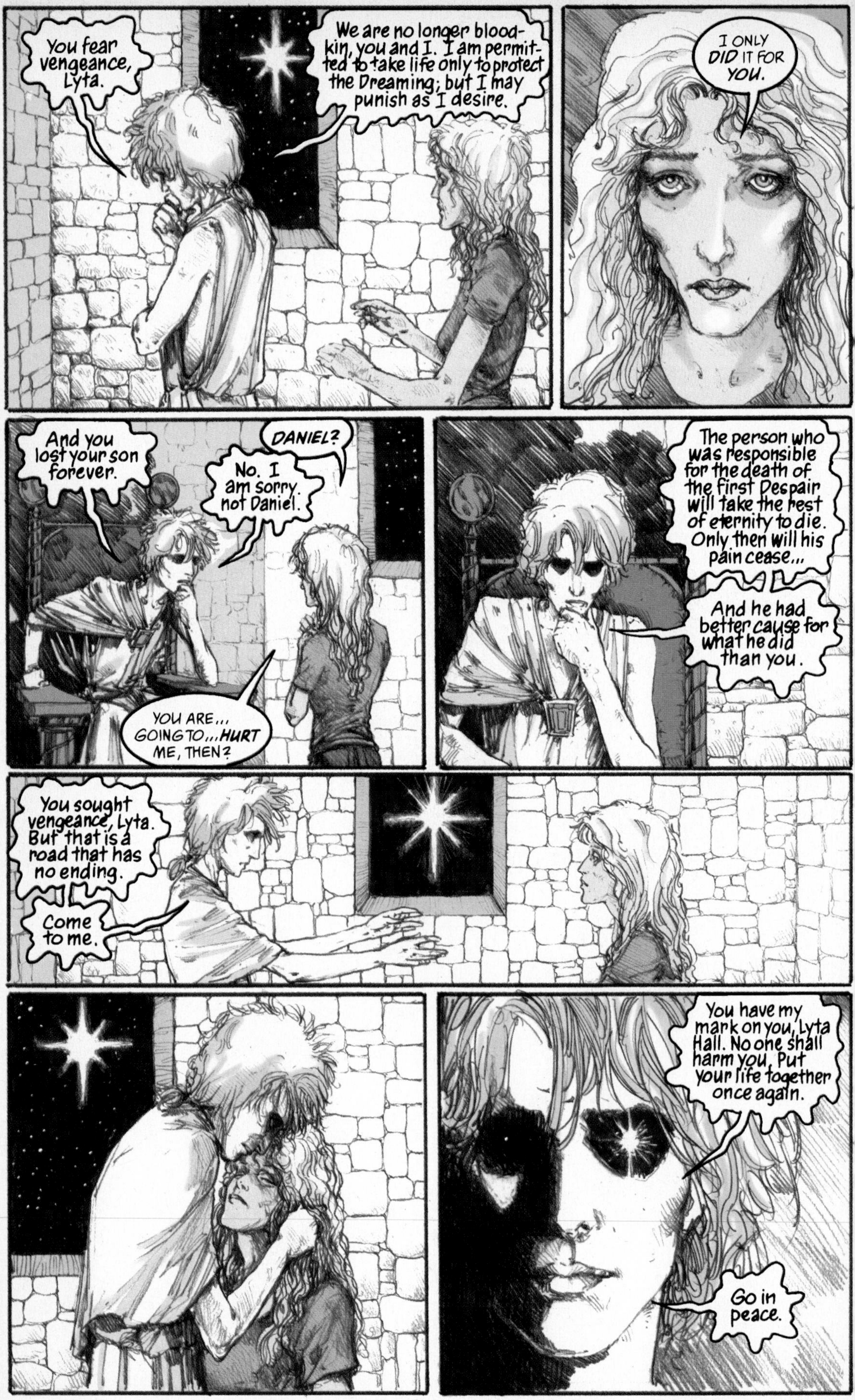
You fear vengeance, Lyta.
We are no longer blood-kin, you and I. I am permitted to take life only to protect the Dreaming; but I may punish as I desire.
I ONLY DID IT FOR YOU.
And you lost your son forever.
DANIEL?
No. I am sorry. not Daniel.
YOU ARE... GOING TO... HURT ME, THEN?
The person who was responsible for the death of the first Despair will take the rest of eternity to die. Only then will his pain cease...
And he had better cause for what he did than you.
You sought vengeance, Lyta. But that is a road that has no ending.
Come to me.
You have my mark on you, Lyta Hall. No one shall harm you. Put your life together once again.
Go in peace.

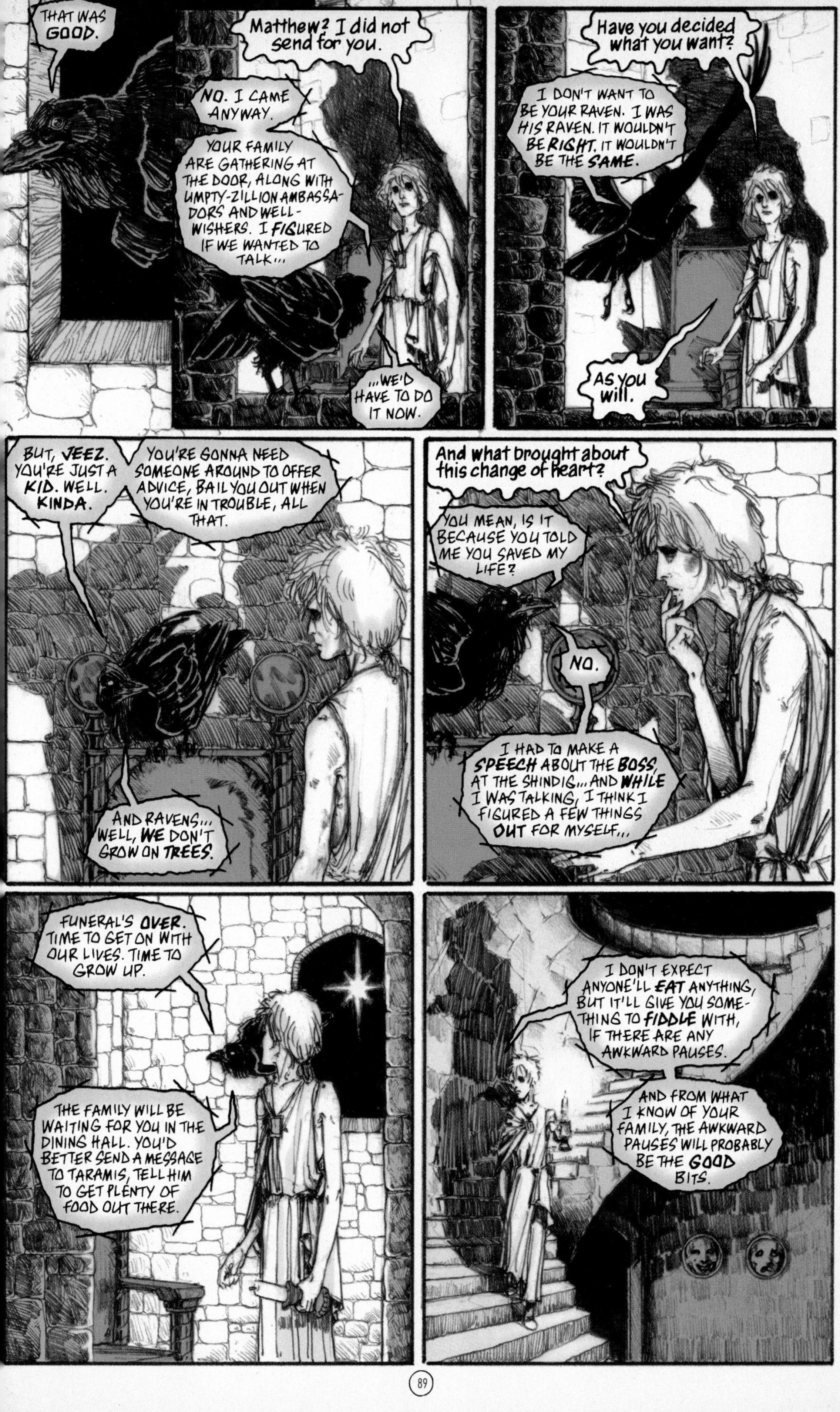
THAT WAS GOOD.
Matthew? I did not send for you.
NO. I CAME ANYWAY.
YOUR FAMILY ARE GATHERING AT THE DOOR, ALONG WITH UMPTY-ZILLION AMBASSADORS AND WELL-WISHERS. I FIGURED IF WE WANTED TO TALK...
...WE'D HAVE TO DO IT NOW.
Have you decided what you want?
I DON'T WANT TO BE YOUR RAVEN. I WAS HIS RAVEN. IT WOULDN'T BE RIGHT. IT WOULDN'T BE THE SAME.
As you will.
BUT, JEEZ. YOU'RE JUST A KID. WELL. KINDA.
YOU'RE GONNA NEED SOMEONE AROUND TO OFFER ADVICE, BAIL YOU OUT WHEN YOU'RE IN TROUBLE, ALL THAT.
AND RAVENS... WELL, WE DON'T GROW ON TREES.
And what brought about this change of heart?
YOU MEAN, IS IT BECAUSE YOU TOLD ME YOU SAVED MY LIFE?
NO.
I HAD TO MAKE A SPEECH ABOUT THE BOSS, AT THE SHINDIG... AND WHILE I WAS TALKING, I THINK I FIGURED A FEW THINGS OUT FOR MYSELF...
FUNERAL'S OVER. TIME TO GET ON WITH OUR LIVES. TIME TO GROW UP.
THE FAMILY WILL BE WAITING FOR YOU IN THE DINING HALL. YOU'D BETTER SEND A MESSAGE TO TARAMIS, TELL HIM TO GET PLENTY OF FOOD OUT THERE.
I DON'T EXPECT ANYONE'LL EAT ANYTHING, BUT IT'LL GIVE YOU SOMETHING TO FIDDLE WITH, IF THERE ARE ANY AWKWARD PAUSES.
AND FROM WHAT I KNOW OF YOUR FAMILY, THE AWKWARD PAUSES WILL PROBABLY BE THE GOOD BITS.

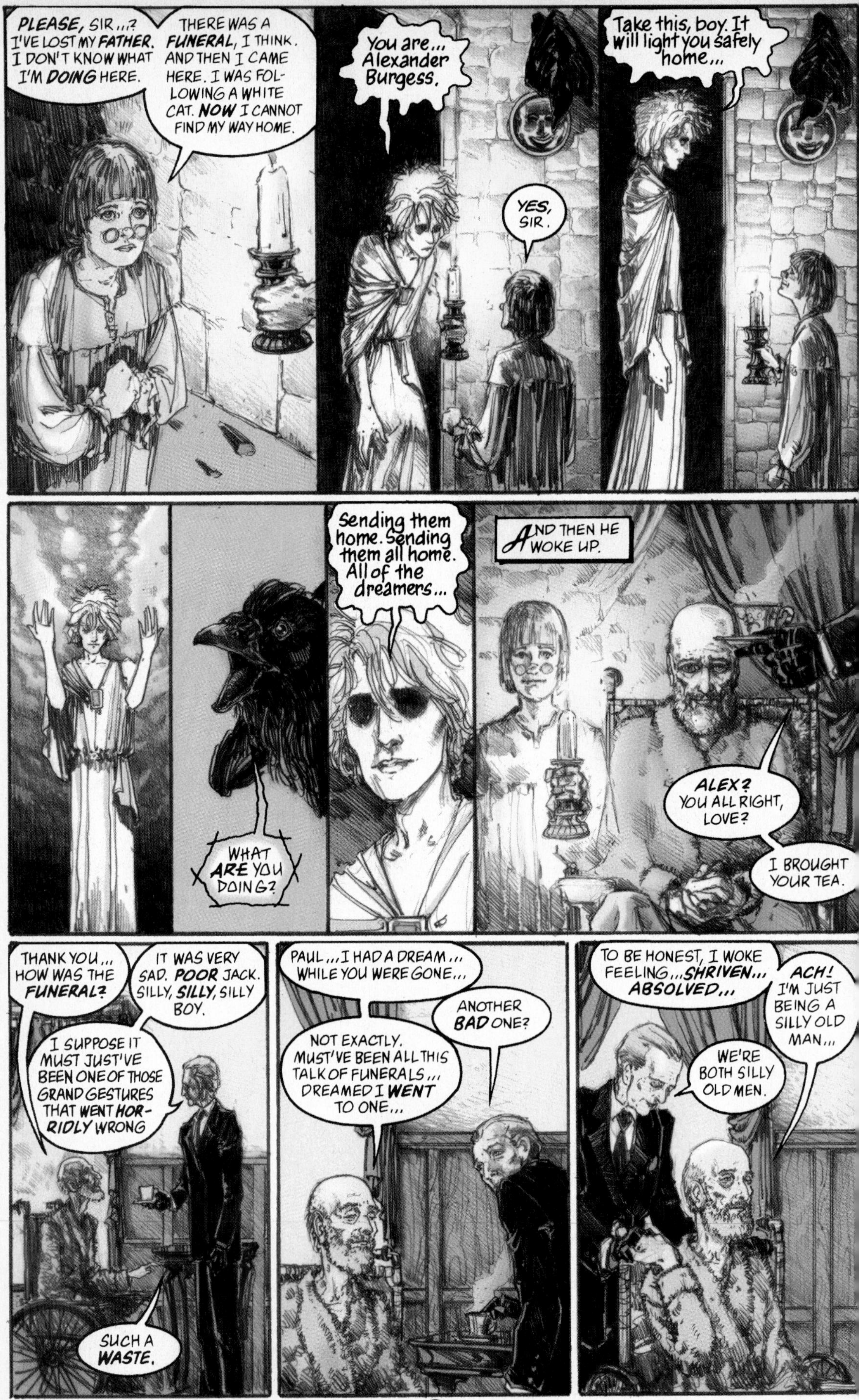
PLEASE, SIR...? I'VE LOST MY FATHER. I DON'T KNOW WHAT I'M DOING HERE.
THERE WAS A FUNERAL, I THINK. AND THEN I CAME HERE. I WAS FOLLOWING A WHITE CAT. NOW I CANNOT FIND MY WAY HOME.
You are... Alexander Burgess.
YES, SIR.
Take this, boy. It will light you safely home...
WHAT ARE YOU DOING?
Sending them home. Sending them all home. All of the dreamers...
AND THEN HE WOKE UP.
ALEX? YOU ALL RIGHT, LOVE?
I BROUGHT YOUR TEA.
THANK YOU... HOW WAS THE FUNERAL?
IT WAS VERY SAD. POOR JACK. SILLY, SILLY, SILLY BOY.
I SUPPOSE IT MUST JUST'VE BEEN ONE OF THOSE GRAND GESTURES THAT WENT HORRIDLY WRONG
SUCH A WASTE.
PAUL... I HAD A DREAM... WHILE YOU WERE GONE...
ANOTHER BAD ONE?
NOT EXACTLY. MUST'VE BEEN ALL THIS TALK OF FUNERALS... DREAMED I WENT TO ONE...
TO BE HONEST, I WOKE FEELING... SHRIVEN... ABSOLVED...
ACH! I'M JUST BEING A SILLY OLD MAN...
WE'RE BOTH SILLY OLD MEN.

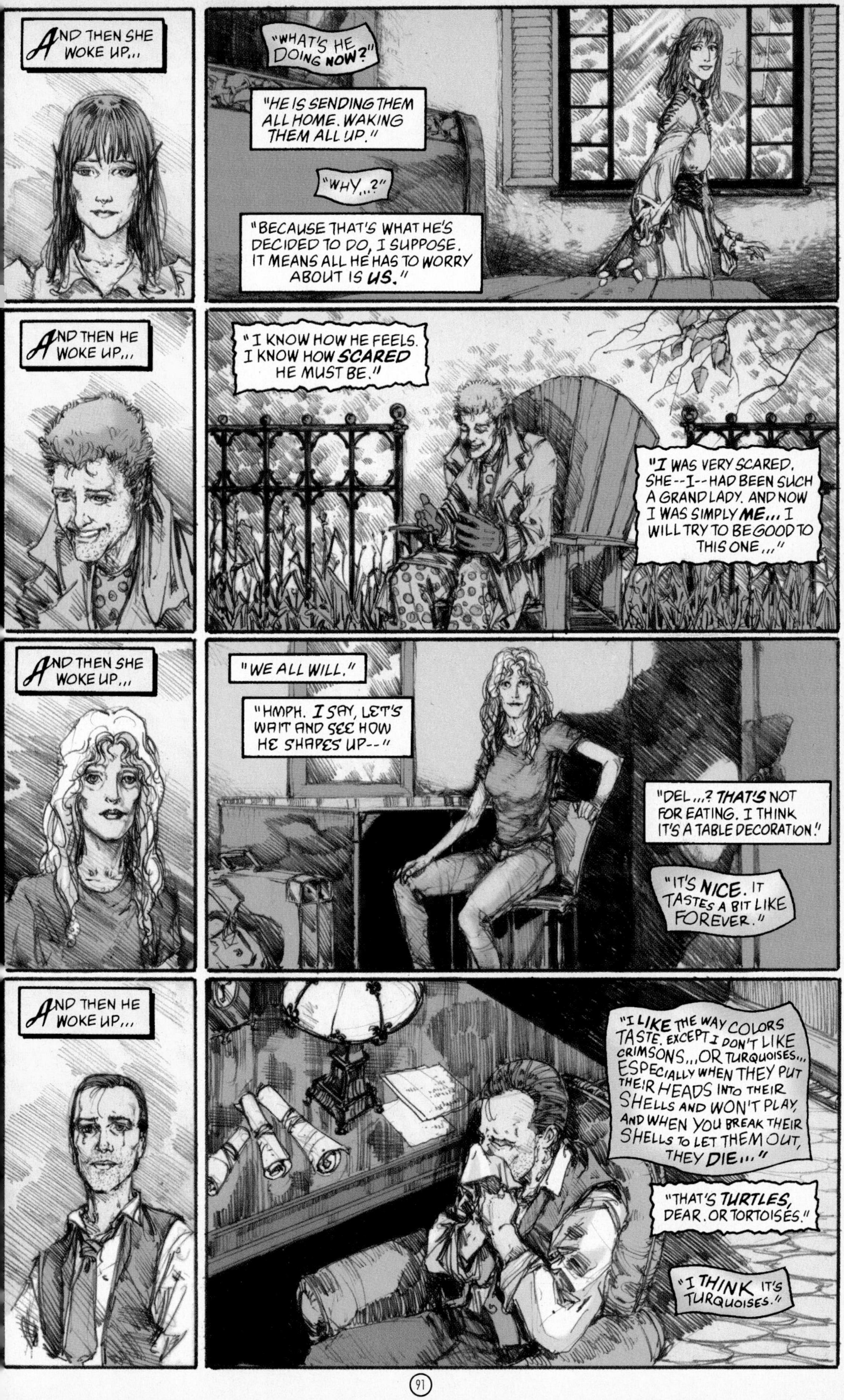
AND THEN SHE WOKE UP...
"WHAT'S HE DOING NOW?"
"HE IS SENDING THEM ALL HOME. WAKING THEM ALL UP."
"WHY...?"
"BECAUSE THAT'S WHAT HE'S DECIDED TO DO, I SUPPOSE. IT MEANS ALL HE HAS TO WORRY ABOUT IS US."
AND THEN HE WOKE UP...
"I KNOW HOW HE FEELS. I KNOW HOW SCARED HE MUST BE."
"I WAS VERY SCARED. SHE--I--HAD BEEN SUCH A GRAND LADY. AND NOW I WAS SIMPLY ME... I WILL TRY TO BE GOOD TO THIS ONE..."
AND THEN SHE WOKE UP...
"WE ALL WILL."
"HMPH. I SAY, LET'S WAIT AND SEE HOW HE SHAPES UP--"
"DEL...? THAT'S NOT FOR EATING. I THINK IT'S A TABLE DECORATION."
"IT'S NICE. IT TASTES A BIT LIKE FOREVER."
AND THEN HE WOKE UP...
"I LIKE THE WAY COLORS TASTE. EXCEPT I DON'T LIKE CRIMSONS...OR TURQUOISES... ESPECIALLY WHEN THEY PUT THEIR HEADS INTO THEIR SHELLS AND WON'T PLAY, AND WHEN YOU BREAK THEIR SHELLS TO LET THEM OUT, THEY DIE..."
"THAT'S TURTLES, DEAR. OR TORTOISES."
"I THINK IT'S TURQUOISES."

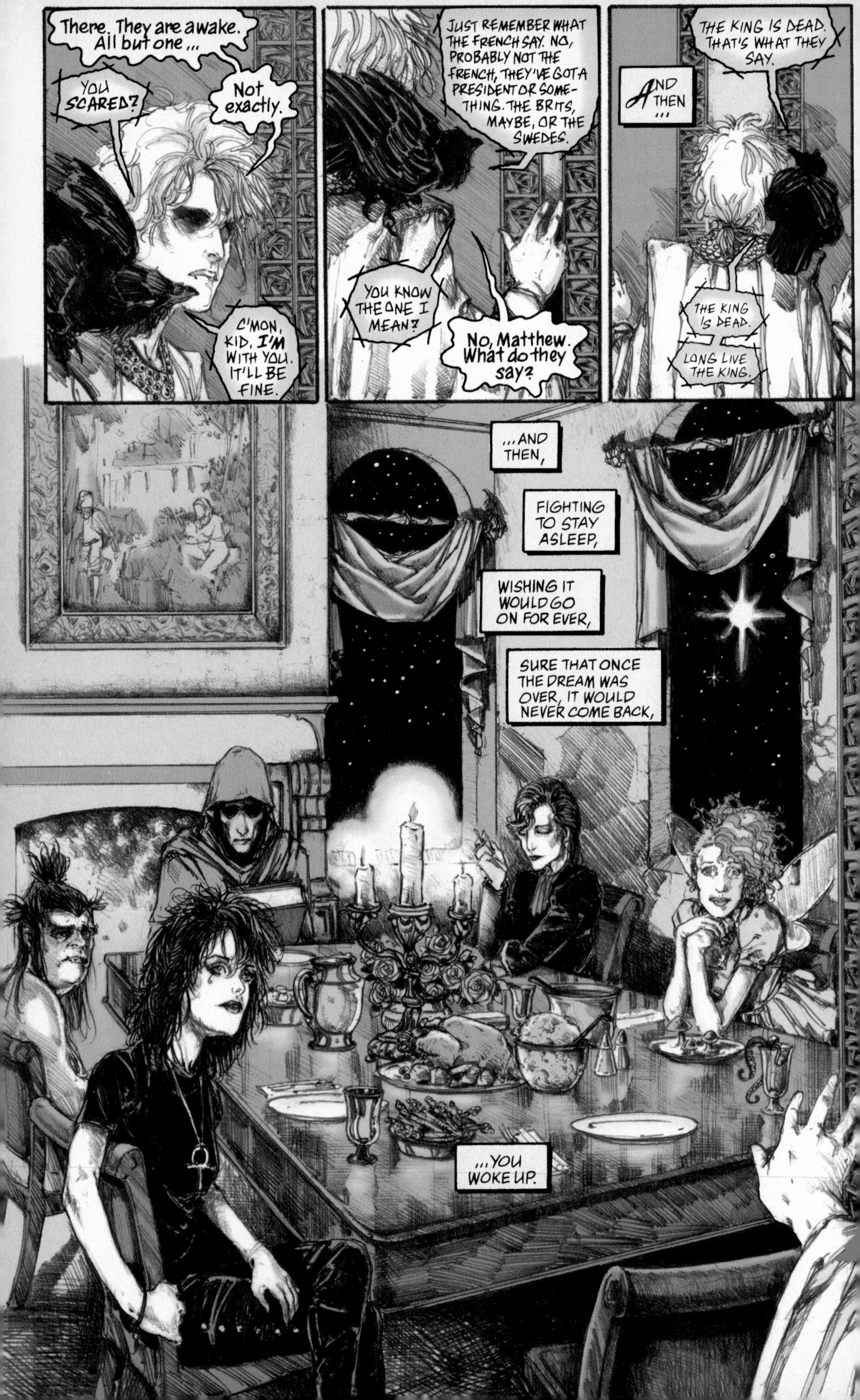

There. They are awake. All but one...
YOU SCARED?
Not exactly.
C'MON, KID. I'M WITH YOU. IT'LL BE FINE.
JUST REMEMBER WHAT THE FRENCH SAY. NO, PROBABLY NOT THE FRENCH, THEY'VE GOT A PRESIDENT OR SOMETHING. THE BRITS, MAYBE, OR THE SWEDES.
YOU KNOW THE ONE I MEAN?
No, Matthew. What do they say?
THE KING IS DEAD. THAT'S WHAT THEY SAY.
AND THEN ...
THE KING IS DEAD.
LONG LIVE THE KING.
...AND THEN,
FIGHTING TO STAY ASLEEP,
WISHING IT WOULD GO ON FOR EVER,
SURE THAT ONCE THE DREAM WAS OVER, IT WOULD NEVER COME BACK,
...YOU WOKE UP.

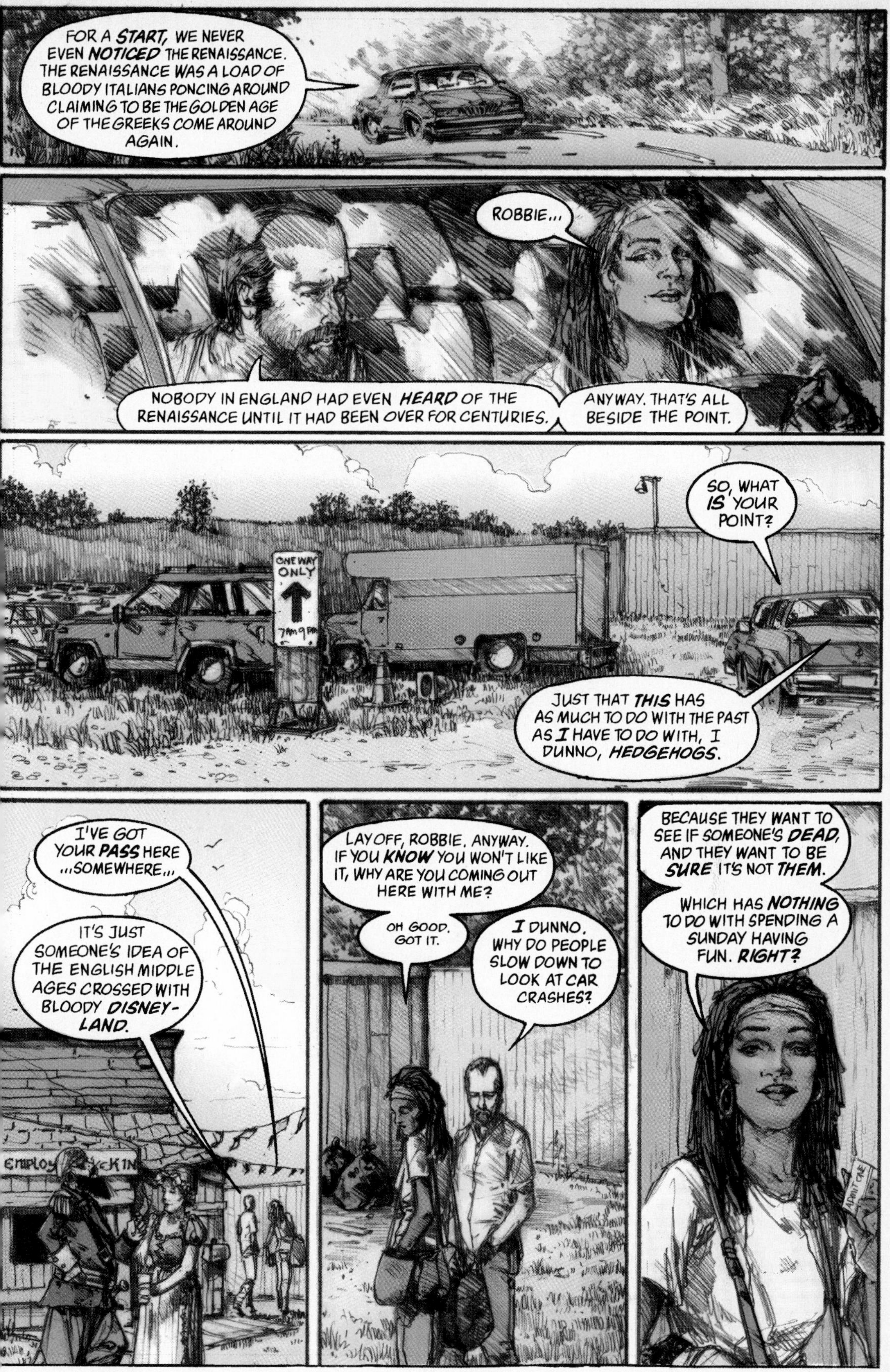
FOR A START, WE NEVER EVEN NOTICED THE RENAISSANCE. THE RENAISSANCE WAS A LOAD OF BLOODY ITALIANS PONCING AROUND CLAIMING TO BE THE GOLDEN AGE OF THE GREEKS COME AROUND AGAIN.
ROBBIE...
NOBODY IN ENGLAND HAD EVEN HEARD OF THE RENAISSANCE UNTIL IT HAD BEEN OVER FOR CENTURIES.
ANYWAY. THAT'S ALL BESIDE THE POINT.
SO, WHAT IS YOUR POINT?
ONE WAY ONLY
JUST THAT THIS HAS AS MUCH TO DO WITH THE PAST AS I HAVE TO DO WITH, I DUNNO, HEDGEHOGS.
I'VE GOT YOUR PASS HERE ...SOMEWHERE...
IT'S JUST SOMEONE'S IDEA OF THE ENGLISH MIDDLE AGES CROSSED WITH BLOODY DISNEY-LAND.
LAY OFF, ROBBIE. ANYWAY. IF YOU KNOW YOU WON'T LIKE IT, WHY ARE YOU COMING OUT HERE WITH ME?
OH GOOD. GOT IT.
I DUNNO. WHY DO PEOPLE SLOW DOWN TO LOOK AT CAR CRASHES?
BECAUSE THEY WANT TO SEE IF SOMEONE'S DEAD, AND THEY WANT TO BE SURE IT'S NOT THEM.
WHICH HAS NOTHING TO DO WITH SPENDING A SUNDAY HAVING FUN. RIGHT?

HERE WE GO.

RIGHT, ROBBIE, STAND GUARD. AND TURN AROUND WHILE YOU'RE DOING IT.

BUT--

UH-*UH*. NO PEEKING.

AH WELL. ONE MORE YEAR AS A LADY OF THE COURT. YOU KNOW WHAT *I* WISH, ROBBIE?

YO HO HO, GUENEVERE.

HAVEN'T A *CLUE*, LOVE.

WHO'S *THAT*? IS THAT *YOU*, GERRY?

SURE IS.

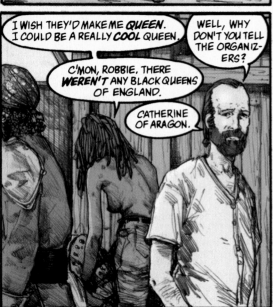

I WISH THEY'D MAKE ME *QUEEN*. I COULD BE A REALLY *COOL* QUEEN.

WELL, WHY DON'T YOU TELL THE ORGANIZERS?

C'MON, ROBBIE, THERE *WEREN'T* ANY BLACK QUEENS OF ENGLAND.

CATHERINE OF ARAGON.

SHE WASN'T BLACK, SHE WAS *SPANISH*.

THERE WERE A LOT OF MOORS AND AFRICANS IN SPAIN AND ITALY IN THE OLD DAYS. REMEMBER *OTHELLO*? TRUST ME, IF CATHERINE OF ARAGON HAD BEEN IN ALABAMA IN THE 1950'S THEY'D HAVE MADE HER RIDE IN THE BACK OF THE BUS.

ROBBIE, YOU'RE SO *FULL* OF IT.

NAH. I THINK YOU'D MAKE A *GREAT* QUEEN.

HISTORICAL? FROM WHAT YOU'VE TOLD ME, *NOTHING* IN THIS BLOODY PLACE IS HISTORICAL.

ROBBIE.... IT'S NOT HISTORICAL

YOU CAN TURN AROUND NOW, ROBBIE, LACE ME UP.

OOF. GENTLY.

I'VE GOT A GOOD MIND TO GO AND TALK TO THE ORGANIZERS.

NO, YOU DON'T.

....I *MIGHT* DO.

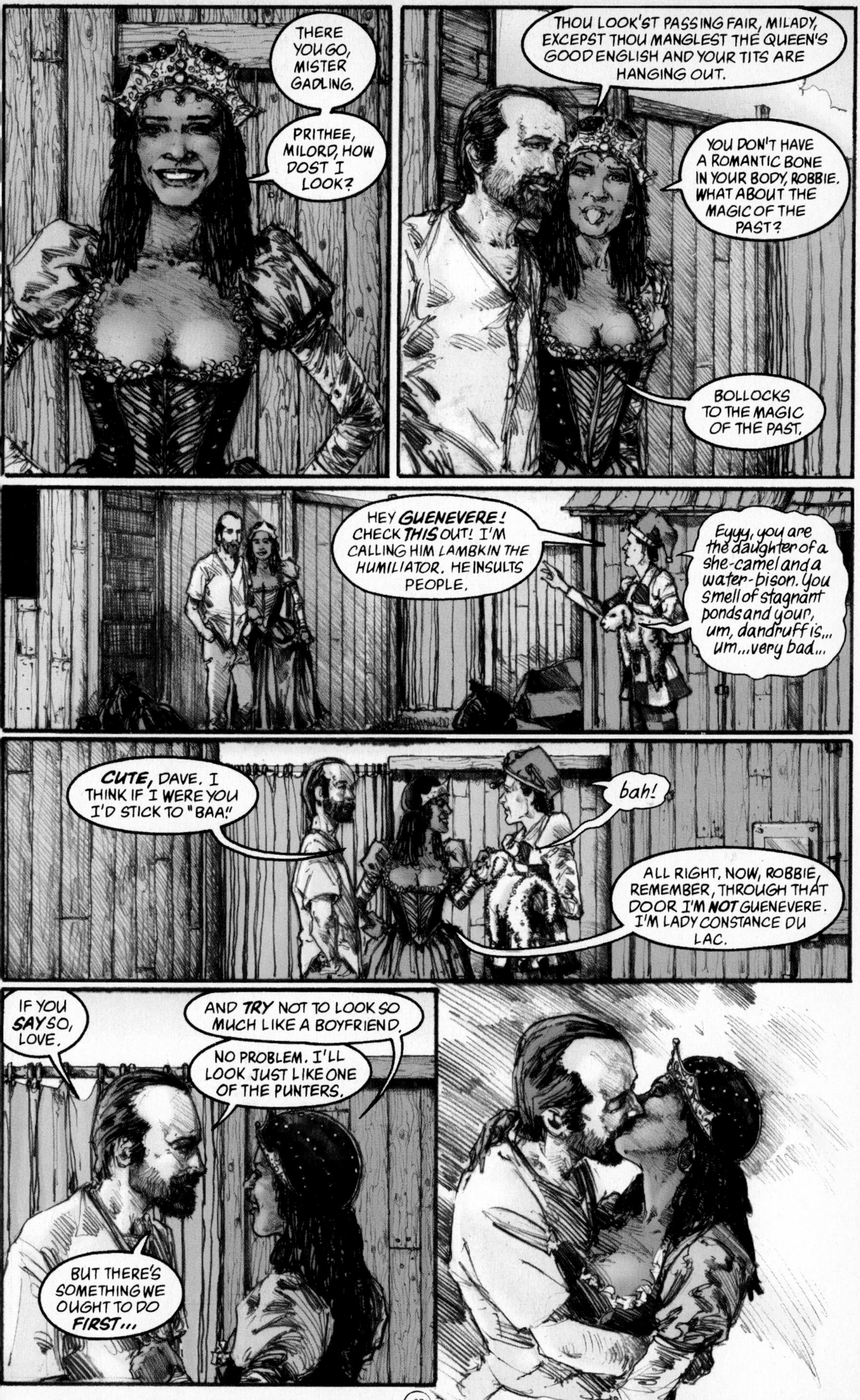

THERE YOU GO, MISTER GADLING.
PRITHEE, MILORD, HOW DOST I LOOK?
THOU LOOK'ST PASSING FAIR, MILADY, EXCEPST THOU MANGLEST THE QUEEN'S GOOD ENGLISH AND YOUR TITS ARE HANGING OUT.
YOU DON'T HAVE A ROMANTIC BONE IN YOUR BODY, ROBBIE. WHAT ABOUT THE MAGIC OF THE PAST?
BOLLOCKS TO THE MAGIC OF THE PAST.
HEY GUENEVERE! CHECK THIS OUT! I'M CALLING HIM LAMBKIN THE HUMILIATOR. HE INSULTS PEOPLE.
Eyyy, you are the daughter of a she-camel and a water-bison. You smell of stagnant ponds and your, um, dandruff is... um... very bad...
CUTE, DAVE. I THINK IF I WERE YOU I'D STICK TO "BAA!"
bah!
ALL RIGHT, NOW, ROBBIE, REMEMBER, THROUGH THAT DOOR I'M NOT GUENEVERE. I'M LADY CONSTANCE DU LAC.
IF YOU SAY SO, LOVE.
AND TRY NOT TO LOOK SO MUCH LIKE A BOYFRIEND.
NO PROBLEM. I'LL LOOK JUST LIKE ONE OF THE PUNTERS.
BUT THERE'S SOMETHING WE OUGHT TO DO FIRST...

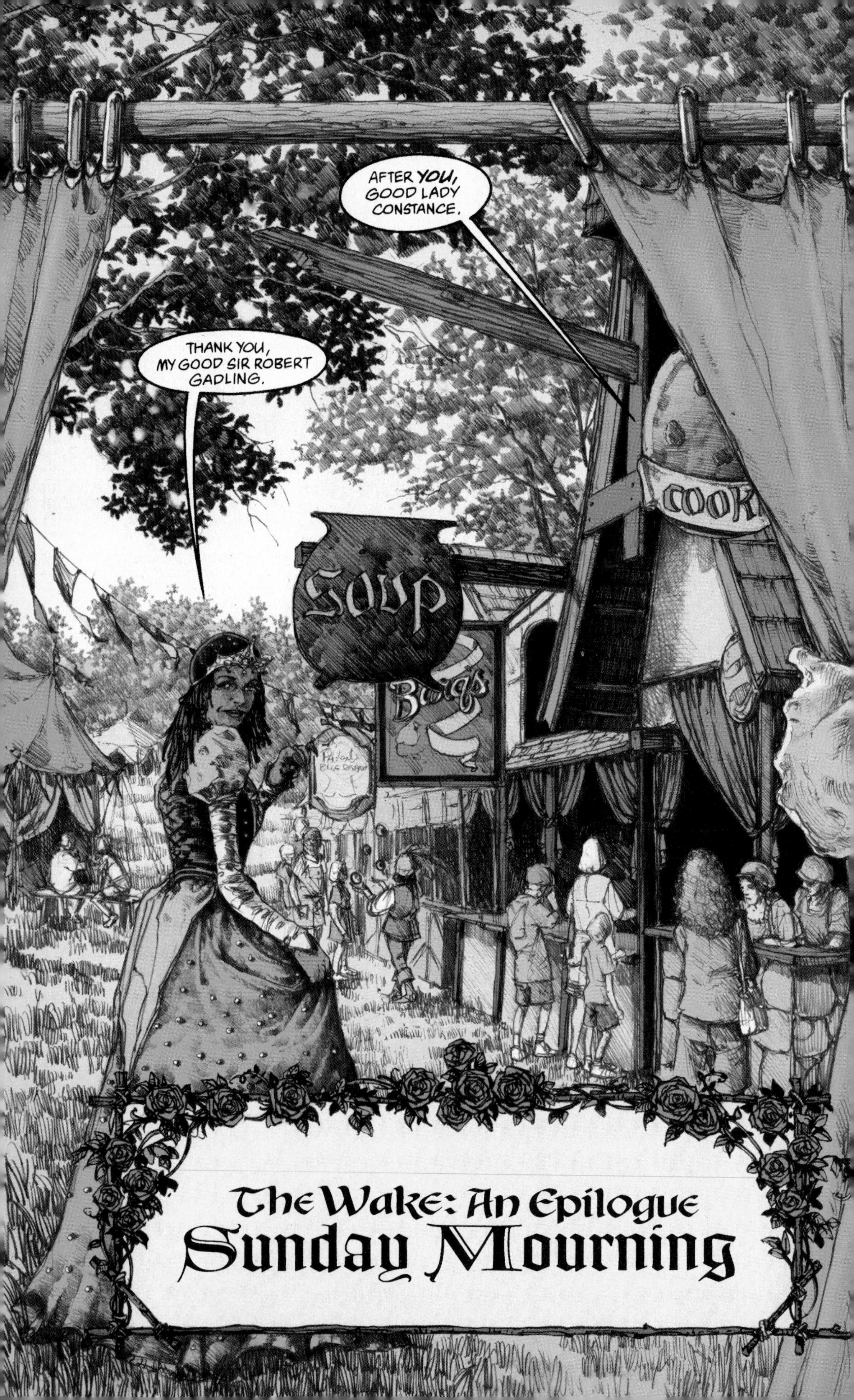
AFTER YOU, GOOD LADY CONSTANCE.
THANK YOU, MY GOOD SIR ROBERT GADLING.
SOUP
COOK
The Wake: An Epilogue
Sunday Mourning

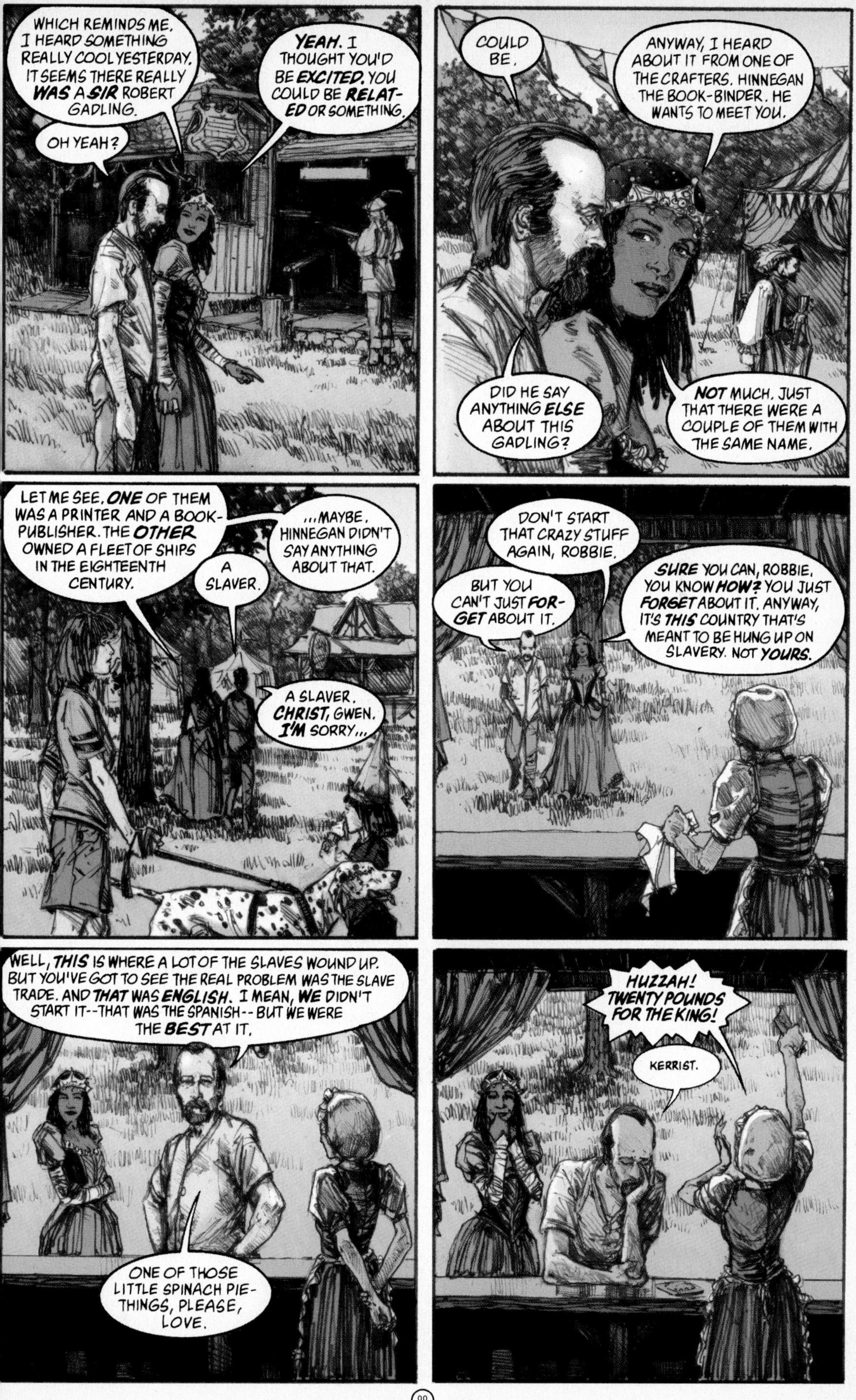
WHICH REMINDS ME. I HEARD SOMETHING REALLY COOL YESTERDAY. IT SEEMS THERE REALLY WAS A SIR ROBERT GADLING.
OH YEAH?
YEAH. I THOUGHT YOU'D BE EXCITED. YOU COULD BE RELATED OR SOMETHING.
COULD BE.
ANYWAY, I HEARD ABOUT IT FROM ONE OF THE CRAFTERS. HINNEGAN THE BOOK-BINDER. HE WANTS TO MEET YOU.
DID HE SAY ANYTHING ELSE ABOUT THIS GADLING?
NOT MUCH. JUST THAT THERE WERE A COUPLE OF THEM WITH THE SAME NAME.
LET ME SEE. ONE OF THEM WAS A PRINTER AND A BOOK-PUBLISHER. THE OTHER OWNED A FLEET OF SHIPS IN THE EIGHTEENTH CENTURY.
...MAYBE. HINNEGAN DIDN'T SAY ANYTHING ABOUT THAT.
A SLAVER.
A SLAVER. CHRIST, GWEN. I'M SORRY...
DON'T START THAT CRAZY STUFF AGAIN, ROBBIE.
BUT YOU CAN'T JUST FORGET ABOUT IT.
SURE YOU CAN, ROBBIE. YOU KNOW HOW? YOU JUST FORGET ABOUT IT. ANYWAY, IT'S THIS COUNTRY THAT'S MEANT TO BE HUNG UP ON SLAVERY. NOT YOURS.
WELL, THIS IS WHERE A LOT OF THE SLAVES WOUND UP. BUT YOU'VE GOT TO SEE THE REAL PROBLEM WAS THE SLAVE TRADE. AND THAT WAS ENGLISH. I MEAN, WE DIDN'T START IT--THAT WAS THE SPANISH--BUT WE WERE THE BEST AT IT.
ONE OF THOSE LITTLE SPINACH PIE-THINGS, PLEASE, LOVE.
HUZZAH! TWENTY POUNDS FOR THE KING!
KERRIST.

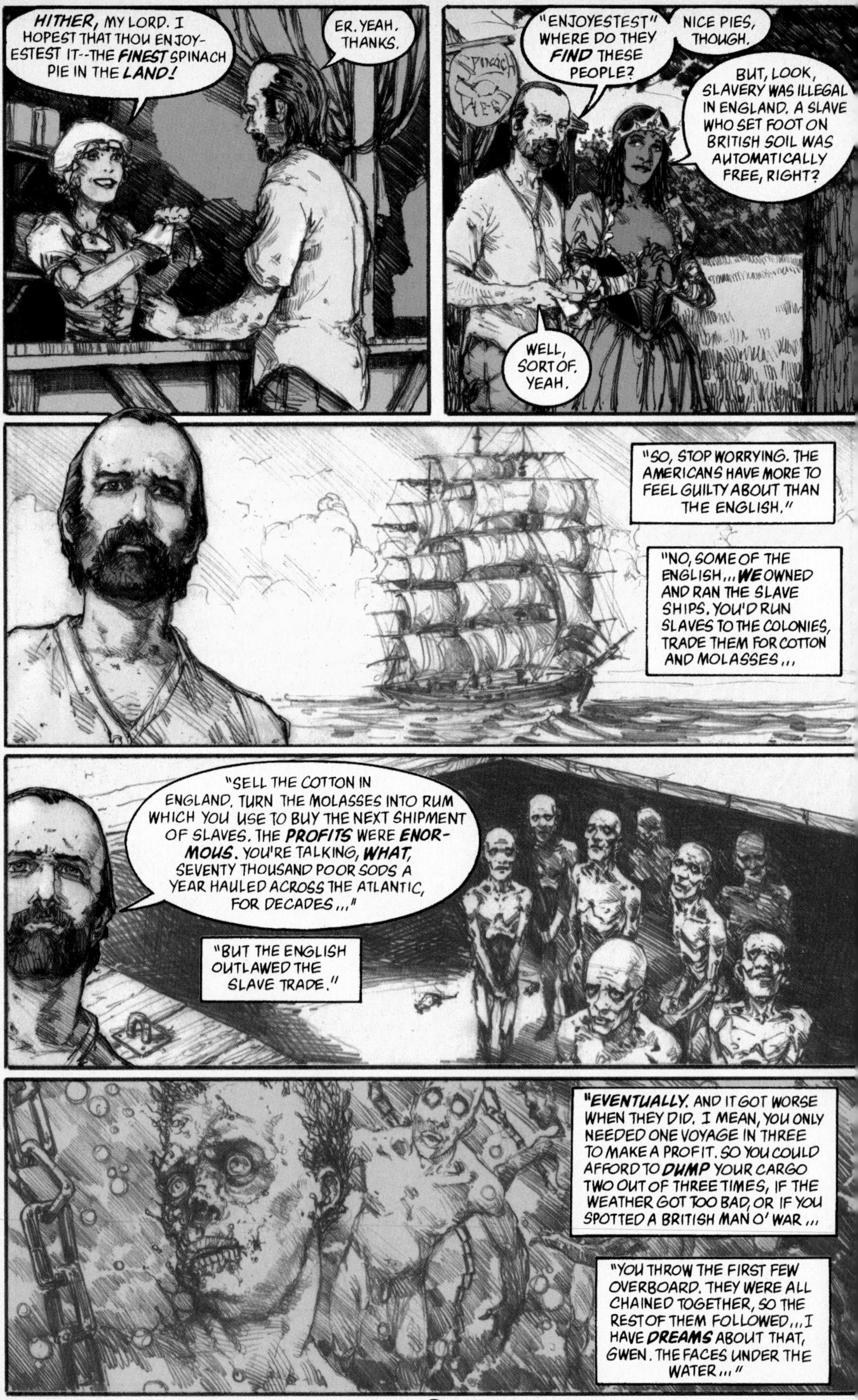
HITHER, MY LORD. I HOPEST THAT THOU ENJOYESTEST IT--THE FINEST SPINACH PIE IN THE LAND!
ER. YEAH. THANKS.
"ENJOYESTEST" WHERE DO THEY FIND THESE PEOPLE?
NICE PIES, THOUGH.
BUT, LOOK, SLAVERY WAS ILLEGAL IN ENGLAND. A SLAVE WHO SET FOOT ON BRITISH SOIL WAS AUTOMATICALLY FREE, RIGHT?
WELL, SORT OF. YEAH.
"SO, STOP WORRYING. THE AMERICANS HAVE MORE TO FEEL GUILTY ABOUT THAN THE ENGLISH."
"NO, SOME OF THE ENGLISH... WE OWNED AND RAN THE SLAVE SHIPS. YOU'D RUN SLAVES TO THE COLONIES, TRADE THEM FOR COTTON AND MOLASSES...
"SELL THE COTTON IN ENGLAND, TURN THE MOLASSES INTO RUM WHICH YOU USE TO BUY THE NEXT SHIPMENT OF SLAVES. THE PROFITS WERE ENORMOUS. YOU'RE TALKING, WHAT, SEVENTY THOUSAND POOR SODS A YEAR HAULED ACROSS THE ATLANTIC, FOR DECADES..."
"BUT THE ENGLISH OUTLAWED THE SLAVE TRADE."
"EVENTUALLY. AND IT GOT WORSE WHEN THEY DID. I MEAN, YOU ONLY NEEDED ONE VOYAGE IN THREE TO MAKE A PROFIT. SO YOU COULD AFFORD TO DUMP YOUR CARGO TWO OUT OF THREE TIMES, IF THE WEATHER GOT TOO BAD, OR IF YOU SPOTTED A BRITISH MAN O' WAR...
"YOU THROW THE FIRST FEW OVERBOARD. THEY WERE ALL CHAINED TOGETHER, SO THE REST OF THEM FOLLOWED... I HAVE DREAMS ABOUT THAT, GWEN. THE FACES UNDER THE WATER..."

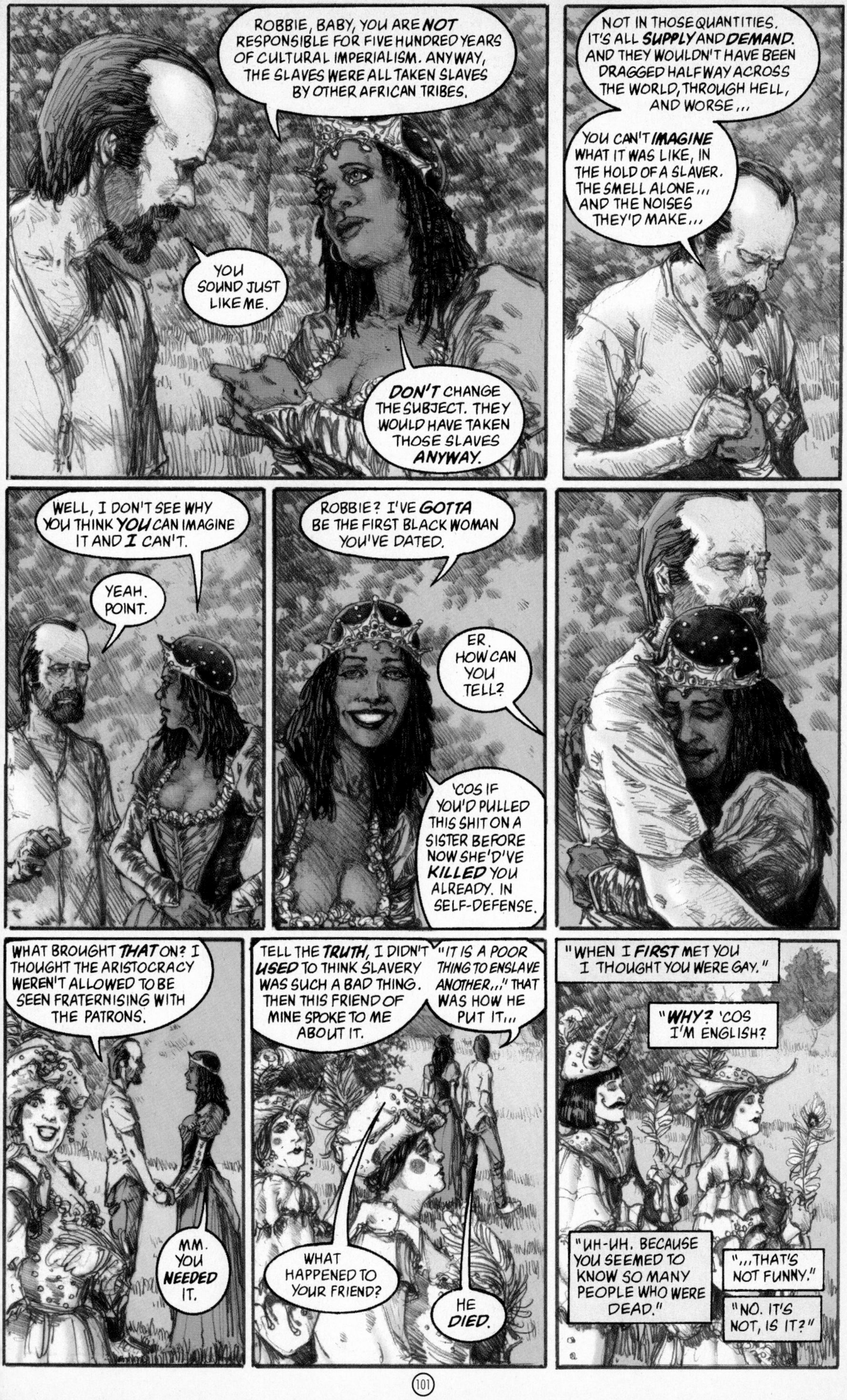
ROBBIE, BABY, YOU ARE NOT RESPONSIBLE FOR FIVE HUNDRED YEARS OF CULTURAL IMPERIALISM. ANYWAY, THE SLAVES WERE ALL TAKEN SLAVES BY OTHER AFRICAN TRIBES.
YOU SOUND JUST LIKE ME.
DON'T CHANGE THE SUBJECT. THEY WOULD HAVE TAKEN THOSE SLAVES ANYWAY.
NOT IN THOSE QUANTITIES. IT'S ALL SUPPLY AND DEMAND. AND THEY WOULDN'T HAVE BEEN DRAGGED HALFWAY ACROSS THE WORLD, THROUGH HELL, AND WORSE...
YOU CAN'T IMAGINE WHAT IT WAS LIKE, IN THE HOLD OF A SLAVER. THE SMELL ALONE... AND THE NOISES THEY'D MAKE...
WELL, I DON'T SEE WHY YOU THINK YOU CAN IMAGINE IT AND I CAN'T.
YEAH. POINT.
ROBBIE? I'VE GOTTA BE THE FIRST BLACK WOMAN YOU'VE DATED.
ER. HOW CAN YOU TELL?
'COS IF YOU'D PULLED THIS SHIT ON A SISTER BEFORE NOW SHE'D'VE KILLED YOU ALREADY. IN SELF-DEFENSE.
WHAT BROUGHT THAT ON? I THOUGHT THE ARISTOCRACY WEREN'T ALLOWED TO BE SEEN FRATERNISING WITH THE PATRONS.
MM. YOU NEEDED IT.
TELL THE TRUTH, I DIDN'T USED TO THINK SLAVERY WAS SUCH A BAD THING. THEN THIS FRIEND OF MINE SPOKE TO ME ABOUT IT.
"IT IS A POOR THING TO ENSLAVE ANOTHER..." THAT WAS HOW HE PUT IT...
WHAT HAPPENED TO YOUR FRIEND?
HE DIED.
"WHEN I FIRST MET YOU I THOUGHT YOU WERE GAY."
"WHY? 'COS I'M ENGLISH?
"UH-UH. BECAUSE YOU SEEMED TO KNOW SO MANY PEOPLE WHO WERE DEAD."
"...THAT'S NOT FUNNY."
"NO. IT'S NOT, IS IT?"

OKAY, IT'S THE OPENING PARADE NOW. THEN THERE'S A FEAST AT MIDDAY, AND I'LL BE NEEDED FOR THAT. BUT YOU'VE GOT A COPY OF MY GRID, ASK ANYONE.

I'LL JUST WANDER ROUND AND AMUSE MESELF, IF THAT'S ALL RIGHT WITH YOU.

FINNEGANS PRINTER AND PAPERMAKER

ye HUGE SALE

THESE BOOKS ARE ALL *BLANK*.

BEST *KIND*. Y'CAN WRITE ANYTHING IN THEM. ANY BOOK IN THE WORLD STARTS WITH BLANK PAGES. WRITE YOUR DREAMS OR POEMS, SECRETS OR RECIPES. HAND BOUND. HAND SEWN. I *MAKE* THE PAPER AND I *TAN* THE LEATHER.

YEAH. GWEN SAID.

YOU'RE GUENEVERE'S BOYFRIEND, THEN.

YEAH.

WHAT'S Y'*NAME*?

ROBBIE. ROBBIE GADLING.

THAT'S WHAT GUENEVERE SAID.

THERE WAS A *ROBT.* GADLING, WHO WAS A BOOKBINDER AND PRINTER BACK A FEW HUNDRED YEARS. MADE *WONDERFUL* BOOKS. ANY RELATION?

YOU STAY THERE. LET ME *SHOW* YOU SOMETHING.

COULD BE.

HERE Y'GO. EACH OF THESE IS A GENUINE GADLING AND COMPANY BOOK. I PAID THE MOON AND STARS FOR THEM, BUT IF YOU'RE A SERIOUS BOOKBINDER, Y'GOT TO SEE HOW THEY DID IT IN THE OLD DAYS.

THOSE *OLD* FELLERS, THEY MUST'VE FOR*GOTTEN* MORE ABOUT BOOK BINDING AND PRINTING THAN *SOME* OF US'LL EVER *KNOW*.

COULD BE.

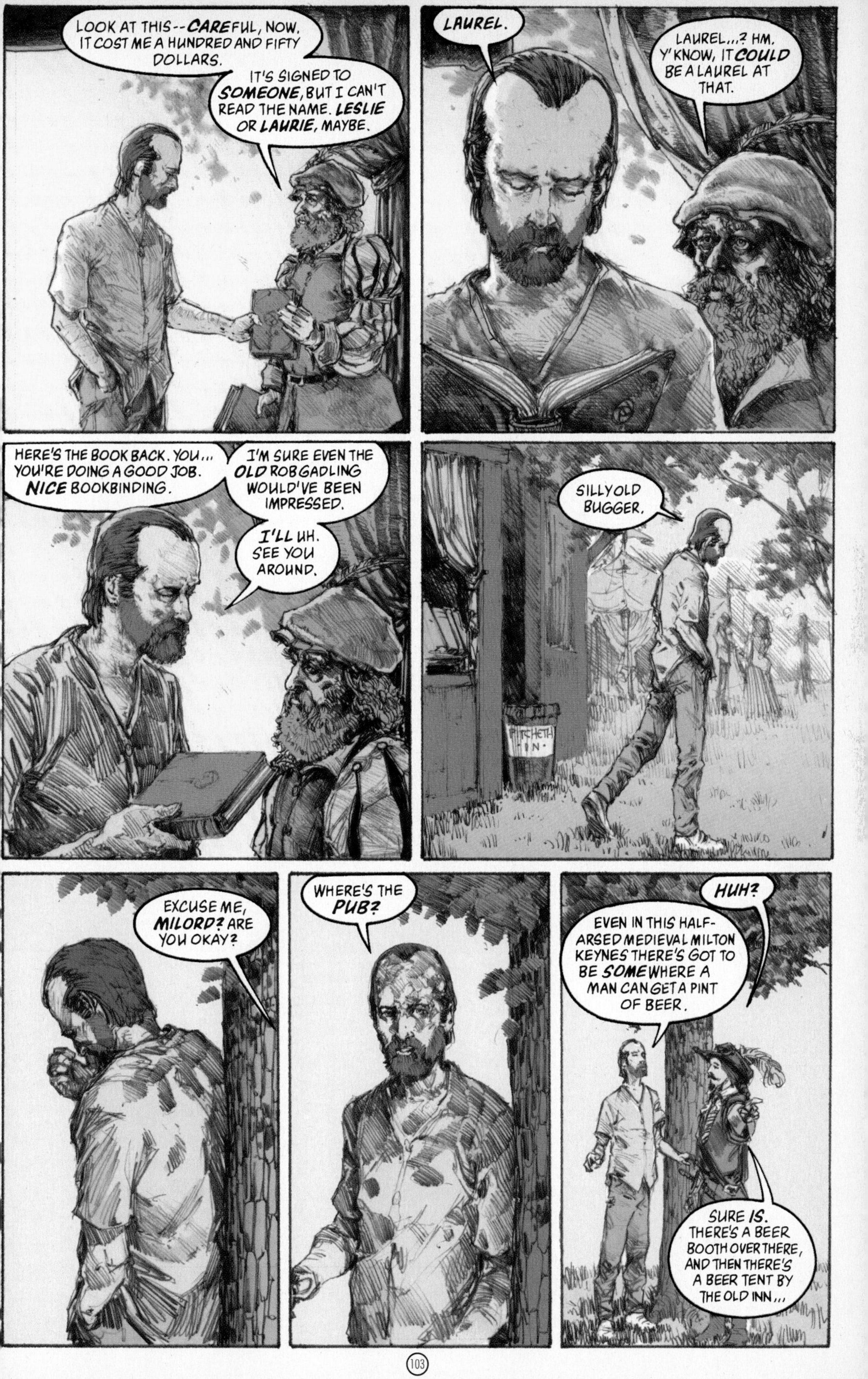
LOOK AT THIS--CAREFUL, NOW. IT COST ME A HUNDRED AND FIFTY DOLLARS.
IT'S SIGNED TO SOMEONE, BUT I CAN'T READ THE NAME. LESLIE OR LAURIE, MAYBE.
LAUREL.
LAUREL...? HM. Y'KNOW, IT COULD BE A LAUREL AT THAT.
HERE'S THE BOOK BACK. YOU... YOU'RE DOING A GOOD JOB. NICE BOOKBINDING.
I'M SURE EVEN THE OLD ROB GADLING WOULD'VE BEEN IMPRESSED.
I'LL UH. SEE YOU AROUND.
SILLY OLD BUGGER.
PITCHETH INN
EXCUSE ME, MILORD? ARE YOU OKAY?
WHERE'S THE PUB?
HUH?
EVEN IN THIS HALF-ARSED MEDIEVAL MILTON KEYNES THERE'S GOT TO BE SOMEWHERE A MAN CAN GET A PINT OF BEER.
SURE IS. THERE'S A BEER BOOTH OVER THERE, AND THEN THERE'S A BEER TENT BY THE OLD INN...

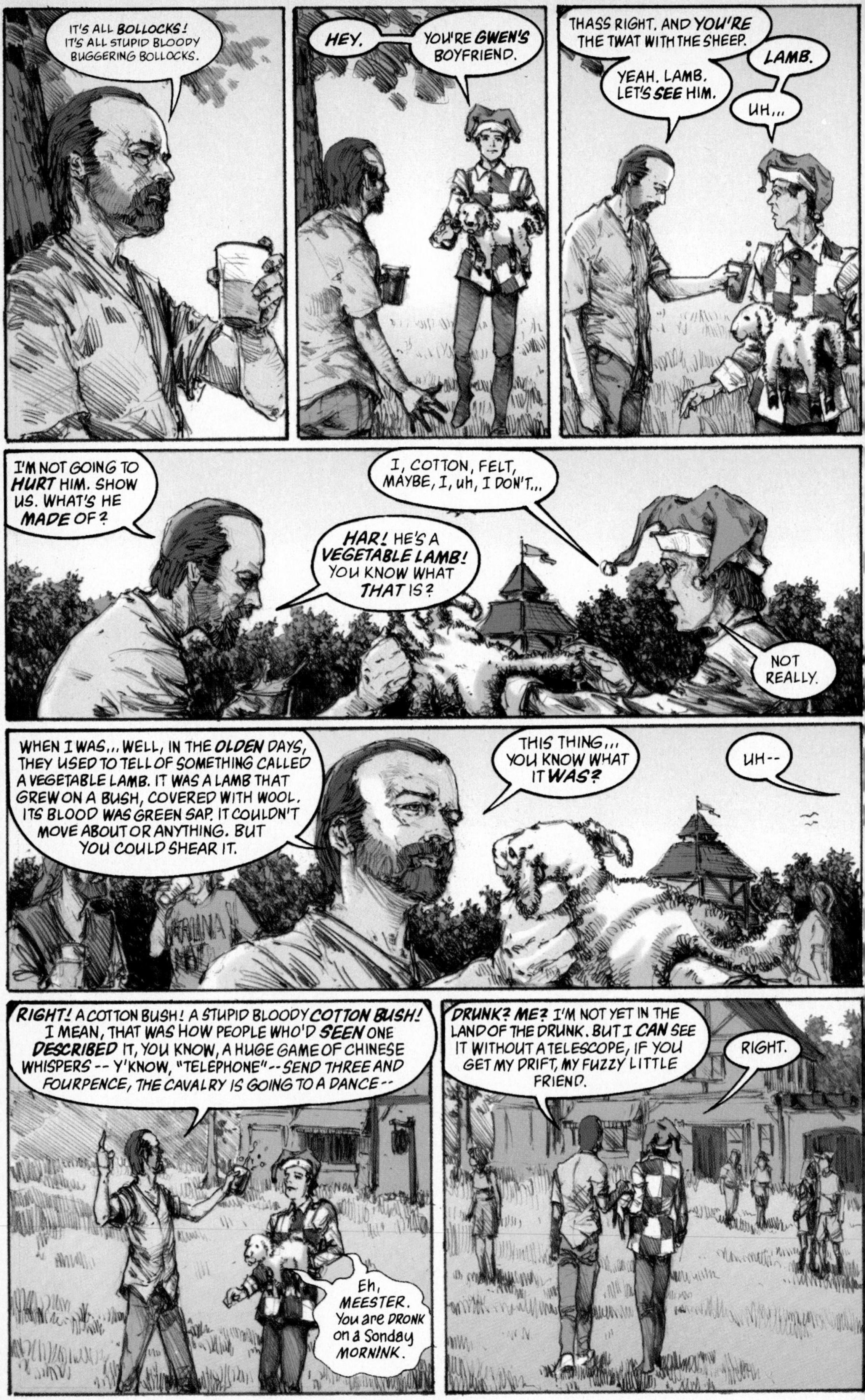
IT'S ALL BOLLOCKS! IT'S ALL STUPID BLOODY BUGGERING BOLLOCKS.
HEY.
YOU'RE GWEN'S BOYFRIEND.
THASS RIGHT. AND YOU'RE THE TWAT WITH THE SHEEP.
LAMB.
YEAH. LAMB. LET'S SEE HIM.
UH...
I'M NOT GOING TO HURT HIM. SHOW US. WHAT'S HE MADE OF?
I, COTTON, FELT, MAYBE, I, uh, I DON'T...
HAR! HE'S A VEGETABLE LAMB! YOU KNOW WHAT THAT IS?
NOT REALLY.
WHEN I WAS... WELL, IN THE OLDEN DAYS, THEY USED TO TELL OF SOMETHING CALLED A VEGETABLE LAMB. IT WAS A LAMB THAT GREW ON A BUSH, COVERED WITH WOOL. ITS BLOOD WAS GREEN SAP. IT COULDN'T MOVE ABOUT OR ANYTHING. BUT YOU COULD SHEAR IT.
THIS THING... YOU KNOW WHAT IT WAS?
UH--
RIGHT! A COTTON BUSH! A STUPID BLOODY COTTON BUSH! I MEAN, THAT WAS HOW PEOPLE WHO'D SEEN ONE DESCRIBED IT, YOU KNOW, A HUGE GAME OF CHINESE WHISPERS -- Y'KNOW, "TELEPHONE" -- SEND THREE AND FOURPENCE, THE CAVALRY IS GOING TO A DANCE --
Eh, MEESTER. You are DRONK on a Sonday MORNINK.
DRUNK? ME? I'M NOT YET IN THE LAND OF THE DRUNK. BUT I CAN SEE IT WITHOUT A TELESCOPE, IF YOU GET MY DRIFT, MY FUZZY LITTLE FRIEND.
RIGHT.

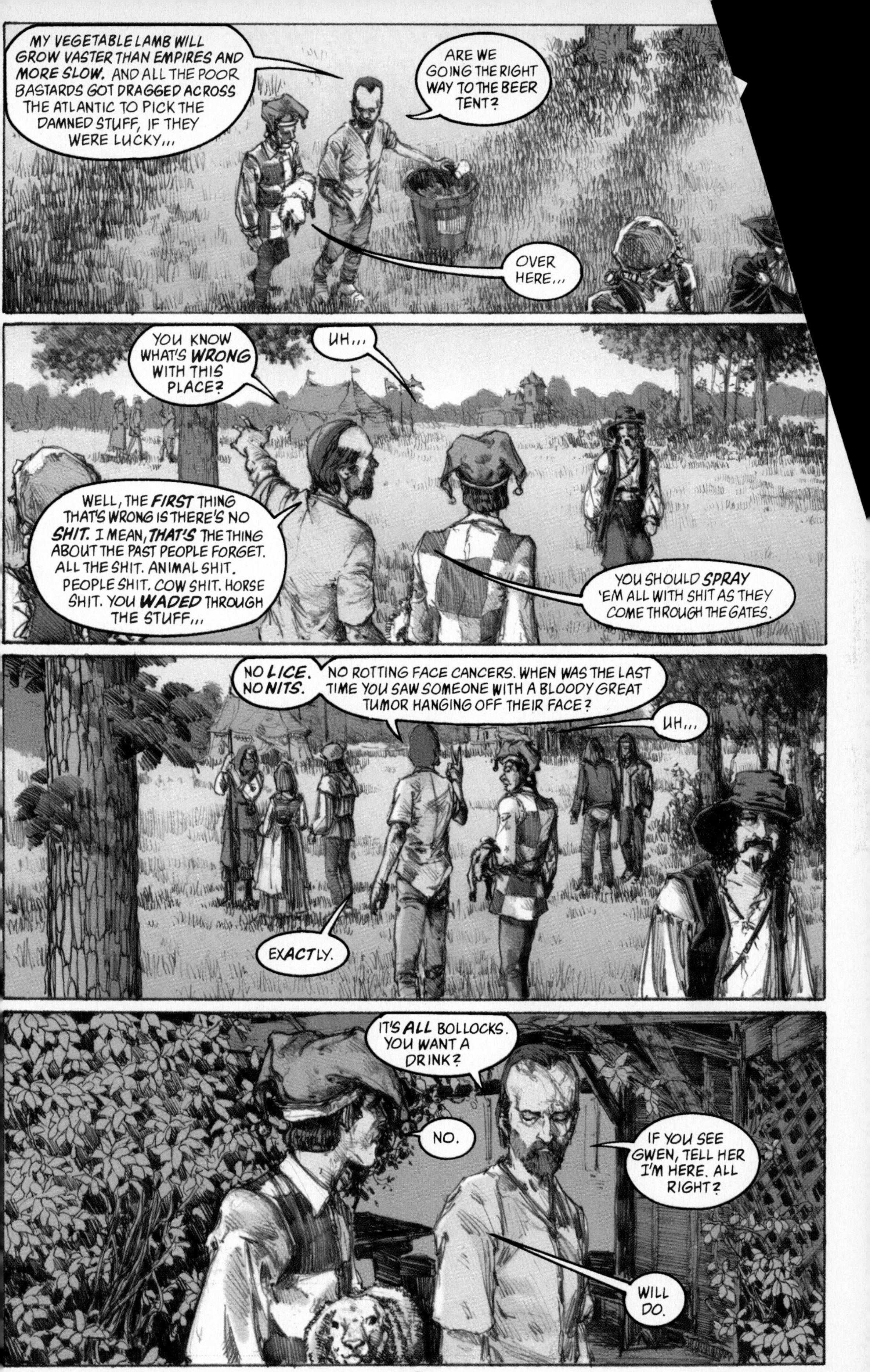
MY VEGETABLE LAMB WILL GROW VASTER THAN EMPIRES AND MORE SLOW. AND ALL THE POOR BASTARDS GOT DRAGGED ACROSS THE ATLANTIC TO PICK THE DAMNED STUFF, IF THEY WERE LUCKY...
ARE WE GOING THE RIGHT WAY TO THE BEER TENT?
OVER HERE...
YOU KNOW WHAT'S WRONG WITH THIS PLACE?
UH...
WELL, THE FIRST THING THAT'S WRONG IS THERE'S NO SHIT. I MEAN, THAT'S THE THING ABOUT THE PAST PEOPLE FORGET. ALL THE SHIT. ANIMAL SHIT. PEOPLE SHIT. COW SHIT. HORSE SHIT. YOU WADED THROUGH THE STUFF...
YOU SHOULD SPRAY 'EM ALL WITH SHIT AS THEY COME THROUGH THE GATES.
NO LICE. NO NITS.
NO ROTTING FACE CANCERS. WHEN WAS THE LAST TIME YOU SAW SOMEONE WITH A BLOODY GREAT TUMOR HANGING OFF THEIR FACE?
UH...
EXACTLY.
IT'S ALL BOLLOCKS. YOU WANT A DRINK?
NO.
IF YOU SEE GWEN, TELL HER I'M HERE. ALL RIGHT?
WILL DO.

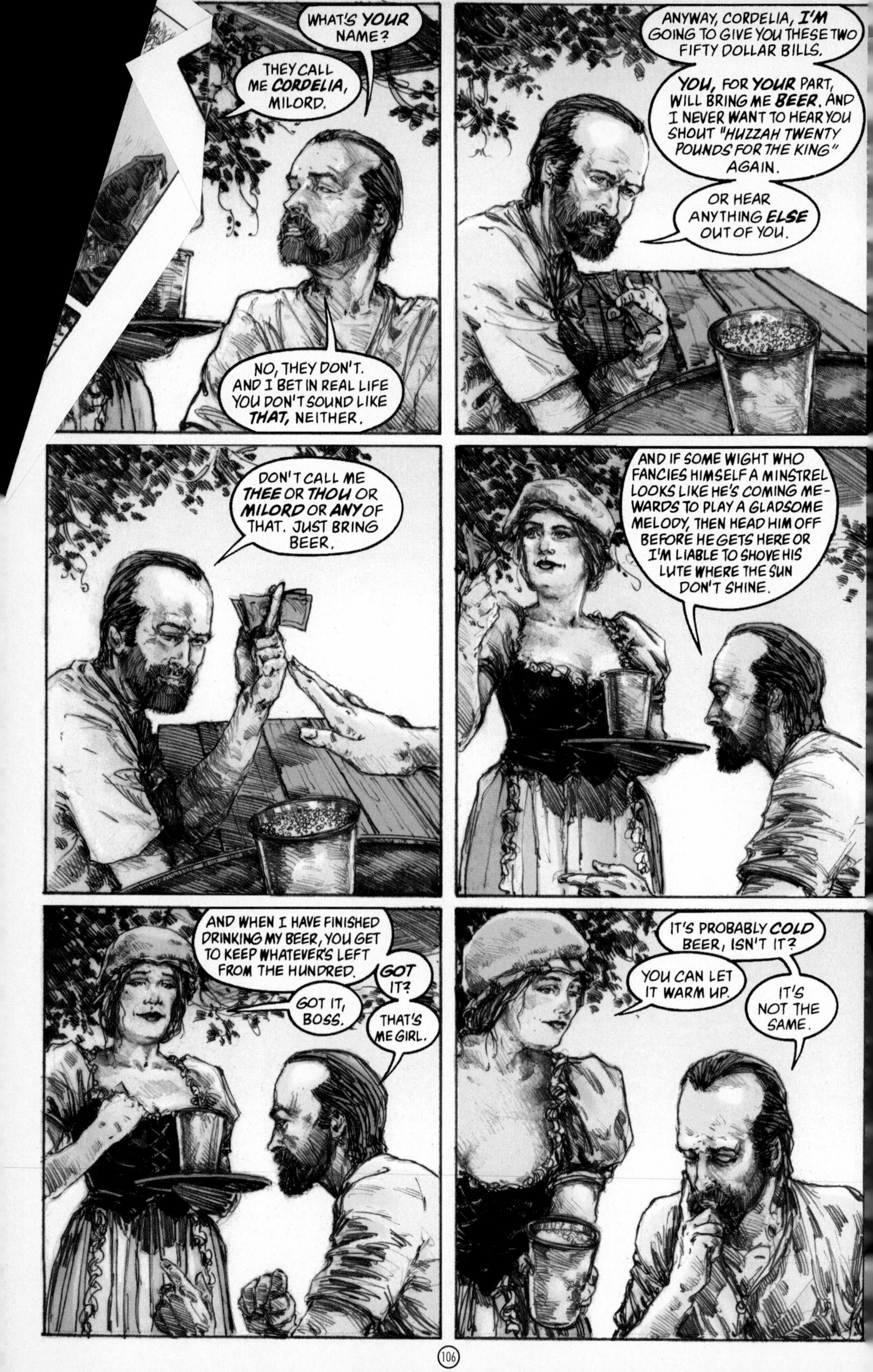

WHAT'S YOUR NAME?
THEY CALL ME CORDELIA, MILORD.
NO, THEY DON'T. AND I BET IN REAL LIFE YOU DON'T SOUND LIKE THAT, NEITHER.
ANYWAY, CORDELIA, I'M GOING TO GIVE YOU THESE TWO FIFTY DOLLAR BILLS.
YOU, FOR YOUR PART, WILL BRING ME BEER. AND I NEVER WANT TO HEAR YOU SHOUT "HUZZAH TWENTY POUNDS FOR THE KING" AGAIN.
OR HEAR ANYTHING ELSE OUT OF YOU.
DON'T CALL ME THEE OR THOU OR MILORD OR ANY OF THAT. JUST BRING BEER.
AND IF SOME WIGHT WHO FANCIES HIMSELF A MINSTREL LOOKS LIKE HE'S COMING ME-WARDS TO PLAY A GLADSOME MELODY, THEN HEAD HIM OFF BEFORE HE GETS HERE OR I'M LIABLE TO SHOVE HIS LUTE WHERE THE SUN DON'T SHINE.
AND WHEN I HAVE FINISHED DRINKING MY BEER, YOU GET TO KEEP WHATEVER'S LEFT FROM THE HUNDRED.
GOT IT?
GOT IT, BOSS.
THAT'S ME GIRL.
IT'S PROBABLY COLD BEER, ISN'T IT?
YOU CAN LET IT WARM UP.
IT'S NOT THE SAME.

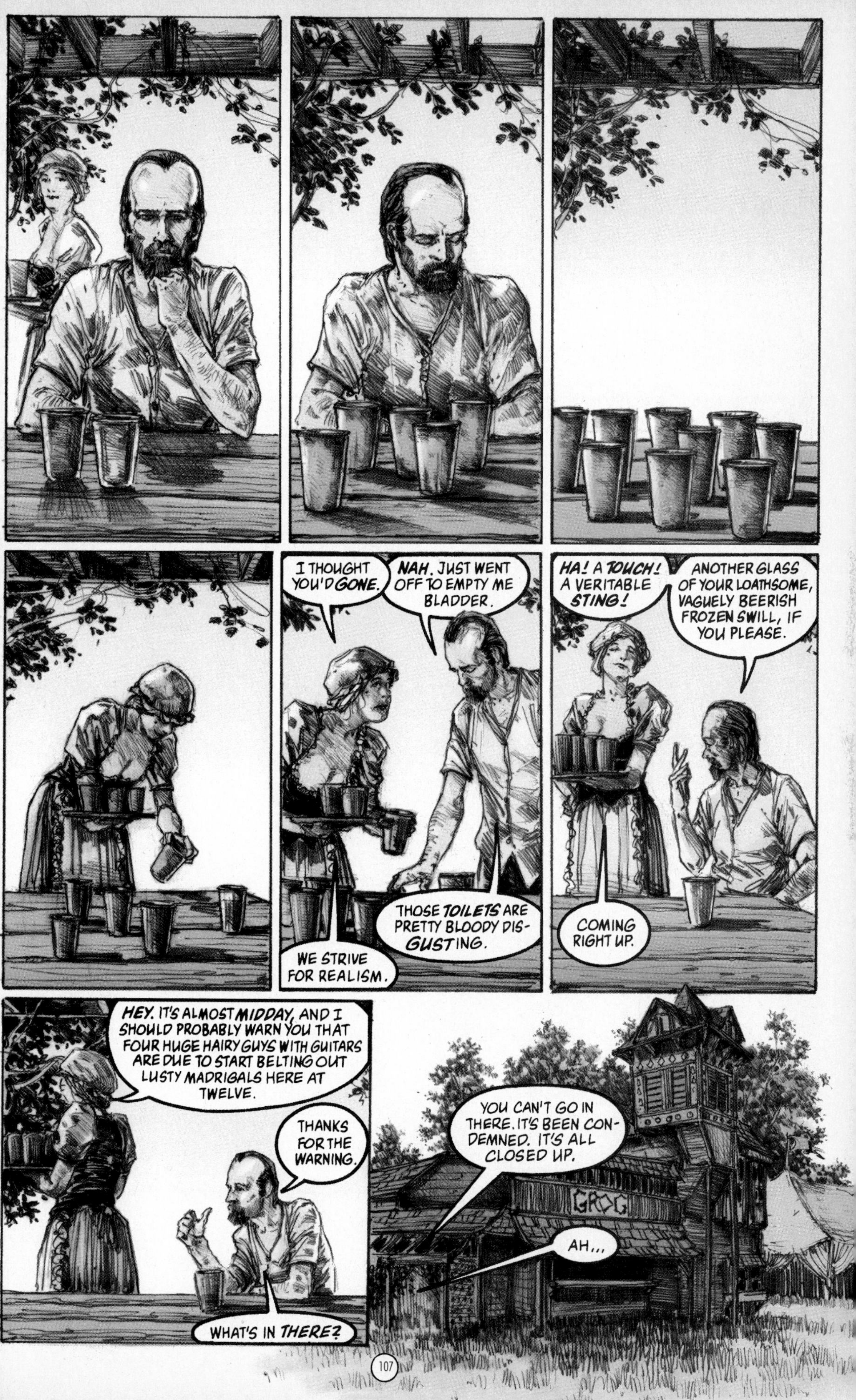

I THOUGHT YOU'D GONE.
NAH. JUST WENT OFF TO EMPTY ME BLADDER.
THOSE TOILETS ARE PRETTY BLOODY DIS-GUSTING.
WE STRIVE FOR REALISM.
HA! A TOUCH! A VERITABLE STING!
ANOTHER GLASS OF YOUR LOATHSOME, VAGUELY BEERISH FROZEN SWILL, IF YOU PLEASE.
COMING RIGHT UP.
HEY. IT'S ALMOST MIDDAY, AND I SHOULD PROBABLY WARN YOU THAT FOUR HUGE HAIRY GUYS WITH GUITARS ARE DUE TO START BELTING OUT LUSTY MADRIGALS HERE AT TWELVE.
THANKS FOR THE WARNING.
WHAT'S IN THERE?
YOU CAN'T GO IN THERE. IT'S BEEN CON-DEMNED. IT'S ALL CLOSED UP.
AH...
GROG

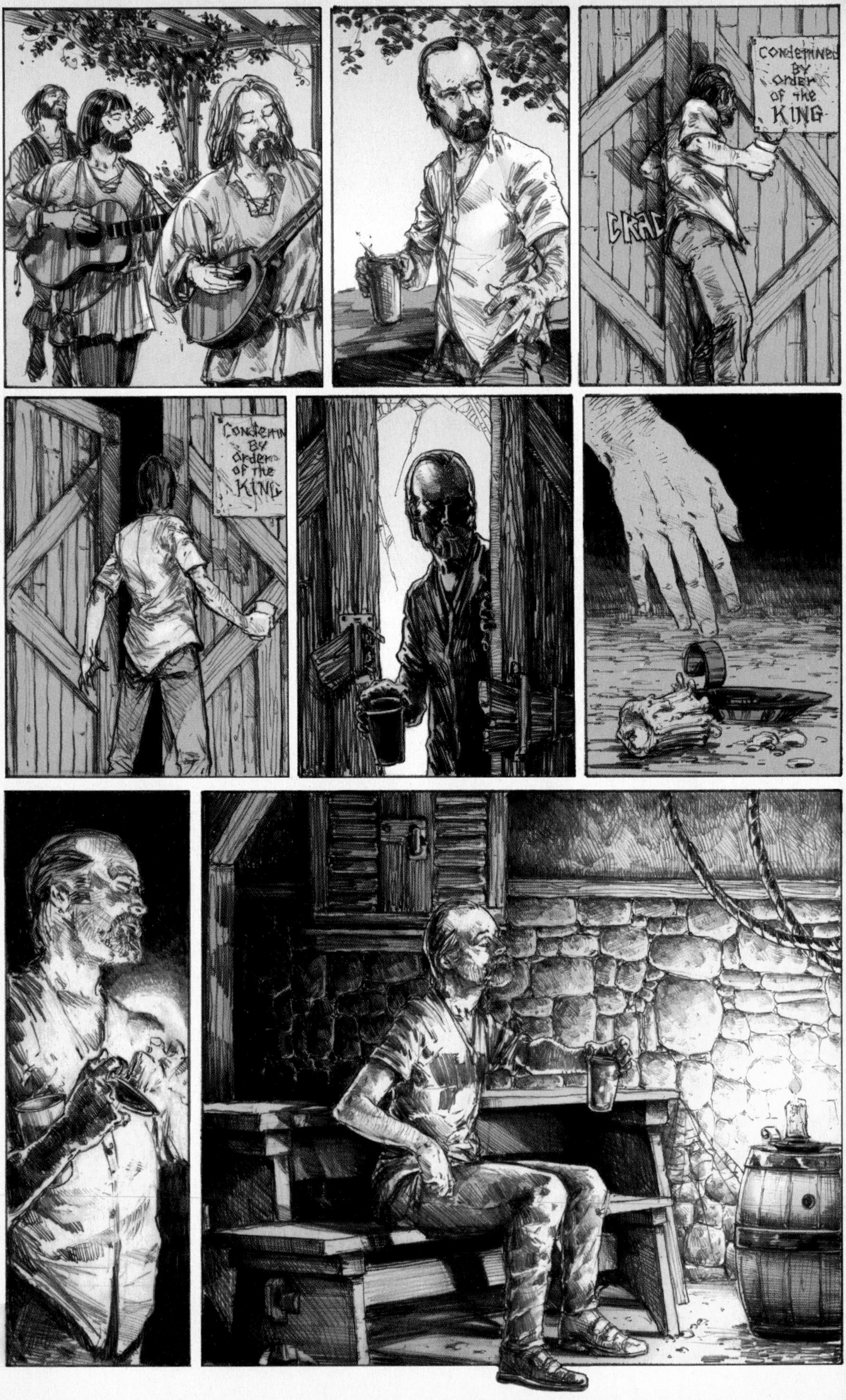
CONDEMNED BY ORDER OF THE KING
CRAC
BY ORDER OF THE KING

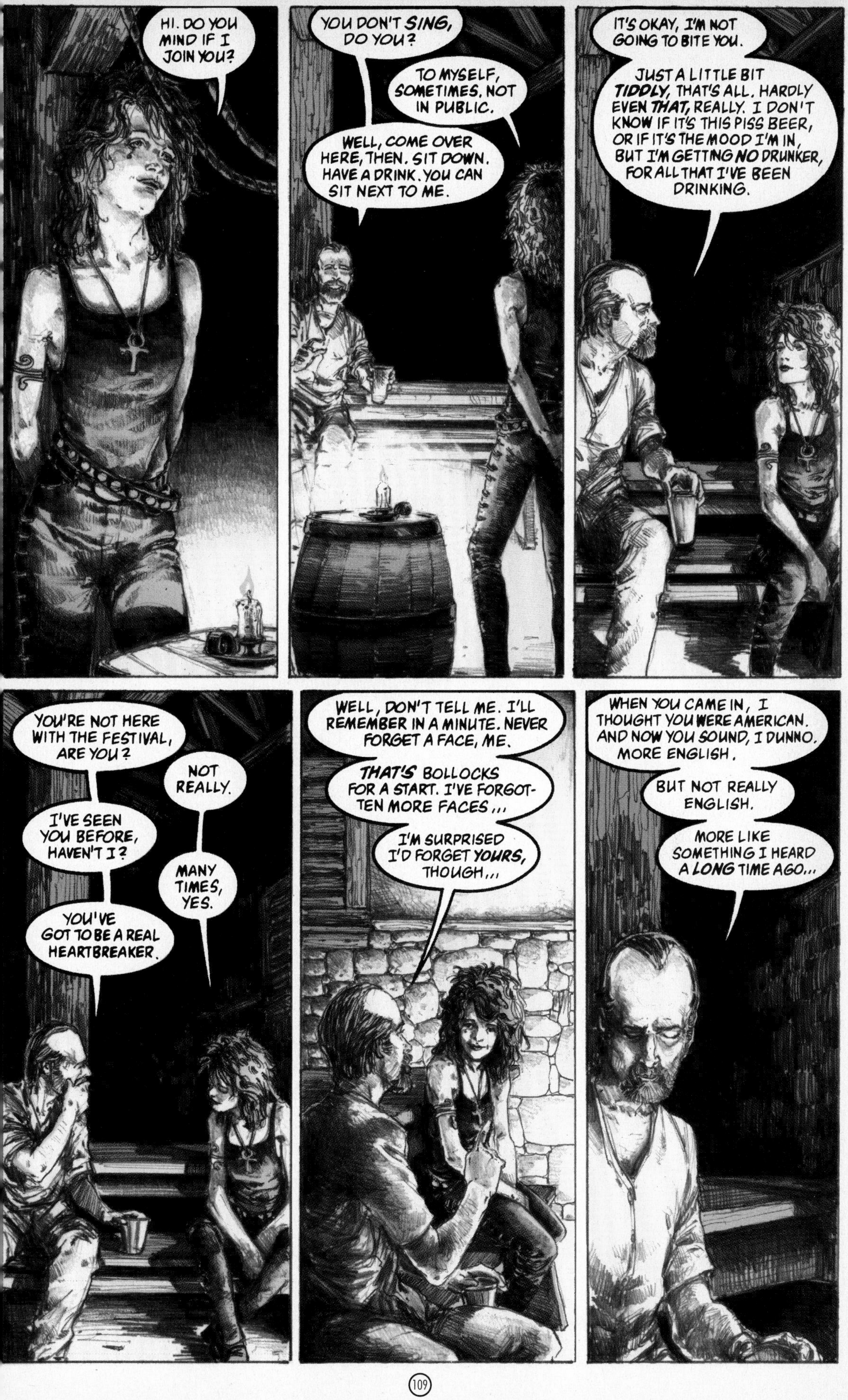
HI. DO YOU MIND IF I JOIN YOU?
YOU DON'T SING, DO YOU?
TO MYSELF, SOMETIMES. NOT IN PUBLIC.
WELL, COME OVER HERE, THEN. SIT DOWN. HAVE A DRINK. YOU CAN SIT NEXT TO ME.
IT'S OKAY, I'M NOT GOING TO BITE YOU.
JUST A LITTLE BIT TIDDLY, THAT'S ALL. HARDLY EVEN THAT, REALLY. I DON'T KNOW IF IT'S THIS PISS BEER, OR IF IT'S THE MOOD I'M IN, BUT I'M GETTING NO DRUNKER, FOR ALL THAT I'VE BEEN DRINKING.
YOU'RE NOT HERE WITH THE FESTIVAL, ARE YOU?
NOT REALLY.
I'VE SEEN YOU BEFORE, HAVEN'T I?
MANY TIMES, YES.
YOU'VE GOT TO BE A REAL HEARTBREAKER.
WELL, DON'T TELL ME. I'LL REMEMBER IN A MINUTE. NEVER FORGET A FACE, ME.
THAT'S BOLLOCKS FOR A START. I'VE FORGOTTEN MORE FACES...
I'M SURPRISED I'D FORGET YOURS, THOUGH...
WHEN YOU CAME IN, I THOUGHT YOU WERE AMERICAN. AND NOW YOU SOUND, I DUNNO. MORE ENGLISH.
BUT NOT REALLY ENGLISH.
MORE LIKE SOMETHING I HEARD A LONG TIME AGO...

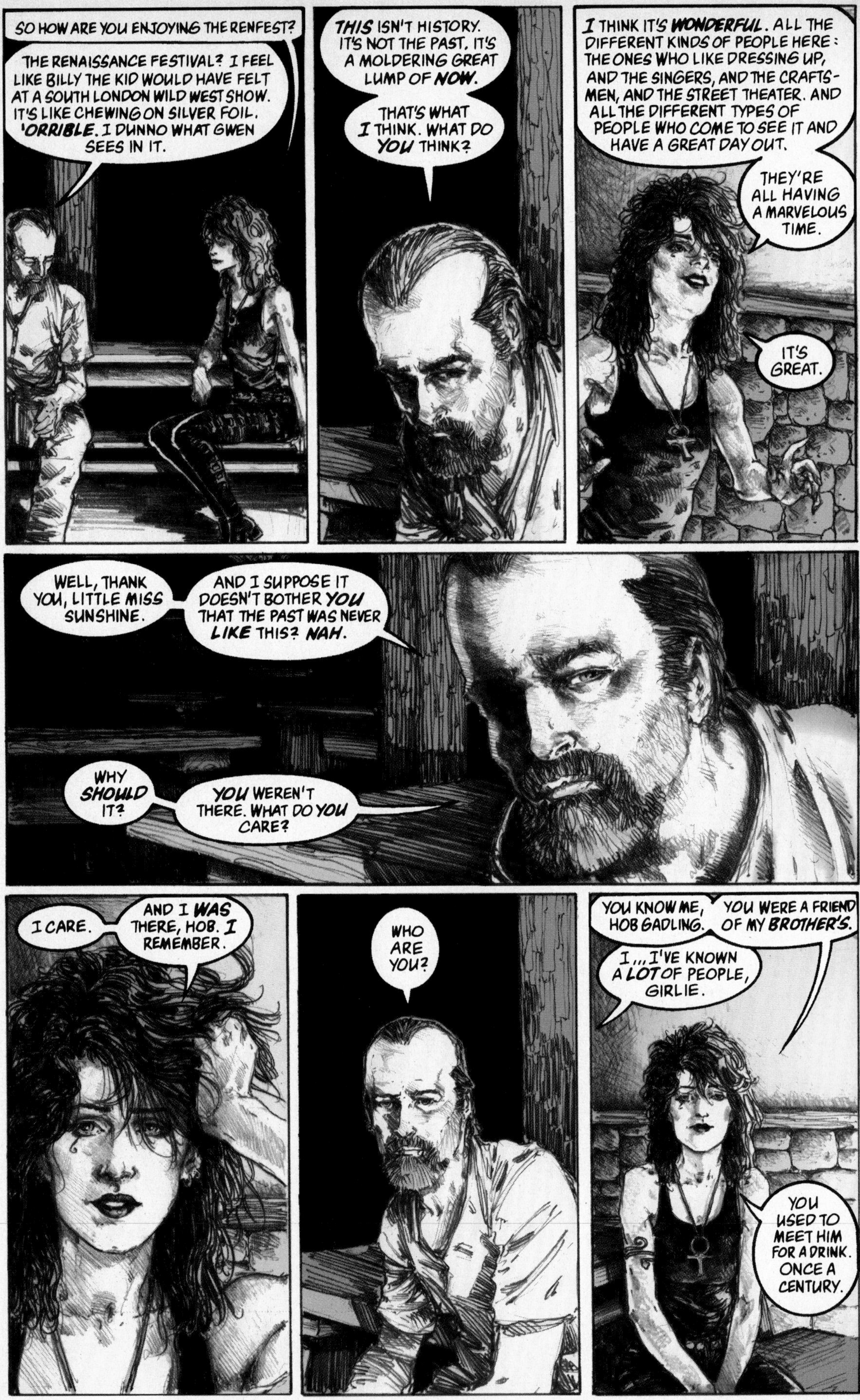
SO HOW ARE YOU ENJOYING THE RENFEST?
THE RENAISSANCE FESTIVAL? I FEEL LIKE BILLY THE KID WOULD HAVE FELT AT A SOUTH LONDON WILD WEST SHOW. IT'S LIKE CHEWING ON SILVER FOIL. 'ORRIBLE. I DUNNO WHAT GWEN SEES IN IT.
THIS ISN'T HISTORY. IT'S NOT THE PAST. IT'S A MOLDERING GREAT LUMP OF NOW.
THAT'S WHAT I THINK. WHAT DO YOU THINK?
I THINK IT'S WONDERFUL. ALL THE DIFFERENT KINDS OF PEOPLE HERE: THE ONES WHO LIKE DRESSING UP, AND THE SINGERS, AND THE CRAFTS-MEN, AND THE STREET THEATER. AND ALL THE DIFFERENT TYPES OF PEOPLE WHO COME TO SEE IT AND HAVE A GREAT DAY OUT.
THEY'RE ALL HAVING A MARVELOUS TIME.
IT'S GREAT.
WELL, THANK YOU, LITTLE MISS SUNSHINE.
AND I SUPPOSE IT DOESN'T BOTHER YOU THAT THE PAST WAS NEVER LIKE THIS? NAH.
WHY SHOULD IT?
YOU WEREN'T THERE. WHAT DO YOU CARE?
I CARE.
AND I WAS THERE, HOB. I REMEMBER.
WHO ARE YOU?
YOU KNOW ME, HOB GADLING.
YOU WERE A FRIEND OF MY BROTHER'S.
I,,,I'VE KNOWN A LOT OF PEOPLE, GIRLIE.
YOU USED TO MEET HIM FOR A DRINK. ONCE A CENTURY.

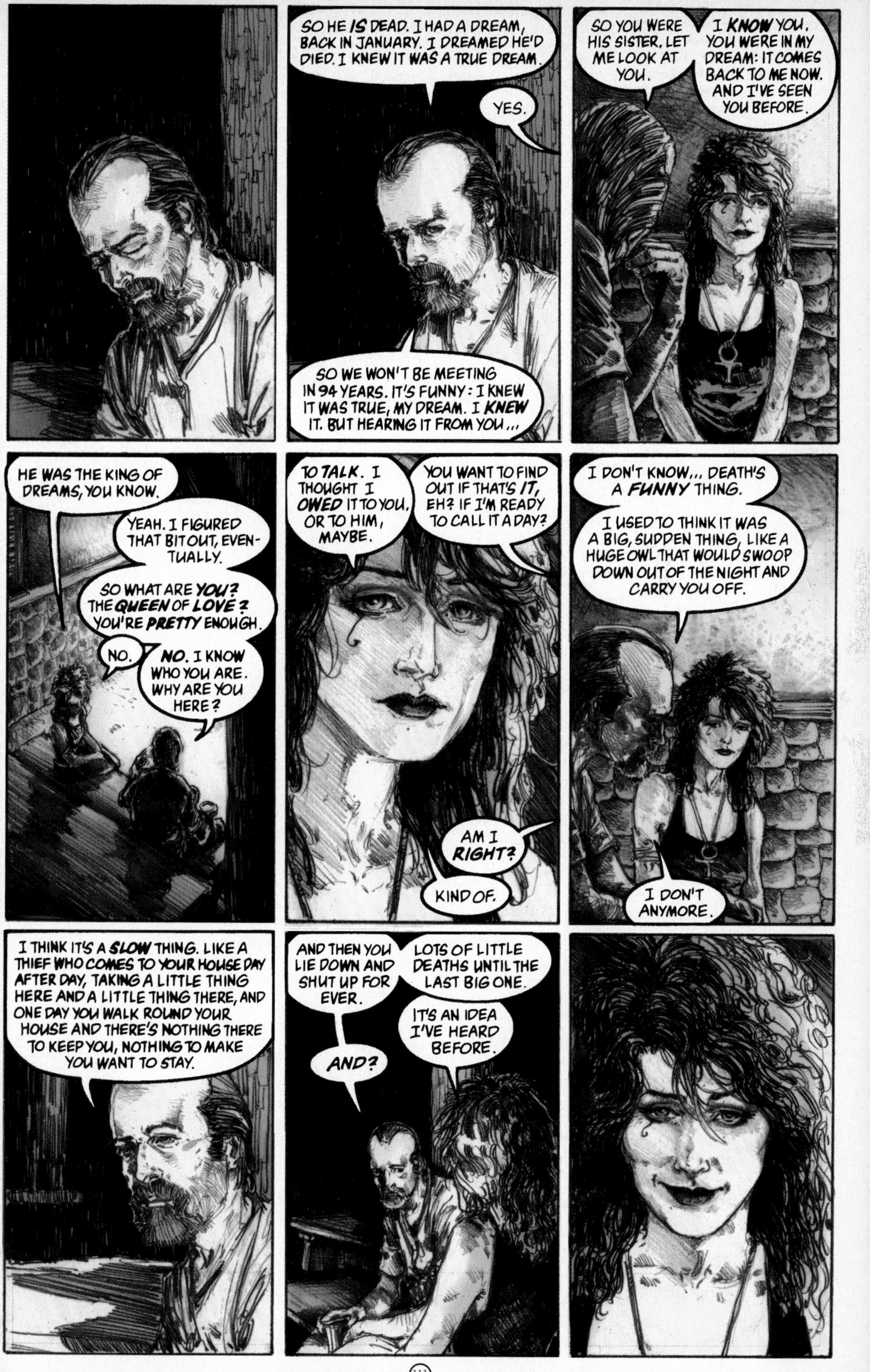

SO HE IS DEAD. I HAD A DREAM, BACK IN JANUARY. I DREAMED HE'D DIED. I KNEW IT WAS A TRUE DREAM.
YES.
SO WE WON'T BE MEETING IN 94 YEARS. IT'S FUNNY: I KNEW IT WAS TRUE, MY DREAM. I KNEW IT. BUT HEARING IT FROM YOU...
SO YOU WERE HIS SISTER. LET ME LOOK AT YOU.
I KNOW YOU. YOU WERE IN MY DREAM: IT COMES BACK TO ME NOW. AND I'VE SEEN YOU BEFORE.
HE WAS THE KING OF DREAMS, YOU KNOW.
YEAH. I FIGURED THAT BIT OUT, EVENTUALLY.
SO WHAT ARE YOU? THE QUEEN OF LOVE? YOU'RE PRETTY ENOUGH.
NO.
NO. I KNOW WHO YOU ARE. WHY ARE YOU HERE?
TO TALK. I THOUGHT I OWED IT TO YOU, OR TO HIM, MAYBE.
YOU WANT TO FIND OUT IF THAT'S IT, EH? IF I'M READY TO CALL IT A DAY?
AM I RIGHT?
KIND OF.
I DON'T KNOW... DEATH'S A FUNNY THING.
I USED TO THINK IT WAS A BIG, SUDDEN THING, LIKE A HUGE OWL THAT WOULD SWOOP DOWN OUT OF THE NIGHT AND CARRY YOU OFF.
I DON'T ANYMORE.
I THINK IT'S A SLOW THING. LIKE A THIEF WHO COMES TO YOUR HOUSE DAY AFTER DAY, TAKING A LITTLE THING HERE AND A LITTLE THING THERE, AND ONE DAY YOU WALK ROUND YOUR HOUSE AND THERE'S NOTHING THERE TO KEEP YOU, NOTHING TO MAKE YOU WANT TO STAY.
AND THEN YOU LIE DOWN AND SHUT UP FOR EVER.
LOTS OF LITTLE DEATHS UNTIL THE LAST BIG ONE.
AND?
IT'S AN IDEA I'VE HEARD BEFORE.

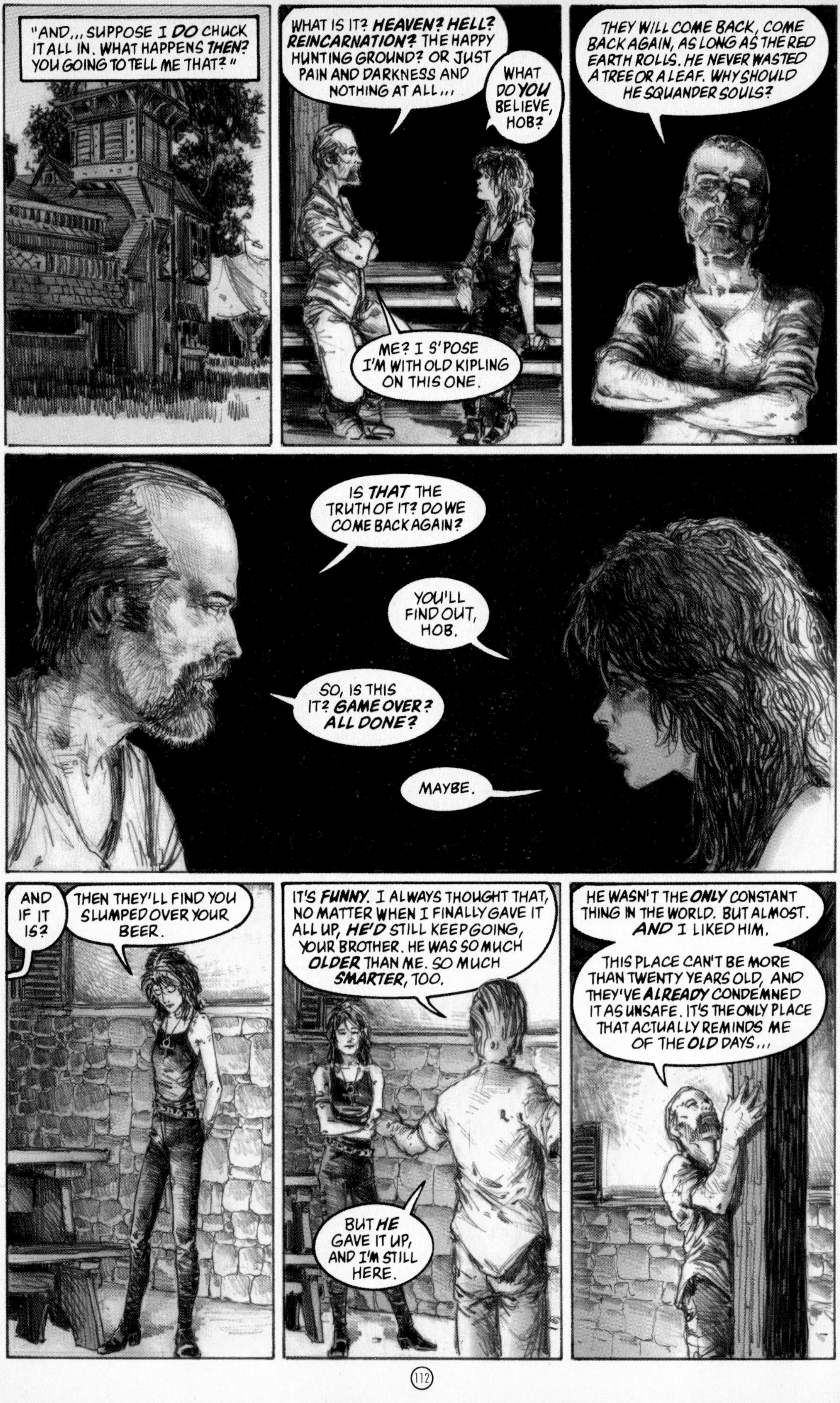
"AND,,, SUPPOSE I DO CHUCK IT ALL IN. WHAT HAPPENS THEN? YOU GOING TO TELL ME THAT?"
WHAT IS IT? HEAVEN? HELL? REINCARNATION? THE HAPPY HUNTING GROUND? OR JUST PAIN AND DARKNESS AND NOTHING AT ALL,,,
WHAT DO YOU BELIEVE, HOB?
ME? I S'POSE I'M WITH OLD KIPLING ON THIS ONE.
THEY WILL COME BACK, COME BACK AGAIN, AS LONG AS THE RED EARTH ROLLS. HE NEVER WASTED A TREE OR A LEAF. WHY SHOULD HE SQUANDER SOULS?
IS THAT THE TRUTH OF IT? DO WE COME BACK AGAIN?
YOU'LL FIND OUT, HOB.
SO, IS THIS IT? GAME OVER? ALL DONE?
MAYBE.
AND IF IT IS?
THEN THEY'LL FIND YOU SLUMPED OVER YOUR BEER.
IT'S FUNNY. I ALWAYS THOUGHT THAT, NO MATTER WHEN I FINALLY GAVE IT ALL UP, HE'D STILL KEEP GOING, YOUR BROTHER. HE WAS SO MUCH OLDER THAN ME. SO MUCH SMARTER, TOO.
BUT HE GAVE IT UP, AND I'M STILL HERE.
HE WASN'T THE ONLY CONSTANT THING IN THE WORLD. BUT ALMOST. AND I LIKED HIM.
THIS PLACE CAN'T BE MORE THAN TWENTY YEARS OLD, AND THEY'VE ALREADY CONDEMNED IT AS UNSAFE. IT'S THE ONLY PLACE THAT ACTUALLY REMINDS ME OF THE OLD DAYS,,,

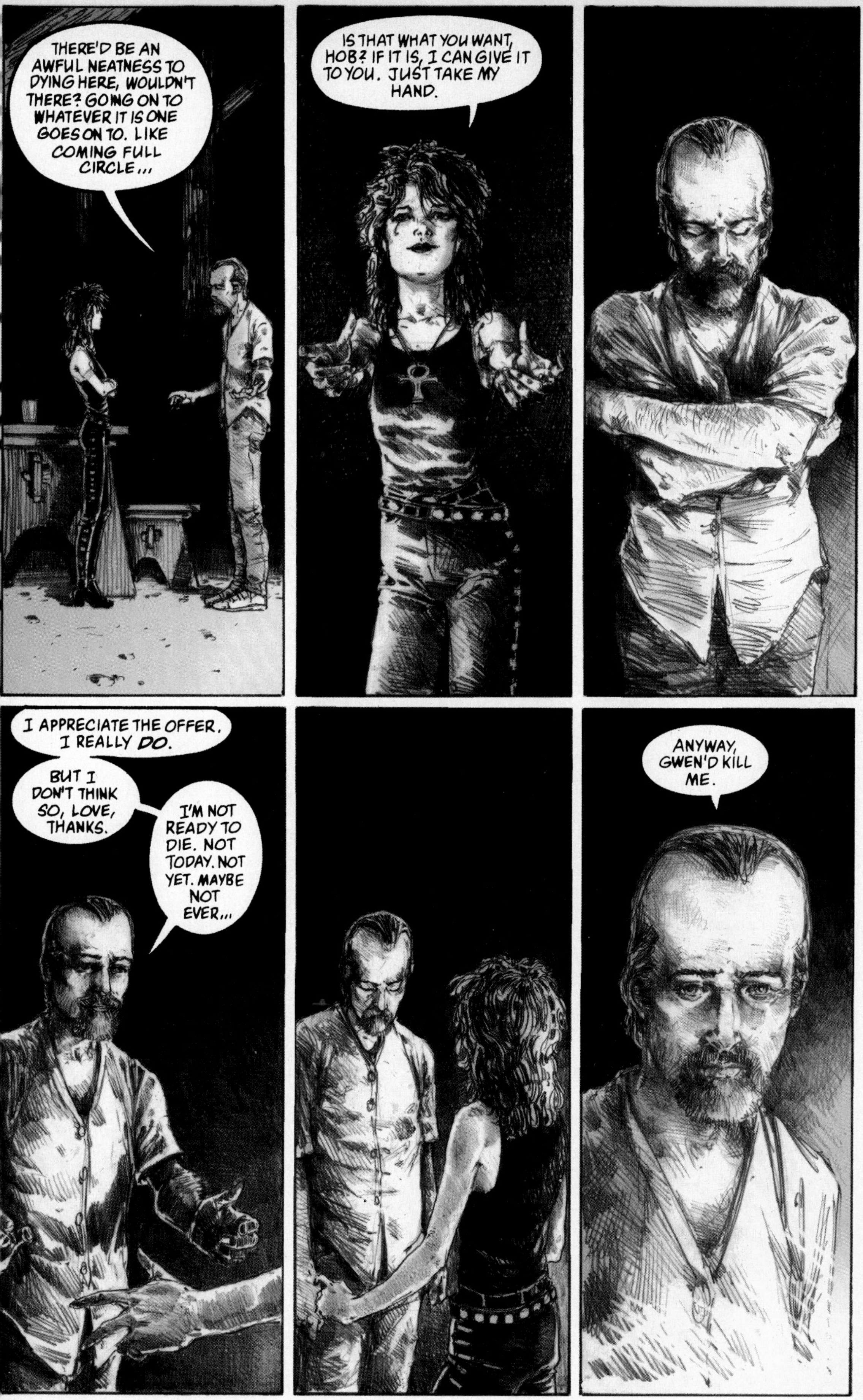
THERE'D BE AN AWFUL NEATNESS TO DYING HERE, WOULDN'T THERE? GOING ON TO WHATEVER IT IS ONE GOES ON TO. LIKE COMING FULL CIRCLE...
IS THAT WHAT YOU WANT, HOB? IF IT IS, I CAN GIVE IT TO YOU. JUST TAKE MY HAND.
I APPRECIATE THE OFFER. I REALLY DO.
BUT I DON'T THINK SO, LOVE, THANKS.
I'M NOT READY TO DIE. NOT TODAY. NOT YET. MAYBE NOT EVER...
ANYWAY, GWEN'D KILL ME.

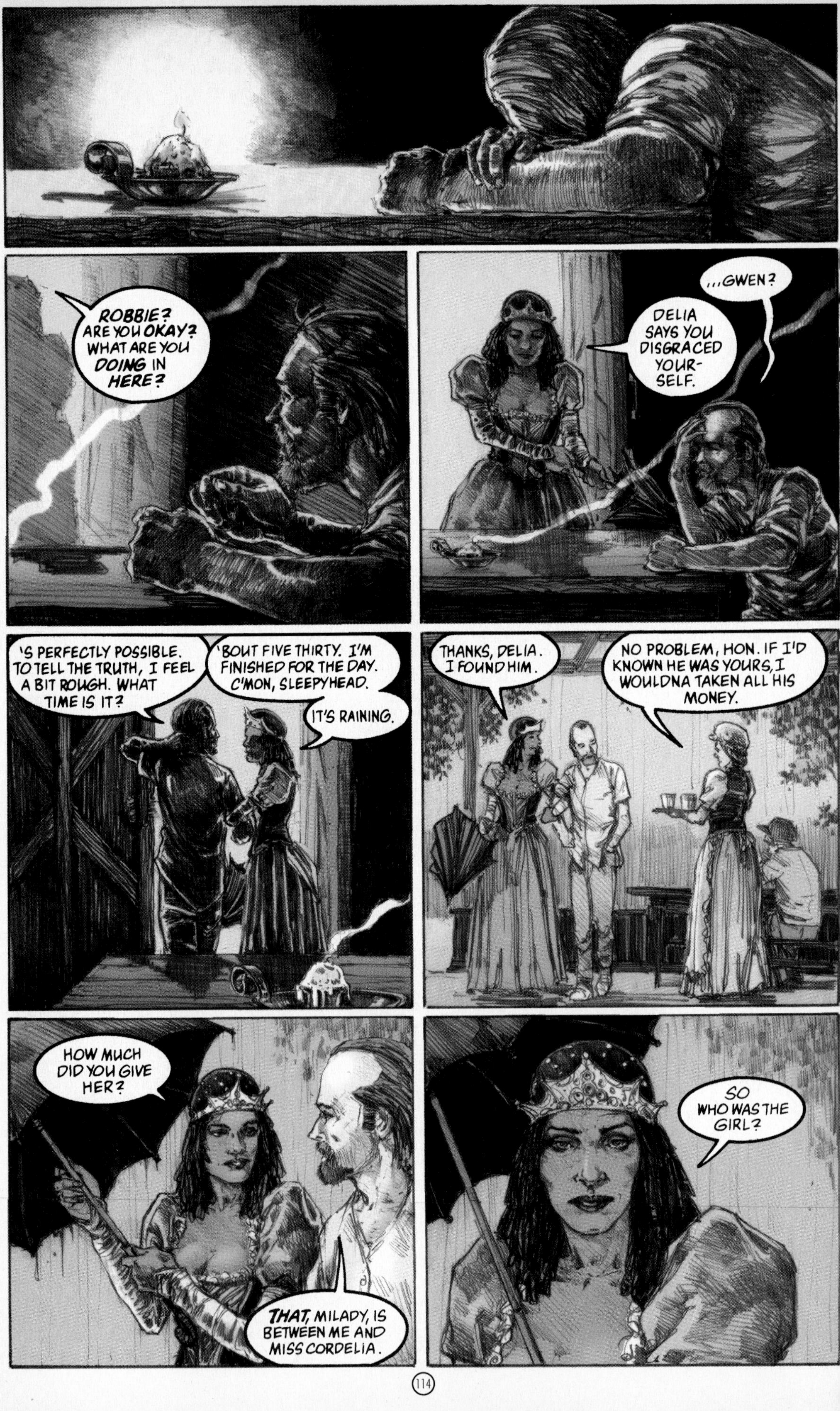
ROBBIE? ARE YOU OKAY? WHAT ARE YOU DOING IN HERE?
DELIA SAYS YOU DISGRACED YOURSELF.
...GWEN?
'S PERFECTLY POSSIBLE. TO TELL THE TRUTH, I FEEL A BIT ROUGH. WHAT TIME IS IT?
'BOUT FIVE THIRTY. I'M FINISHED FOR THE DAY. C'MON, SLEEPYHEAD.
IT'S RAINING.
THANKS, DELIA. I FOUND HIM.
NO PROBLEM, HON. IF I'D KNOWN HE WAS YOURS, I WOULDNA TAKEN ALL HIS MONEY.
HOW MUCH DID YOU GIVE HER?
THAT, MILADY, IS BETWEEN ME AND MISS CORDELIA.
SO WHO WAS THE GIRL?

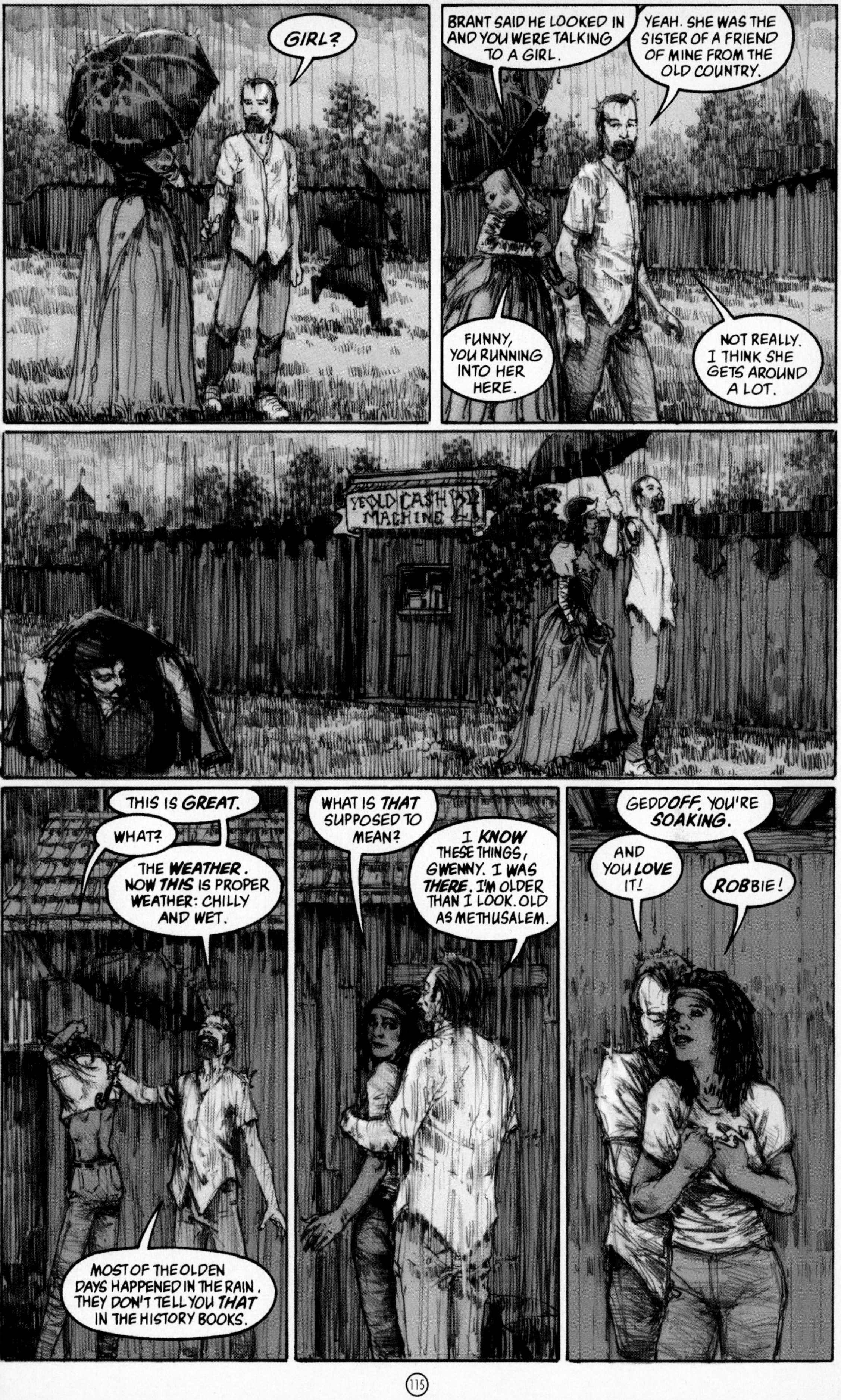
GIRL?
BRANT SAID HE LOOKED IN AND YOU WERE TALKING TO A GIRL.
YEAH. SHE WAS THE SISTER OF A FRIEND OF MINE FROM THE OLD COUNTRY.
FUNNY, YOU RUNNING INTO HER HERE.
NOT REALLY. I THINK SHE GETS AROUND A LOT.
YE OLD CASH MACHINE
THIS IS GREAT.
WHAT?
THE WEATHER. NOW THIS IS PROPER WEATHER: CHILLY AND WET.
MOST OF THE OLDEN DAYS HAPPENED IN THE RAIN. THEY DON'T TELL YOU THAT IN THE HISTORY BOOKS.
WHAT IS THAT SUPPOSED TO MEAN?
I KNOW THESE THINGS, GWENNY. I WAS THERE. I'M OLDER THAN I LOOK. OLD AS METHUSALEM.
GEDDOFF. YOU'RE SOAKING.
AND YOU LOVE IT!
ROBBIE!

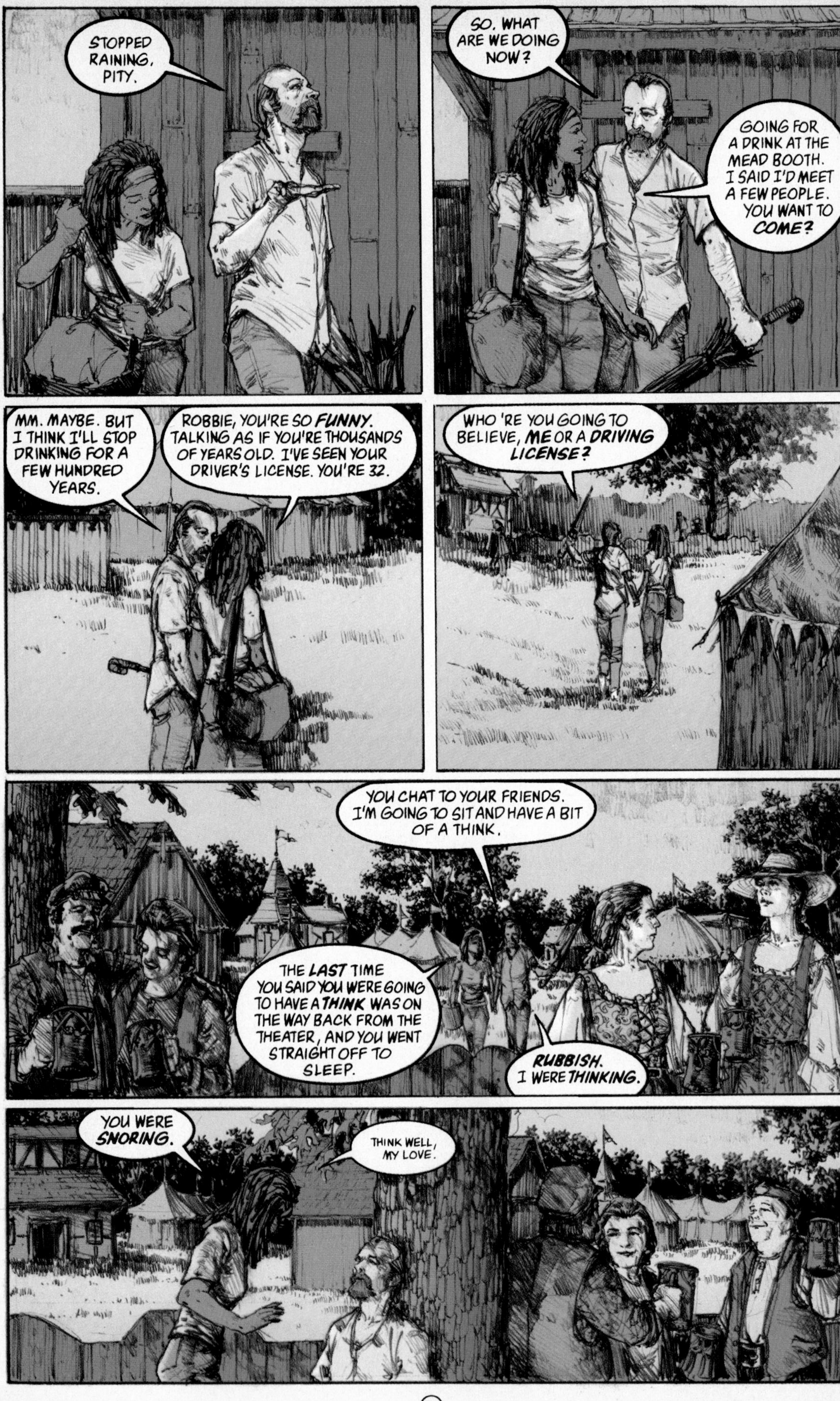
STOPPED RAINING. PITY.
SO, WHAT ARE WE DOING NOW?
GOING FOR A DRINK AT THE MEAD BOOTH. I SAID I'D MEET A FEW PEOPLE. YOU WANT TO COME?
MM. MAYBE. BUT I THINK I'LL STOP DRINKING FOR A FEW HUNDRED YEARS.
ROBBIE, YOU'RE SO FUNNY. TALKING AS IF YOU'RE THOUSANDS OF YEARS OLD. I'VE SEEN YOUR DRIVER'S LICENSE. YOU'RE 32.
WHO 'RE YOU GOING TO BELIEVE, ME OR A DRIVING LICENSE?
YOU CHAT TO YOUR FRIENDS. I'M GOING TO SIT AND HAVE A BIT OF A THINK.
THE LAST TIME YOU SAID YOU WERE GOING TO HAVE A THINK WAS ON THE WAY BACK FROM THE THEATER, AND YOU WENT STRAIGHT OFF TO SLEEP.
RUBBISH. I WERE THINKING.
YOU WERE SNORING.
THINK WELL, MY LOVE.

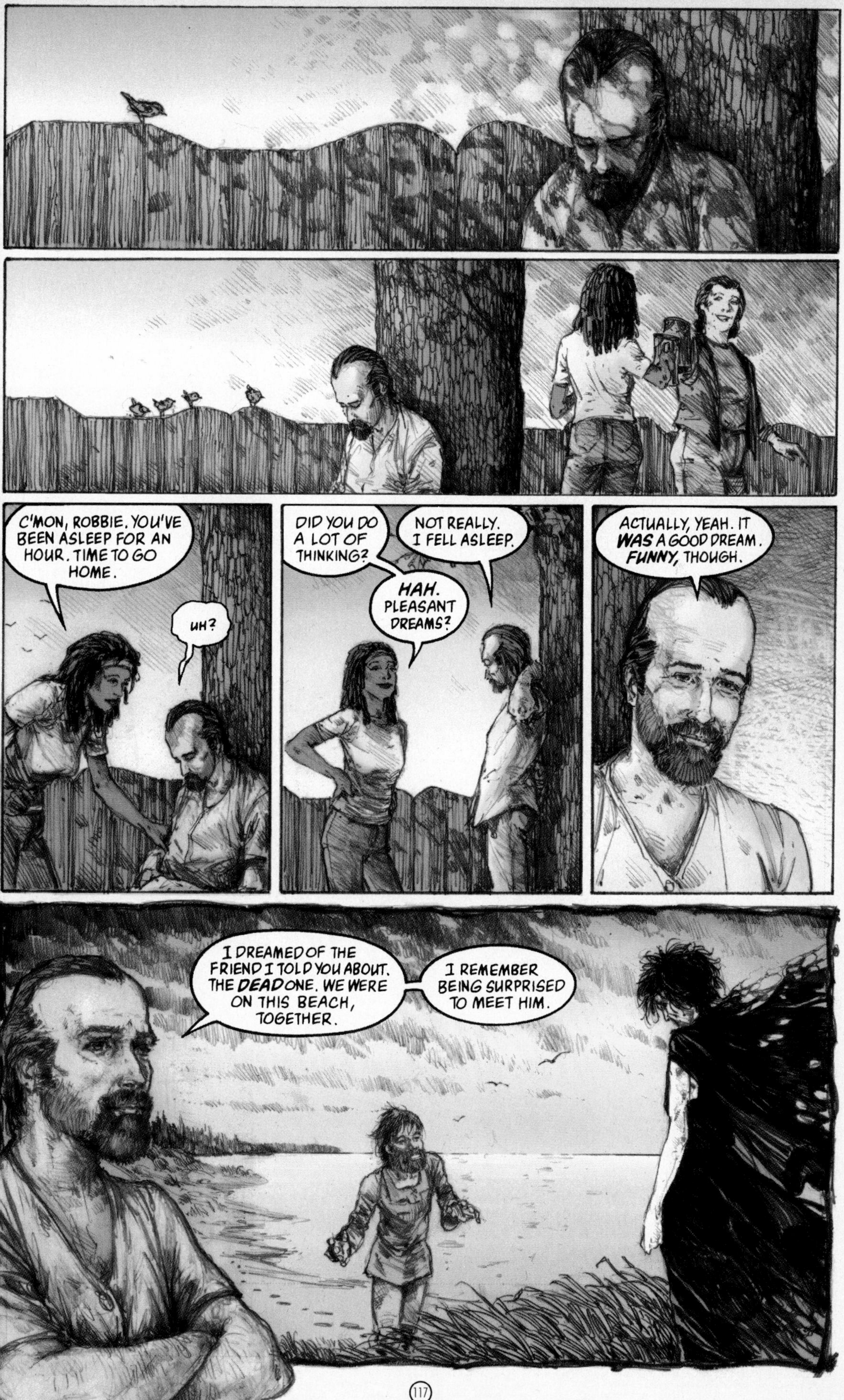
C'MON, ROBBIE. YOU'VE BEEN ASLEEP FOR AN HOUR. TIME TO GO HOME.
UH?
DID YOU DO A LOT OF THINKING?
NOT REALLY. I FELL ASLEEP.
HAH. PLEASANT DREAMS?
ACTUALLY, YEAH. IT WAS A GOOD DREAM. FUNNY, THOUGH.
I DREAMED OF THE FRIEND I TOLD YOU ABOUT. THE DEAD ONE. WE WERE ON THIS BEACH, TOGETHER.
I REMEMBER BEING SURPRISED TO MEET HIM.

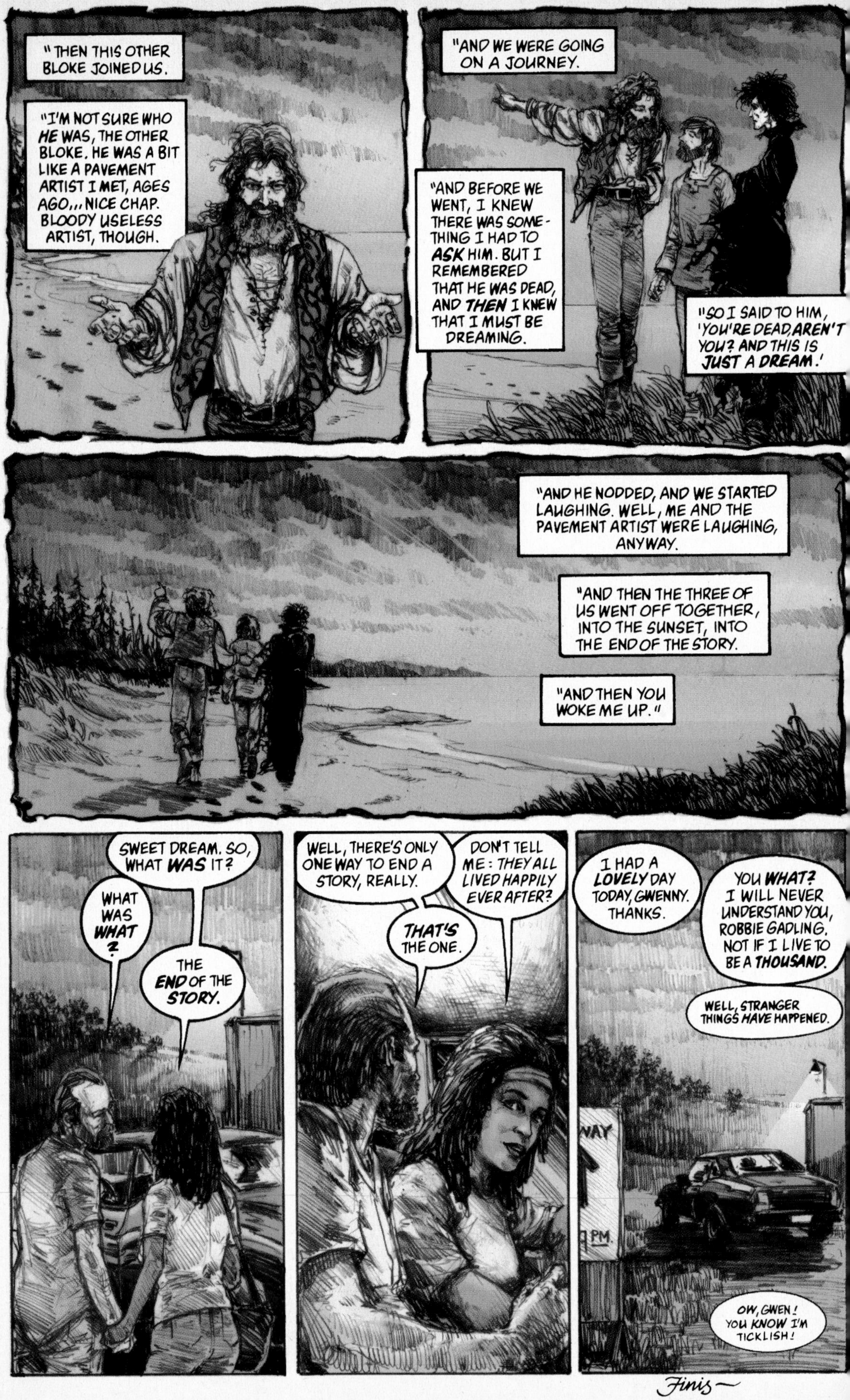

"THEN THIS OTHER BLOKE JOINED US.
"I'M NOT SURE WHO HE WAS, THE OTHER BLOKE. HE WAS A BIT LIKE A PAVEMENT ARTIST I MET, AGES AGO... NICE CHAP. BLOODY USELESS ARTIST, THOUGH.
"AND WE WERE GOING ON A JOURNEY.
"AND BEFORE WE WENT, I KNEW THERE WAS SOMETHING I HAD TO ASK HIM. BUT I REMEMBERED THAT HE WAS DEAD, AND THEN I KNEW THAT I MUST BE DREAMING.
"SO I SAID TO HIM, 'YOU'RE DEAD, AREN'T YOU? AND THIS IS JUST A DREAM.'
"AND HE NODDED, AND WE STARTED LAUGHING. WELL, ME AND THE PAVEMENT ARTIST WERE LAUGHING, ANYWAY.
"AND THEN THE THREE OF US WENT OFF TOGETHER, INTO THE SUNSET, INTO THE END OF THE STORY.
"AND THEN YOU WOKE ME UP."
SWEET DREAM. SO, WHAT WAS IT?
WHAT WAS WHAT?
THE END OF THE STORY.
WELL, THERE'S ONLY ONE WAY TO END A STORY, REALLY.
DON'T TELL ME: THEY ALL LIVED HAPPILY EVER AFTER?
THAT'S THE ONE.
I HAD A LOVELY DAY TODAY, GWENNY. THANKS.
YOU WHAT? I WILL NEVER UNDERSTAND YOU, ROBBIE GADLING. NOT IF I LIVE TO BE A THOUSAND.
WELL, STRANGER THINGS HAVE HAPPENED.
WAY
PM.
OW, GWEN! YOU KNOW I'M TICKLISH!
Finis—

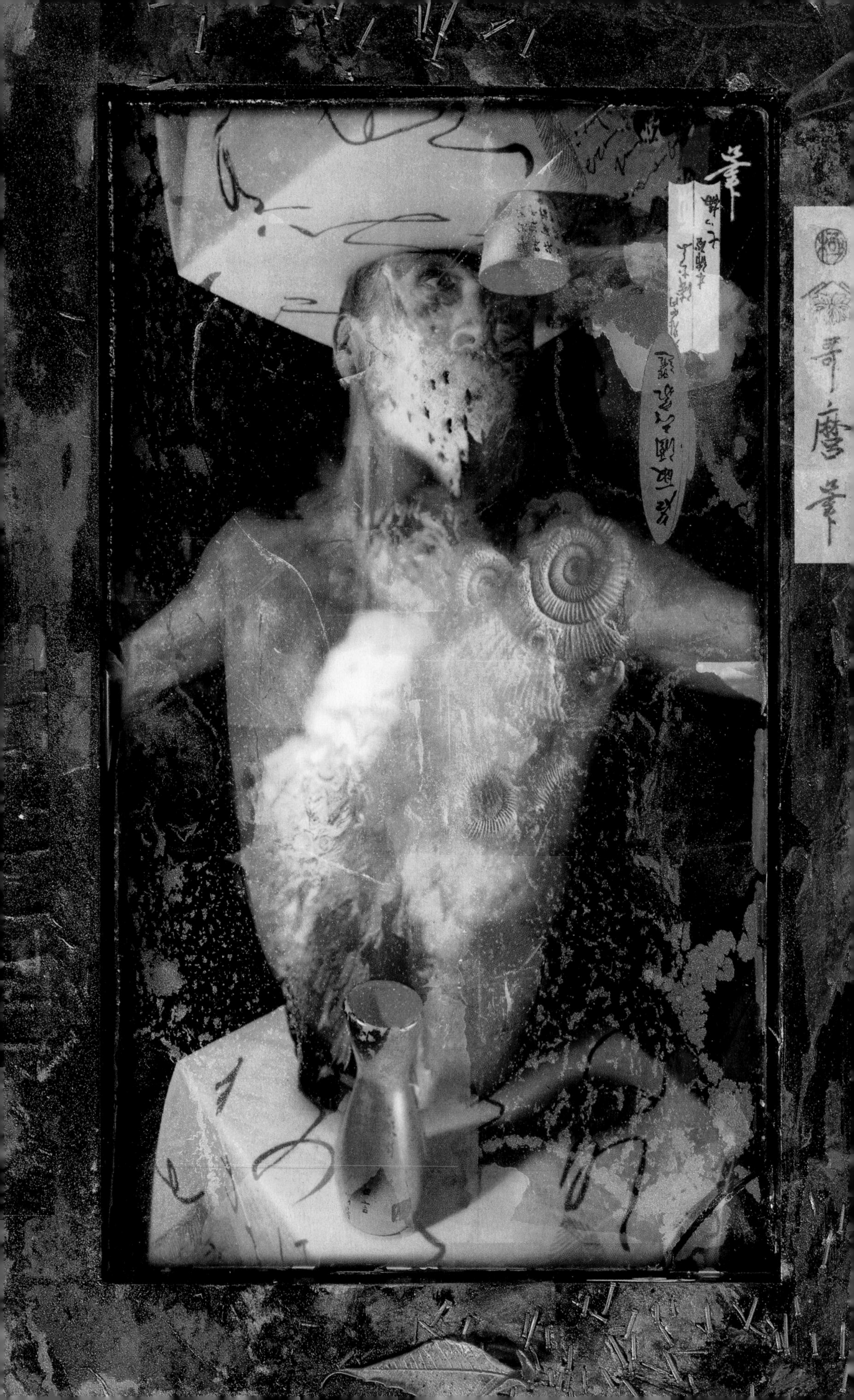

When I was a child I lived amid the mulberry groves.
In summer the mulberry trees would stain the green grass
with crimson pulp.

Birds of a thousand colors danced in the sky when I was a boy.
They brightened the day with their intricate songs.
"We are who we choose to be," sang the goldfinch, when the sun
was high.
"I dream about dreams about dreams," sang the nightingale,
under the pale moon.

The girls in my village had lips like plums,
were lovelier by far
Than other girls in other villages,
in the days of my youth.

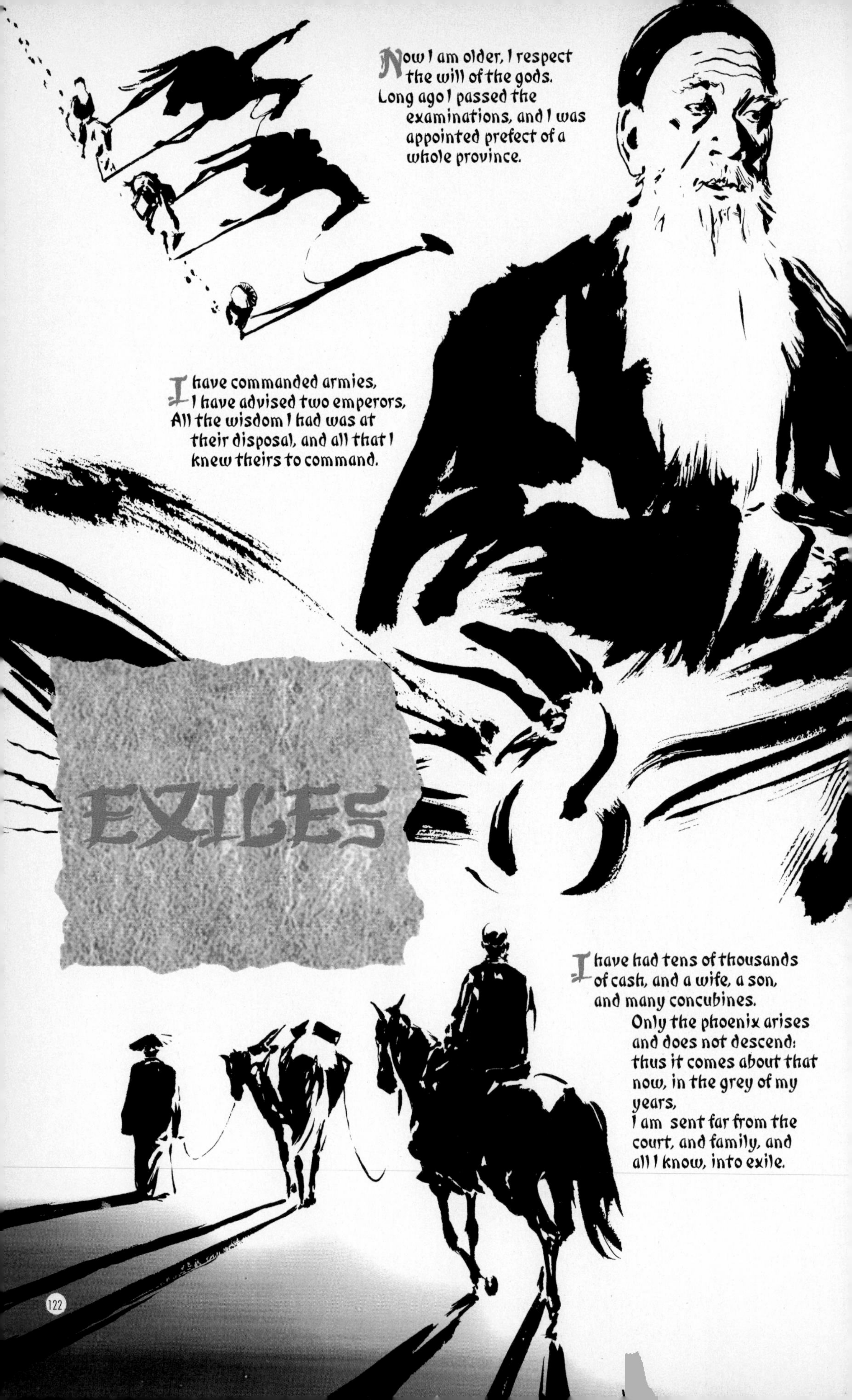
Now I am older, I respect the will of the gods. Long ago I passed the examinations, and I was appointed prefect of a whole province.
I have commanded armies, I have advised two emperors, All the wisdom I had was at their disposal, and all that I knew theirs to command.
EXILES
I have had tens of thousands of cash, and a wife, a son, and many concubines.
Only the phoenix arises and does not descend: thus it comes about that now, in the grey of my years, I am sent far from the court, and family, and all I know, into exile.

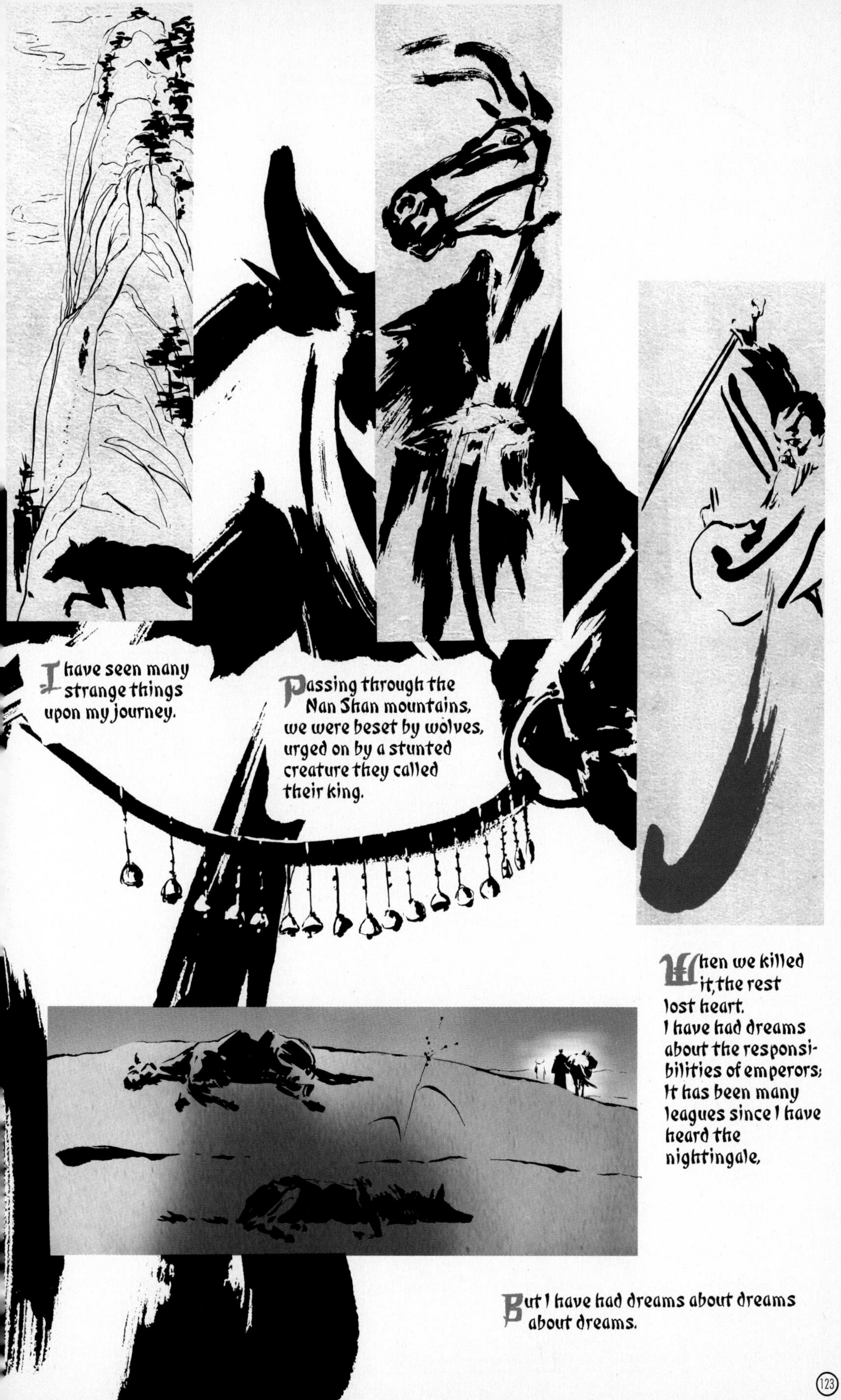
I have seen many strange things upon my journey.
Passing through the Nan Shan mountains, we were beset by wolves, urged on by a stunted creature they called their king.
When we killed it, the rest lost heart.
I have had dreams about the responsibilities of emperors;
It has been many leagues since I have heard the nightingale,
But I have had dreams about dreams about dreams.

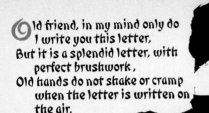

Old friend, in my mind only do
I write you this letter,
But it is a splendid letter, with
perfect brushwork,
Old hands do not shake or cramp
when the letter is written on
the air.

When my son was born the
emperor commanded
fireworks,
They burst on the night sky
like sunflowers of light.
Now my son is dead and I am
in exile.

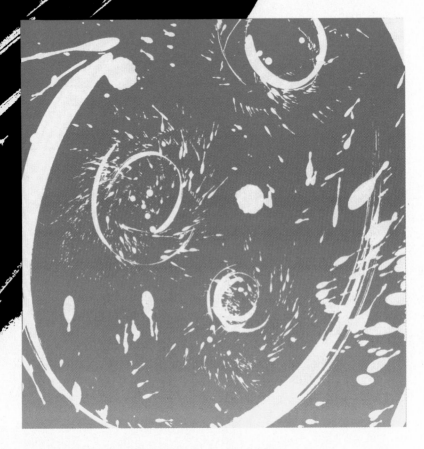

The desert is grey: Grey sand beneath grey skies,
and I say to my guide,"This desert is grey," and he agrees.
He is a man from a local village.
I ask the name of the desert, but my guide says nothing.
It has a name of ill omen, and ill omens have become my life.

My son allied himself with the people of the White Lotus.
"You are lucky that I have left you your head,"
the Emperor told me.

And now I am here, sand in my beard and
eyes and ears, thoughts washing into grey and sand,
Dreams, like sea-foam, washing over everything.

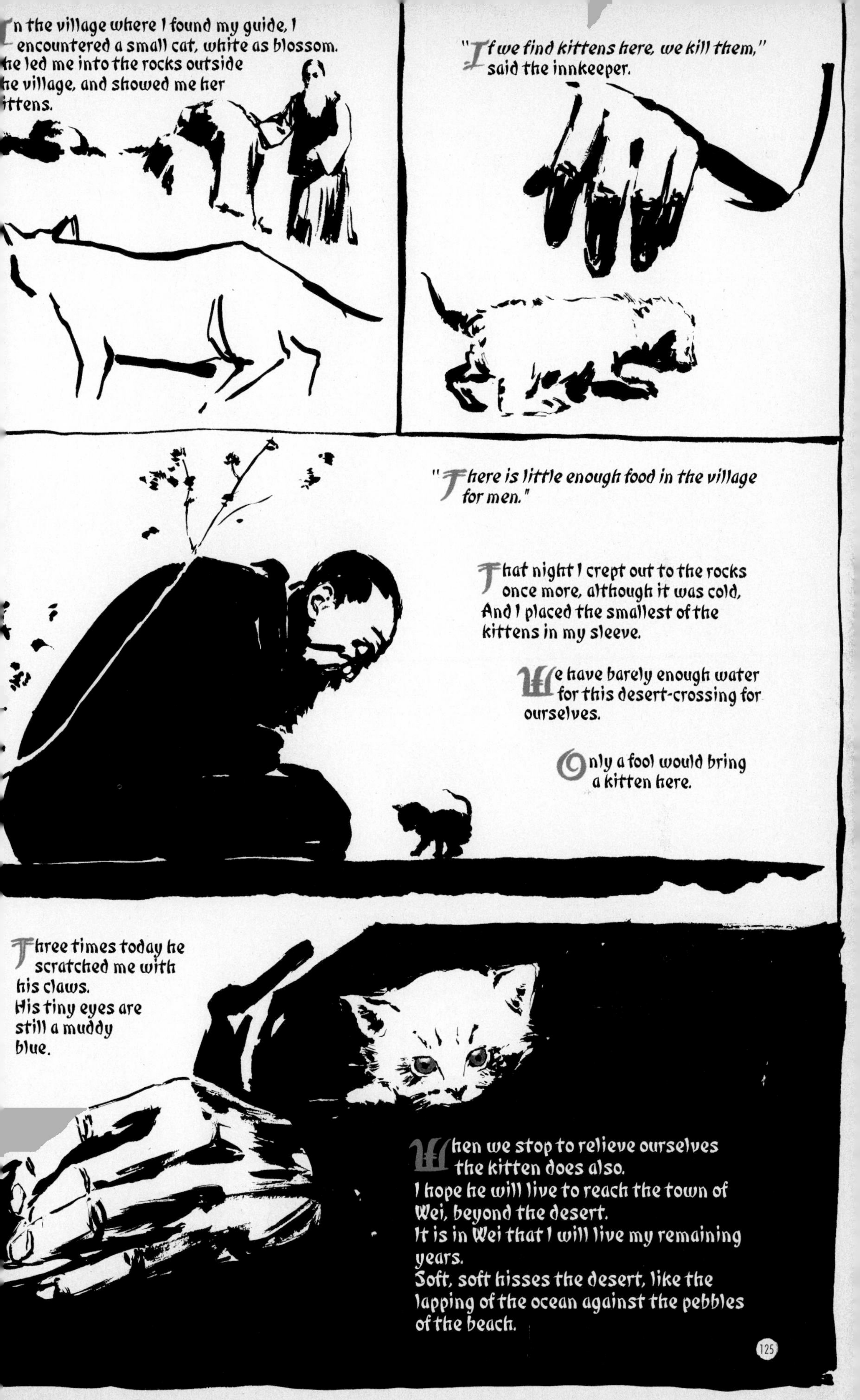
In the village where I found my guide, I encountered a small cat, white as blossom.
he led me into the rocks outside
he village, and showed me her
ittens.
"If we find kittens here, we kill them," said the innkeeper.
"There is little enough food in the village for men."
That night I crept out to the rocks once more, although it was cold, And I placed the smallest of the kittens in my sleeve.
We have barely enough water for this desert-crossing for ourselves.
Only a fool would bring a kitten here.
Three times today he scratched me with his claws.
His tiny eyes are still a muddy blue.
When we stop to relieve ourselves the kitten does also.
I hope he will live to reach the town of Wei, beyond the desert.
It is in Wei that I will live my remaining years.
Soft, soft hisses the desert, like the lapping of the ocean against the pebbles of the beach.

DID YOU SAY SOMETHING, MASTER?

I SAID NOTHING.

I BEG YOUR PARDON, MASTER, I THOUGHT I HEARD YOU SPEAK.

I AM COMPOSING LETTERS THAT I SHALL, PERHAPS, WRITE, WHEN THIS JOURNEYING IS DONE, AND WE ARE SAFE. IT IS HOW I OCCUPY MY MIND AS WE TRAVEL. IS THERE SOMETHING *YOU* DO TO OCCUPY *YOUR* MIND?

I PRAY, MASTER, THAT THE ALL-HIGHEST, AND ALL THE LESSER GODS, WILL SEE US SAFELY ACROSS THE DESERT. ALSO, I HOPE.

I HAVE HEARD THAT ILLUSIONS BREED IN THIS DESERT, THAT GHOSTS AND FOX-SPIRITS WANDER IT, STEALING TRAVELLERS AND LEADING THEM OFF THE PATH.

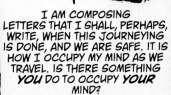

IT IS TRUE, MASTER.

HOW LONG DO WE HAVE UNTIL NIGHTFALL?

SEVERAL HOURS, MASTER.

AND UNTIL WE CROSS THE DESERT?

AT LEAST ONE MORE DAY, MASTER.

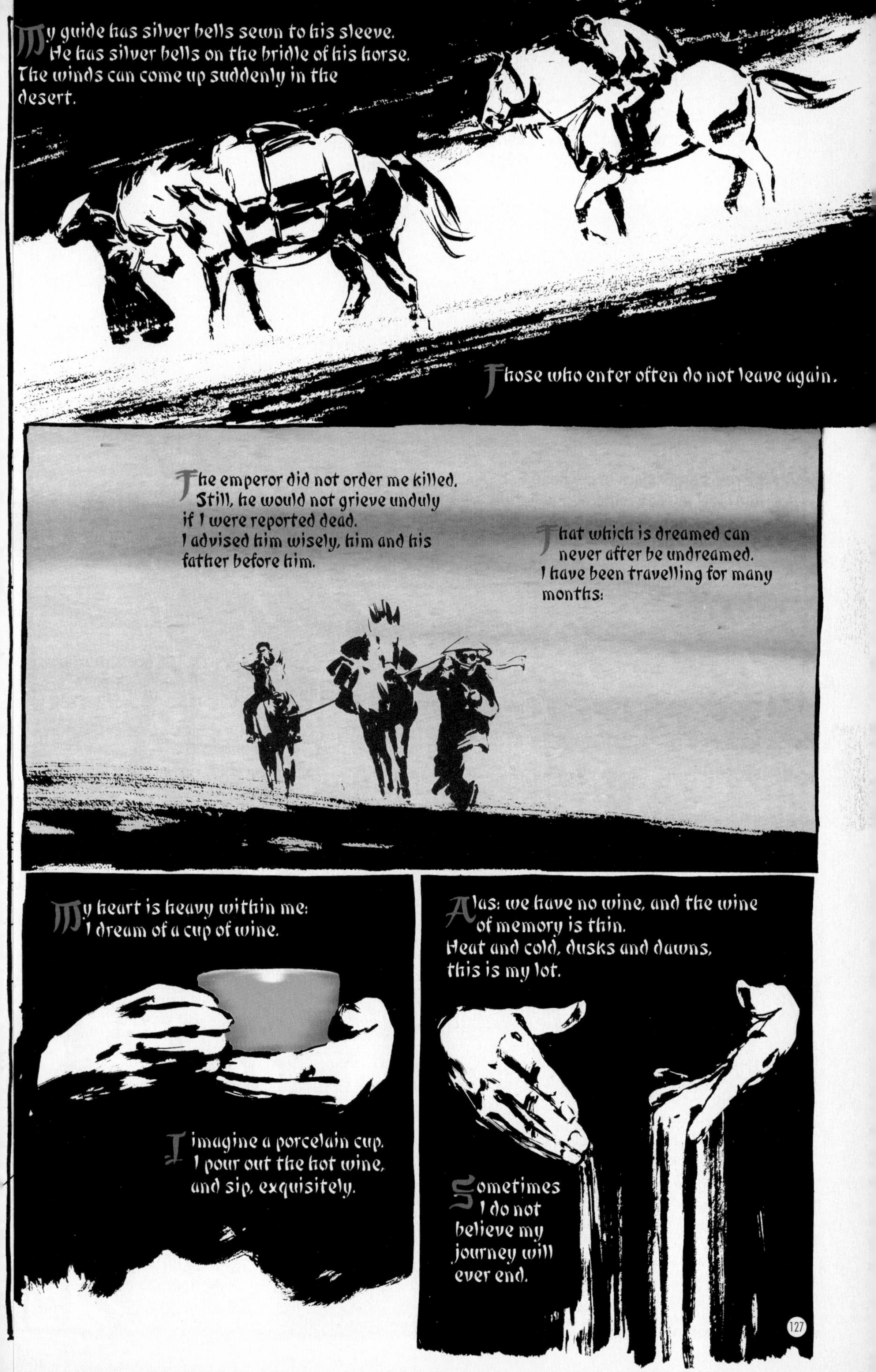
My guide has silver bells sewn to his sleeve.
He has silver bells on the bridle of his horse.
The winds can come up suddenly in the desert.
Those who enter often do not leave again.
The emperor did not order me killed.
Still, he would not grieve unduly if I were reported dead.
I advised him wisely, him and his father before him.
That which is dreamed can never after be undreamed.
I have been travelling for many months:
My heart is heavy within me:
I dream of a cup of wine.
I imagine a porcelain cup.
I pour out the hot wine, and sip, exquisitely.
Alas: we have no wine, and the wine of memory is thin.
Heat and cold, dusks and dawns, this is my lot.
Sometimes I do not believe my journey will ever end.

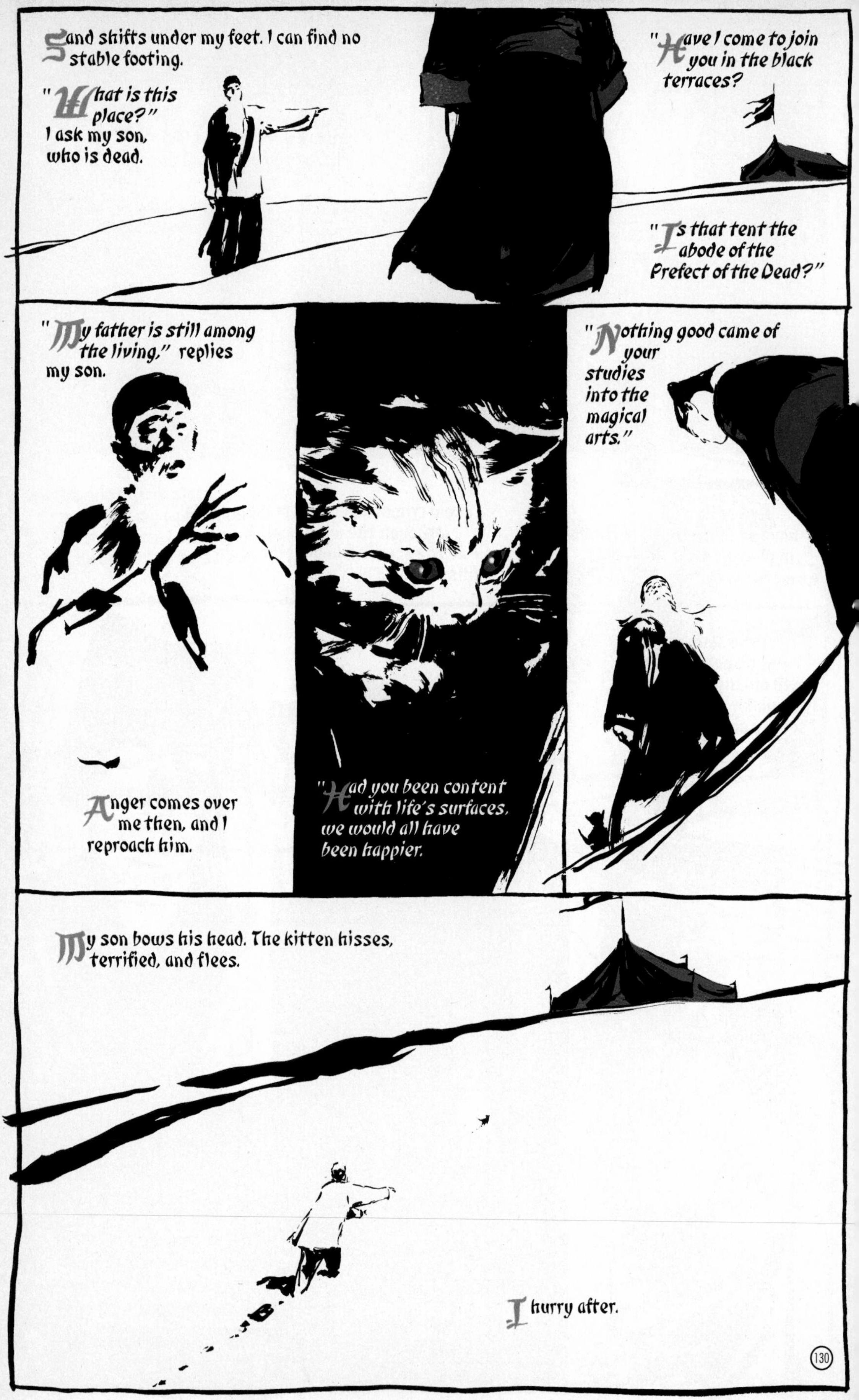
Sand shifts under my feet. I can find no stable footing.
"What is this place?" I ask my son, who is dead.
"Have I come to join you in the black terraces?
"Is that tent the abode of the Prefect of the Dead?"
"My father is still among the living," replies my son.
Anger comes over me then, and I reproach him.
"Had you been content with life's surfaces, we would all have been happier.
"Nothing good came of your studies into the magical arts."
My son bows his head. The kitten hisses, terrified, and flees.
I hurry after.

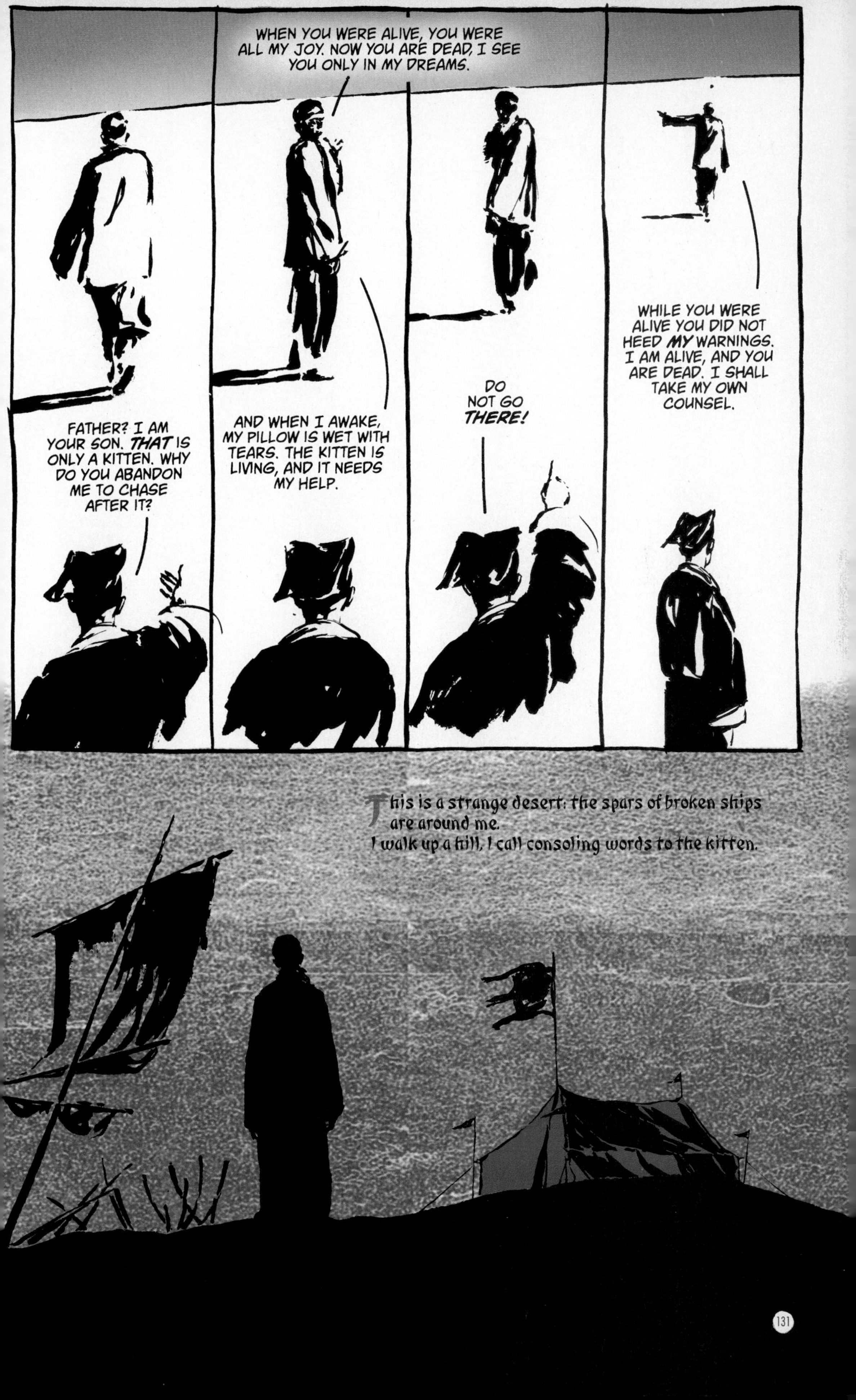
WHEN YOU WERE ALIVE, YOU WERE ALL MY JOY. NOW YOU ARE DEAD, I SEE YOU ONLY IN MY DREAMS.
FATHER? I AM YOUR SON. THAT IS ONLY A KITTEN. WHY DO YOU ABANDON ME TO CHASE AFTER IT?
AND WHEN I AWAKE, MY PILLOW IS WET WITH TEARS. THE KITTEN IS LIVING, AND IT NEEDS MY HELP.
DO NOT GO THERE!
WHILE YOU WERE ALIVE YOU DID NOT HEED MY WARNINGS. I AM ALIVE, AND YOU ARE DEAD. I SHALL TAKE MY OWN COUNSEL.
This is a strange desert: the spars of broken ships are around me.
I walk up a hill, I call consoling words to the kitten.

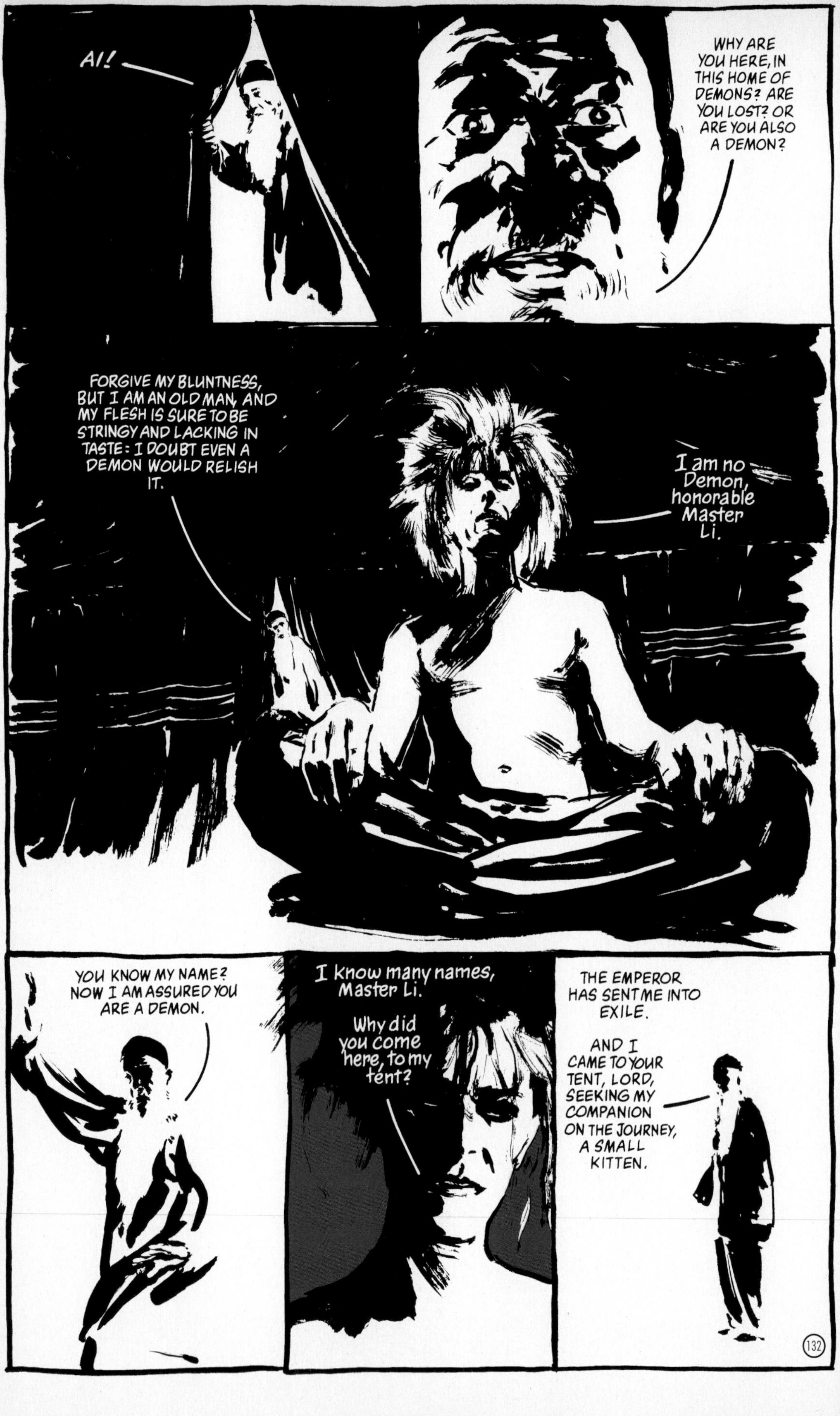
AI!
WHY ARE YOU HERE, IN THIS HOME OF DEMONS? ARE YOU LOST? OR ARE YOU ALSO A DEMON?
FORGIVE MY BLUNTNESS, BUT I AM AN OLD MAN, AND MY FLESH IS SURE TO BE STRINGY AND LACKING IN TASTE: I DOUBT EVEN A DEMON WOULD RELISH IT.
I am no Demon, honorable Master Li.
YOU KNOW MY NAME? NOW I AM ASSURED YOU ARE A DEMON.
I know many names, Master Li.
Why did you come here, to my tent?
THE EMPEROR HAS SENT ME INTO EXILE.
AND I CAME TO YOUR TENT, LORD, SEEKING MY COMPANION ON THE JOURNEY, A SMALL KITTEN.

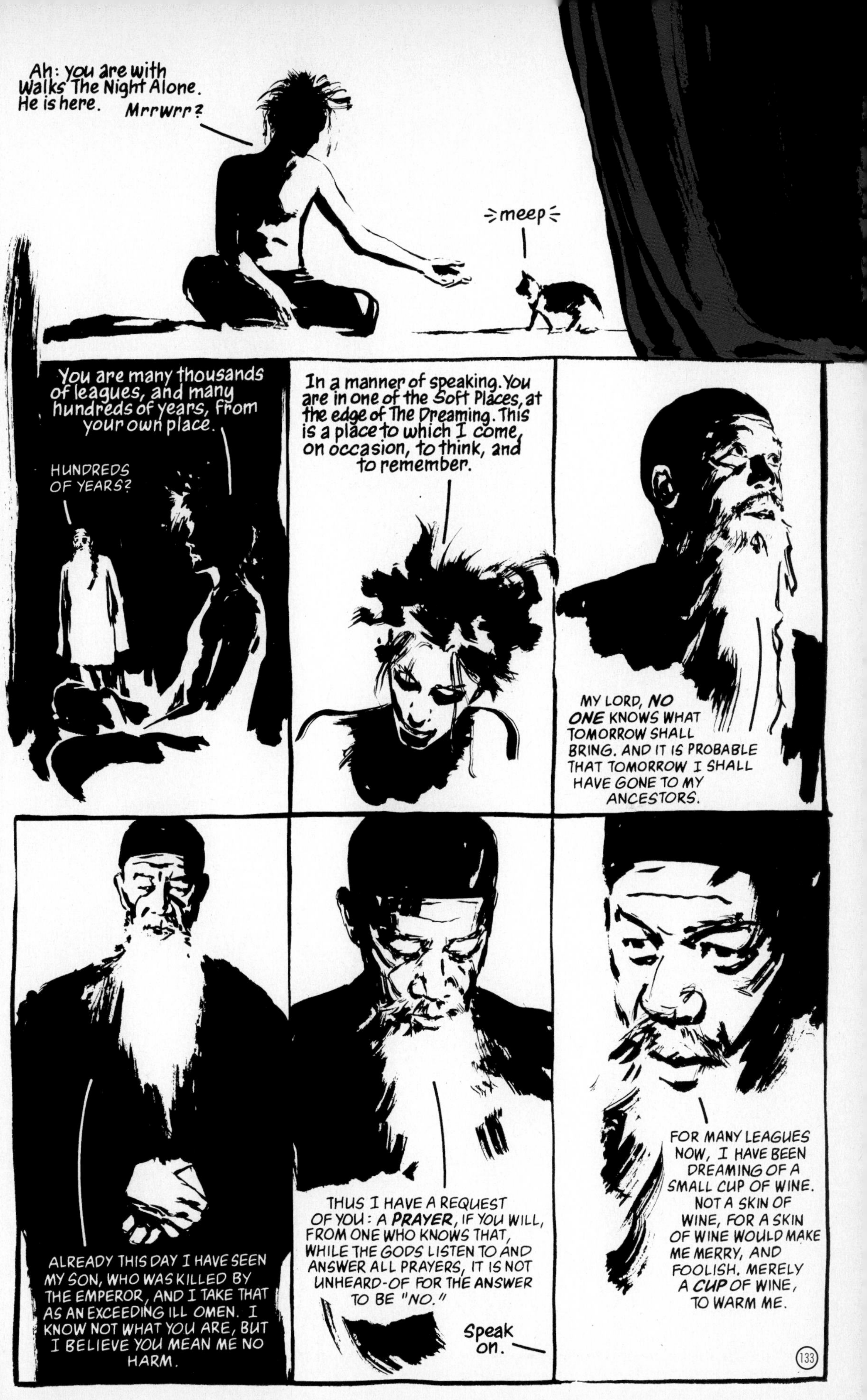
Ah: you are with Walks The Night Alone. He is here.
Mrrwrr?
meep
You are many thousands of leagues, and many hundreds of years, from your own place.
HUNDREDS OF YEARS?
In a manner of speaking. You are in one of the Soft Places, at the edge of The Dreaming. This is a place to which I come, on occasion, to think, and to remember.
MY LORD, NO ONE KNOWS WHAT TOMORROW SHALL BRING. AND IT IS PROBABLE THAT TOMORROW I SHALL HAVE GONE TO MY ANCESTORS.
ALREADY THIS DAY I HAVE SEEN MY SON, WHO WAS KILLED BY THE EMPEROR, AND I TAKE THAT AS AN EXCEEDING ILL OMEN. I KNOW NOT WHAT YOU ARE, BUT I BELIEVE YOU MEAN ME NO HARM.
THUS I HAVE A REQUEST OF YOU: A PRAYER, IF YOU WILL, FROM ONE WHO KNOWS THAT, WHILE THE GODS LISTEN TO AND ANSWER ALL PRAYERS, IT IS NOT UNHEARD-OF FOR THE ANSWER TO BE "NO."
Speak on.
FOR MANY LEAGUES NOW, I HAVE BEEN DREAMING OF A SMALL CUP OF WINE. NOT A SKIN OF WINE, FOR A SKIN OF WINE WOULD MAKE ME MERRY, AND FOOLISH. MERELY A CUP OF WINE, TO WARM ME.

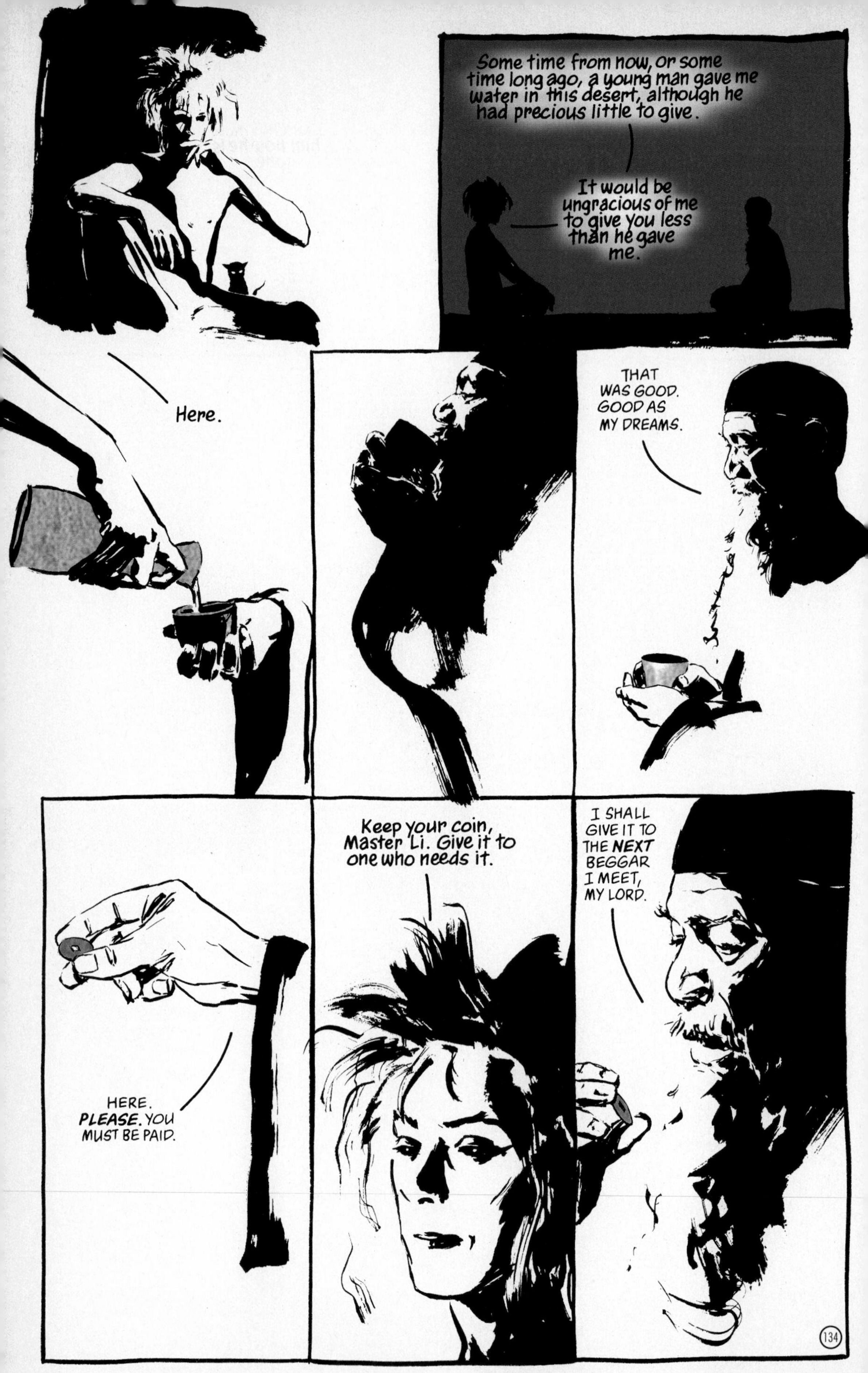
Some time from now, or some time long ago, a young man gave me water in this desert, although he had precious little to give.
It would be ungracious of me to give you less than he gave me.
Here.
THAT WAS GOOD. GOOD AS MY DREAMS.
HERE. *PLEASE.* YOU MUST BE PAID.
Keep your coin, Master Li. Give it to one who needs it.
I SHALL GIVE IT TO THE *NEXT* BEGGAR I MEET, MY LORD.

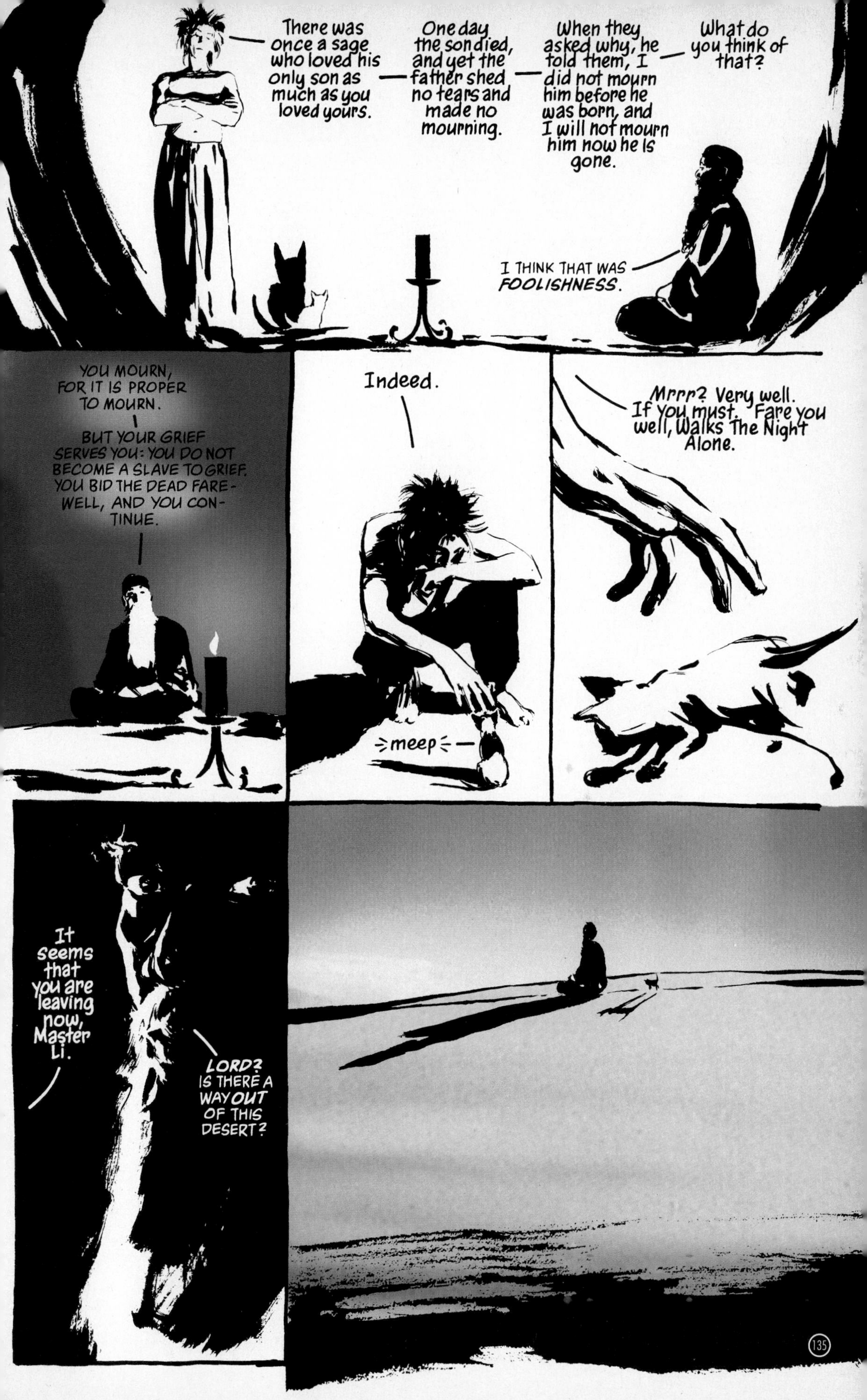

There was once a sage who loved his only son as much as you loved yours.
One day the son died, and yet the father shed no tears and made no mourning.
When they asked why, he told them, I did not mourn him before he was born, and I will not mourn him now he is gone.
What do you think of that?
I THINK THAT WAS FOOLISHNESS.
YOU MOURN, FOR IT IS PROPER TO MOURN.
BUT YOUR GRIEF SERVES YOU: YOU DO NOT BECOME A SLAVE TO GRIEF. YOU BID THE DEAD FARE-WELL, AND YOU CON-TINUE.
Indeed.
meep
Mrrr? Very well. If you must. Fare you well, Walks The Night Alone.
It seems that you are leaving now, Master Li.
LORD? IS THERE A WAY OUT OF THIS DESERT?

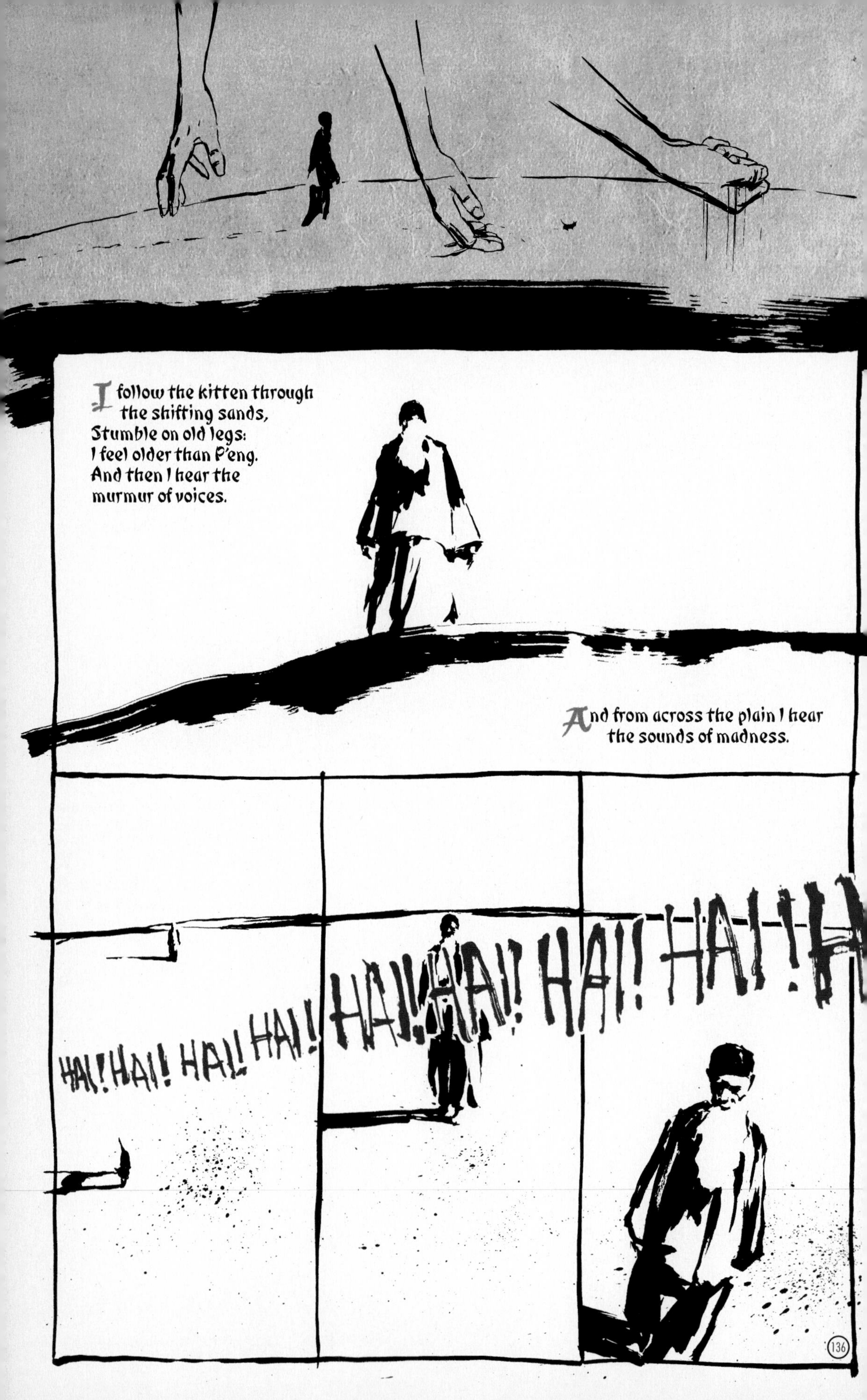
I follow the kitten through the shifting sands,
Stumble on old legs:
I feel older than P'eng.
And then I hear the murmur of voices.
And from across the plain I hear the sounds of madness.
HAI! HAI! HAI! HAI! HAI! HAI! HAI! HAI!

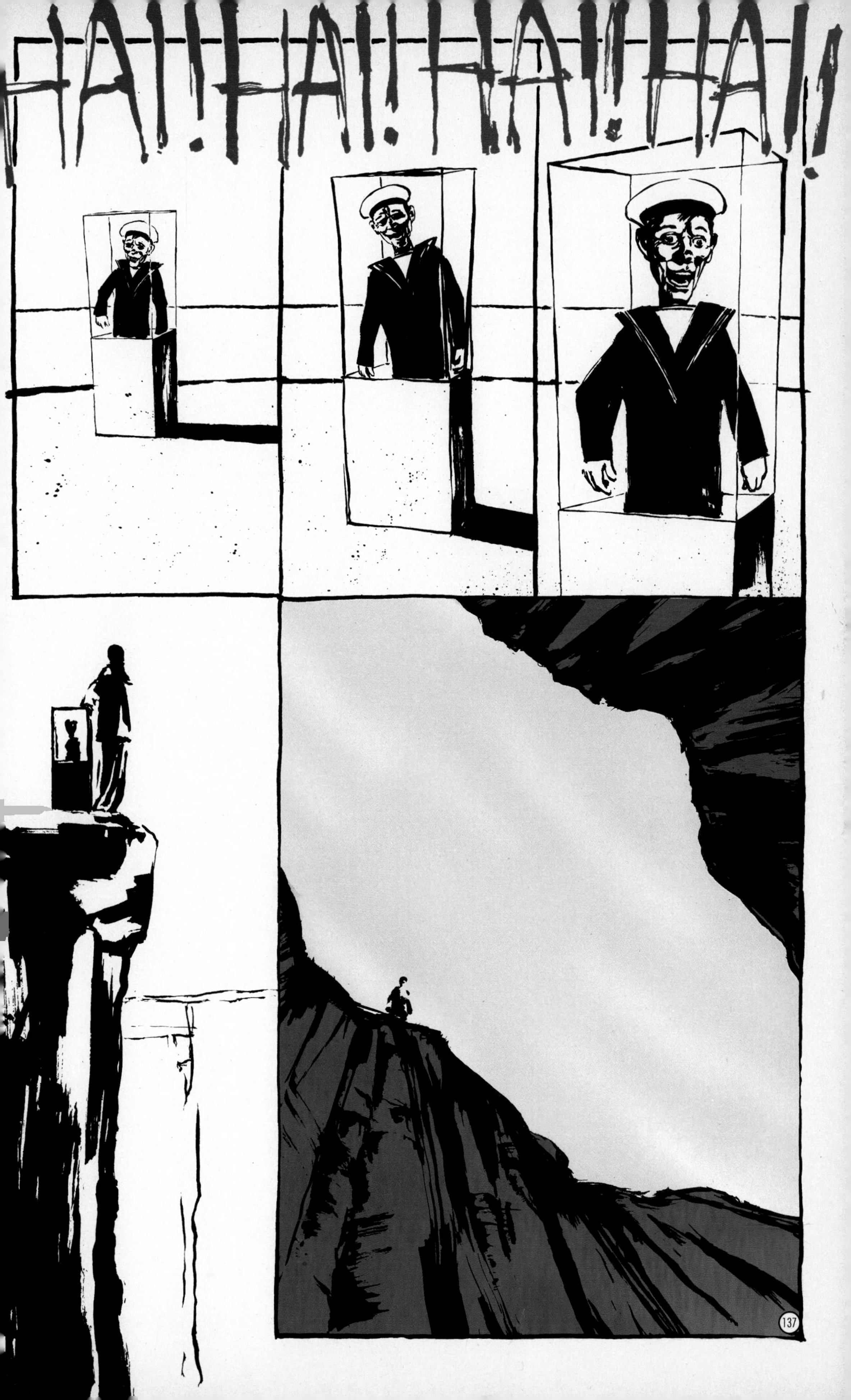
HA! HA! HA! HA!

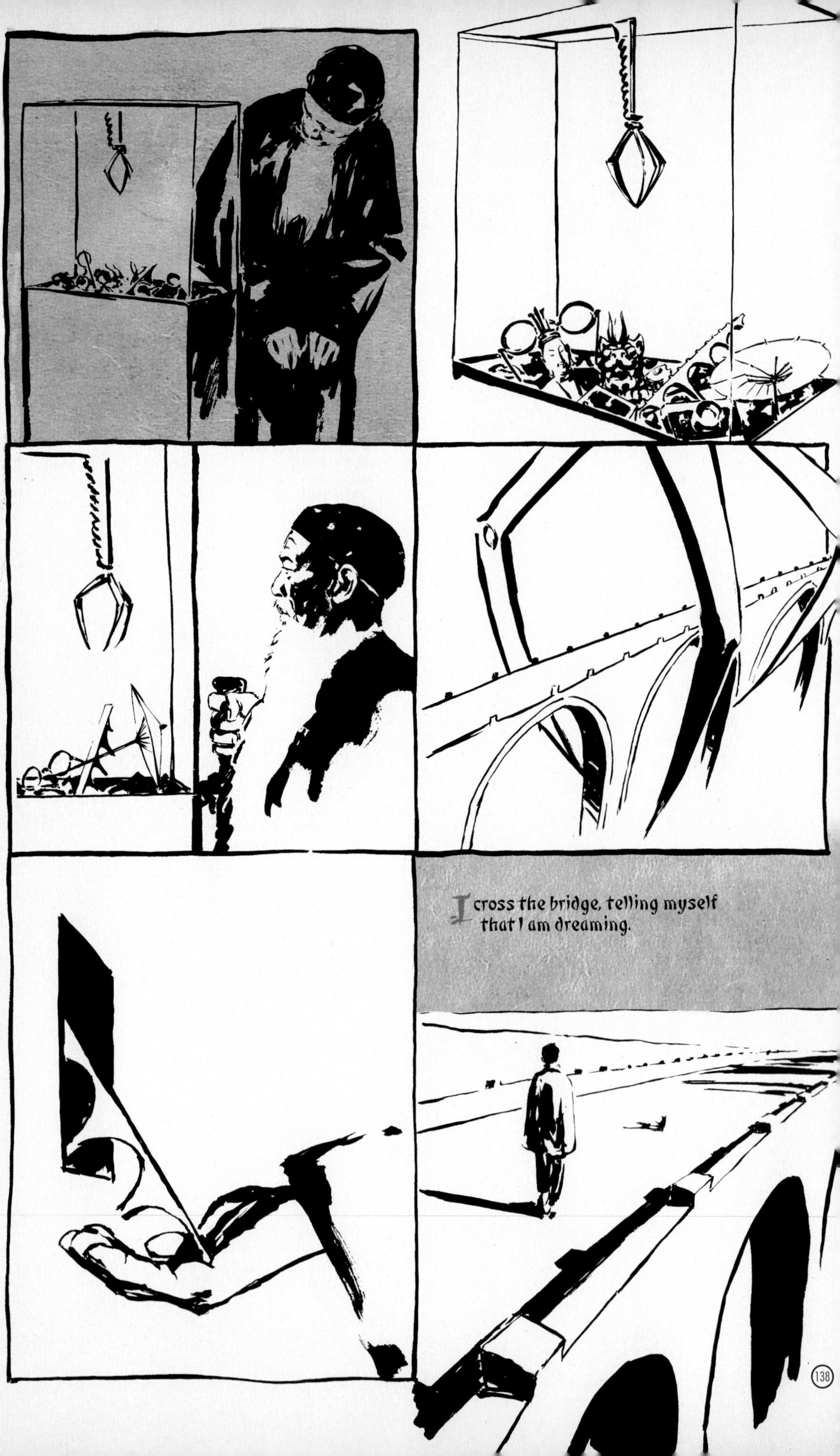
I cross the bridge, telling myself that I am dreaming.

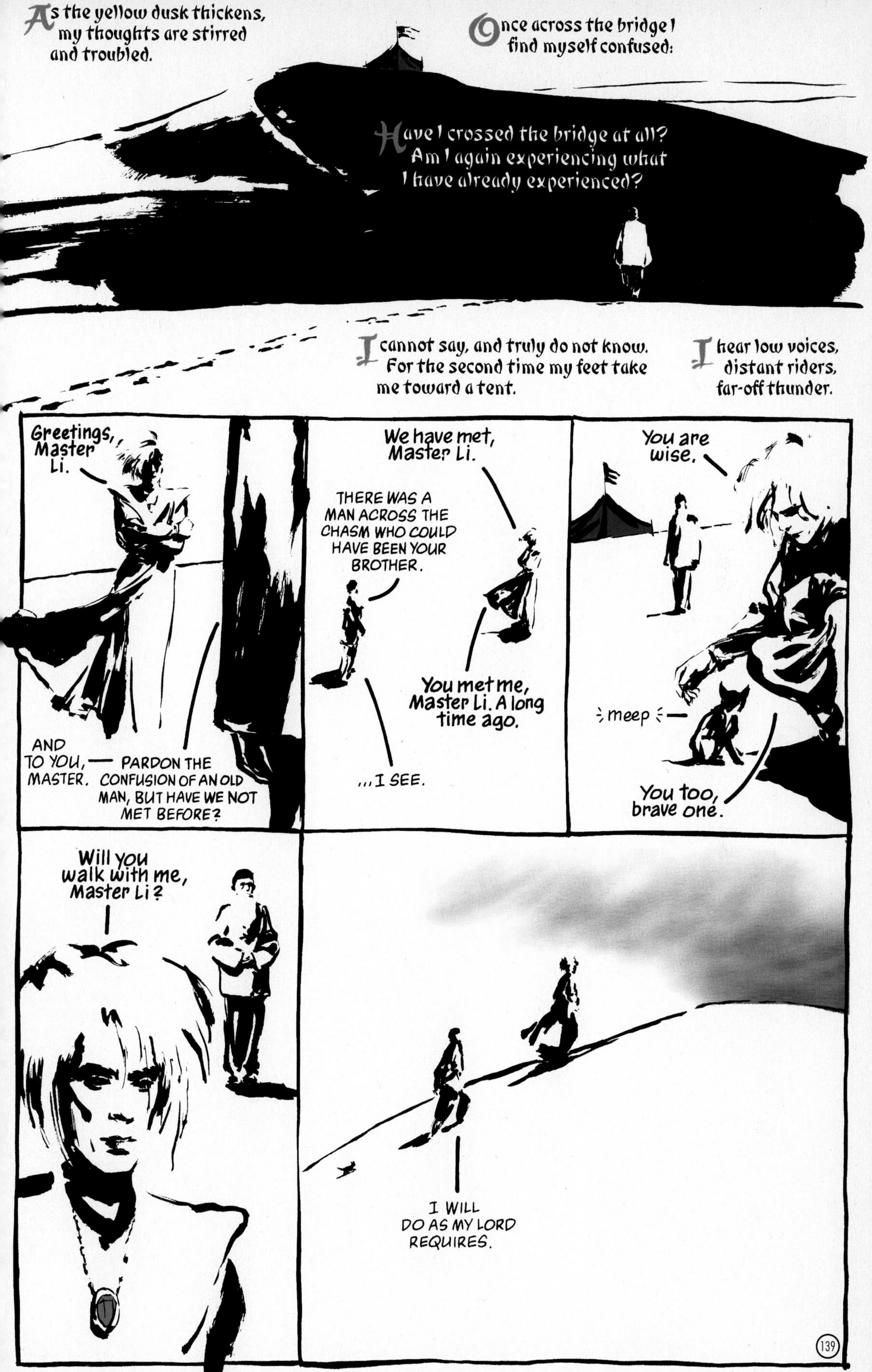

As the yellow dusk thickens, my thoughts are stirred and troubled.
Once across the bridge I find myself confused:
Have I crossed the bridge at all? Am I again experiencing what I have already experienced?
I cannot say, and truly do not know. For the second time my feet take me toward a tent.
I hear low voices, distant riders, far-off thunder.
Greetings, Master Li.
AND TO YOU, MASTER.
PARDON THE CONFUSION OF AN OLD MAN, BUT HAVE WE NOT MET BEFORE?
We have met, Master Li.
THERE WAS A MAN ACROSS THE CHASM WHO COULD HAVE BEEN YOUR BROTHER.
You met me, Master Li. A long time ago.
...I SEE.
You are wise.
meep
You too, brave one.
Will you walk with me, Master Li?
I WILL DO AS MY LORD REQUIRES.

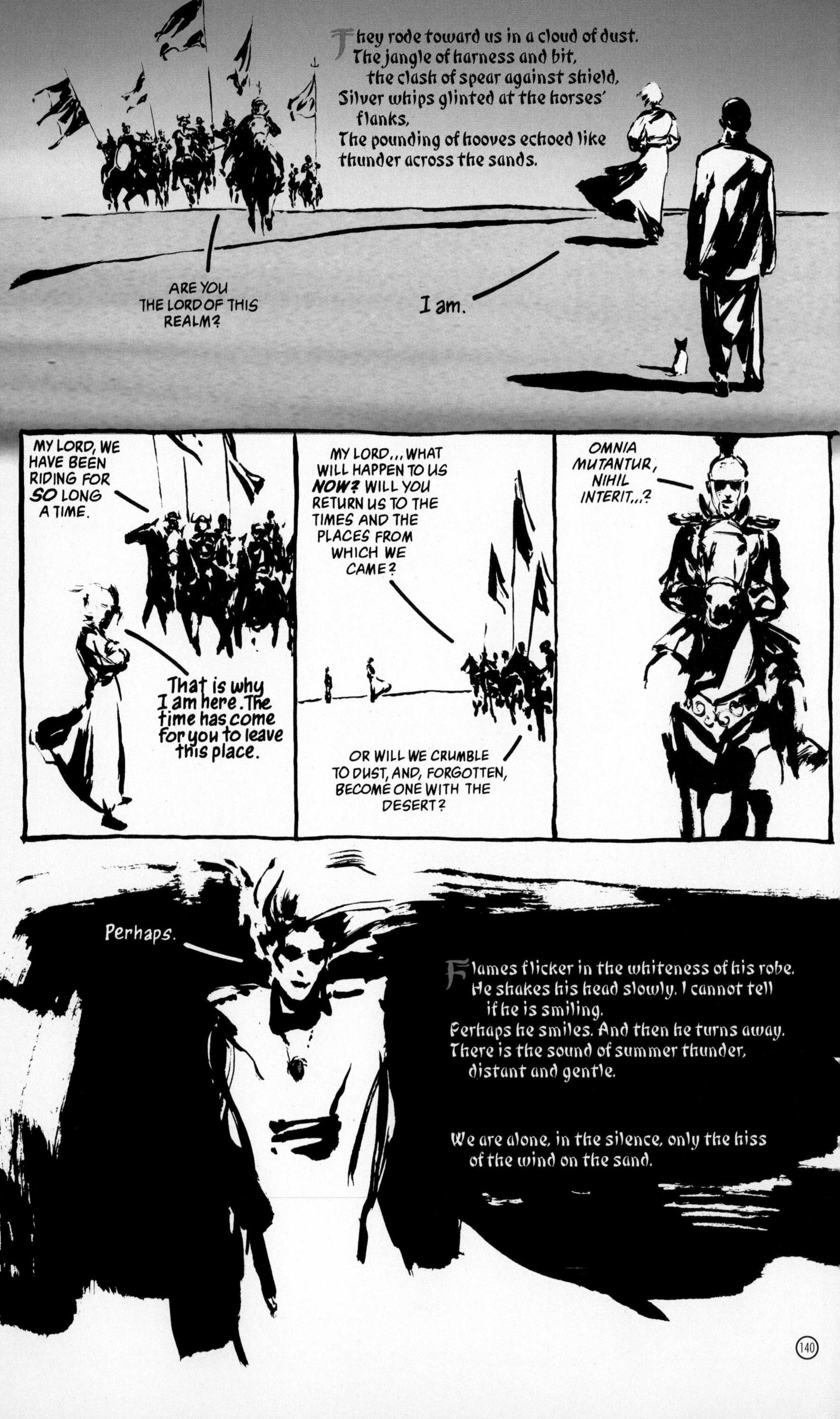
They rode toward us in a cloud of dust.
The jangle of harness and bit,
the clash of spear against shield,
Silver whips glinted at the horses' flanks,
The pounding of hooves echoed like thunder across the sands.
ARE YOU THE LORD OF THIS REALM?
I am.
MY LORD, WE HAVE BEEN RIDING FOR SO LONG A TIME.
That is why I am here. The time has come for you to leave this place.
MY LORD... WHAT WILL HAPPEN TO US NOW? WILL YOU RETURN US TO THE TIMES AND THE PLACES FROM WHICH WE CAME?
OR WILL WE CRUMBLE TO DUST, AND, FORGOTTEN, BECOME ONE WITH THE DESERT?
OMNIA MUTANTUR, NIHIL INTERIT...?
Perhaps.
Flames flicker in the whiteness of his robe.
He shakes his head slowly. I cannot tell if he is smiling.
Perhaps he smiles. And then he turns away.
There is the sound of summer thunder, distant and gentle.
We are alone, in the silence, only the hiss of the wind on the sand.

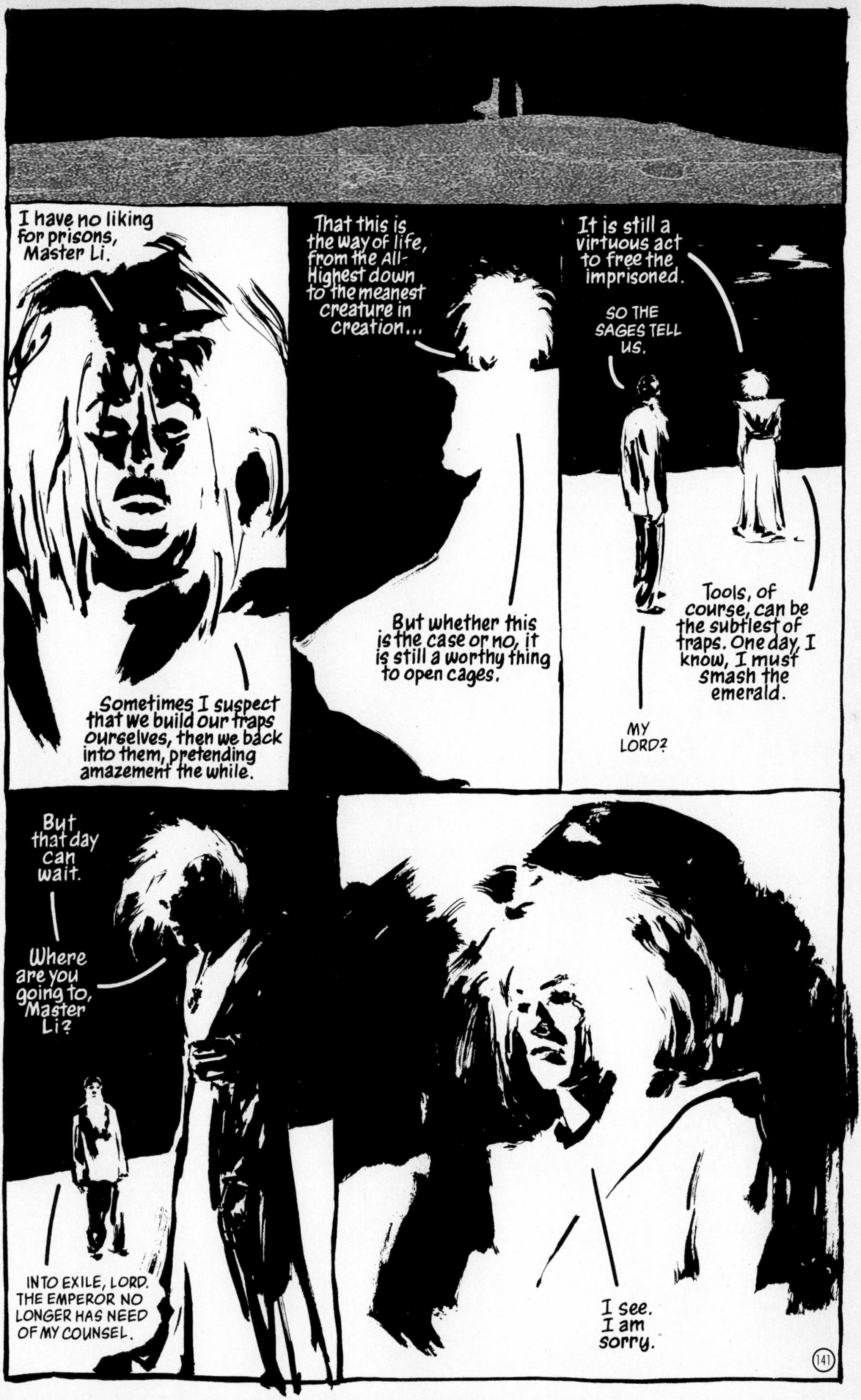
I have no liking for prisons, Master Li.
Sometimes I suspect that we build our traps ourselves, then we back into them, pretending amazement the while.
That this is the way of life, from the All-Highest down to the meanest creature in creation...
But whether this is the case or no, it is still a worthy thing to open cages.
It is still a virtuous act to free the imprisoned.
SO THE SAGES TELL US.
Tools, of course, can be the subtlest of traps. One day, I know, I must smash the emerald.
MY LORD?
But that day can wait.
Where are you going to, Master Li?
INTO EXILE, LORD. THE EMPEROR NO LONGER HAS NEED OF MY COUNSEL.
I see. I am sorry.
141

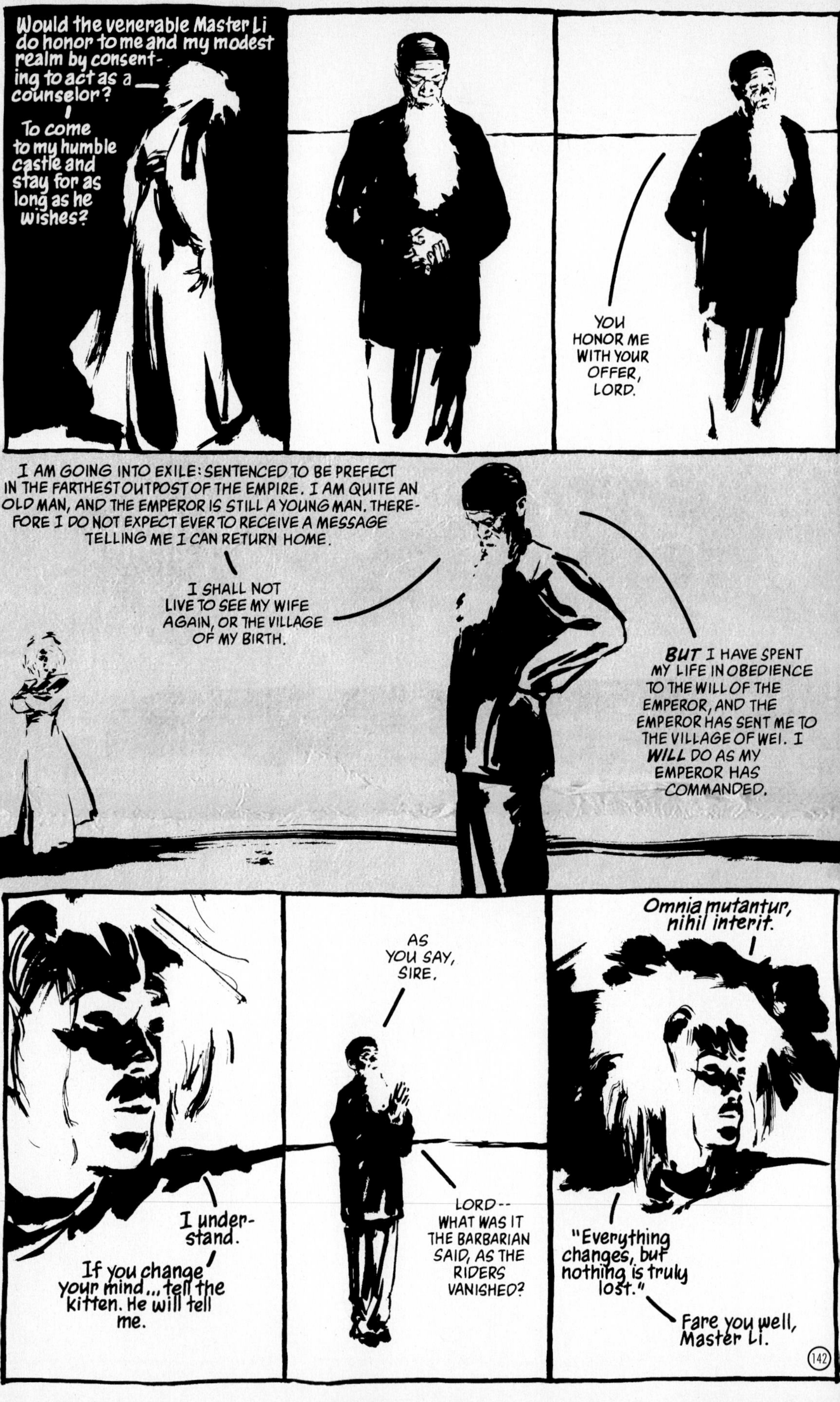
Would the venerable Master Li do honor to me and my modest realm by consenting to act as a counselor?
To come to my humble castle and stay for as long as he wishes?
YOU HONOR ME WITH YOUR OFFER, LORD.
I AM GOING INTO EXILE: SENTENCED TO BE PREFECT IN THE FARTHEST OUTPOST OF THE EMPIRE. I AM QUITE AN OLD MAN, AND THE EMPEROR IS STILL A YOUNG MAN. THEREFORE I DO NOT EXPECT EVER TO RECEIVE A MESSAGE TELLING ME I CAN RETURN HOME.
I SHALL NOT LIVE TO SEE MY WIFE AGAIN, OR THE VILLAGE OF MY BIRTH.
BUT I HAVE SPENT MY LIFE IN OBEDIENCE TO THE WILL OF THE EMPEROR, AND THE EMPEROR HAS SENT ME TO THE VILLAGE OF WEI. I WILL DO AS MY EMPEROR HAS COMMANDED.
I understand.
If you change your mind... tell the kitten. He will tell me.
AS YOU SAY, SIRE.
LORD-- WHAT WAS IT THE BARBARIAN SAID, AS THE RIDERS VANISHED?
Omnia mutantur, nihil interit.
"Everything changes, but nothing is truly lost."
Fare you well, Master Li.

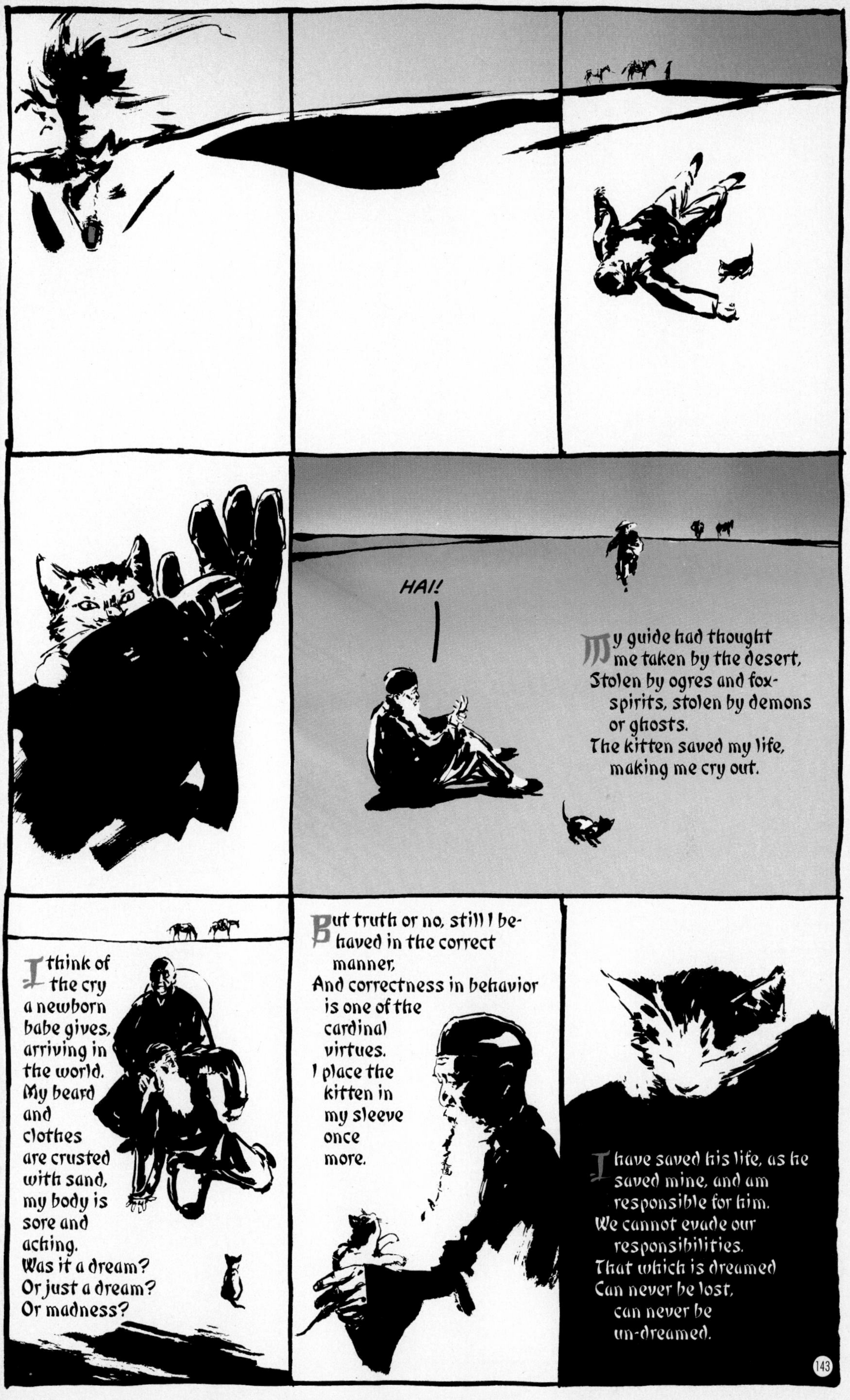
HAI!
My guide had thought me taken by the desert,
Stolen by ogres and fox-spirits, stolen by demons or ghosts.
The kitten saved my life, making me cry out.
I think of the cry a newborn babe gives, arriving in the world.
My beard and clothes are crusted with sand, my body is sore and aching.
Was it a dream?
Or just a dream?
Or madness?
But truth or no, still I behaved in the correct manner,
And correctness in behavior is one of the cardinal virtues.
I place the kitten in my sleeve once more.
I have saved his life, as he saved mine, and am responsible for him.
We cannot evade our responsibilities.
That which is dreamed
Can never be lost,
can never be un-dreamed.

I shall truly set brush to paper when I reach the village of Wei, old frie...
My thoughts go to you; and to my wife, alone and disgraced in the Co...
And to my son.

I am banished to the grey waste at the end of the world,
    but I mourn myself no longer; I cherish the pain in my hand.
I imagine the taste of the mulberries in the violet dusk.
And tomorrow I shall arrive in the town of Wei.

Only the phoenix arises
    and does not descend.
And everything changes.

And nothing...
    truly los...

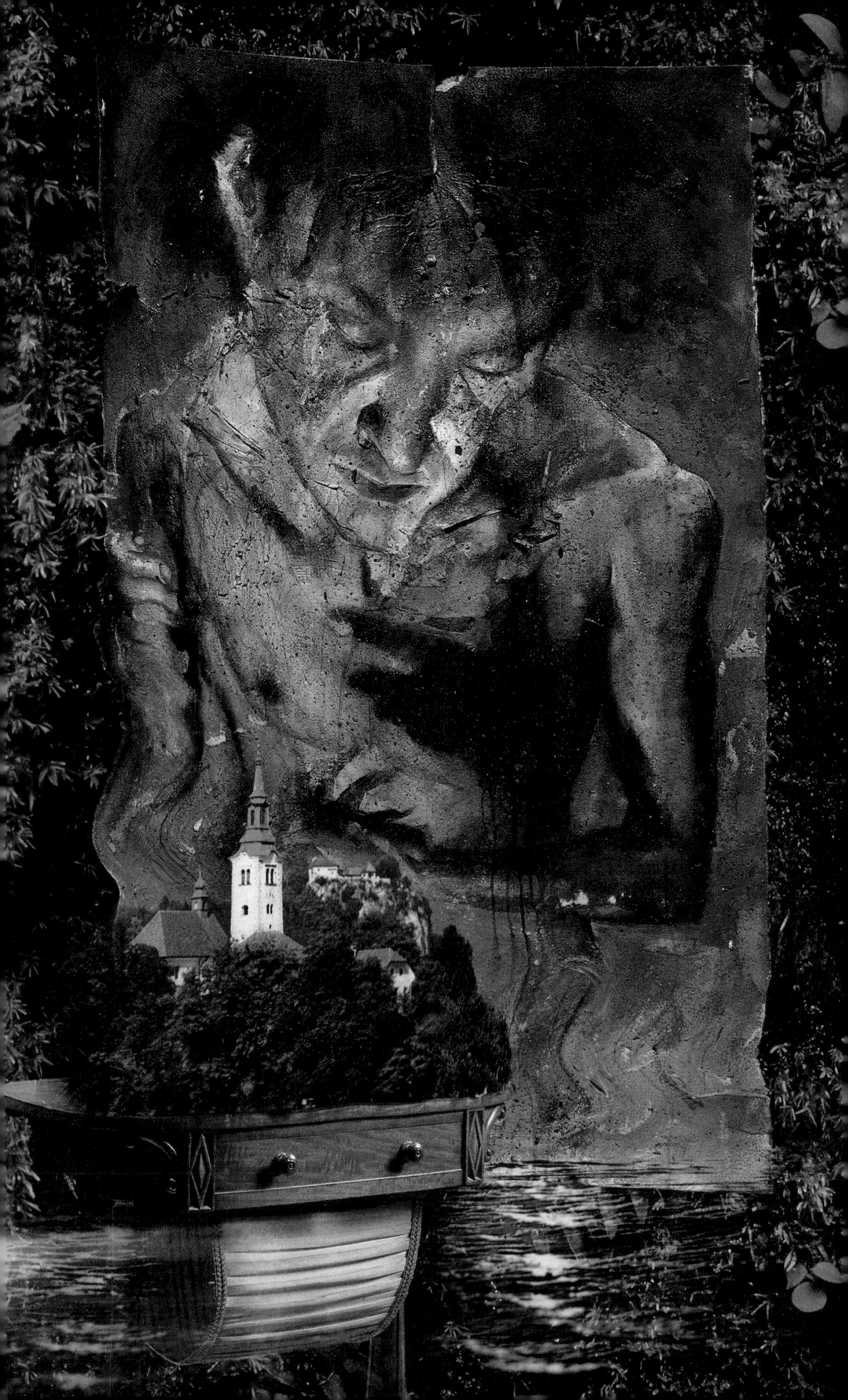

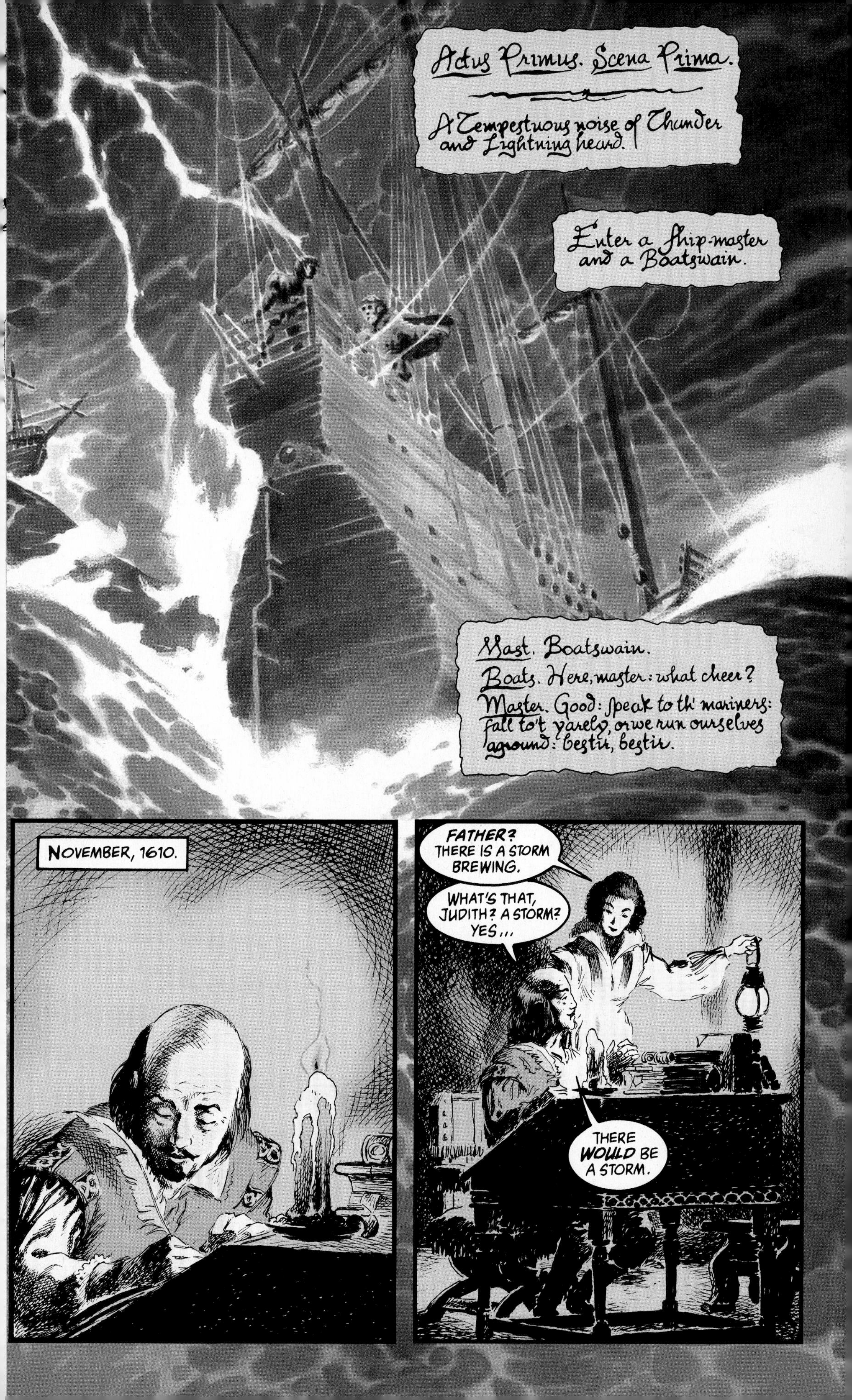
Actus Primus. Scena Prima.
A Tempestuous noise of Thunder and Lightning heard.
Enter a Ship-master and a Boatswain.
Mast. Boatswain.
Boats. Here, master: what cheer?
Master. Good: speak to th' mariners: fall to't yarely, or we run ourselves aground: bestir, bestir.
NOVEMBER, 1610.
FATHER? THERE IS A STORM BREWING.
WHAT'S THAT, JUDITH? A STORM? YES...
THERE WOULD BE A STORM.

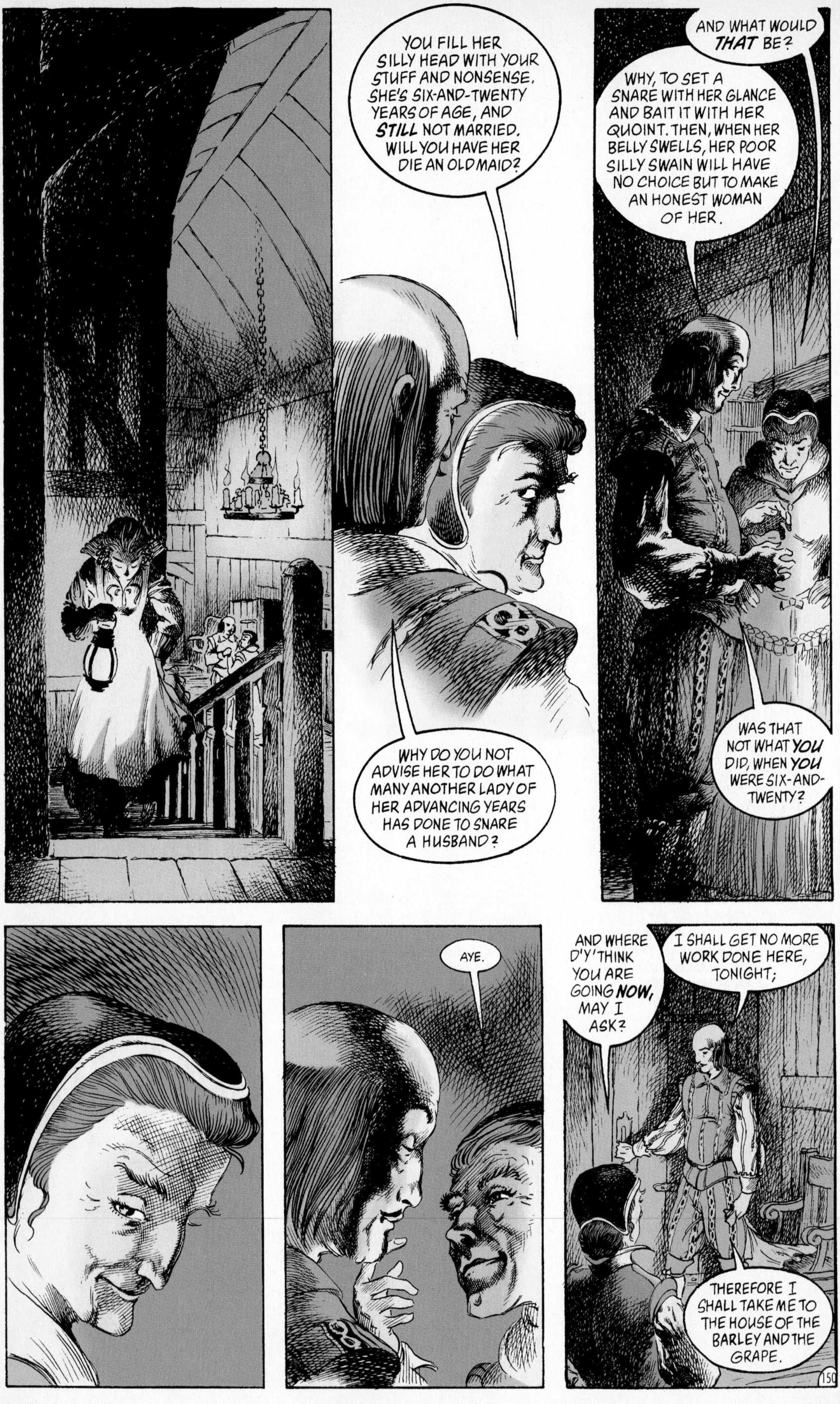

YOU FILL HER SILLY HEAD WITH YOUR STUFF AND NONSENSE. SHE'S SIX-AND-TWENTY YEARS OF AGE, AND STILL NOT MARRIED. WILL YOU HAVE HER DIE AN OLD MAID?
WHY DO YOU NOT ADVISE HER TO DO WHAT MANY ANOTHER LADY OF HER ADVANCING YEARS HAS DONE TO SNARE A HUSBAND?
AND WHAT WOULD THAT BE?
WHY, TO SET A SNARE WITH HER GLANCE AND BAIT IT WITH HER QUOINT. THEN, WHEN HER BELLY SWELLS, HER POOR SILLY SWAIN WILL HAVE NO CHOICE BUT TO MAKE AN HONEST WOMAN OF HER.
WAS THAT NOT WHAT YOU DID, WHEN YOU WERE SIX-AND-TWENTY?
AYE.
I SHALL GET NO MORE WORK DONE HERE, TONIGHT;
AND WHERE D'Y'THINK YOU ARE GOING NOW, MAY I ASK?
THEREFORE I SHALL TAKE ME TO THE HOUSE OF THE BARLEY AND THE GRAPE.

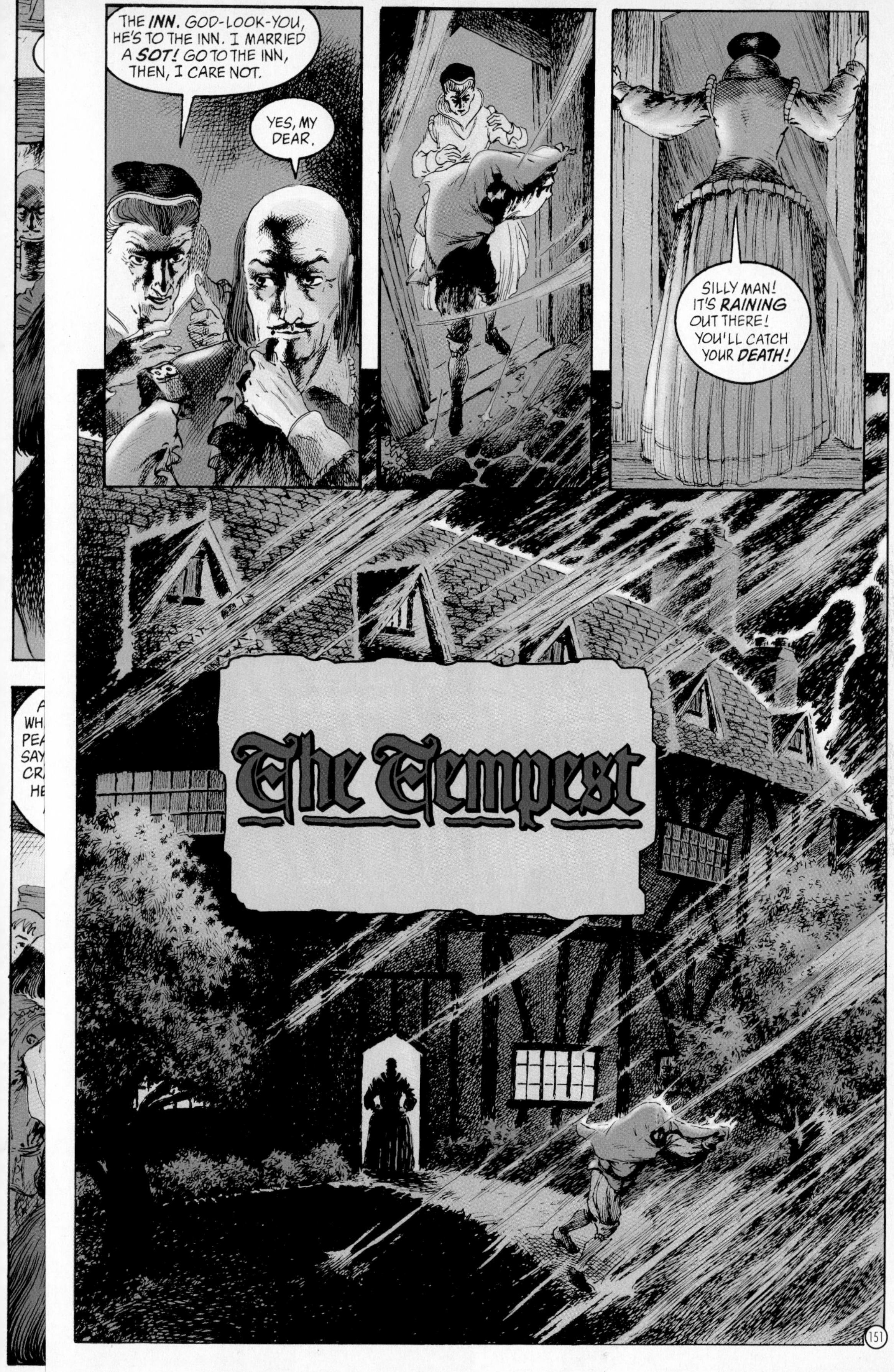
THE INN. GOD-LOOK-YOU, HE'S TO THE INN. I MARRIED A SOT! GO TO THE INN, THEN, I CARE NOT.
YES, MY DEAR.
SILLY MAN! IT'S RAINING OUT THERE! YOU'LL CATCH YOUR DEATH!
The Tempest

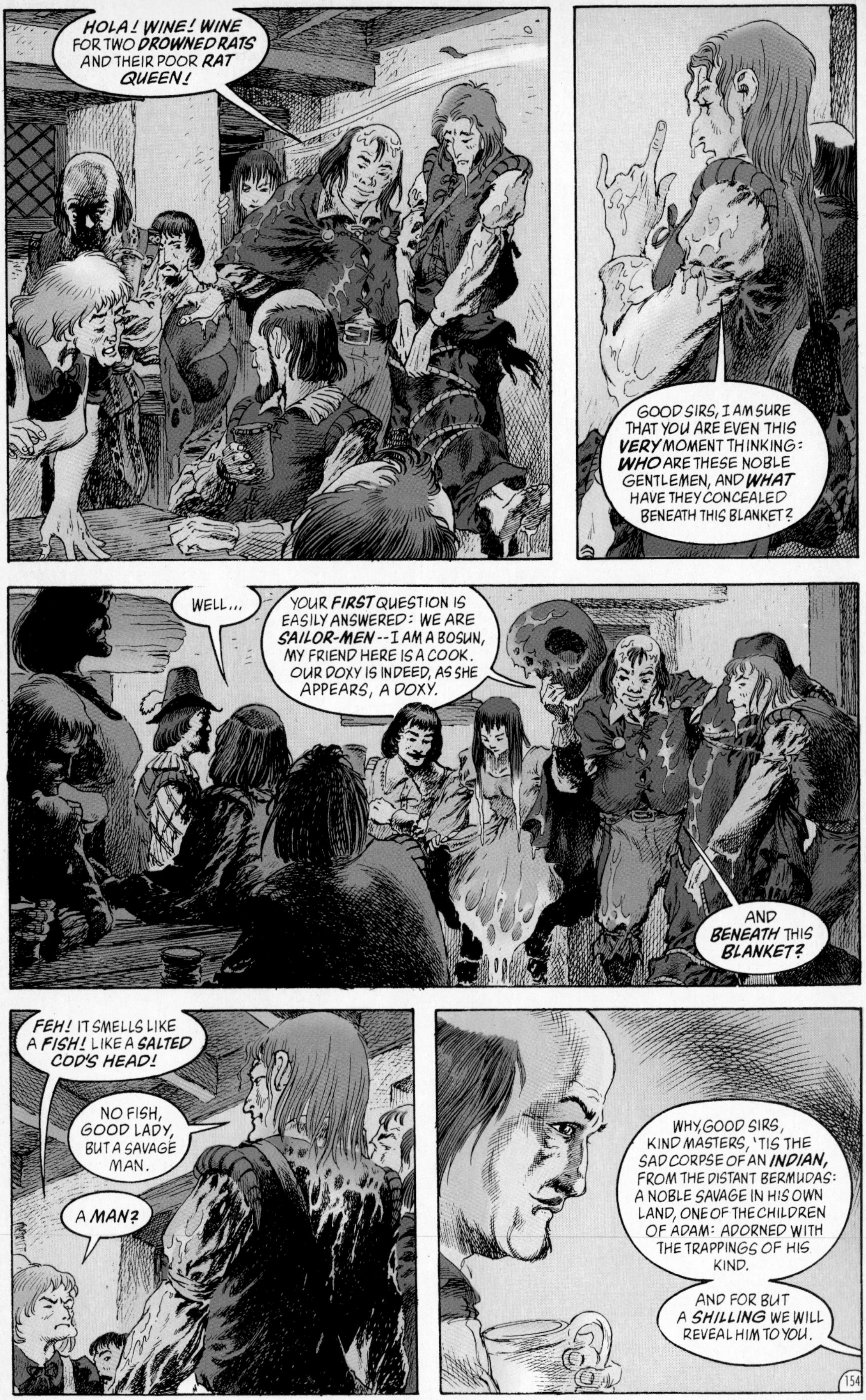
HOLA! WINE! WINE FOR TWO DROWNED RATS AND THEIR POOR RAT QUEEN!
GOOD SIRS, I AM SURE THAT YOU ARE EVEN THIS VERY MOMENT THINKING: WHO ARE THESE NOBLE GENTLEMEN, AND WHAT HAVE THEY CONCEALED BENEATH THIS BLANKET?
WELL...
YOUR FIRST QUESTION IS EASILY ANSWERED: WE ARE SAILOR-MEN--I AM A BOSUN, MY FRIEND HERE IS A COOK. OUR DOXY IS INDEED, AS SHE APPEARS, A DOXY.
AND BENEATH THIS BLANKET?
FEH! IT SMELLS LIKE A FISH! LIKE A SALTED COD'S HEAD!
NO FISH, GOOD LADY, BUT A SAVAGE MAN.
A MAN?
WHY, GOOD SIRS, KIND MASTERS, 'TIS THE SAD CORPSE OF AN INDIAN, FROM THE DISTANT BERMUDAS: A NOBLE SAVAGE IN HIS OWN LAND, ONE OF THE CHILDREN OF ADAM: ADORNED WITH THE TRAPPINGS OF HIS KIND.
AND FOR BUT A SHILLING WE WILL REVEAL HIM TO YOU.

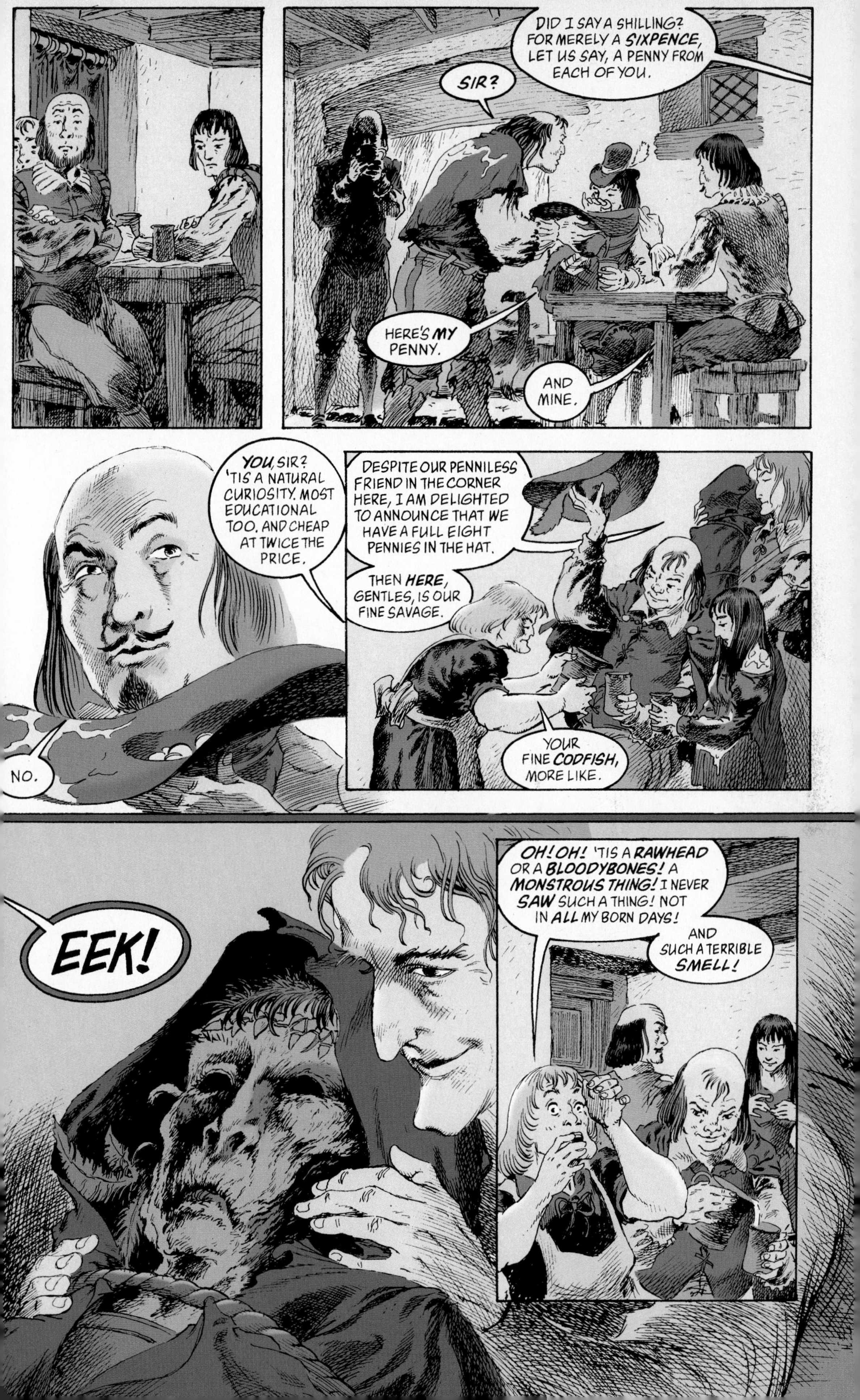
SIR?
DID I SAY A SHILLING? FOR MERELY A SIXPENCE, LET US SAY, A PENNY FROM EACH OF YOU.
HERE'S MY PENNY.
AND MINE.
YOU, SIR? 'TIS A NATURAL CURIOSITY. MOST EDUCATIONAL TOO, AND CHEAP AT TWICE THE PRICE.
NO.
DESPITE OUR PENNILESS FRIEND IN THE CORNER HERE, I AM DELIGHTED TO ANNOUNCE THAT WE HAVE A FULL EIGHT PENNIES IN THE HAT.
THEN HERE, GENTLES, IS OUR FINE SAVAGE.
YOUR FINE CODFISH, MORE LIKE.
EEK!
OH! OH! 'TIS A RAWHEAD OR A BLOODYBONES! A MONSTROUS THING! I NEVER SAW SUCH A THING! NOT IN ALL MY BORN DAYS!
AND SUCH A TERRIBLE SMELL!

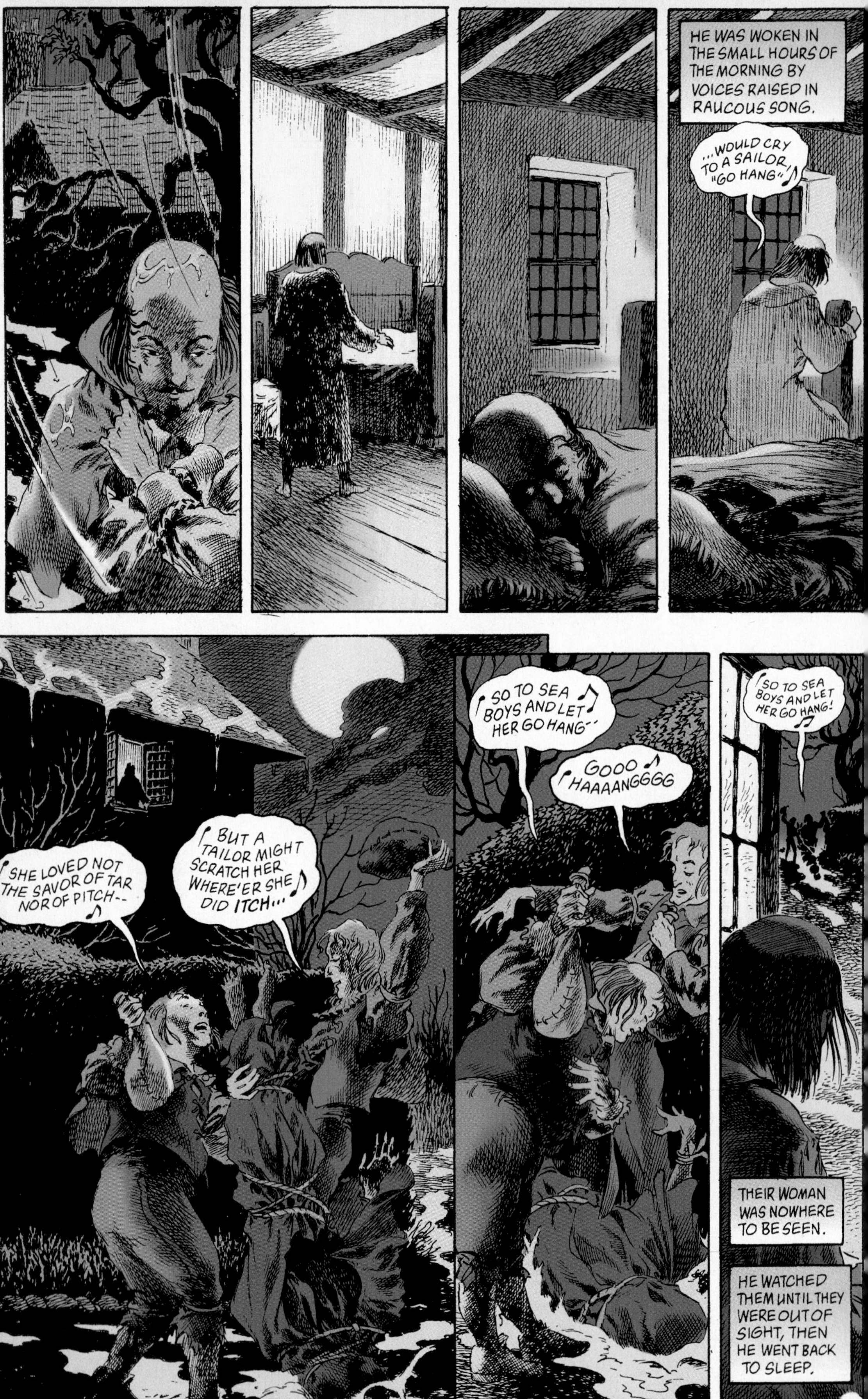
HE WAS WOKEN IN THE SMALL HOURS OF THE MORNING BY VOICES RAISED IN RAUCOUS SONG.
...WOULD CRY TO A SAILOR "GO HANG"
SHE LOVED NOT THE SAVOR OF TAR NOR OF PITCH--
BUT A TAILOR MIGHT SCRATCH HER WHERE'ER SHE DID ITCH...
SO TO SEA BOYS AND LET HER GO HANG--
GOOO HAAAANGGGG
SO TO SEA BOYS AND LET HER GO HANG!
THEIR WOMAN WAS NOWHERE TO BE SEEN.
HE WATCHED THEM UNTIL THEY WERE OUT OF SIGHT, THEN HE WENT BACK TO SLEEP.
156

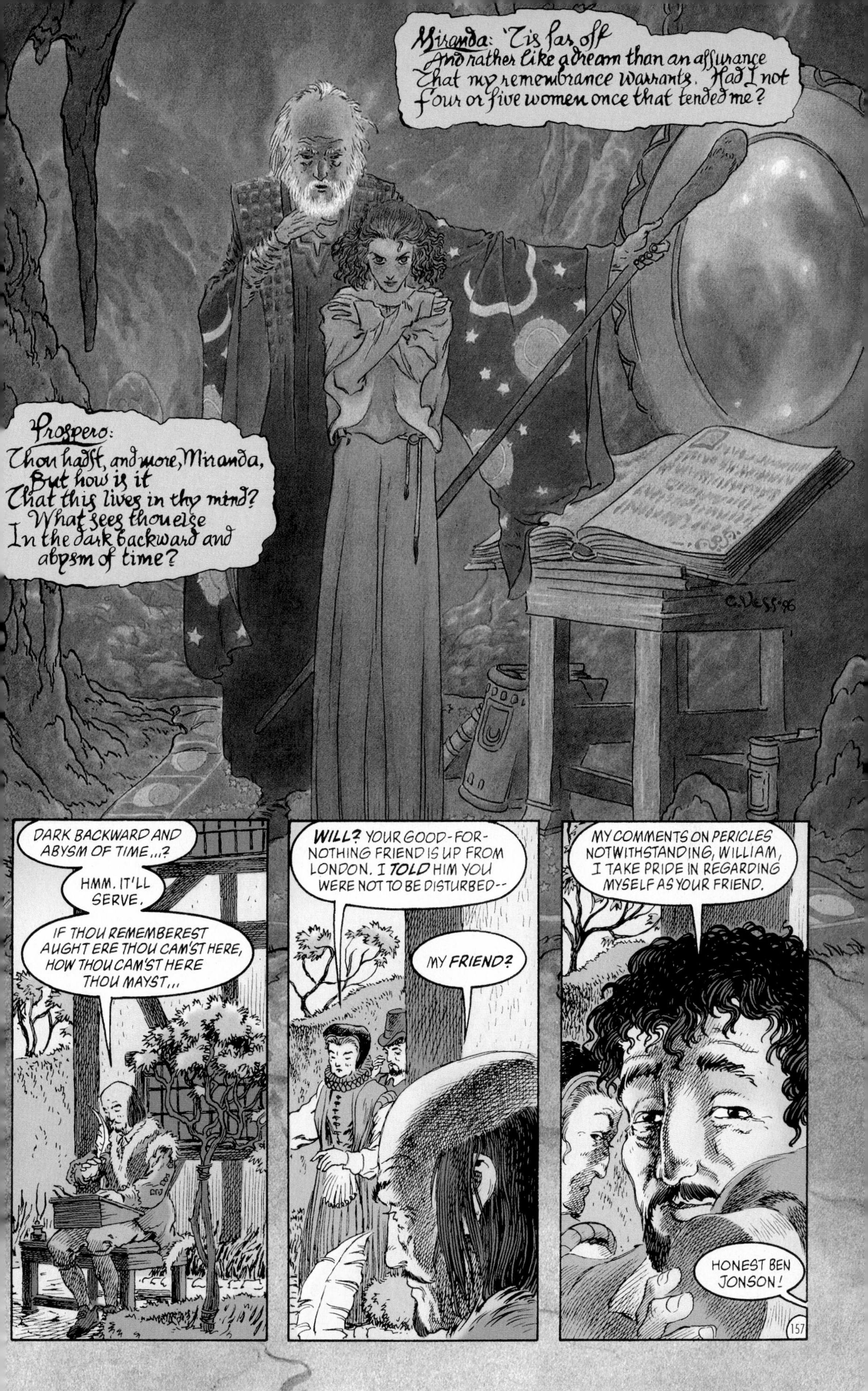
Miranda: 'Tis far off
And rather like a dream than an assurance
That my remembrance warrants. Had I not
four or five women once that tended me?
Prospero:
Thou hadst, and more, Miranda,
But how is it
That this lives in thy mind?
What sees thou else
In the dark backward and
abysm of time?
C. VESS '96
DARK BACKWARD AND ABYSM OF TIME...?
HMM. IT'LL SERVE.
IF THOU REMEMBEREST AUGHT ERE THOU CAM'ST HERE, HOW THOU CAM'ST HERE THOU MAYST...
WILL? YOUR GOOD-FOR-NOTHING FRIEND IS UP FROM LONDON. I TOLD HIM YOU WERE NOT TO BE DISTURBED--
MY FRIEND?
MY COMMENTS ON PERICLES NOTWITHSTANDING, WILLIAM, I TAKE PRIDE IN REGARDING MYSELF AS YOUR FRIEND.
HONEST BEN JONSON!

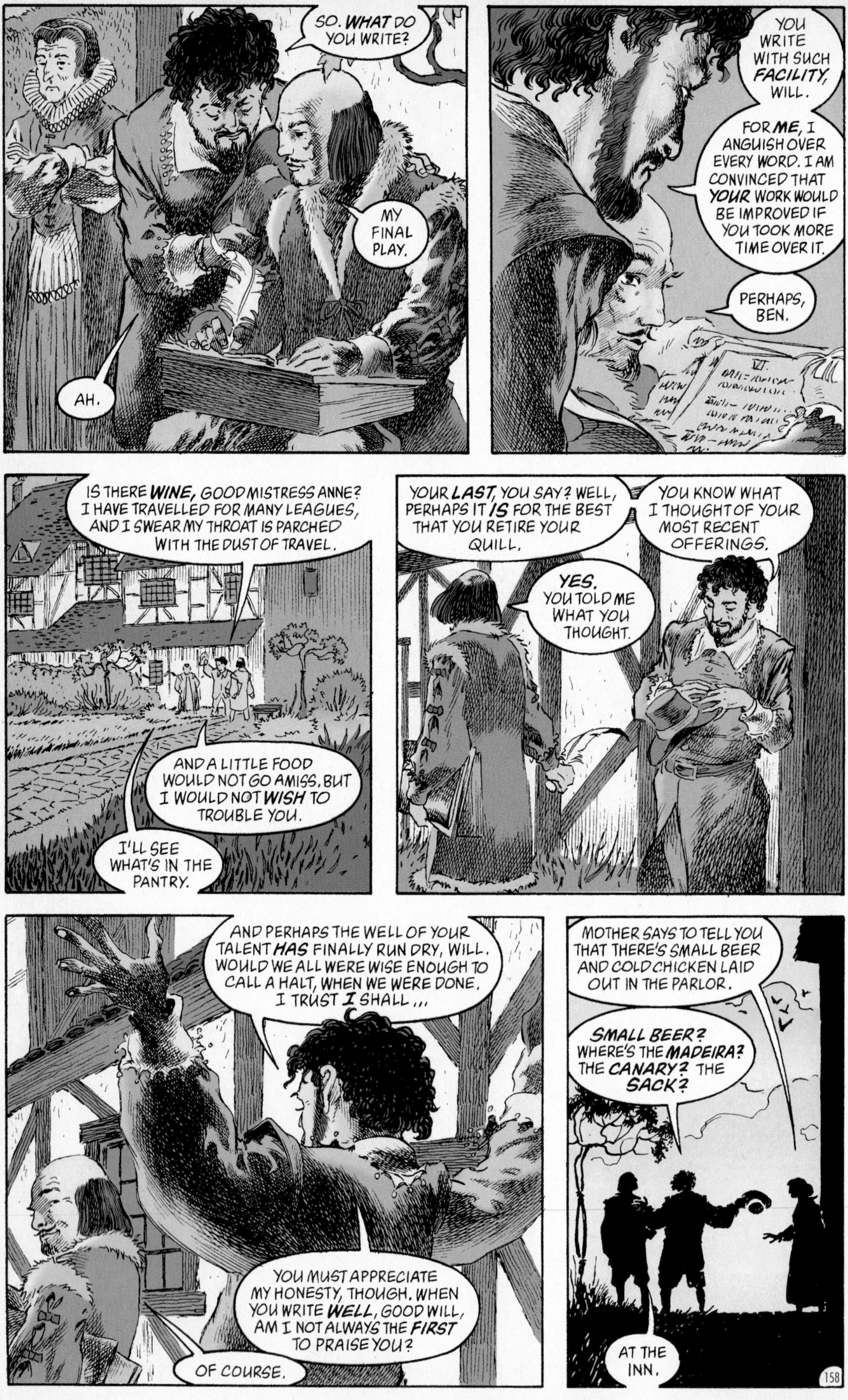
SO. WHAT DO YOU WRITE?
MY FINAL PLAY.
AH.
YOU WRITE WITH SUCH FACILITY, WILL.
FOR ME, I ANGUISH OVER EVERY WORD. I AM CONVINCED THAT YOUR WORK WOULD BE IMPROVED IF YOU TOOK MORE TIME OVER IT.
PERHAPS, BEN.
IS THERE WINE, GOOD MISTRESS ANNE? I HAVE TRAVELLED FOR MANY LEAGUES, AND I SWEAR MY THROAT IS PARCHED WITH THE DUST OF TRAVEL.
AND A LITTLE FOOD WOULD NOT GO AMISS, BUT I WOULD NOT WISH TO TROUBLE YOU.
I'LL SEE WHAT'S IN THE PANTRY.
YOUR LAST, YOU SAY? WELL, PERHAPS IT IS FOR THE BEST THAT YOU RETIRE YOUR QUILL.
YOU KNOW WHAT I THOUGHT OF YOUR MOST RECENT OFFERINGS.
YES. YOU TOLD ME WHAT YOU THOUGHT.
AND PERHAPS THE WELL OF YOUR TALENT HAS FINALLY RUN DRY, WILL. WOULD WE ALL WERE WISE ENOUGH TO CALL A HALT, WHEN WE WERE DONE. I TRUST I SHALL ...
YOU MUST APPRECIATE MY HONESTY, THOUGH. WHEN YOU WRITE WELL, GOOD WILL, AM I NOT ALWAYS THE FIRST TO PRAISE YOU?
OF COURSE.
MOTHER SAYS TO TELL YOU THAT THERE'S SMALL BEER AND COLD CHICKEN LAID OUT IN THE PARLOR.
SMALL BEER? WHERE'S THE MADEIRA? THE CANARY? THE SACK?
AT THE INN.

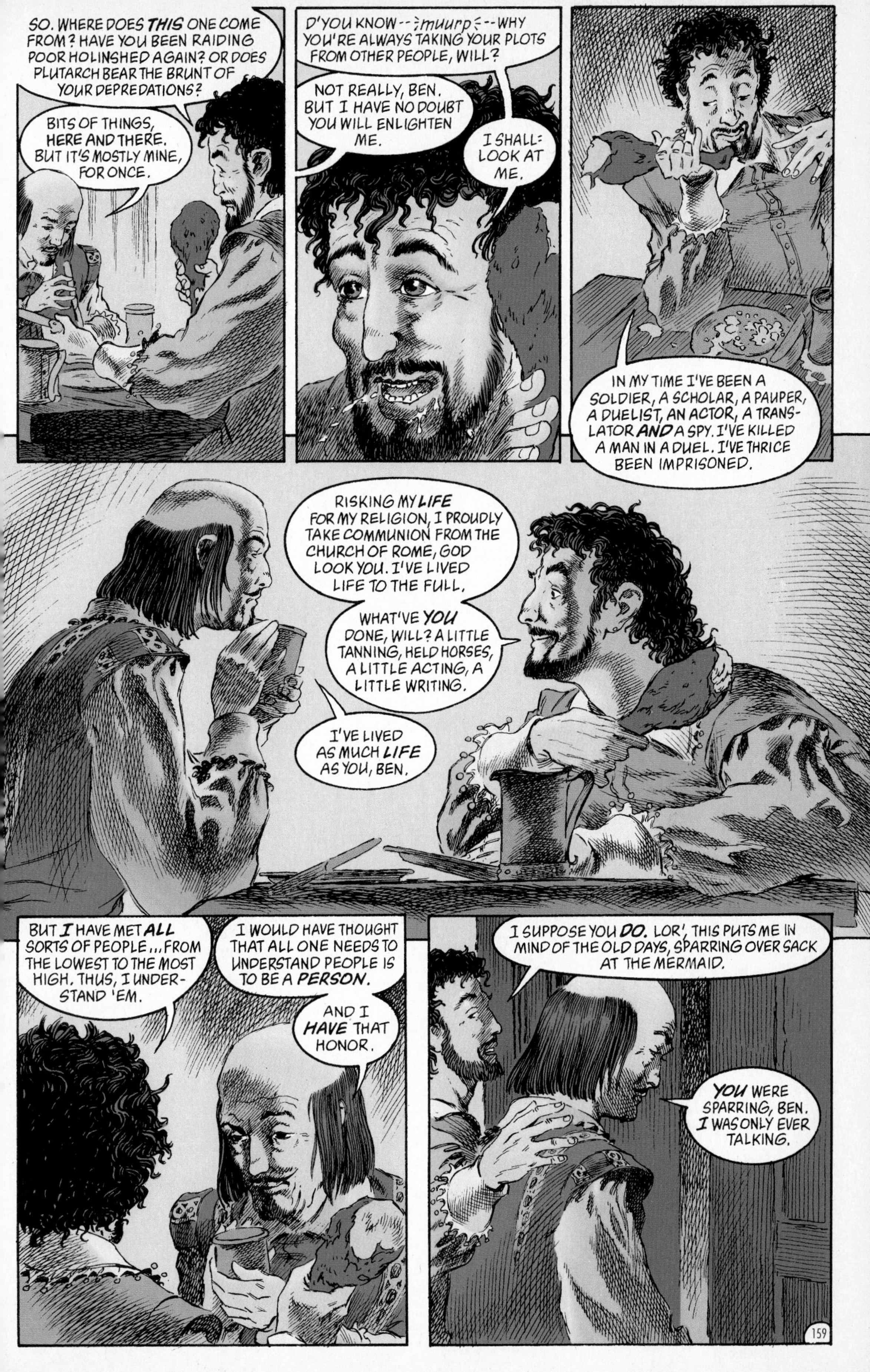

SO. WHERE DOES THIS ONE COME FROM? HAVE YOU BEEN RAIDING POOR HOLINSHED AGAIN? OR DOES PLUTARCH BEAR THE BRUNT OF YOUR DEPREDATIONS?
BITS OF THINGS, HERE AND THERE. BUT IT'S MOSTLY MINE, FOR ONCE.
D'YOU KNOW-- ;muurp; --WHY YOU'RE ALWAYS TAKING YOUR PLOTS FROM OTHER PEOPLE, WILL?
NOT REALLY, BEN. BUT I HAVE NO DOUBT YOU WILL ENLIGHTEN ME.
I SHALL: LOOK AT ME.
IN MY TIME I'VE BEEN A SOLDIER, A SCHOLAR, A PAUPER, A DUELIST, AN ACTOR, A TRANSLATOR AND A SPY. I'VE KILLED A MAN IN A DUEL. I'VE THRICE BEEN IMPRISONED.
RISKING MY LIFE FOR MY RELIGION, I PROUDLY TAKE COMMUNION FROM THE CHURCH OF ROME, GOD LOOK YOU. I'VE LIVED LIFE TO THE FULL.
WHAT'VE YOU DONE, WILL? A LITTLE TANNING, HELD HORSES, A LITTLE ACTING, A LITTLE WRITING.
I'VE LIVED AS MUCH LIFE AS YOU, BEN.
BUT I HAVE MET ALL SORTS OF PEOPLE... FROM THE LOWEST TO THE MOST HIGH. THUS, I UNDERSTAND 'EM.
I WOULD HAVE THOUGHT THAT ALL ONE NEEDS TO UNDERSTAND PEOPLE IS TO BE A PERSON.
AND I HAVE THAT HONOR.
I SUPPOSE YOU DO. LOR', THIS PUTS ME IN MIND OF THE OLD DAYS, SPARRING OVER SACK AT THE MERMAID.
YOU WERE SPARRING, BEN. I WAS ONLY EVER TALKING.

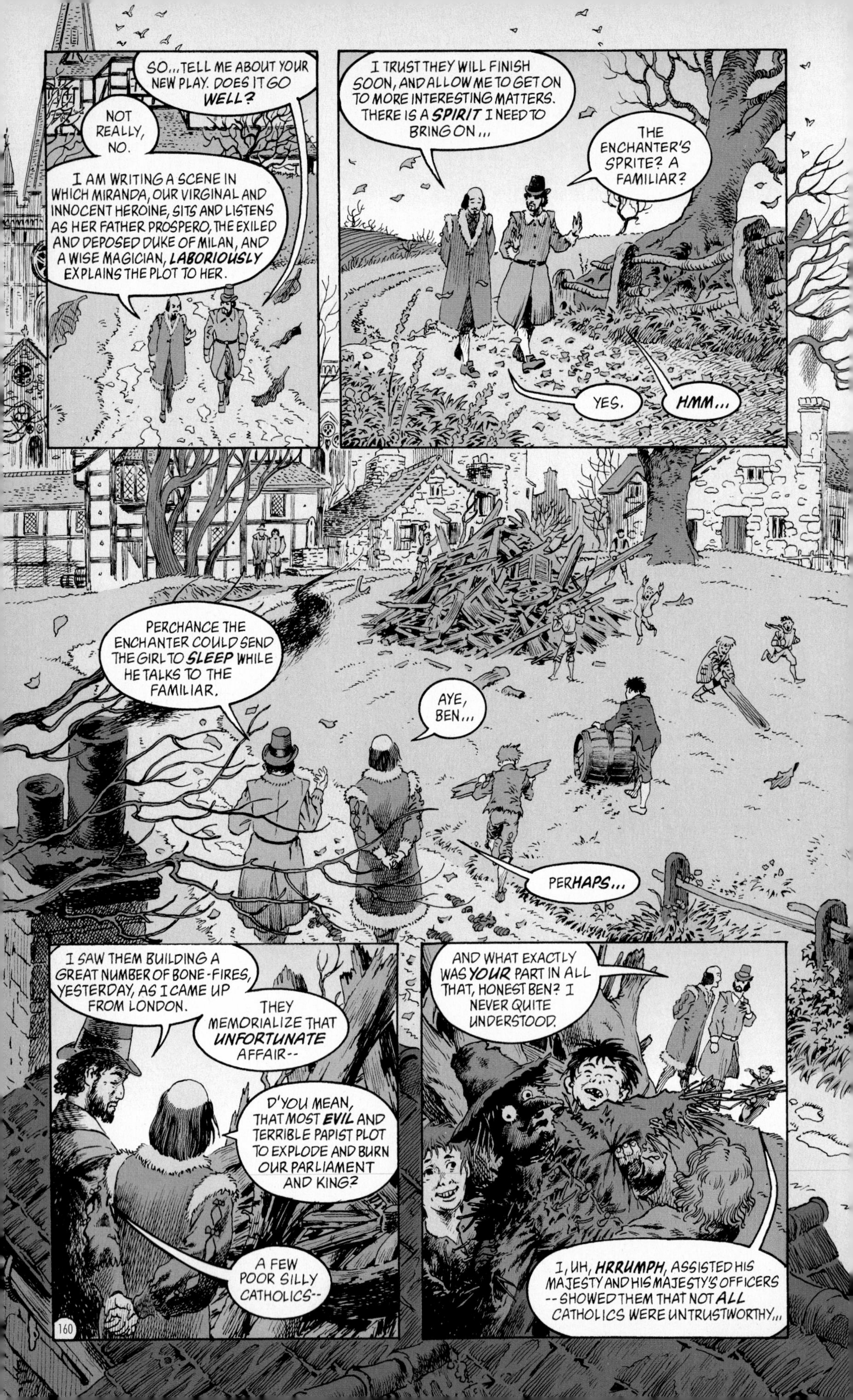

SO... TELL ME ABOUT YOUR NEW PLAY. DOES IT GO WELL?
NOT REALLY, NO.
I AM WRITING A SCENE IN WHICH MIRANDA, OUR VIRGINAL AND INNOCENT HEROINE, SITS AND LISTENS AS HER FATHER PROSPERO, THE EXILED AND DEPOSED DUKE OF MILAN, AND A WISE MAGICIAN, LABORIOUSLY EXPLAINS THE PLOT TO HER.
I TRUST THEY WILL FINISH SOON, AND ALLOW ME TO GET ON TO MORE INTERESTING MATTERS. THERE IS A SPIRIT I NEED TO BRING ON...
THE ENCHANTER'S SPRITE? A FAMILIAR?
YES.
HMM...
PERCHANCE THE ENCHANTER COULD SEND THE GIRL TO SLEEP WHILE HE TALKS TO THE FAMILIAR.
AYE, BEN...
PERHAPS...
I SAW THEM BUILDING A GREAT NUMBER OF BONE-FIRES, YESTERDAY, AS I CAME UP FROM LONDON.
THEY MEMORIALIZE THAT UNFORTUNATE AFFAIR--
D'YOU MEAN, THAT MOST EVIL AND TERRIBLE PAPIST PLOT TO EXPLODE AND BURN OUR PARLIAMENT AND KING?
A FEW POOR SILLY CATHOLICS--
AND WHAT EXACTLY WAS YOUR PART IN ALL THAT, HONEST BEN? I NEVER QUITE UNDERSTOOD.
I, UH, HRRUMPH, ASSISTED HIS MAJESTY AND HIS MAJESTY'S OFFICERS -- SHOWED THEM THAT NOT ALL CATHOLICS WERE UNTRUSTWORTHY...

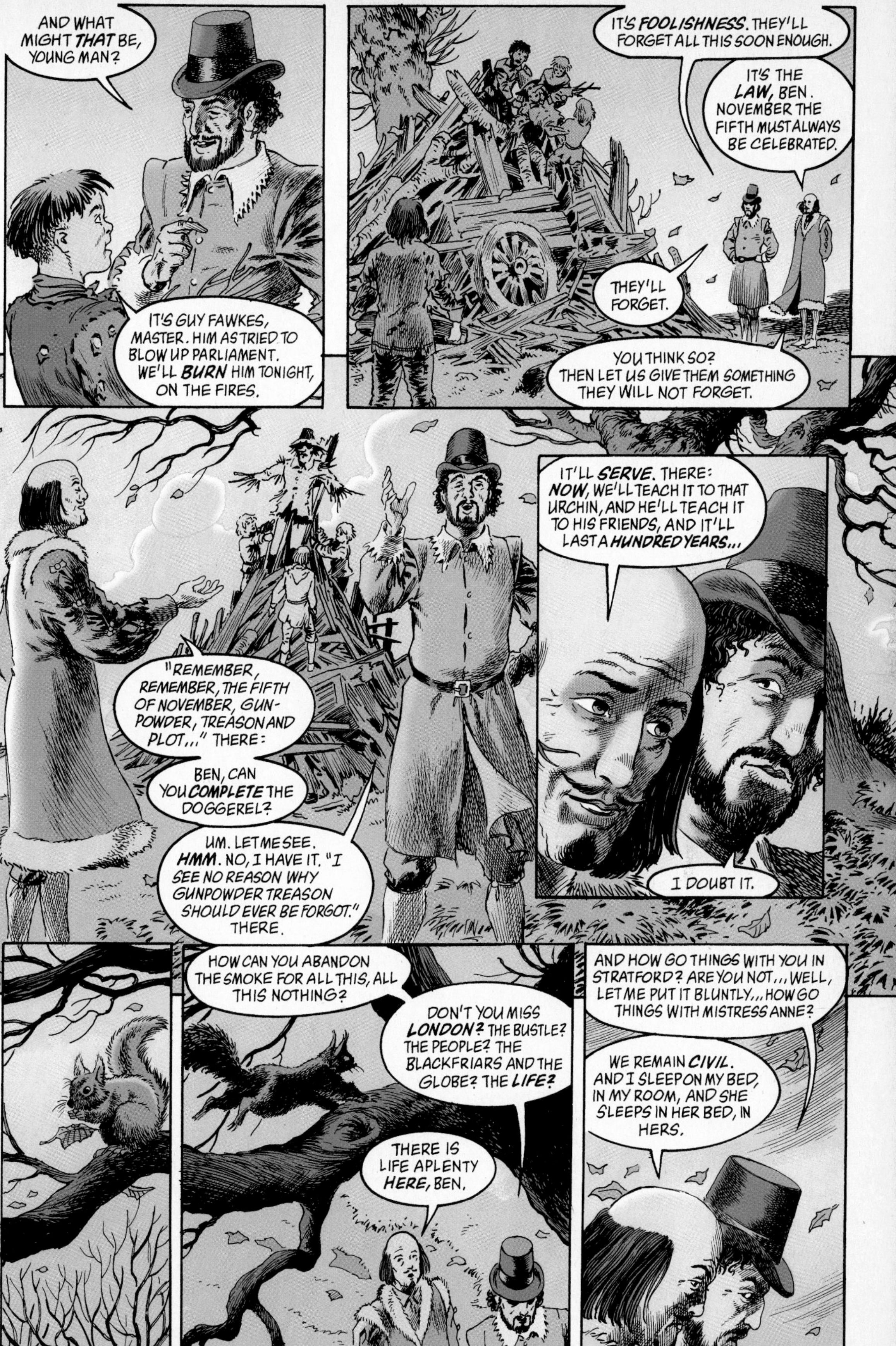
AND WHAT MIGHT THAT BE, YOUNG MAN?
IT'S GUY FAWKES, MASTER. HIM AS TRIED TO BLOW UP PARLIAMENT. WE'LL BURN HIM TONIGHT, ON THE FIRES.
IT'S FOOLISHNESS. THEY'LL FORGET ALL THIS SOON ENOUGH.
IT'S THE LAW, BEN. NOVEMBER THE FIFTH MUST ALWAYS BE CELEBRATED.
THEY'LL FORGET.
YOU THINK SO? THEN LET US GIVE THEM SOMETHING THEY WILL NOT FORGET.
"REMEMBER, REMEMBER, THE FIFTH OF NOVEMBER, GUNPOWDER, TREASON AND PLOT..." THERE:
BEN, CAN YOU COMPLETE THE DOGGEREL?
UM. LET ME SEE. HMM. NO, I HAVE IT. "I SEE NO REASON WHY GUNPOWDER TREASON SHOULD EVER BE FORGOT." THERE.
IT'LL SERVE. THERE: NOW, WE'LL TEACH IT TO THAT URCHIN, AND HE'LL TEACH IT TO HIS FRIENDS, AND IT'LL LAST A HUNDRED YEARS...
I DOUBT IT.
HOW CAN YOU ABANDON THE SMOKE FOR ALL THIS, ALL THIS NOTHING?
DON'T YOU MISS LONDON? THE BUSTLE? THE PEOPLE? THE BLACKFRIARS AND THE GLOBE? THE LIFE?
THERE IS LIFE APLENTY HERE, BEN.
AND HOW GO THINGS WITH YOU IN STRATFORD? ARE YOU NOT... WELL, LET ME PUT IT BLUNTLY... HOW GO THINGS WITH MISTRESS ANNE?
WE REMAIN CIVIL. AND I SLEEP ON MY BED, IN MY ROOM, AND SHE SLEEPS IN HER BED, IN HERS.
AH.

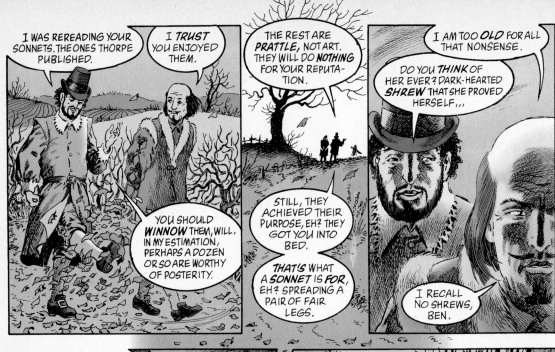

I WAS REREADING YOUR SONNETS. THE ONES THORPE PUBLISHED.

I TRUST YOU ENJOYED THEM.

THE REST ARE PRATTLE, NOT ART. THEY WILL DO NOTHING FOR YOUR REPUTATION.

I AM TOO OLD FOR ALL THAT NONSENSE.

DO YOU THINK OF HER EVER? DARK-HEARTED SHREW THAT SHE PROVED HERSELF...

YOU SHOULD WINNOW THEM, WILL. IN MY ESTIMATION, PERHAPS A DOZEN OR SO ARE WORTHY OF POSTERITY.

STILL, THEY ACHIEVED THEIR PURPOSE, EH? THEY GOT YOU INTO BED.

THAT'S WHAT A SONNET IS FOR, EH? SPREADING A PAIR OF FAIR LEGS.

I RECALL NO SHREWS, BEN.

AH, WILL. YOU ARE TOO GOOD-NATURED A FELLOW. I HAVE NEVER HEARD YOU SAY A BAD WORD ABOUT A LIVING SOUL.

WHAT NOW?

THIS WILL BE MY LAST PLAY, BEN.

SO YOU SAID.

IN SPITE OF ANYTHING I MIGHT HAVE SAID ABOUT PERICLES ...WELL... YOU ARE A BORN PLAYWRIGHT, WILL. IT'S IN YOUR BLOOD, AND IN YOUR BONES. I AM SURE IT WILL TAKE THE COLD OF DEATH TO TUG THE PEN FROM YOUR HAND.

I HOPE NOT. I SHALL BE PLEASED TO PUT DOWN MY PEN.

TRULY?

TRULY.

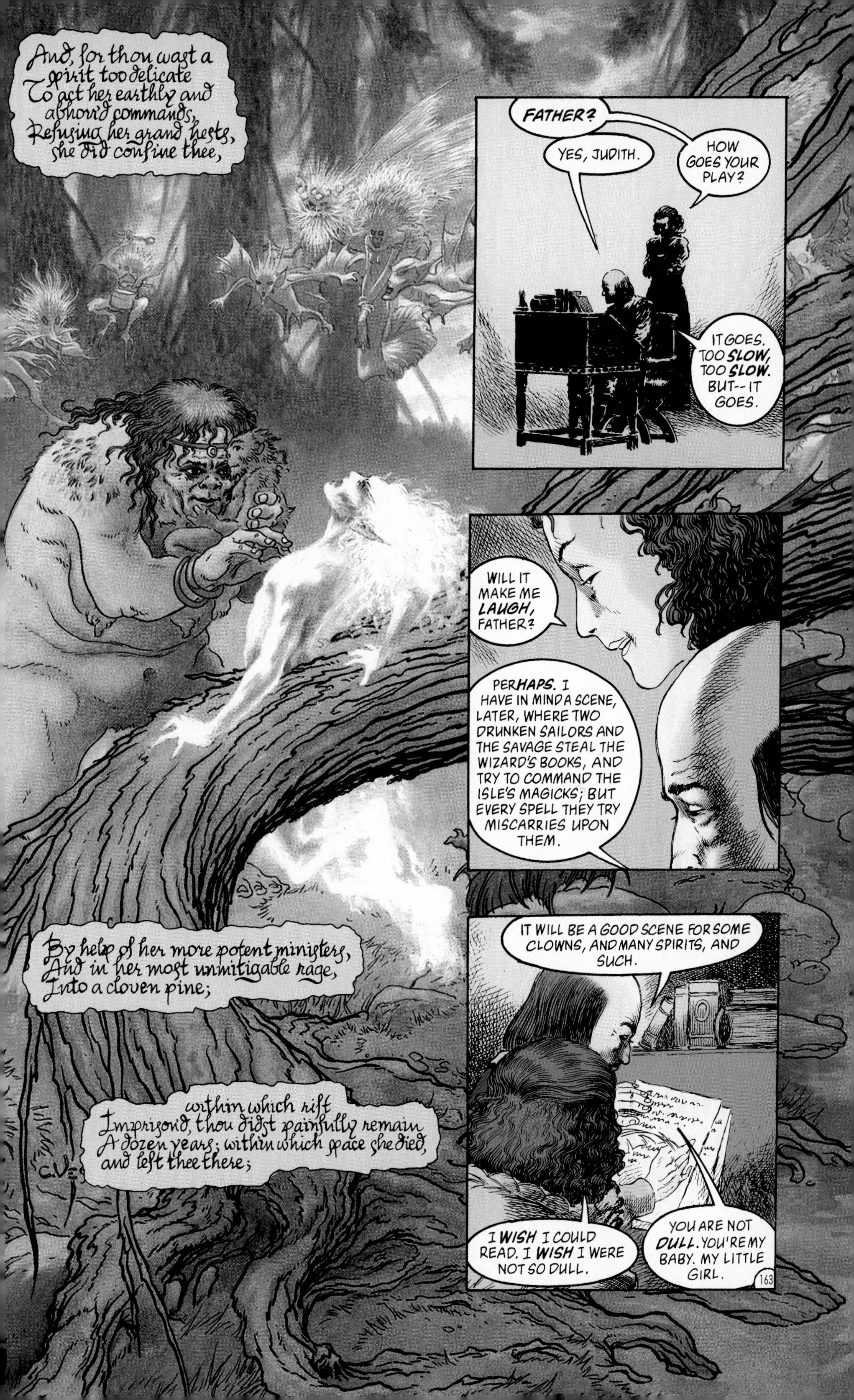
And, for thou wast a spirit too delicate
To act her earthly and abhorr'd commands,
Refusing her grand hests, she did confine thee,
FATHER?
YES, JUDITH.
HOW GOES YOUR PLAY?
IT GOES. TOO SLOW, TOO SLOW. BUT--IT GOES.
WILL IT MAKE ME LAUGH, FATHER?
PERHAPS. I HAVE IN MIND A SCENE, LATER, WHERE TWO DRUNKEN SAILORS AND THE SAVAGE STEAL THE WIZARD'S BOOKS, AND TRY TO COMMAND THE ISLE'S MAGICKS; BUT EVERY SPELL THEY TRY MISCARRIES UPON THEM.
By help of her more potent ministers,
And in her most unmitigable rage,
Into a cloven pine;
IT WILL BE A GOOD SCENE FOR SOME CLOWNS, AND MANY SPIRITS, AND SUCH.
within which rift
Imprison'd, thou didst painfully remain
A dozen years; within which space she died,
and left thee there;
I WISH I COULD READ. I WISH I WERE NOT SO DULL.
YOU ARE NOT DULL. YOU'RE MY BABY. MY LITTLE GIRL.

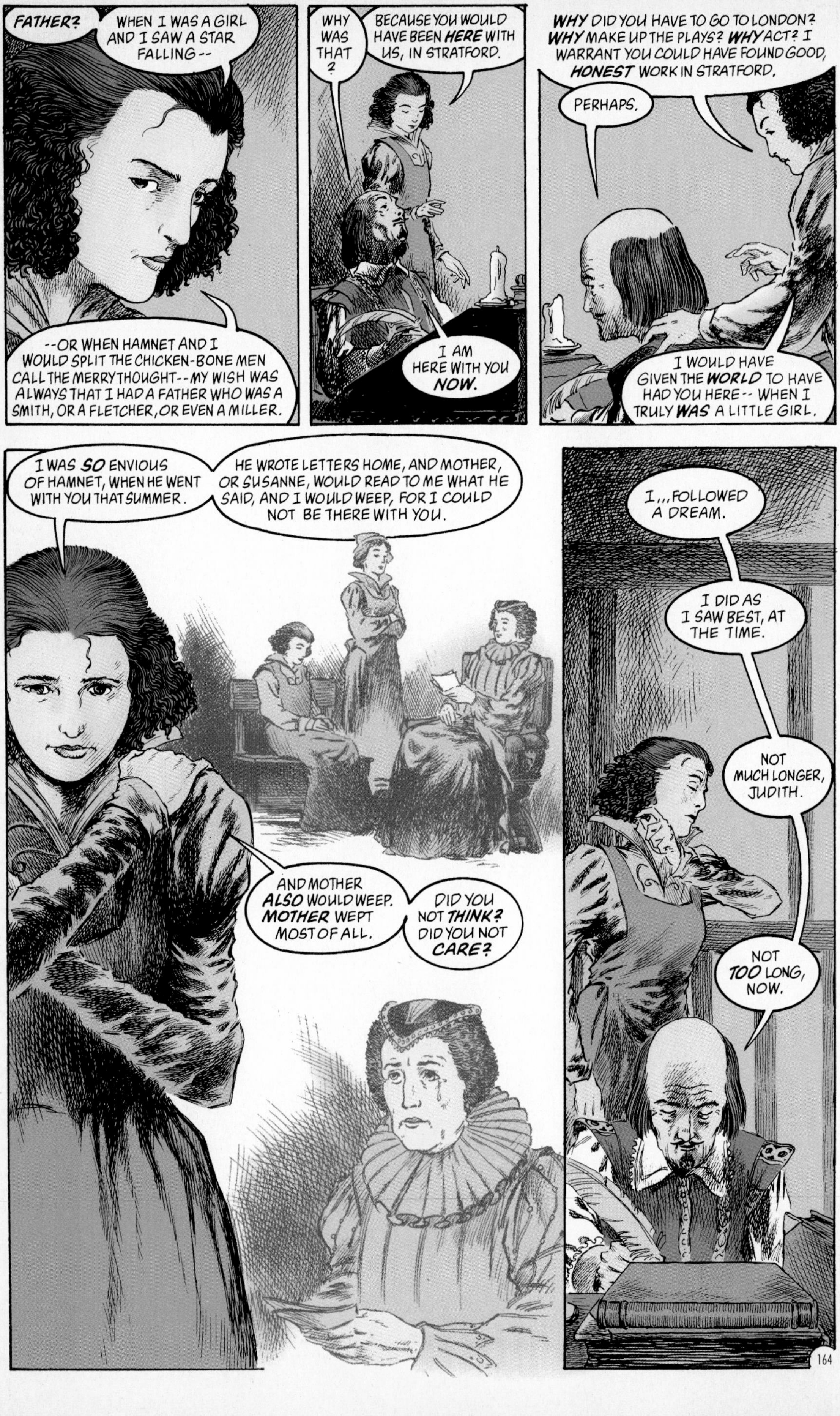
FATHER?
WHEN I WAS A GIRL AND I SAW A STAR FALLING--
--OR WHEN HAMNET AND I WOULD SPLIT THE CHICKEN-BONE MEN CALL THE MERRYTHOUGHT--MY WISH WAS ALWAYS THAT I HAD A FATHER WHO WAS A SMITH, OR A FLETCHER, OR EVEN A MILLER.
WHY WAS THAT?
BECAUSE YOU WOULD HAVE BEEN HERE WITH US, IN STRATFORD.
I AM HERE WITH YOU NOW.
WHY DID YOU HAVE TO GO TO LONDON? WHY MAKE UP THE PLAYS? WHY ACT? I WARRANT YOU COULD HAVE FOUND GOOD, HONEST WORK IN STRATFORD.
PERHAPS.
I WOULD HAVE GIVEN THE WORLD TO HAVE HAD YOU HERE-- WHEN I TRULY WAS A LITTLE GIRL.
I WAS SO ENVIOUS OF HAMNET, WHEN HE WENT WITH YOU THAT SUMMER.
HE WROTE LETTERS HOME, AND MOTHER, OR SUSANNE, WOULD READ TO ME WHAT HE SAID, AND I WOULD WEEP, FOR I COULD NOT BE THERE WITH YOU.
AND MOTHER ALSO WOULD WEEP. MOTHER WEPT MOST OF ALL.
DID YOU NOT THINK? DID YOU NOT CARE?
I...FOLLOWED A DREAM.
I DID AS I SAW BEST, AT THE TIME.
NOT MUCH LONGER, JUDITH.
NOT TOO LONG, NOW.

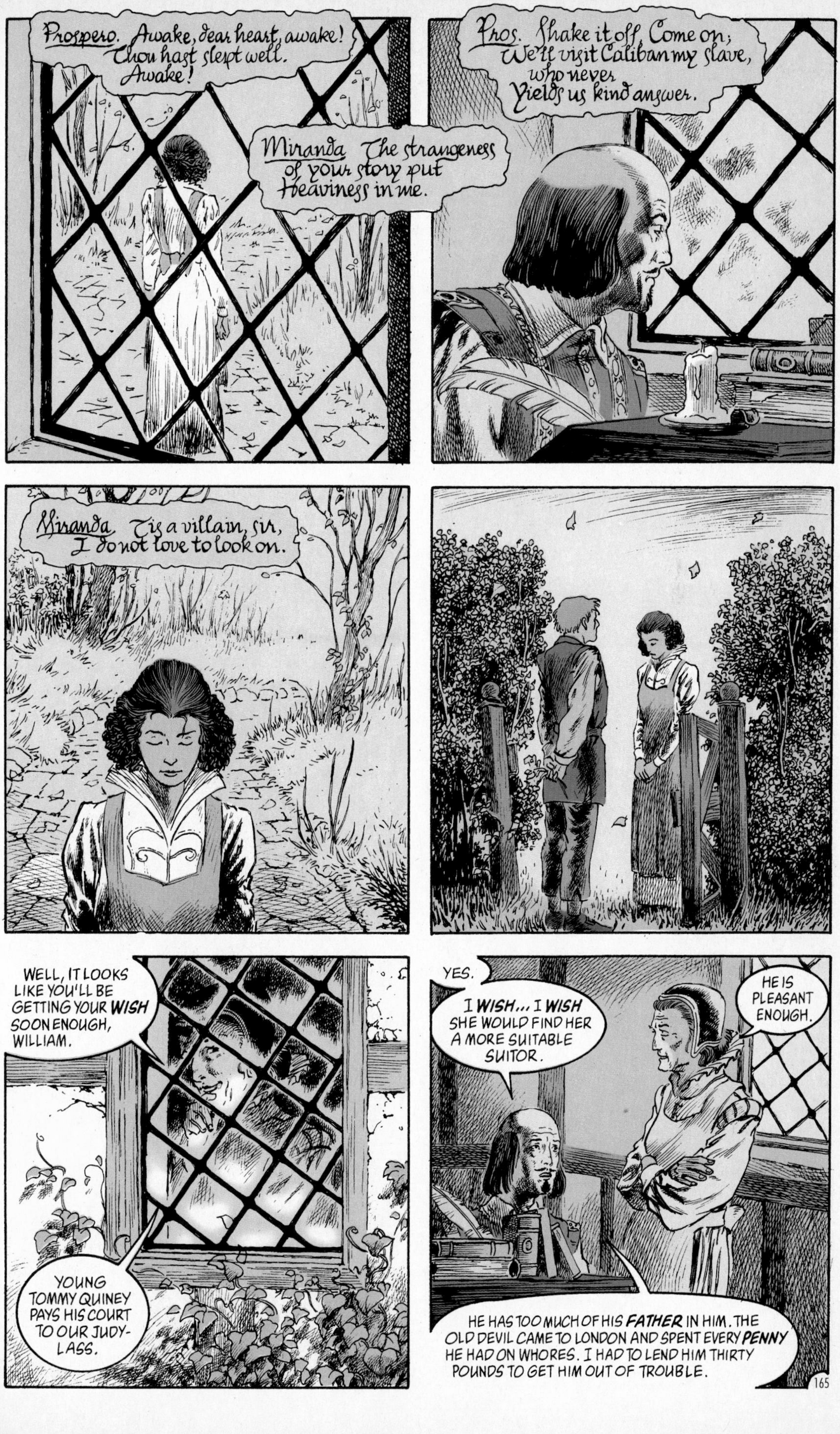
Prospero. Awake, dear heart, awake! Thou hast slept well. Awake!
Miranda The strangeness of your story put Heaviness in me.
Pros. Shake it off. Come on; We'll visit Caliban my slave, who never Yields us kind answer.
Miranda 'Tis a villain, sir, I do not love to look on.
WELL, IT LOOKS LIKE YOU'LL BE GETTING YOUR WISH SOON ENOUGH, WILLIAM.
YOUNG TOMMY QUINEY PAYS HIS COURT TO OUR JUDY-LASS.
YES.
I WISH... I WISH SHE WOULD FIND HER A MORE SUITABLE SUITOR.
HE IS PLEASANT ENOUGH.
HE HAS TOO MUCH OF HIS FATHER IN HIM. THE OLD DEVIL CAME TO LONDON AND SPENT EVERY PENNY HE HAD ON WHORES. I HAD TO LEND HIM THIRTY POUNDS TO GET HIM OUT OF TROUBLE.

"YOU ARE **NEVER** SATISFIED, MY WILL. YOU DO NOT WANT WHAT YOU WANTED AS SOON AS YOU **HAVE** IT, BUT MUST **ALWAYS** BE PINING AND PLAINING AFTER SOMETHING MORE."

WHAT WIN **I**, IF I GAIN THE THING I SEEK? A DREAM, A BREATH, A FROTH OF FLEETING JOY. WHO BUYS A MINUTE'S MIRTH TO WAIL A WEEK? OR SELLS ETERNITY TO GET A TOY?

MORE OF YOUR PRETTY-PLAY-NONSENSE? WELL, I CAN GIVE YOU THE ANSWER TO **THAT** ONE.

"WHO BUYS A MINUTE'S MIRTH TO WAIL A WEEK?" THAT'S **PEOPLE** DO THAT. LIKE OLD QUINEY SPENDING HIS PENNIES ON THE WHORES OF LONDON TOWN.

YOU KNOW THE TROUBLE WITH **YOU**, WILL? YOU LIVE IN **WORDS**, NOT IN THE REAL WORLD. YOU **THINK** TOO MUCH. YOU **DREAM** TOO MUCH.

WHEREAS **I** CONSIDER MYSELF A PRACTICAL MAN.

OF **COURSE** YOU DO, MY DEAR.

PRACTICAL MEN **ALWAYS** DESERT THEIR WIVES AND RUN AWAY TO MAKE UP PRETTY TALES; AND WRITE PRETTY SONNETS TO PRETTY GIRLS AND PRETTY BOYS.

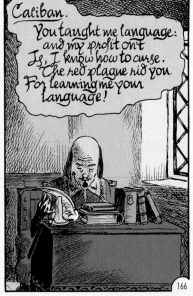

Caliban.
You taught me language:
and my profit on't
Is, I know how to curse.
The red plague rid you
For learning me your
language!

166

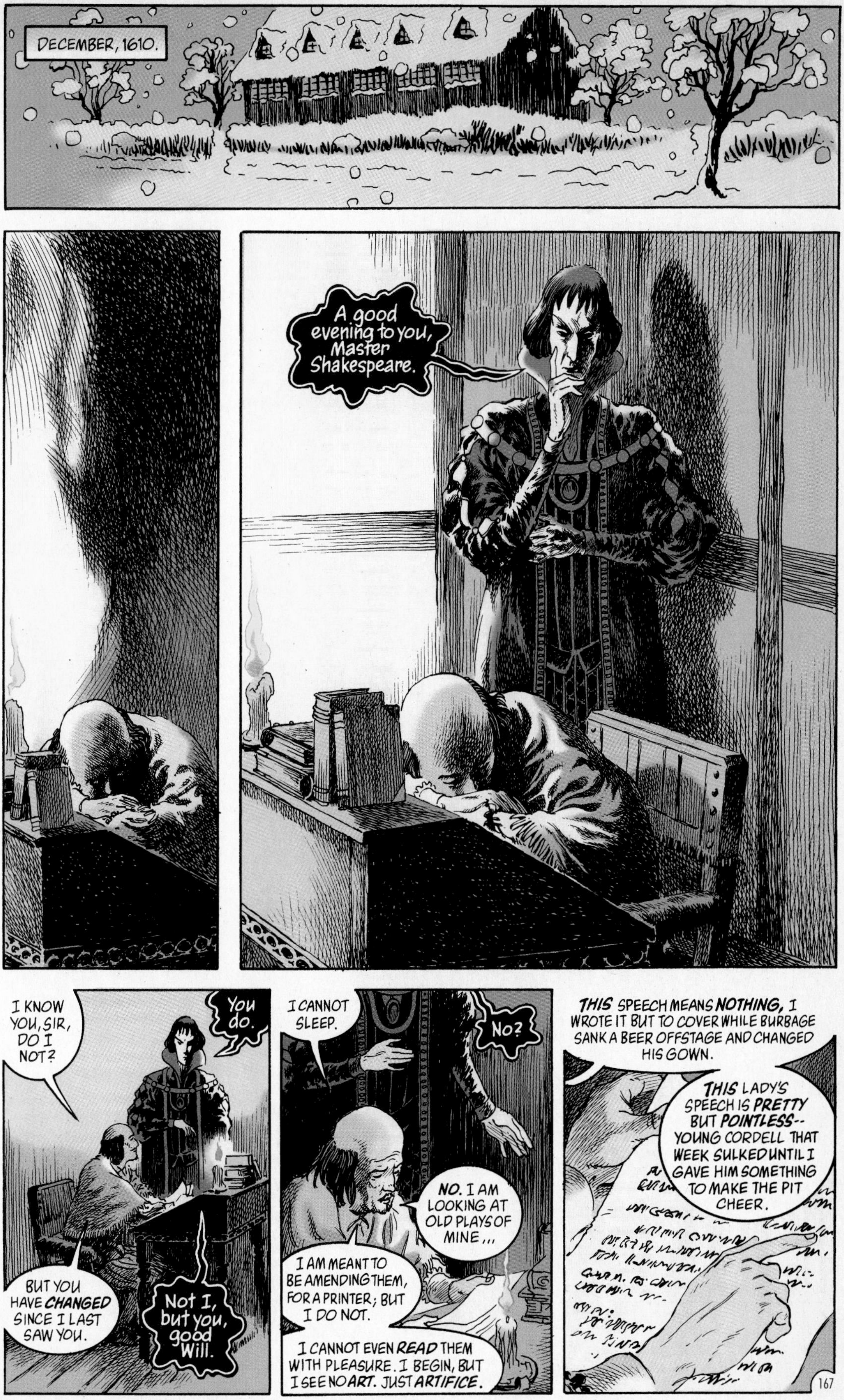

DECEMBER, 1610.
A good evening to you, Master Shakespeare.
I KNOW YOU, SIR, DO I NOT?
You do.
BUT YOU HAVE CHANGED SINCE I LAST SAW YOU.
Not I, but you, good Will.
I CANNOT SLEEP.
No?
NO. I AM LOOKING AT OLD PLAYS OF MINE...
I AM MEANT TO BE AMENDING THEM, FOR A PRINTER; BUT I DO NOT.
I CANNOT EVEN READ THEM WITH PLEASURE. I BEGIN, BUT I SEE NO ART. JUST ARTIFICE.
THIS SPEECH MEANS NOTHING, I WROTE IT BUT TO COVER WHILE BURBAGE SANK A BEER OFFSTAGE AND CHANGED HIS GOWN.
THIS LADY'S SPEECH IS PRETTY BUT POINTLESS-- YOUNG CORDELL THAT WEEK SULKED UNTIL I GAVE HIM SOMETHING TO MAKE THE PIT CHEER.

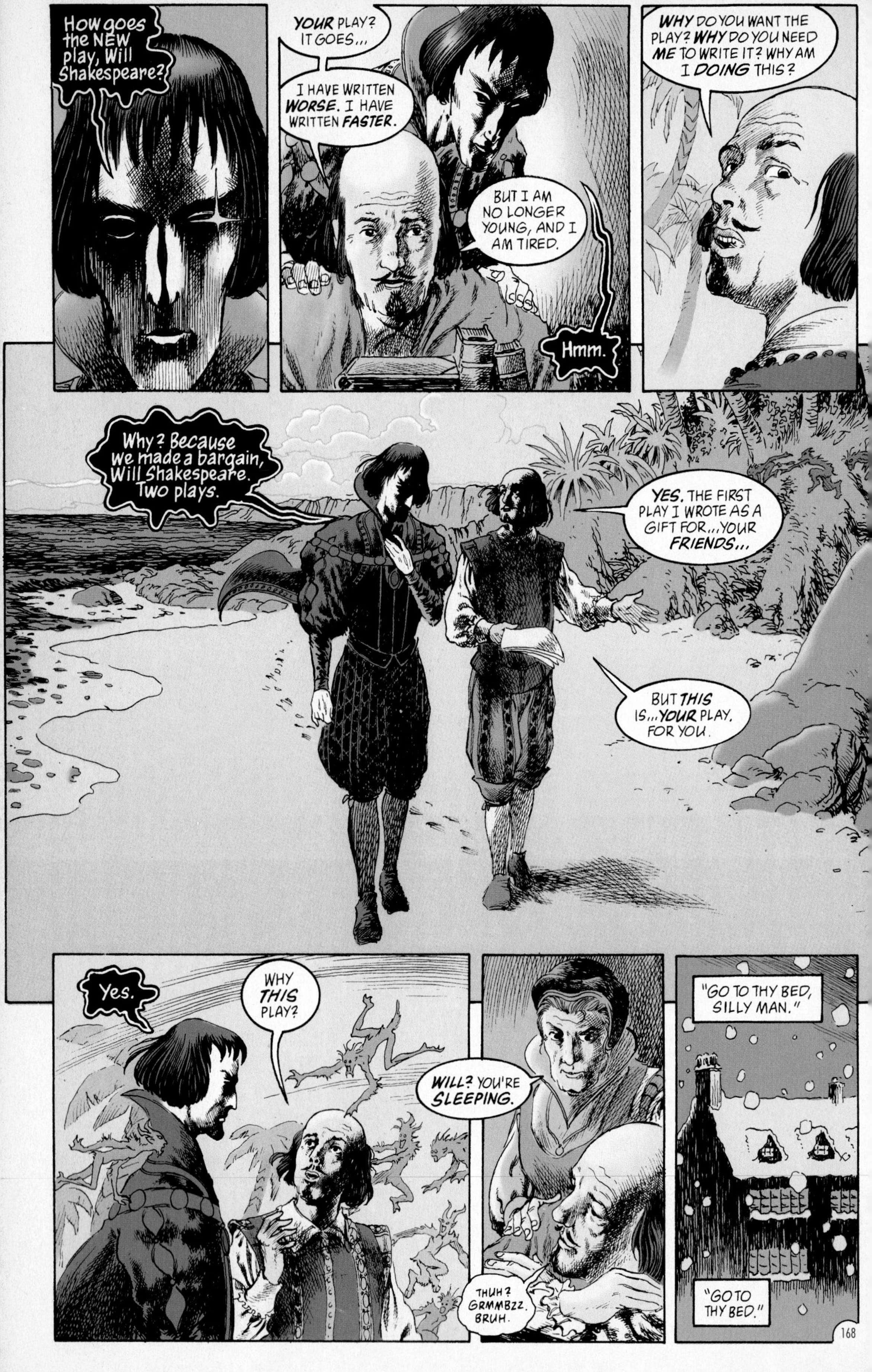
How goes the NEW play, Will Shakespeare?
YOUR PLAY? IT GOES...
I HAVE WRITTEN WORSE. I HAVE WRITTEN FASTER.
BUT I AM NO LONGER YOUNG, AND I AM TIRED.
Hmm.
WHY DO YOU WANT THE PLAY? WHY DO YOU NEED ME TO WRITE IT? WHY AM I DOING THIS?
Why? Because we made a bargain, Will Shakespeare. Two plays.
YES. THE FIRST PLAY I WROTE AS A GIFT FOR... YOUR FRIENDS...
BUT THIS IS... YOUR PLAY. FOR YOU.
Yes.
WHY THIS PLAY?
WILL? YOU'RE SLEEPING.
THUH? GRMMBZZ. BRUH.
"GO TO THY BED, SILLY MAN."
"GO TO THY BED."

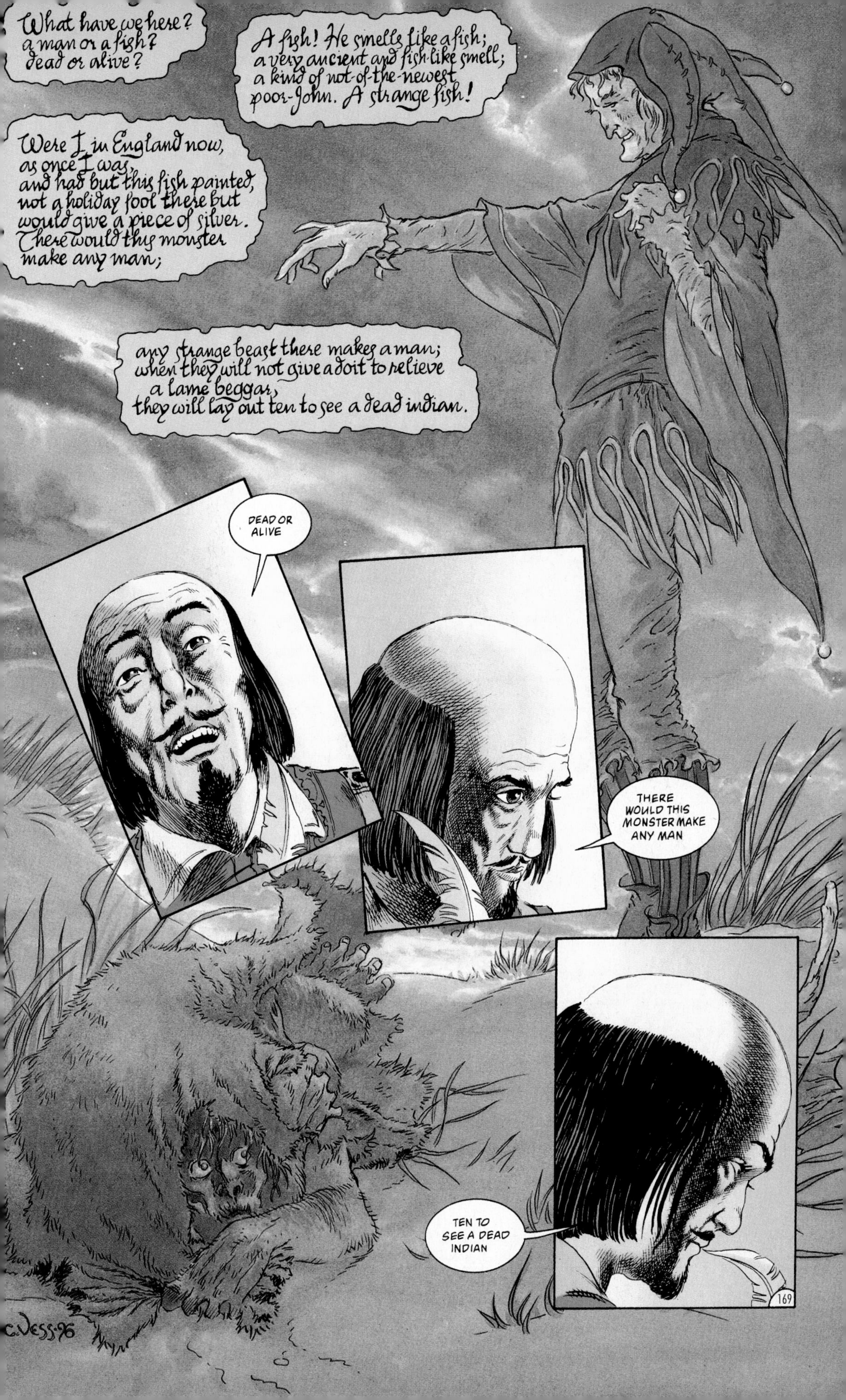
What have we here? a man or a fish? dead or alive?
A fish! He smells like a fish; a very ancient and fish-like smell; a kind of not-of-the-newest poor-John. A strange fish!
Were I in England now, as once I was, and had but this fish painted, not a holiday fool there but would give a piece of silver. There would this monster make any man;
any strange beast there makes a man; when they will not give a doit to relieve a lame beggar, they will lay out ten to see a dead indian.
DEAD OR ALIVE
THERE WOULD THIS MONSTER MAKE ANY MAN
TEN TO SEE A DEAD INDIAN
C.VESS.96

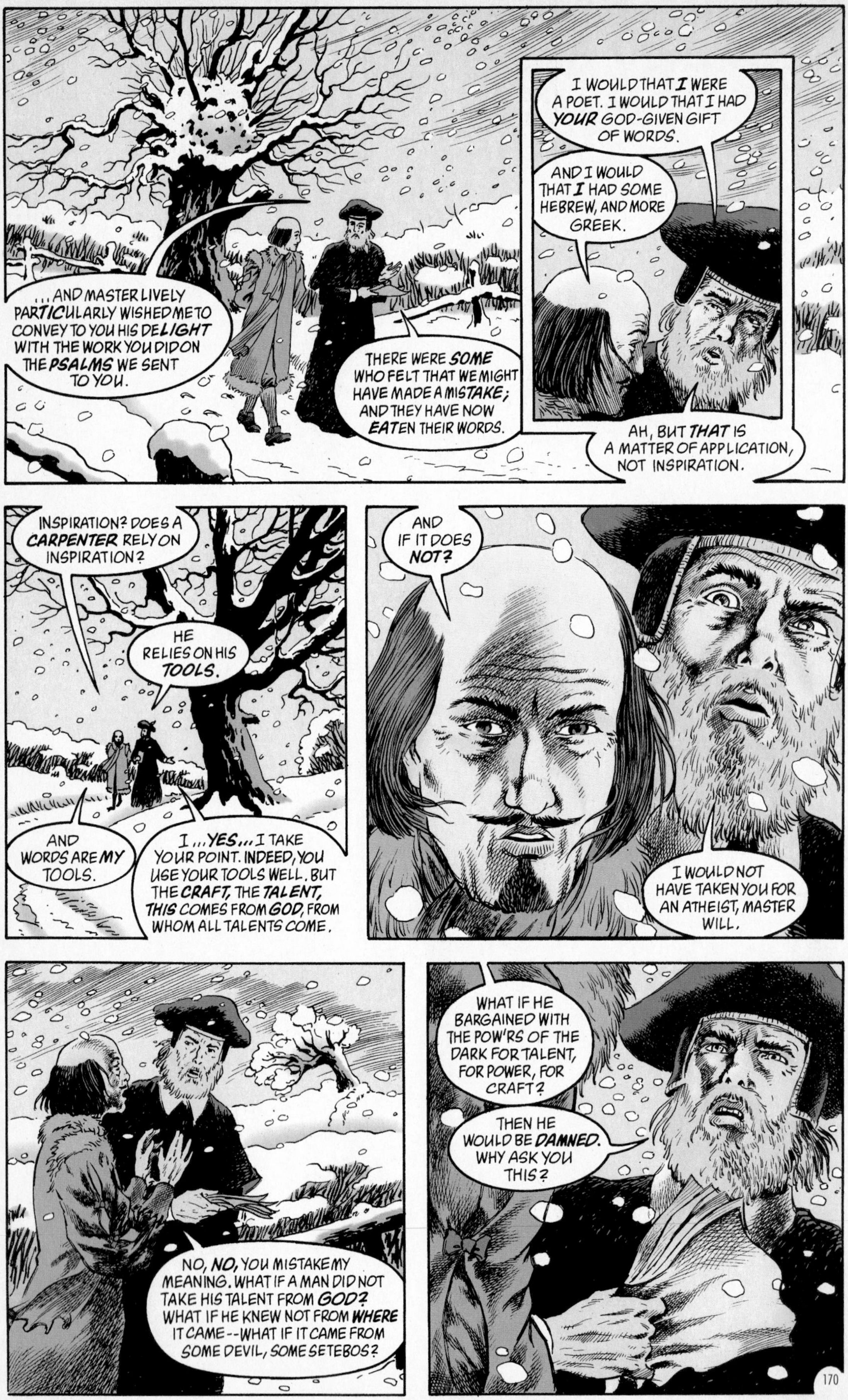
...AND MASTER LIVELY PARTICULARLY WISHED ME TO CONVEY TO YOU HIS DELIGHT WITH THE WORK YOU DID ON THE PSALMS WE SENT TO YOU.
THERE WERE SOME WHO FELT THAT WE MIGHT HAVE MADE A MISTAKE; AND THEY HAVE NOW EATEN THEIR WORDS.
I WOULD THAT I WERE A POET. I WOULD THAT I HAD YOUR GOD-GIVEN GIFT OF WORDS.
AND I WOULD THAT I HAD SOME HEBREW, AND MORE GREEK.
AH, BUT THAT IS A MATTER OF APPLICATION, NOT INSPIRATION.
INSPIRATION? DOES A CARPENTER RELY ON INSPIRATION?
HE RELIES ON HIS TOOLS.
AND WORDS ARE MY TOOLS.
I...YES...I TAKE YOUR POINT. INDEED, YOU USE YOUR TOOLS WELL. BUT THE CRAFT, THE TALENT, THIS COMES FROM GOD, FROM WHOM ALL TALENTS COME.
AND IF IT DOES NOT?
I WOULD NOT HAVE TAKEN YOU FOR AN ATHEIST, MASTER WILL.
NO, NO, YOU MISTAKE MY MEANING. WHAT IF A MAN DID NOT TAKE HIS TALENT FROM GOD? WHAT IF HE KNEW NOT FROM WHERE IT CAME--WHAT IF IT CAME FROM SOME DEVIL, SOME SETEBOS?
WHAT IF HE BARGAINED WITH THE POW'RS OF THE DARK FOR TALENT, FOR POWER, FOR CRAFT?
THEN HE WOULD BE DAMNED. WHY ASK YOU THIS?

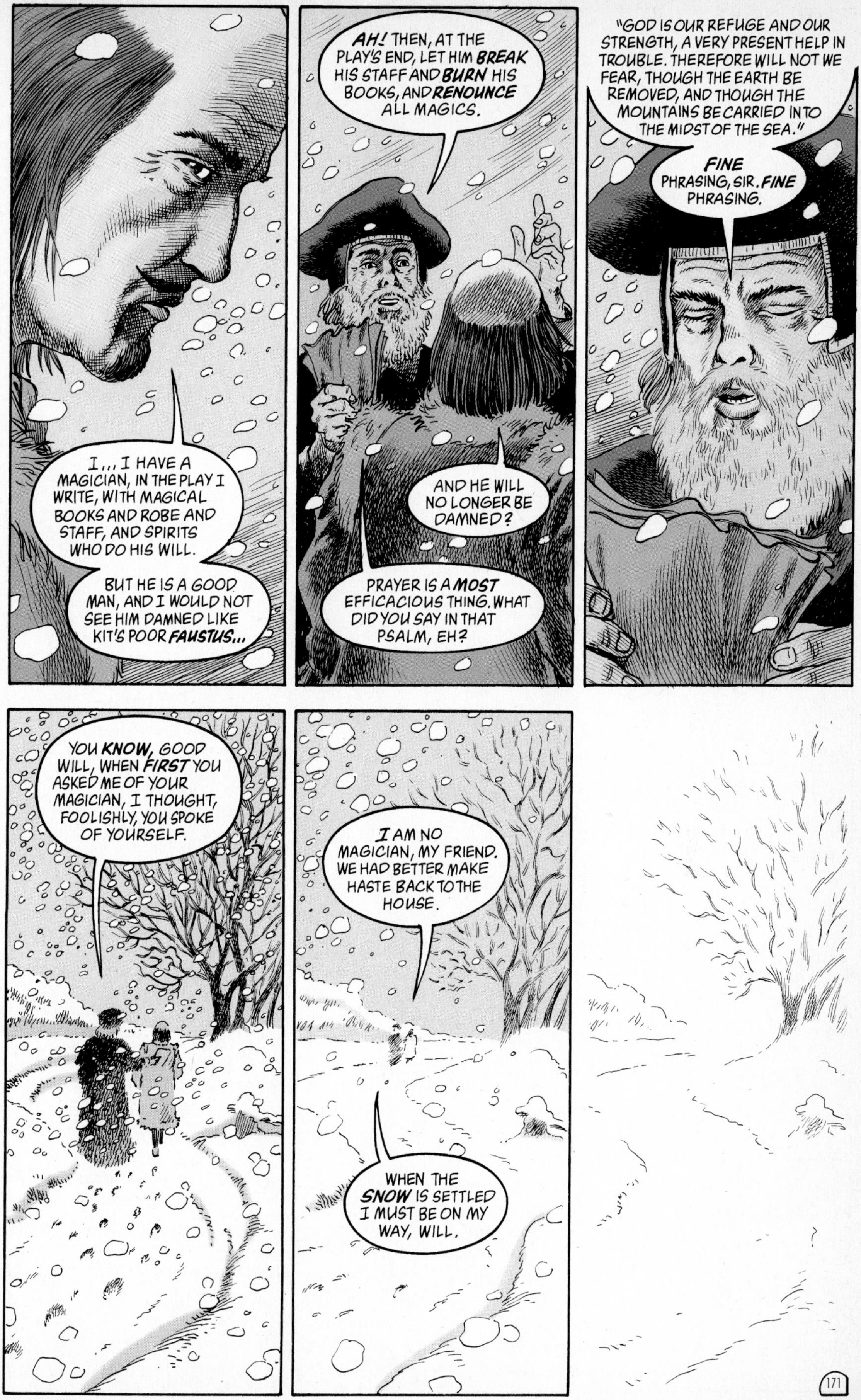
I... I HAVE A MAGICIAN, IN THE PLAY I WRITE, WITH MAGICAL BOOKS AND ROBE AND STAFF, AND SPIRITS WHO DO HIS WILL.
BUT HE IS A GOOD MAN, AND I WOULD NOT SEE HIM DAMNED LIKE KIT'S POOR FAUSTUS...
AH! THEN, AT THE PLAY'S END, LET HIM BREAK HIS STAFF AND BURN HIS BOOKS, AND RENOUNCE ALL MAGICS.
AND HE WILL NO LONGER BE DAMNED?
PRAYER IS A MOST EFFICACIOUS THING. WHAT DID YOU SAY IN THAT PSALM, EH?
"GOD IS OUR REFUGE AND OUR STRENGTH, A VERY PRESENT HELP IN TROUBLE. THEREFORE WILL NOT WE FEAR, THOUGH THE EARTH BE REMOVED, AND THOUGH THE MOUNTAINS BE CARRIED INTO THE MIDST OF THE SEA."
FINE PHRASING, SIR. FINE PHRASING.
YOU KNOW, GOOD WILL, WHEN FIRST YOU ASKED ME OF YOUR MAGICIAN, I THOUGHT, FOOLISHLY, YOU SPOKE OF YOURSELF.
I AM NO MAGICIAN, MY FRIEND. WE HAD BETTER MAKE HASTE BACK TO THE HOUSE.
WHEN THE SNOW IS SETTLED I MUST BE ON MY WAY, WILL.

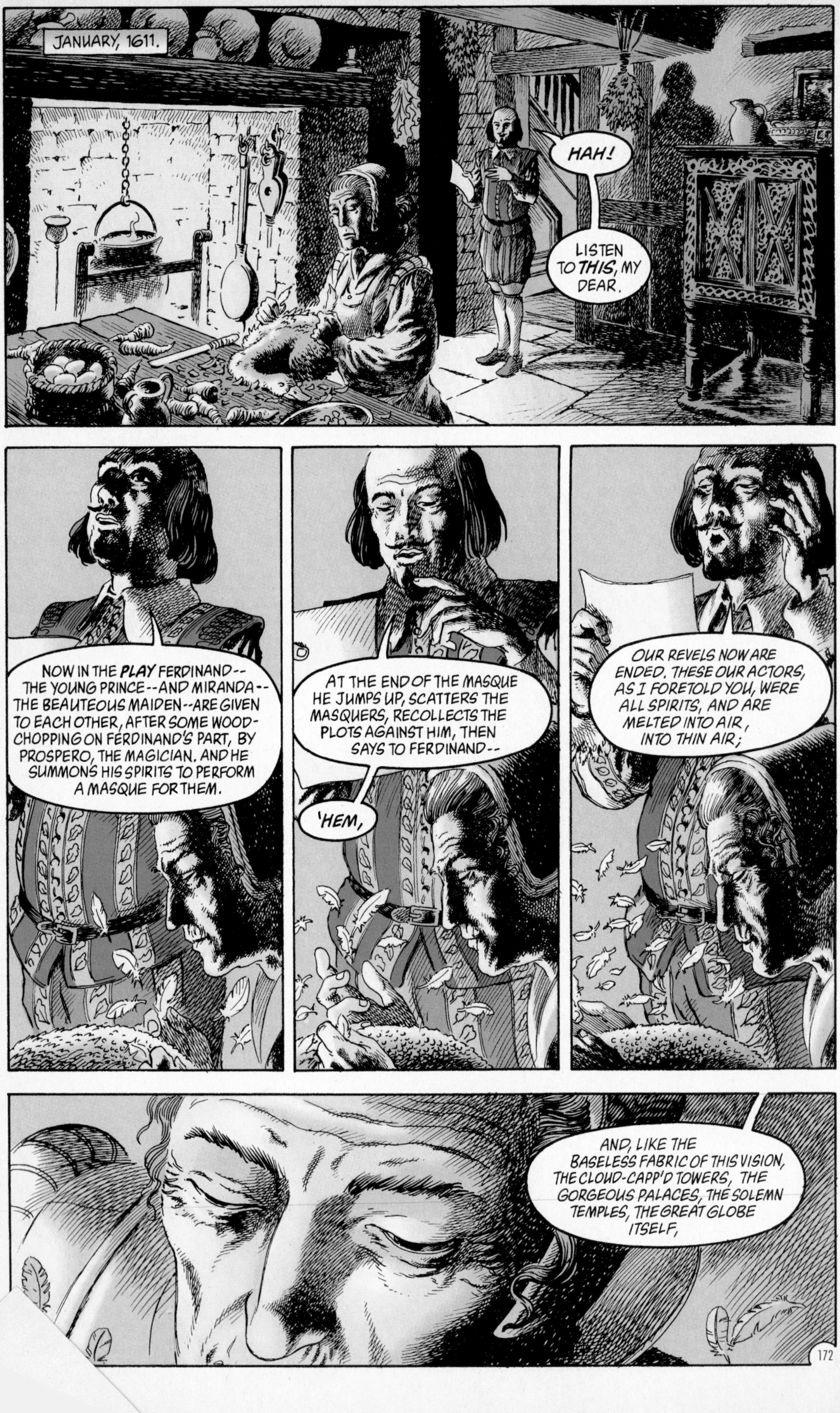
JANUARY, 1611.
HAH!
LISTEN TO THIS, MY DEAR.
NOW IN THE PLAY FERDINAND-- THE YOUNG PRINCE--AND MIRANDA-- THE BEAUTEOUS MAIDEN--ARE GIVEN TO EACH OTHER, AFTER SOME WOOD-CHOPPING ON FERDINAND'S PART, BY PROSPERO, THE MAGICIAN. AND HE SUMMONS HIS SPIRITS TO PERFORM A MASQUE FOR THEM.
AT THE END OF THE MASQUE HE JUMPS UP, SCATTERS THE MASQUERS, RECOLLECTS THE PLOTS AGAINST HIM, THEN SAYS TO FERDINAND--
'HEM,
OUR REVELS NOW ARE ENDED. THESE OUR ACTORS, AS I FORETOLD YOU, WERE ALL SPIRITS, AND ARE MELTED INTO AIR, INTO THIN AIR;
AND, LIKE THE BASELESS FABRIC OF THIS VISION, THE CLOUD-CAPP'D TOWERS, THE GORGEOUS PALACES, THE SOLEMN TEMPLES, THE GREAT GLOBE ITSELF,

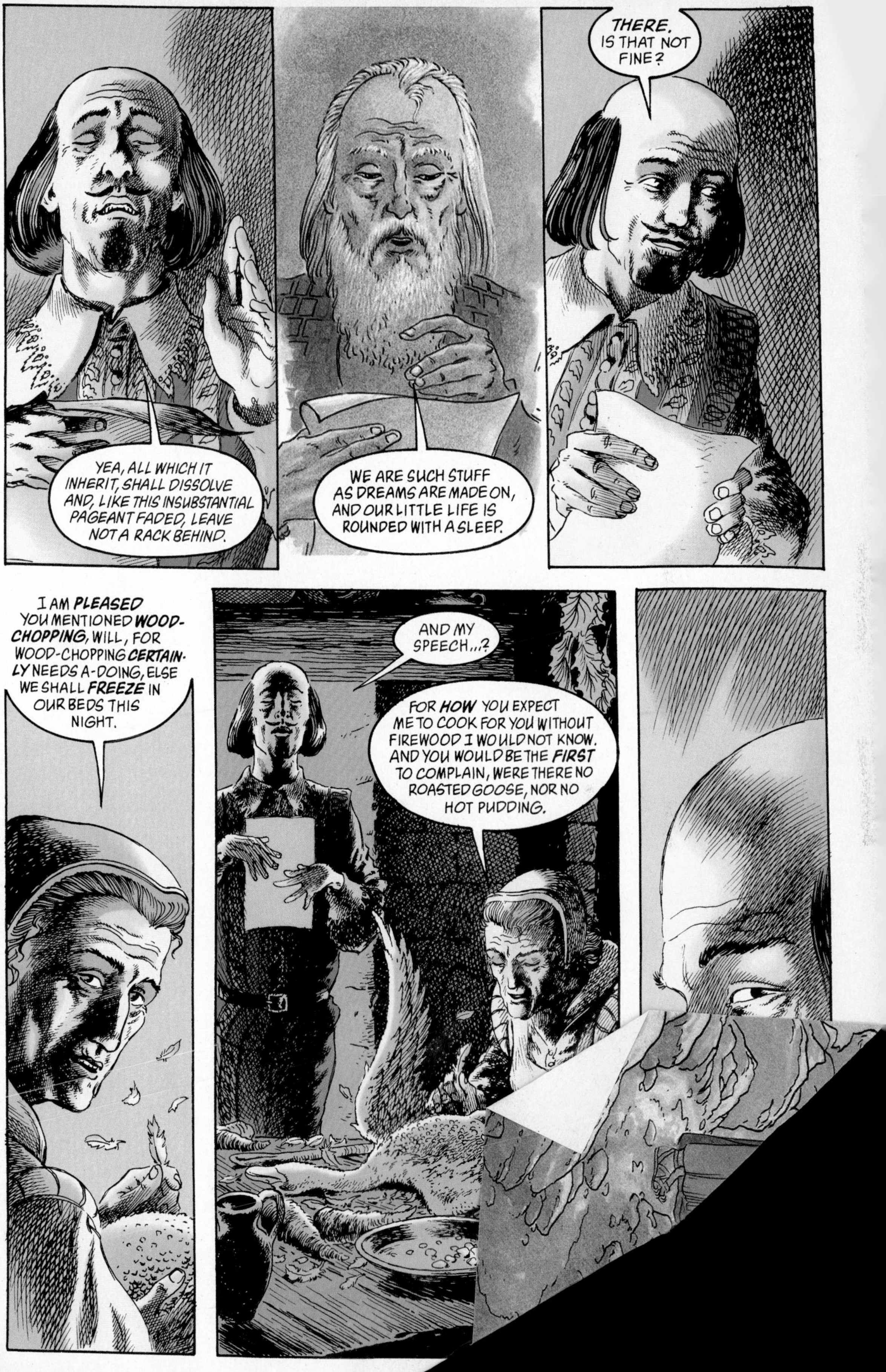
YEA, ALL WHICH IT INHERIT, SHALL DISSOLVE AND, LIKE THIS INSUBSTANTIAL PAGEANT FADED, LEAVE NOT A RACK BEHIND.
WE ARE SUCH STUFF AS DREAMS ARE MADE ON, AND OUR LITTLE LIFE IS ROUNDED WITH A SLEEP.
THERE. IS THAT NOT FINE?
I AM PLEASED YOU MENTIONED WOOD-CHOPPING, WILL, FOR WOOD-CHOPPING CERTAINLY NEEDS A-DOING, ELSE WE SHALL FREEZE IN OUR BEDS THIS NIGHT.
AND MY SPEECH...?
FOR HOW YOU EXPECT ME TO COOK FOR YOU WITHOUT FIREWOOD I WOULD NOT KNOW. AND YOU WOULD BE THE FIRST TO COMPLAIN, WERE THERE NO ROASTED GOOSE, NOR NO HOT PUDDING.

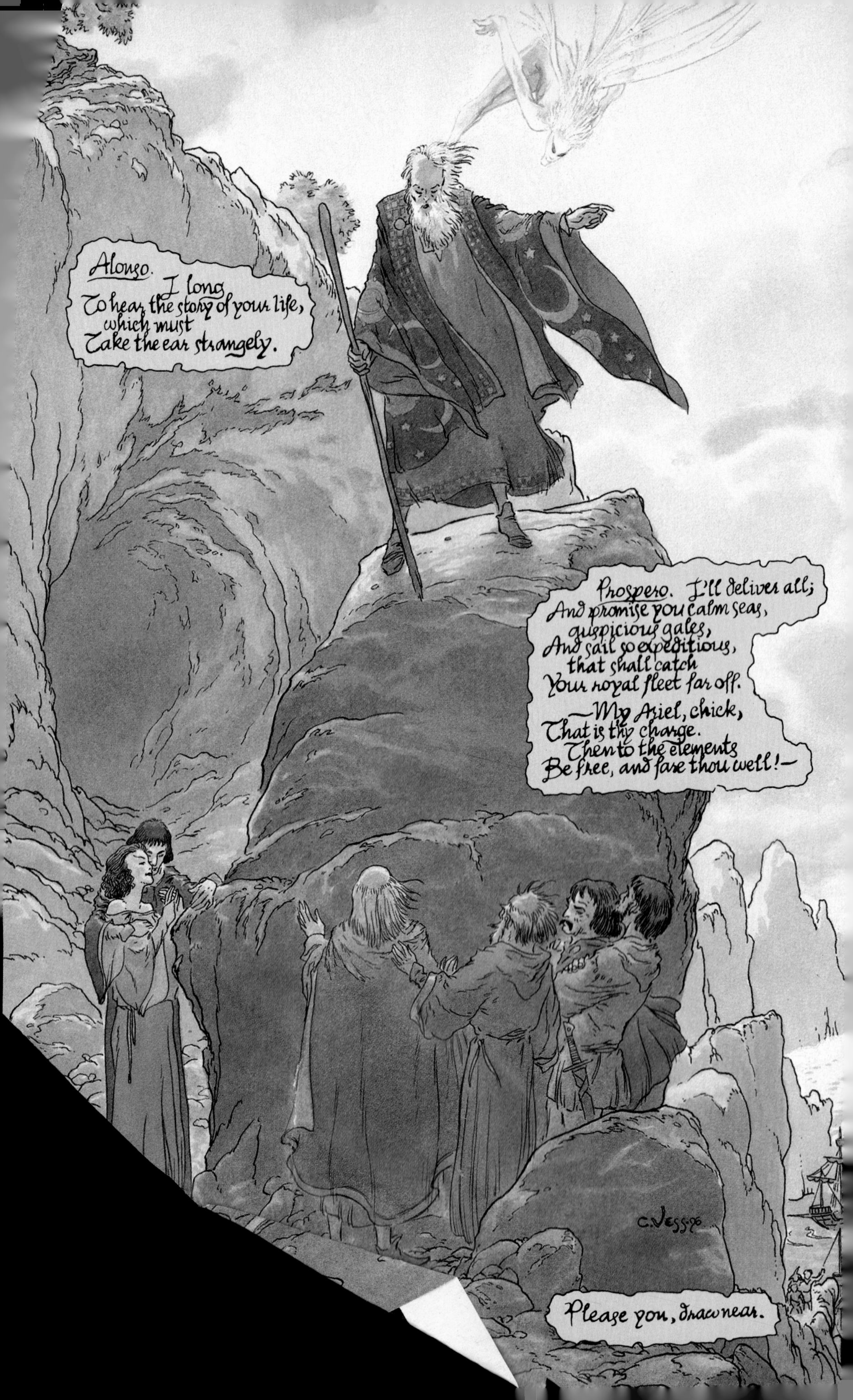
Alonzo. I long
To hear the story of your life, which must
Take the ear strangely.
Prospero. I'll deliver all;
And promise you calm seas, auspicious gales,
And sail so expeditious, that shall catch
Your royal fleet far off.
—My Ariel, chick,
That is thy charge. Then to the elements
Be free, and fare thou well!—
Please you, draw near.
C. Vess '96

Exeunt Omnes.

Is it finished?

IT IS.

Then we are quits, Will Shakespeare. It remains only for me to thank you, and wish you well in your life to come.

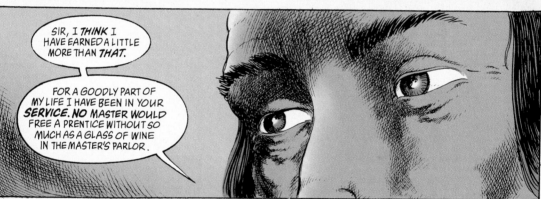

SIR, I *THINK* I HAVE EARNED A LITTLE MORE THAN *THAT.*

FOR A GOODLY PART OF MY LIFE I HAVE BEEN IN YOUR *SERVICE. NO* MASTER WOULD FREE A PRENTICE WITHOUT SO MUCH AS A GLASS OF WINE IN THE MASTER'S PARLOR.

Sir, is this your will?

Sir, it *IS.*

I see. Then we shall take a glass of wine in my house.

YOUR HOUSE. YES. IS IT.... IS IT *FAR?*

Aye. Very far. So tell me, Will: do you see yourself reflected in your tale?

I WOULD BE A *FOOL* IF I DENIED IT. I AM PROSPER, CERTAINLY; AND I TRUST I *SHALL.*

BUT I AM ALSO *ARIEL*--A FLAMING FIRING SPIRIT, CRACKLING LIKE LIGHTNING IN THE SKY.

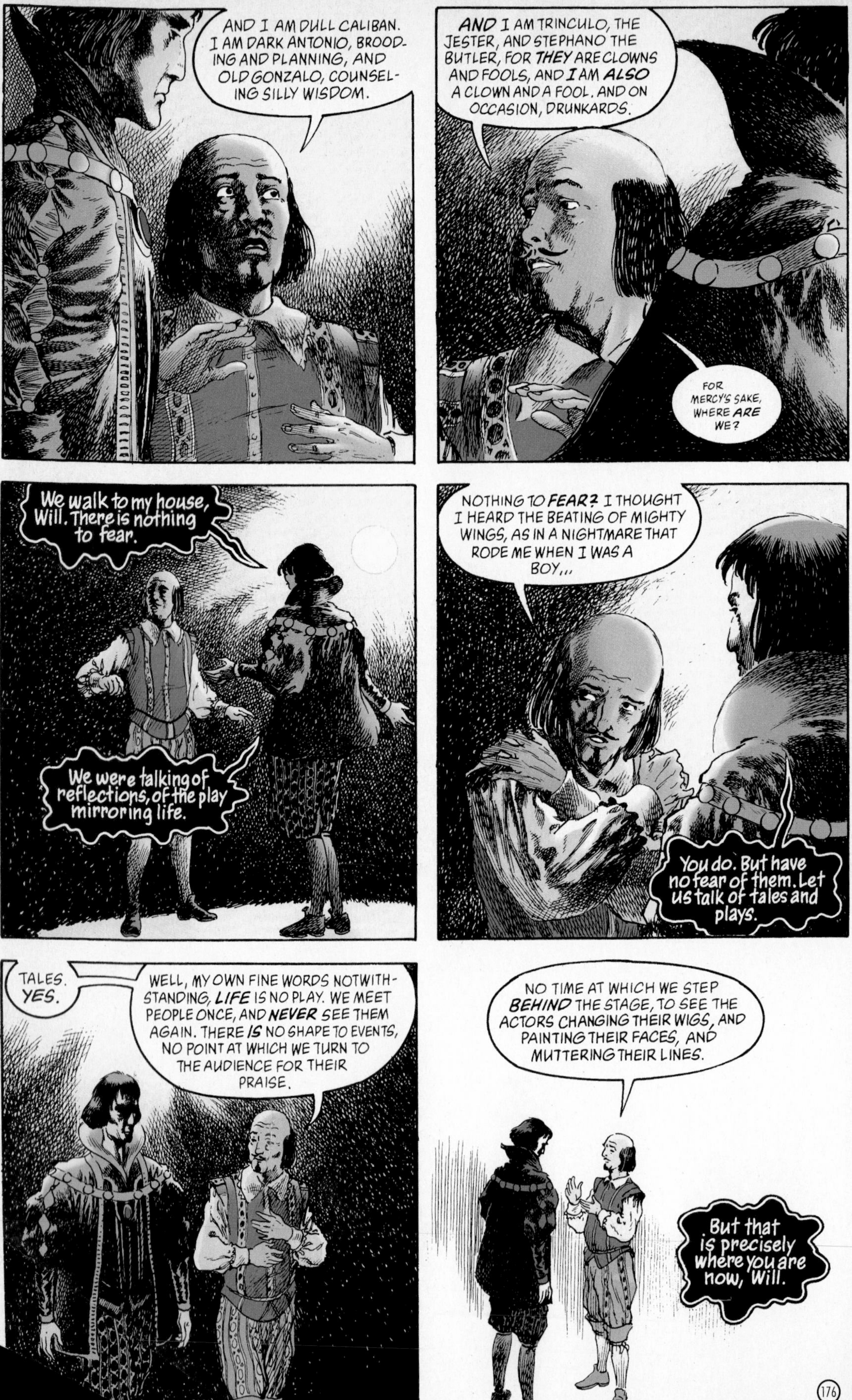
AND I AM DULL CALIBAN. I AM DARK ANTONIO, BROODING AND PLANNING, AND OLD GONZALO, COUNSELING SILLY WISDOM.
AND I AM TRINCULO, THE JESTER, AND STEPHANO THE BUTLER, FOR THEY ARE CLOWNS AND FOOLS, AND I AM ALSO A CLOWN AND A FOOL. AND ON OCCASION, DRUNKARDS.
FOR MERCY'S SAKE, WHERE ARE WE?
We walk to my house, Will. There is nothing to fear.
We were talking of reflections, of the play mirroring life.
NOTHING TO FEAR? I THOUGHT I HEARD THE BEATING OF MIGHTY WINGS, AS IN A NIGHTMARE THAT RODE ME WHEN I WAS A BOY...
You do. But have no fear of them. Let us talk of tales and plays.
TALES. YES.
WELL, MY OWN FINE WORDS NOTWITHSTANDING, LIFE IS NO PLAY. WE MEET PEOPLE ONCE, AND NEVER SEE THEM AGAIN. THERE IS NO SHAPE TO EVENTS, NO POINT AT WHICH WE TURN TO THE AUDIENCE FOR THEIR PRAISE.
NO TIME AT WHICH WE STEP BEHIND THE STAGE, TO SEE THE ACTORS CHANGING THEIR WIGS, AND PAINTING THEIR FACES, AND MUTTERING THEIR LINES.
But that is precisely where you are now, Will.

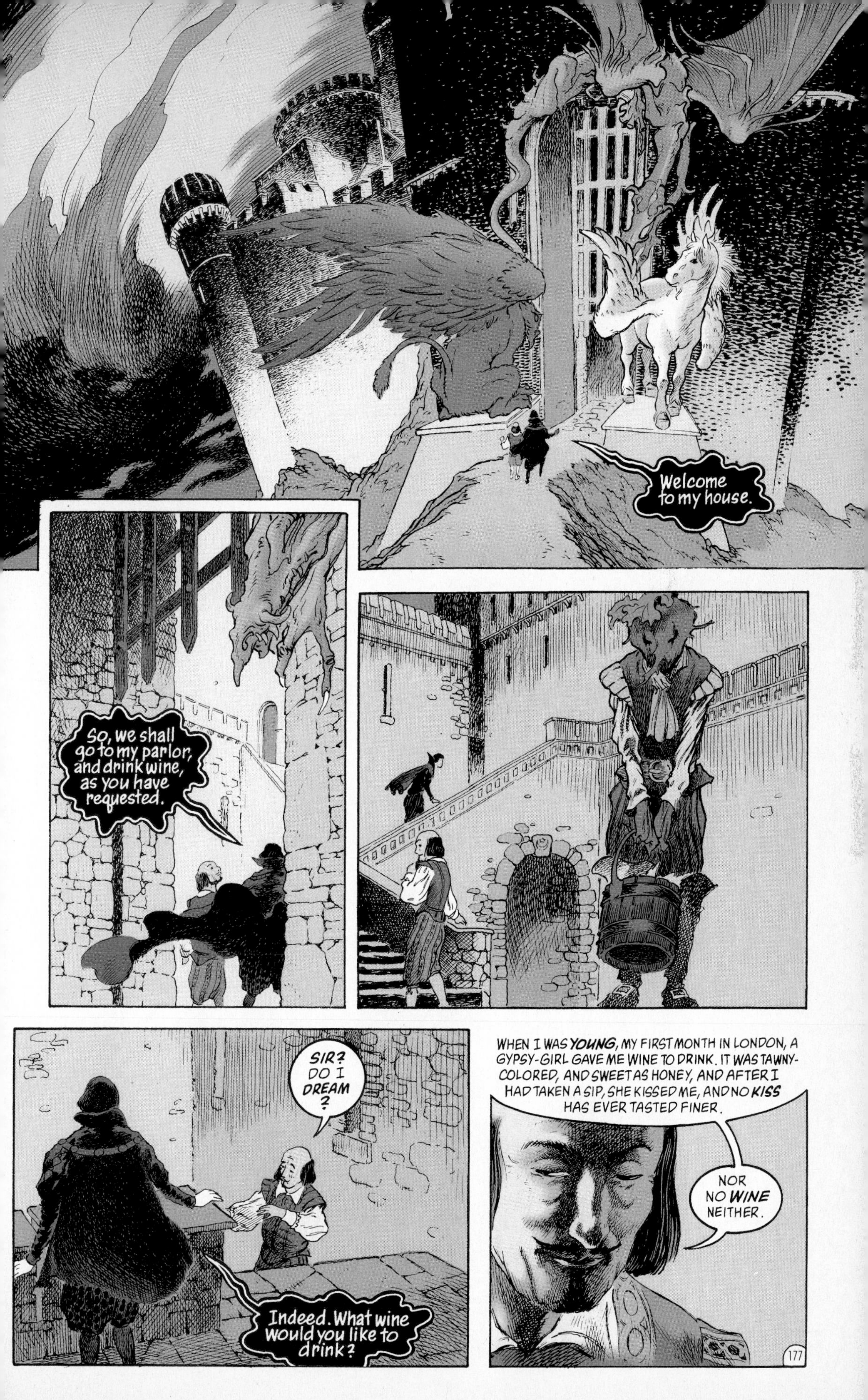
Welcome to my house.
So, we shall go to my parlor, and drink wine, as you have requested.
SIR? DO I DREAM?
Indeed. What wine would you like to drink?
WHEN I WAS YOUNG, MY FIRST MONTH IN LONDON, A GYPSY-GIRL GAVE ME WINE TO DRINK. IT WAS TAWNY-COLORED, AND SWEET AS HONEY, AND AFTER I HAD TAKEN A SIP, SHE KISSED ME, AND NO KISS HAS EVER TASTED FINER.
NOR NO WINE NEITHER.
177

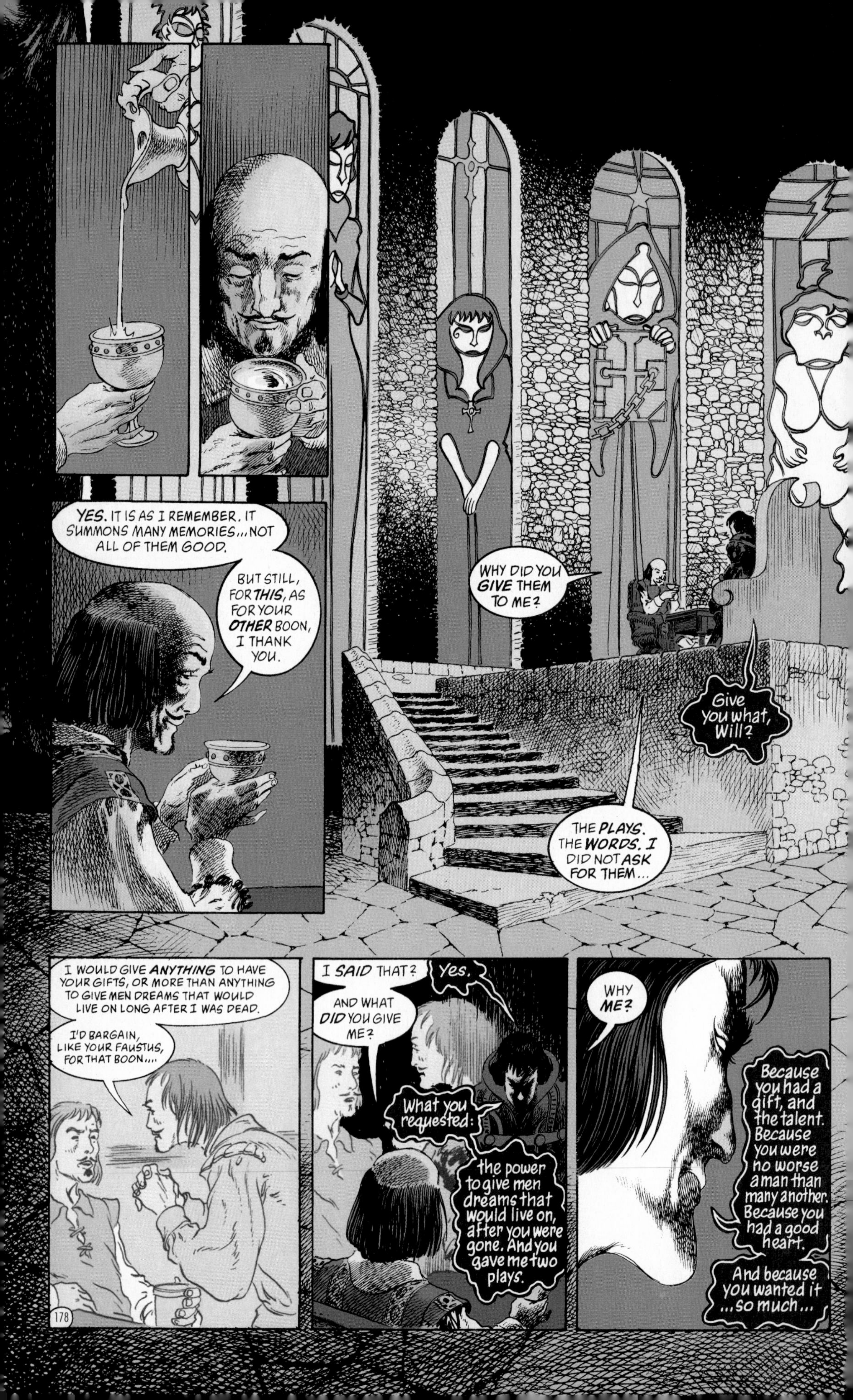
YES. IT IS AS I REMEMBER. IT SUMMONS MANY MEMORIES... NOT ALL OF THEM GOOD.
BUT STILL, FOR THIS, AS FOR YOUR OTHER BOON, I THANK YOU.
WHY DID YOU GIVE THEM TO ME?
Give you what, Will?
THE PLAYS. THE WORDS. I DID NOT ASK FOR THEM...
I WOULD GIVE ANYTHING TO HAVE YOUR GIFTS, OR MORE THAN ANYTHING TO GIVE MEN DREAMS THAT WOULD LIVE ON LONG AFTER I WAS DEAD.
I'D BARGAIN, LIKE YOUR FAUSTUS, FOR THAT BOON...
I SAID THAT?
Yes.
AND WHAT DID YOU GIVE ME?
What you requested:
the power to give men dreams that would live on, after you were gone. And you gave me two plays.
WHY ME?
Because you had a gift, and the talent. Because you were no worse a man than many another. Because you had a good heart.
And because you wanted it ...so much...

YES, I **DID**... I REMEMBER. I WAS SO **YOUNG**. FIVE AND TWENTY...

LOOK AT ME **NOW:** A FAT OLD MAN, LUSTLESS AND LACKLUSTER, WITH MY TWO-SCORE YEARS AND SEVEN...

I DREAM OF BEING NOBODY AT ALL. MY EVERY THIRD THOUGHT IS OF THE GRAVE.

BUT **YOU** MUST HAVE LIVED LONGER THAN TWO SCORE YEARS AND SEVEN.

If I must.

WHAT WOULD HAVE HAPPENED, HAD WE NOT MET, IN THE INN, TWENTY YEARS AGO?

It is not given to any man to know what would have happened.

BUT **YOU** KNOW.

I can hazard an educated guess.

What would have happened? You would have written a handful of other plays, in quality no better than, say, "*The Merrye Devil of Edmonton*", and then you would have come home to Stratford.

You would have taught school, saved a little money. You would have bought a house, let it out, and bought another.

You would have made your money in bricks and mortar-- enough for your family's coat of arms, enough to make them forget your father's setbacks.

You would not have been satisfied with your life; and, from time to time, you would have bored your children with the tales of your years in London, your days on the stage.

AND **HAMNET.** MY BOY. WOULD HE HAVE LIVED?

NO. DO NOT TELL ME THAT. YOU HAVE SAID TOO MUCH ALREADY.

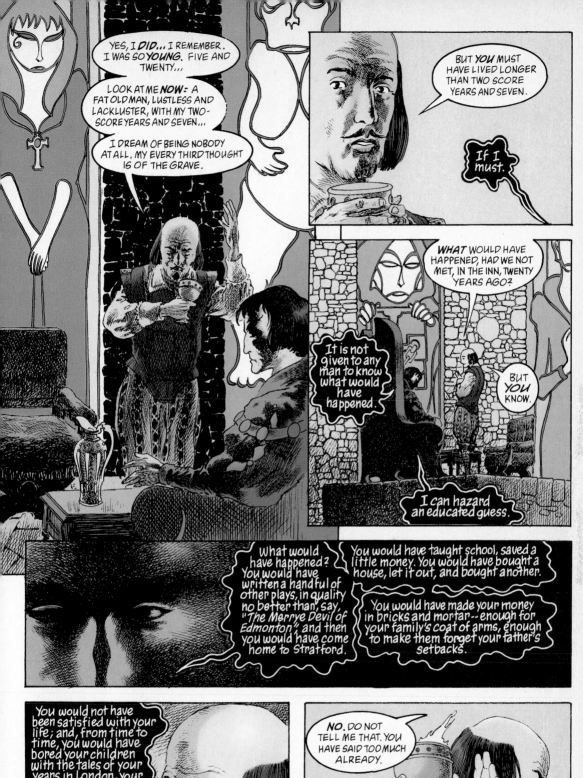

179

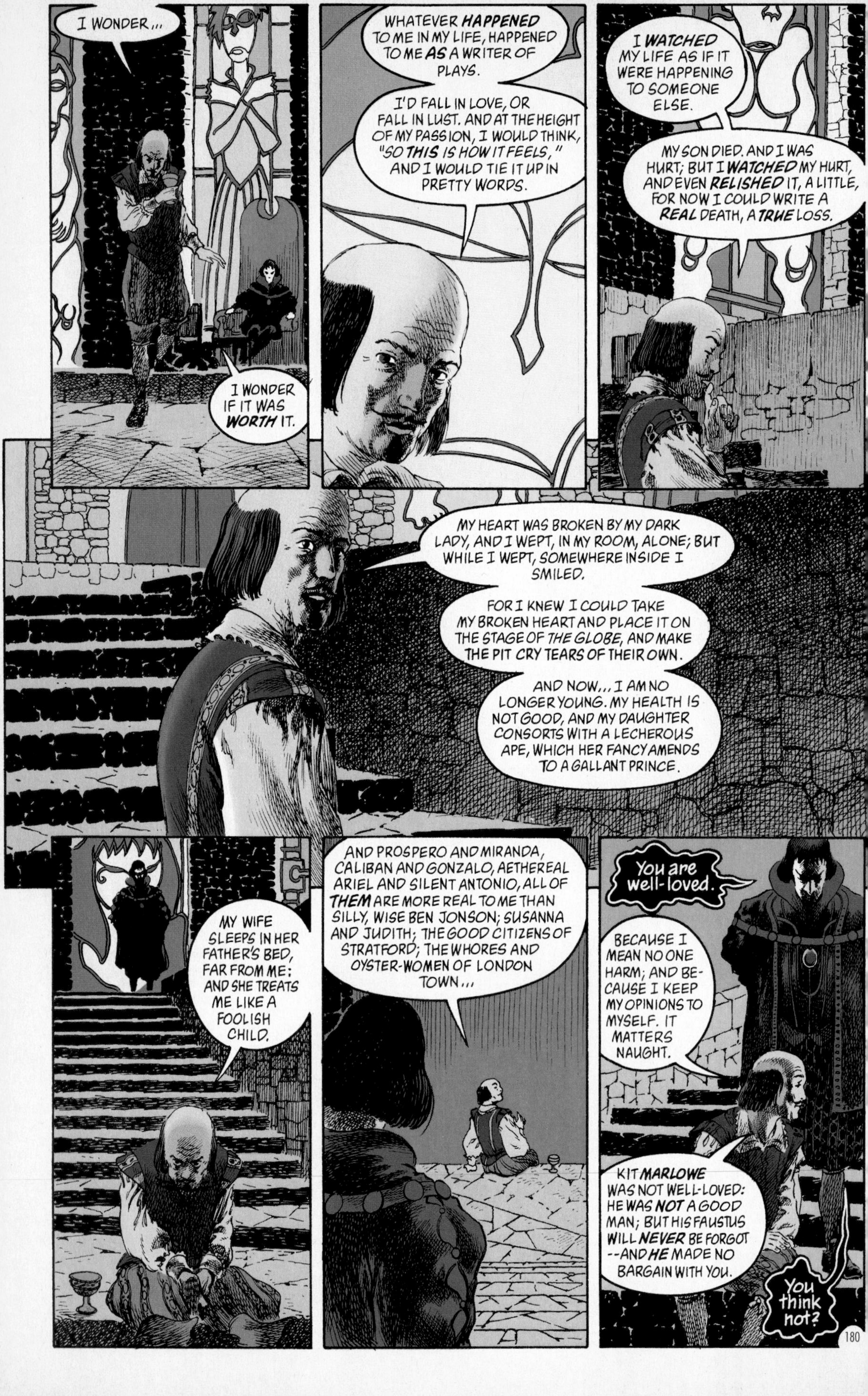
I WONDER...
I WONDER IF IT WAS WORTH IT.
WHATEVER HAPPENED TO ME IN MY LIFE, HAPPENED TO ME AS A WRITER OF PLAYS.
I'D FALL IN LOVE, OR FALL IN LUST. AND AT THE HEIGHT OF MY PASSION, I WOULD THINK, "SO THIS IS HOW IT FEELS," AND I WOULD TIE IT UP IN PRETTY WORDS.
I WATCHED MY LIFE AS IF IT WERE HAPPENING TO SOMEONE ELSE.
MY SON DIED. AND I WAS HURT; BUT I WATCHED MY HURT, AND EVEN RELISHED IT, A LITTLE, FOR NOW I COULD WRITE A REAL DEATH, A TRUE LOSS.
MY HEART WAS BROKEN BY MY DARK LADY, AND I WEPT, IN MY ROOM, ALONE; BUT WHILE I WEPT, SOMEWHERE INSIDE I SMILED.
FOR I KNEW I COULD TAKE MY BROKEN HEART AND PLACE IT ON THE STAGE OF THE GLOBE, AND MAKE THE PIT CRY TEARS OF THEIR OWN.
AND NOW... I AM NO LONGER YOUNG. MY HEALTH IS NOT GOOD, AND MY DAUGHTER CONSORTS WITH A LECHEROUS APE, WHICH HER FANCY AMENDS TO A GALLANT PRINCE.
MY WIFE SLEEPS IN HER FATHER'S BED, FAR FROM ME: AND SHE TREATS ME LIKE A FOOLISH CHILD.
AND PROSPERO AND MIRANDA, CALIBAN AND GONZALO, AETHEREAL ARIEL AND SILENT ANTONIO, ALL OF THEM ARE MORE REAL TO ME THAN SILLY, WISE BEN JONSON; SUSANNA AND JUDITH; THE GOOD CITIZENS OF STRATFORD; THE WHORES AND OYSTER-WOMEN OF LONDON TOWN...
You are well-loved.
BECAUSE I MEAN NO ONE HARM; AND BECAUSE I KEEP MY OPINIONS TO MYSELF. IT MATTERS NAUGHT.
KIT MARLOWE WAS NOT WELL-LOVED: HE WAS NOT A GOOD MAN; BUT HIS FAUSTUS WILL NEVER BE FORGOT --AND HE MADE NO BARGAIN WITH YOU.
You think not?

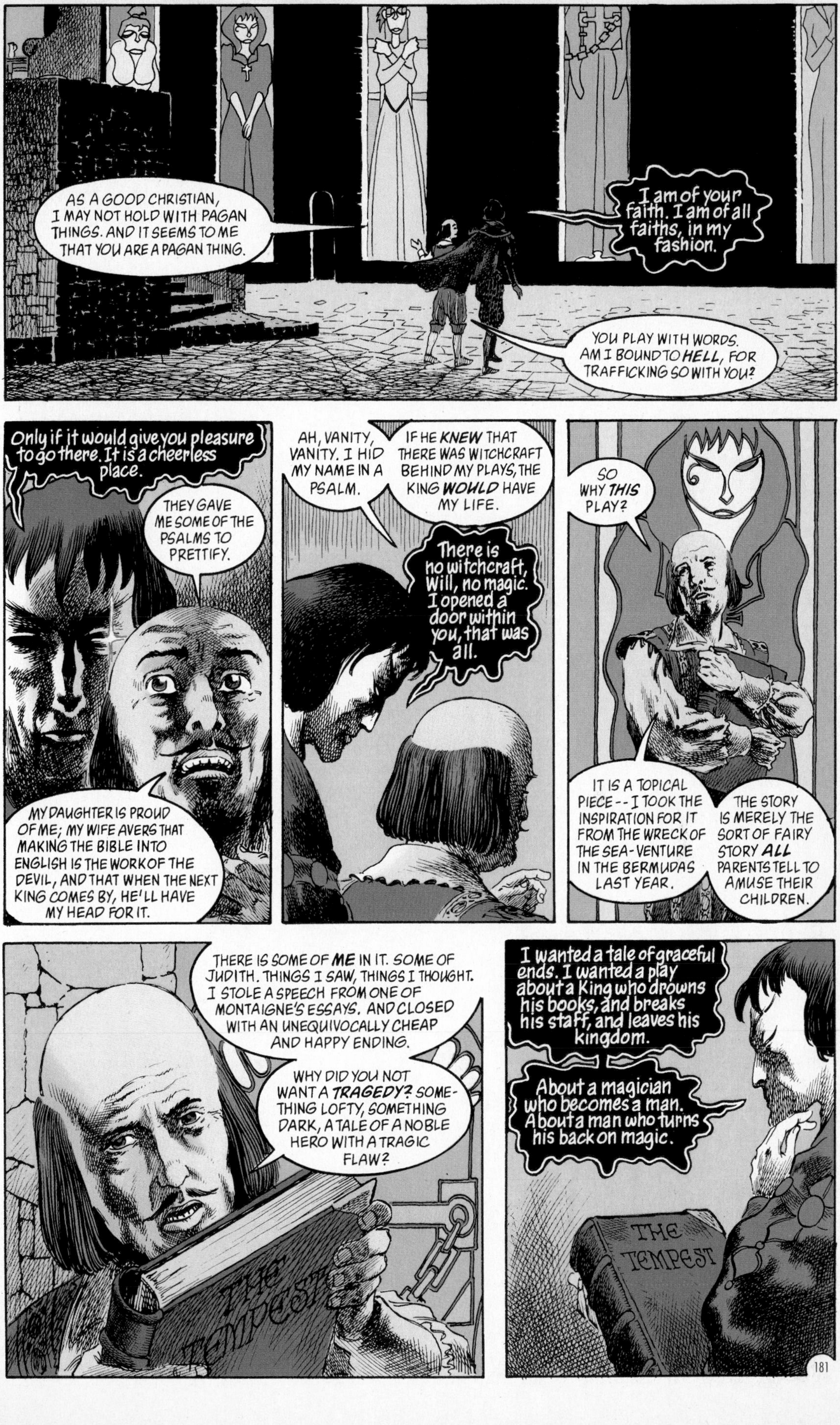
AS A GOOD CHRISTIAN, I MAY NOT HOLD WITH PAGAN THINGS. AND IT SEEMS TO ME THAT YOU ARE A PAGAN THING.
I am of your faith. I am of all faiths, in my fashion.
YOU PLAY WITH WORDS. AM I BOUND TO HELL, FOR TRAFFICKING SO WITH YOU?
Only if it would give you pleasure to go there. It is a cheerless place.
THEY GAVE ME SOME OF THE PSALMS TO PRETTIFY.
MY DAUGHTER IS PROUD OF ME; MY WIFE AVERS THAT MAKING THE BIBLE INTO ENGLISH IS THE WORK OF THE DEVIL, AND THAT WHEN THE NEXT KING COMES BY, HE'LL HAVE MY HEAD FOR IT.
AH, VANITY, VANITY. I HID MY NAME IN A PSALM.
IF HE KNEW THAT THERE WAS WITCHCRAFT BEHIND MY PLAYS, THE KING WOULD HAVE MY LIFE.
There is no witchcraft, Will, no magic. I opened a door within you, that was all.
SO WHY THIS PLAY?
IT IS A TOPICAL PIECE -- I TOOK THE INSPIRATION FOR IT FROM THE WRECK OF THE SEA-VENTURE IN THE BERMUDAS LAST YEAR.
THE STORY IS MERELY THE SORT OF FAIRY STORY ALL PARENTS TELL TO AMUSE THEIR CHILDREN.
THERE IS SOME OF ME IN IT. SOME OF JUDITH. THINGS I SAW, THINGS I THOUGHT. I STOLE A SPEECH FROM ONE OF MONTAIGNE'S ESSAYS. AND CLOSED WITH AN UNEQUIVOCALLY CHEAP AND HAPPY ENDING.
WHY DID YOU NOT WANT A TRAGEDY? SOMETHING LOFTY, SOMETHING DARK, A TALE OF A NOBLE HERO WITH A TRAGIC FLAW?
THE TEMPEST
I wanted a tale of graceful ends. I wanted a play about a King who drowns his books, and breaks his staff, and leaves his kingdom.
About a magician who becomes a man. About a man who turns his back on magic.
THE TEMPEST

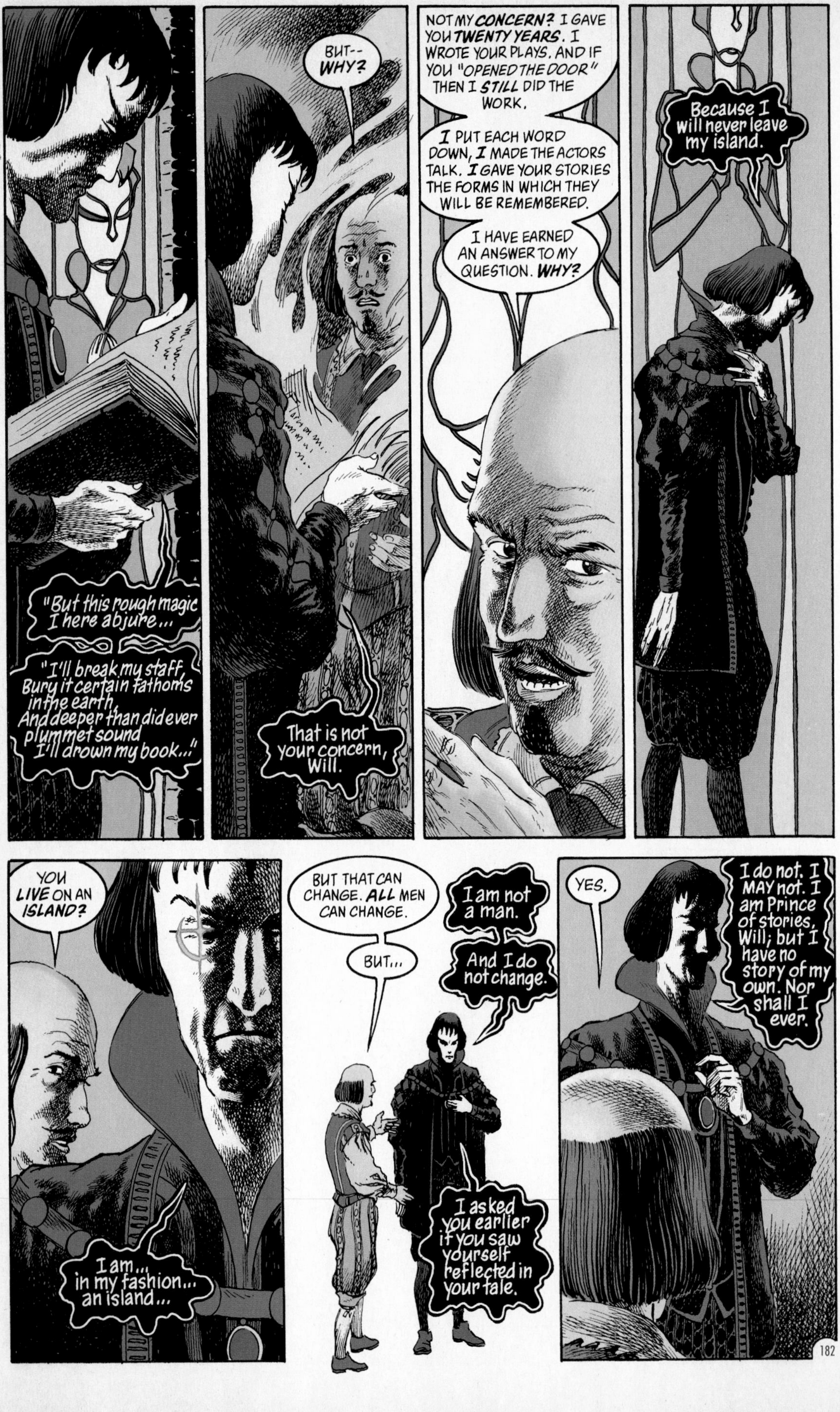
"But this rough magic I here abjure...
"I'll break my staff, Bury it certain fathoms in the earth, And deeper than did ever plummet sound I'll drown my book..."
BUT-- WHY?
That is not your concern, Will.
NOT MY CONCERN? I GAVE YOU TWENTY YEARS. I WROTE YOUR PLAYS. AND IF YOU "OPENED THE DOOR" THEN I STILL DID THE WORK.
I PUT EACH WORD DOWN, I MADE THE ACTORS TALK. I GAVE YOUR STORIES THE FORMS IN WHICH THEY WILL BE REMEMBERED.
I HAVE EARNED AN ANSWER TO MY QUESTION. WHY?
Because I will never leave my island.
YOU LIVE ON AN ISLAND?
I am... in my fashion... an island...
BUT THAT CAN CHANGE. ALL MEN CAN CHANGE.
BUT...
I am not a man.
And I do not change.
I asked you earlier if you saw yourself reflected in your tale.
YES.
I do not. I MAY not. I am Prince of stories, Will; but I have no story of my own. Nor shall I ever.

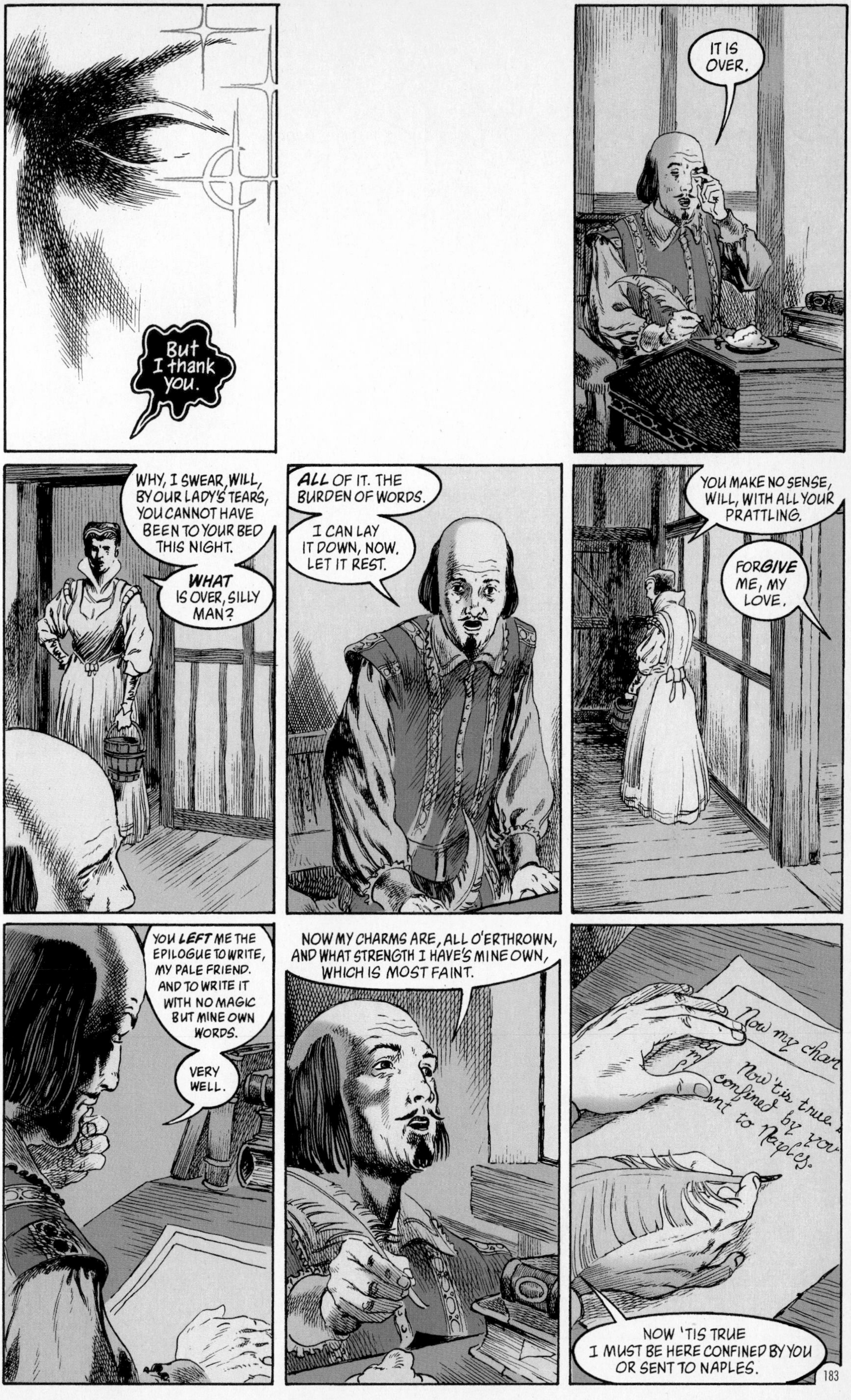
But I thank you.
IT IS OVER.
WHY, I SWEAR, WILL, BY OUR LADY'S TEARS, YOU CANNOT HAVE BEEN TO YOUR BED THIS NIGHT.
WHAT IS OVER, SILLY MAN?
ALL OF IT. THE BURDEN OF WORDS.
I CAN LAY IT DOWN, NOW. LET IT REST.
YOU MAKE NO SENSE, WILL, WITH ALL YOUR PRATTLING.
FORGIVE ME, MY LOVE.
YOU LEFT ME THE EPILOGUE TO WRITE, MY PALE FRIEND. AND TO WRITE IT WITH NO MAGIC BUT MINE OWN WORDS.
VERY WELL.
NOW MY CHARMS ARE, ALL O'ERTHROWN, AND WHAT STRENGTH I HAVE'S MINE OWN, WHICH IS MOST FAINT.
Now my charm
Now 'tis true
confined by you
ent to Naples.
NOW 'TIS TRUE I MUST BE HERE CONFINED BY YOU OR SENT TO NAPLES.

Let me not
Since I have my dukedom got
And pardoned the deceiver, dwell
In this bare island by your spell;

But release me from my bands
With the help of your good hands:

Gentle breath of yours my sails
Must fill, or else my project fails,
Which was to please.

NOW I WANT
SPIRITS TO ENFORCE,
ART TO ENCHANT;

AND MY
ENDING IS DESPAIR
UNLESS I BE RELIEV'D
BY PRAYER,

Which pierces so,
that it assaults
Mercy itself,
and frees all faults.

AS YOU FROM CRIMES
WOULD PARDONED BE,
LET YOUR INDULGENCE
SET ME FREE.

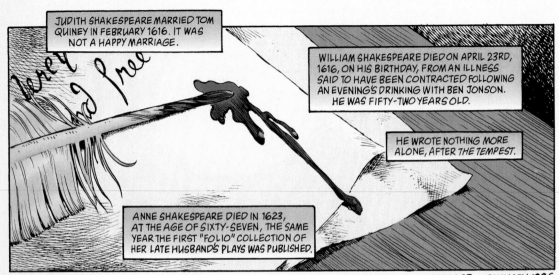

JUDITH SHAKESPEARE MARRIED TOM QUINEY IN FEBRUARY 1616. IT WAS NOT A HAPPY MARRIAGE.

WILLIAM SHAKESPEARE DIED ON APRIL 23RD, 1616, ON HIS BIRTHDAY, FROM AN ILLNESS SAID TO HAVE BEEN CONTRACTED FOLLOWING AN EVENING'S DRINKING WITH BEN JONSON. HE WAS FIFTY-TWO YEARS OLD.

HE WROTE NOTHING MORE ALONE, AFTER *THE TEMPEST*.

ANNE SHAKESPEARE DIED IN 1623, AT THE AGE OF SIXTY-SEVEN, THE SAME YEAR THE FIRST "FOLIO" COLLECTION OF HER LATE HUSBAND'S PLAYS WAS PUBLISHED.

NEIL GAIMAN. OCTOBER 1987 ~ JANUARY 1996.

I have always been bad at goodbyes.

In many ways, that's what these stories are about:
the process of saying goodbye.

My electronic address book contains a
number of people who have died -
friends and colleagues.
Their names and their last known
addresses are still sitting there:
all it would take would be a press
of the delete key to remove them.
But that would be too final a goodbye,
so they remain undeleted.

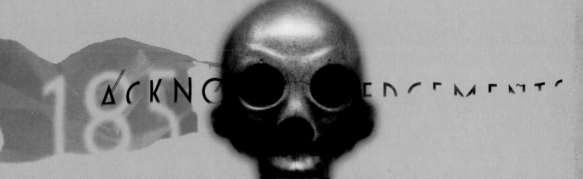

ACKNOWLEDGEMENTS

Roger Zelazny died as I completed
the first chapter of The Wake,
and his memorial informed the second chapter.

The Ten Volumes of Sandman, of which this is the last,
comprise a story about stories. But in looking back over
the nine years between my starting Sandman and writing this,
what comes to mind are not stories, but friends.
Some of whom I have met, many of whom I have still to meet.

To the friends of Sandman, and to my friends, my thanks.

Neil Gaiman

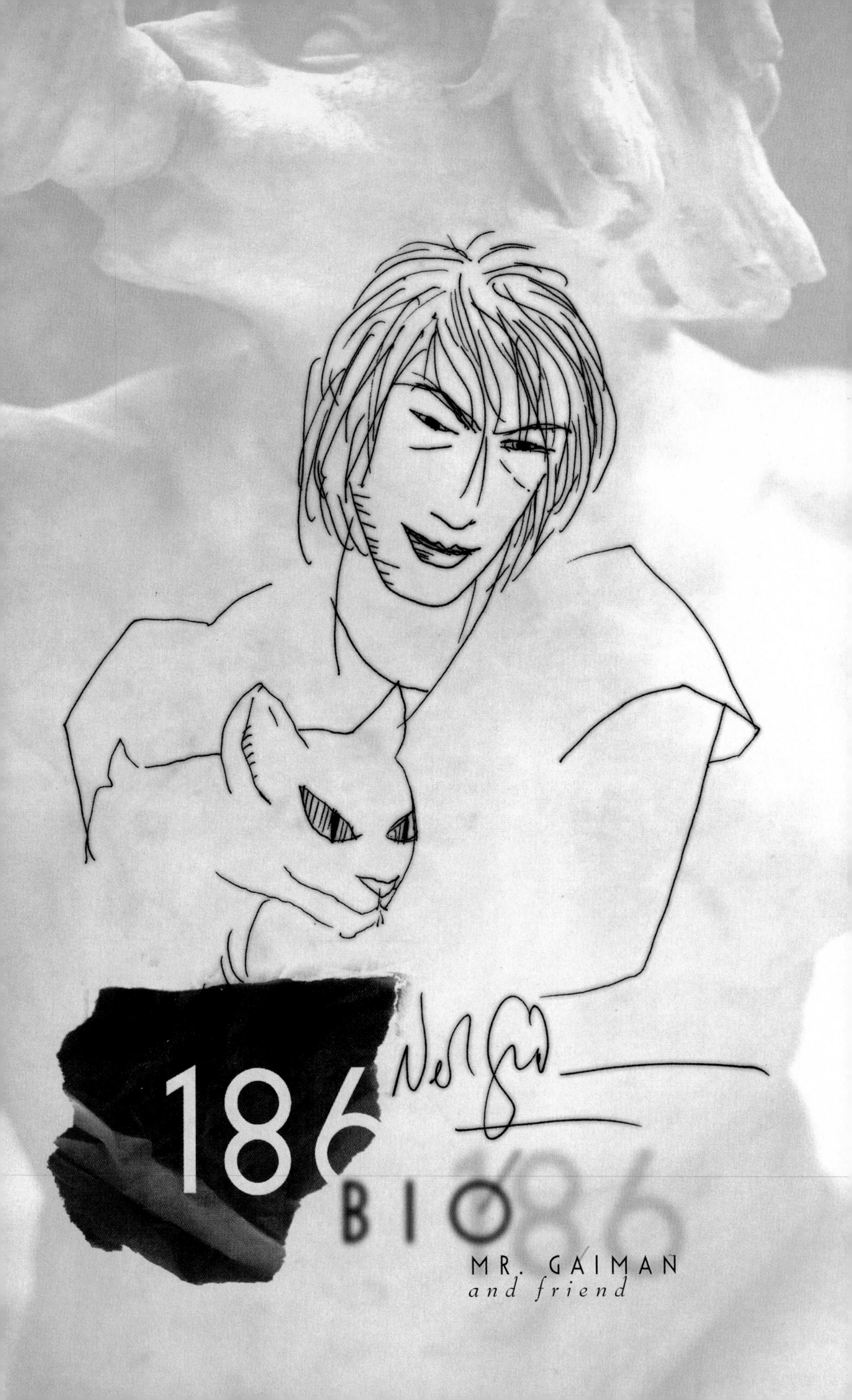
186
BIO
MR. GAIMAN
and friend

GR87HIES
MR. ZULLI

B I O G R A

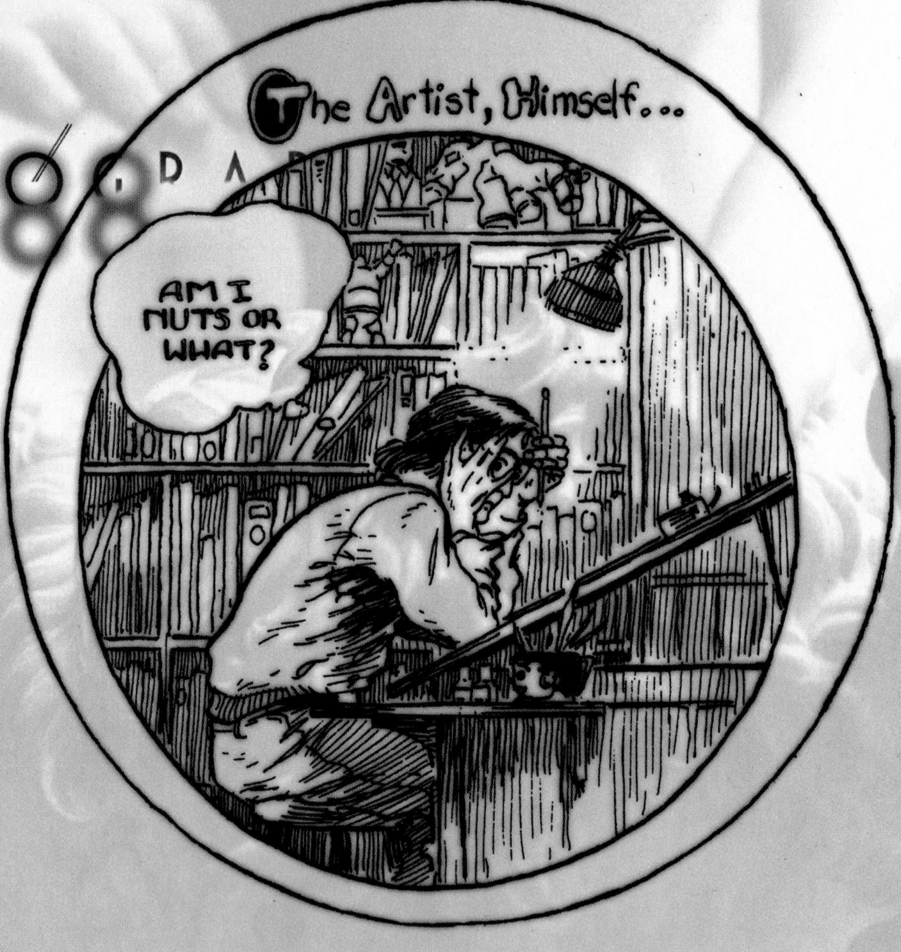
The Artist, Himself...
AM I NUTS OR WHAT?

MR. VESS

189

MR. MUTH

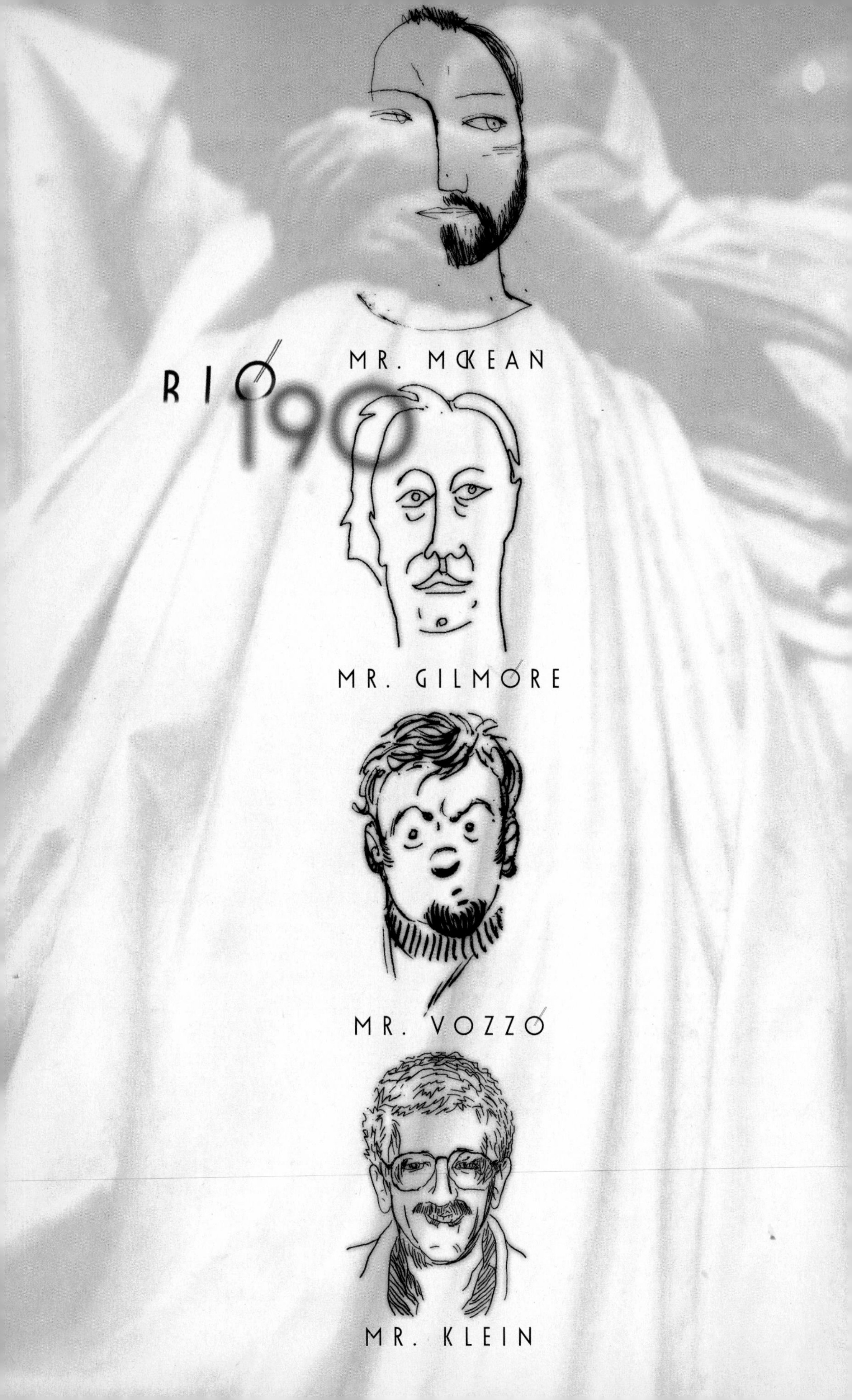
MR. MCKEAN
RIO
190
MR. GILMORE
MR. VOZZO
MR. KLEIN